CURRICULUM VISIONS

COUNTERPOINTS

Studies in the
Postmodern Theory of Education

Joe L. Kincheloe and Shirley R. Steinberg
General Editors

Vol. 151

PETER LANG
New York • Washington, D.C./Baltimore • Bern
Frankfurt am Main • Berlin • Brussels • Vienna • Oxford

CURRICULUM VISIONS

EDITED BY

William E. Doll, Jr.
and Noel Gough

PETER LANG
New York • Washington, D.C./Baltimore • Bern
Frankfurt am Main • Berlin • Brussels • Vienna • Oxford

Library of Congress Cataloging-in-Publication Data

Curriculum visions / edited by William E. Doll, Jr. and Noel Gough.
p. cm. —(Counterpoints; v. 151)
Includes bibliographical references and index.
1. Curriculum planning—Philosophy. 2. Postmodernism and
education. I. Doll, William E. II. Gough, Noel.
III. Counterpoints (New York, N.Y.); v. 151.
LB2806.15 .C887 375'.001—dc21 2001050630
ISBN 0-8204-4999-7
ISSN 1058-1634

Die Deutsche Bibliothek-CIP-Einheitsaufnahme

Curriculum visions / ed. by: William E. Doll, Jr. and Noel Gough.
–New York; Washington, D.C./Baltimore; Bern;
Frankfurt am Main; Berlin; Brussels; Vienna; Oxford: Lang.
(Counterpoints; Vol. 151)
ISBN 0-8204-4999-7

Cover art by Niki Konstantinou
Cover design by Lisa Dillon

We dedicate this book to

Arthur W. "Wells" Foshay

and to

Gwyneth Dow

whose spirits continue to enliven our thoughts.

Contents

Preface

The story of *Curriculum Visions* began in 1991 with an invitation from the commissioning editor of an ambitious series of volumes in education to develop an international handbook on curriculum. To plan this volume, three editors met at a Mendecino farmhouse during the weekend immediately following the annual meeting of the American Educational Research Association in San Francisco in April 1992. The *Handbook of Research on Curriculum*, edited by Philip Jackson (Macmillan, 1992), had just been published, and we wanted our book to complement rather than compete with Jackson's monumental collection. We decided to organize our handbook around past, present, and future perspectives on curriculum, with these three temporal categories being represented, respectively, by the views of senior/emeritus scholars, contemporary theorists, and schoolchildren.

A series of earthquakes and aftershocks struck Mendecino that weekend. We are not superstitious, so conducting our deliberations in a farmhouse subject to sporadic seismic spasms, with fixtures and fittings falling fitfully around us, did not then seem like an omen of ill fortune, but within a few months the publisher had canceled the entire handbook series.

Our new publisher did not want anything quite so grandiose as a "handbook" (and, frankly, we did not want to edit one either). Nevertheless, we retained two parts of our original structure—perspectives past and present—in the revised proposal, with many authors invited and committed to contributing to each part. The project proved to be too daunting for the second publishing house, which was then in the process of repositioning itself in the academic book marketplace, and we agreed to an amicable separation.

We decided to abandon an explicitly historical focus, and, from this point on, only two of us continued as editors. However, we wanted to strengthen our emphasis on perspectives in curriculum inquiry in a way that would be both insightful and forward-looking, and so we chose *curriculum visions* as the organizing principle that best seemed to capture these qualities. The eclecticism of our reconceived book polarized reviewers—they either loved or loathed it—and we parted company from a third publisher. There is a Chinese proverb, "Once is happenstance, twice is coincidence, three times is enemy action," but we still attribute no significance to the earthquakes.

For nearly a decade, this book has existed chiefly in conversations between the editors and among prospective authors, potential publishers, and ourselves. Somewhere along the way, we decided to make some of these conversations visible in the text. To initiate conversation between authors and ourselves, we sent them draft copies of our introductory chapters. Authors were free to write their own visionary essays as they saw fit, but we also wanted to inform them of our thinking so that they would be able, if they wished, to comment on and/or interrogate our assumptions and assertions.

We added another layer of conversation between the editors' and the authors' visions through the "Problematics" that introduce each essay. Finally, readers of the draft chapters who were looking for teaching implications in the various authors' visions were invited into the conversation. These are the "Perspectives" that follow each essay.

We have many people to thank for their assistance and support in bringing this project to its eventual fruition. Annette Gough, Molly Quinn, and Bill Schubert contributed substantially to our initial deliberations (and shared the earthquake experiences). As Noel's partner, Annette continues to be his best and most critical friend. Bill Schubert's participation was invaluable during the first two iterations of this text's development, but he withdrew when we agreed to focus the text more sharply on contemporary visions. Molly began the project as our graduate research assistant and then became one of our visionary authors.

Other graduate students who assisted us very capably and effectively at various times include Anne Pautz and Hongyu Wang. Indeed, we thank all of the graduate students in our curriculum courses at Deakin University, Louisiana State University, and the University of Victoria (British Columbia, Canada) who have helped to refine and improve many aspects of this text by reading and responding constructively to draft chapters. We are especially indebted to Bill's doctoral seminar students of the fall of 1999 who read and critiqued every word of every essay: this book is far better for the sharpness of their eyes (and tongues). They also are responsible for and took leadership roles in generating the perspectives which ask, "Just what do all these visions mean?" Nor can we forget Bill's master's degree students of the spring semesters of 2000 and 2001 who gave much-needed feedback on the overall product and started work on the index.

Noel extends warm thanks to Bill for initiating this project, for his friendship and hospitality, and for his patience with procrastination (also known as "just-in-time management"). Noel also acknowledges with love and gratitude the honesty and expertise of his children, Kate and Simon, as resident reality checkers.

Bill extends his gratitude first to Noel, who, as chief seer, has kept the book honest and the vision clear during all these years. As for Donna, Bill's wife, what can we say? She is brilliant and has patience beyond endurance.

We are grateful to all the authors who suffered through endless writings and rewritings, always keeping their own voices while acknowledging—at times kindly—our work. Thanks also to Niki Konstantin for creating 'Eyeland 2' from which the cover image is excerpted.

Finally, both of us are indebted to Joe Kincheloe and Shirley Steinberg, who found a home for the manuscript in its final version in their Counterpoints series with its nonpareil publisher, Peter Lang. Peggy McConnell and Donna Trueit have been our local exemplary copyeditors, working closely with Jacqueline Pavlovic and Stephanie Achard of Peter Lang. Without these two, the book would not be.

Thank you all.

Wm. E. Doll, Jr.
Louisiana State University

Noel Gough
Deakin University

Voicing Curriculum Visions

Noel Gough

I wander thro' each charter'd street,
Near where the charter'd Thames docs flow,
And mark in every face I meet
Marks of weakness, marks of woe.
In every cry of every Man,
In every Infant's cry of fear,
In every voice, in every ban,
The mind-forg'd manacles I hear.
(William Blake, 1794, "London," ll, 1–8)[1]

I saw the best minds of my generation destroyed by madness, starving
    hysterical naked,
dragging themselves through the negro streets at dawn looking for an angry fix,
angelheaded hipsters burning for the ancient heavenly connection to the
    starry dynamo in the machinery of night,...
who passed through universities with radiant cool eyes hallucinating
    Arkansas and Blake-light tragedy among the scholars of war,...
(Allen Ginsberg, 1956, "Howl," ll, 1–3, 6)

I begin with the first few lines of William Blake's "London" and Allen Ginsberg's "Howl" because I suspect that poets (and connoisseurs of poetry) are more confident and clear about what is named by the elusive terms "vision" and "visionary" than are we curriculum scholars. The unequivocal assertion with which "Howl" begins, "I saw," testifies emphatically to Ginsberg's confidence in his own vision, and I take his gesture to Blake ("hallucinating...Blake-light tragedy") to refer to the types of art that exemplify his sense of the visionary. I first read Blake's "London" (along with other poems from *Songs of Experience*, including "The Tyger," "The Sick Rose," and "A Poison Tree") in my early years at high school, and I recall being struck by the economy of his words and the clarity of his vision—and I mean *vision*, not observation, because I could swear that Blake *saw* "mind-forg'd manacles" even if he wrote "hear" (my visual repertoire at the time was part comic book, part film noir, and I imagined the narrator of "London" as a kind of eighteenth-century private eye with x-ray vision).[2]

As I think about what "curriculum visions" might mean to the authors, editors, and readers of this book, it also seems significant to me that although Blake suffered neglect and even ridicule during his life, Ginsberg's peers immediately recognized "Howl" as a visionary work. As Mary Elizabeth Moore (this volume) might say, with visionary art you either "get it" right away or you don't. In Ginsberg's case, we "got it." Consider, for example, how fellow poet Michael McClure (1994) recalls one of Ginsberg's early public readings of "Howl" at the Six Gallery in San Francisco in December 1955:

> In all of our memories no one had been so outspoken in poetry before—we had gone beyond a point of no return—and we were ready for it....None of us wanted to go back to the gray, chill, militaristic silence, to the intellective void —to the land without poetry—to the spiritual drabness. We wanted to make it new and we wanted to invent it and the process of it as we went into it. We wanted voice and we wanted vision. (13)

We hope that many of the curriculum visions voiced in this book will strike readers with similar immediacy. For example, it is rare to find curriculum scholars being "so outspoken in poetry" as Peter Cole and Pat O'Riley in "Much Rezadieux About (Dewey's) Goats in the Curriculum" (and they clearly reject curriculum as a "land without poetry"). Molly Quinn's "Holy Vision, Wholly Vision-ing" is a similarly forceful rejection of a curriculum field marked by "spiritual drabness." But to be outspoken is not enough. For reasons not unlike those that led Ginsberg and McClure to exemplify artistic vision by reference to Blake, the visions gathered here represent our struggles not only to speak of but also to *enact* curriculum renewal and invention. To read Blake, in McClure's (1994) words (but with my emphasis), is "to *experience* an invention"—an invention based on the "clarity of his perceptions and his rejection of the general propaganda":

> Blake's intuitive meditative imagination employed his unique reconstellation of sensory data, creating new models....Blake's works, like the artifacts of all high artists, are his body. Gestures come so directly from his physical being that their presence is real and physical. Blake appeared to Allen Ginsberg in a vision. In adolescence I dreamed I was Blake. Blake seemed as real a presence as an automobile. (137–38)

Here McClure draws attention to an important connection between the *embodiment* of an artist's vision and the "unique reconstellation of sensory data" from which the artist constructs a durable artifact such as a poem or a painting. To date, we have seen very little evidence of such an understanding of vision in the literature of curriculum inquiry. Indeed, until relatively recently, the conventions of academic writing in education have encouraged authors to represent themselves in texts as if they were "no(t)bodies"—and academics are less likely than artists to be the subjects of biographies that chronicle the connections between their corporeality and their "body" of work. These connections include the relatively mundane effects of the eye's physiology on representations of the "real," such as Monet's myopic "impressions" of diffuse rather than detailed objects and El Greco's astigmatic elongations of the human form.[3]

A surrealistic artist's vision is no less embodied as Salvador Dali demonstrates in the total fusion of his persona and paintings. Dali's alleged dictum "Surrealism is myself" is a confession rather than a boast —and so complete an acceptance of a psychoanalytic view of the unconscious as a narrative stage that he could incarnate himself as a character in his own landscapes of psychic alienation: "Don Quixote in a silk lounge suit, he rides eccentrically across a viscous and overlit desert, protected by nothing more than his furious moustaches" (Ballard, 1996, 91). I live in hope that a curriculum scholar with equivalent clarity of embodied vision might one day produce a critique of the clockwork curriculum (timetables, times tables, time on task) with as real and as compelling a presence as the watches that melt and drip in the timeless melancholy of Dali's "The Persistence of Memory." I saw the best minds of *my* generation preset and programmed by bells and buzzers and buzzwords....

Whether our curriculum visions are realistic, surreal, or abstract, they are all "real and physical" inventions of "real and physical" authors. A curriculum vision begins with an embodied eye/I.

Embodying Curriculum Visions

Although the concept of "vision" that I have sketched here is drawn chiefly from the creative and critical language of beat poets, there is nothing particularly esoteric about it. In everyday speech, too, "vision" refers to the sensory system with/in which we embody much of what counts most to us as knowledge ("*seeing* is believing," and to rely on anything less is "blind faith"). Yet vision in much educational discourse—especially if it is inscribed as "*a* vision"—can also refer to seemingly disembodied, remote, abstract, and even chimerical prospects of futures in which we place little trust (it is usually only with hindsight that we label foresight as having been "visionary"). Because I do not believe that this distrust is altogether misplaced, my purpose in the remainder of this essay is to explore some ways in which we might rehabilitate prospective vision in curriculum inquiry—to consider ways of generating representations of curriculum visions that might themselves be generative (and regenerative) in various forms of curriculum work.

Prospective senses of "vision" are typically found in the overlapping literatures of educational administration, school improvement, and organizational development. For example, Katrine Staessens and Roland Vandenberghe (1994) write:

> "Vision" and "vision-building" play central roles in the construction of a professional culture. The notion of vision captures the goals an organization wants to achieve; it reflects also understandings of the future of an organization...vision as a set of shared goals does not mean the sum of individual goals, but the *degree of consensus* among organizational members about the value of daily activities and decisions in relation to some goals and the future development of the organization. (187–88, emphasis in original)

For these writers, "the degree of goal-consensus is considered to be the main indicator of the existence of a vision" (188). This understanding of vision—as a positive orientation to shared goals that express preferred futures—is commonplace, and I do not doubt that examples of such visions could be compelling in some circumstances. But there are equally commonplace—and no less generative—understandings of vision that lack a focus on the future, positive goal orientation, and consensus. For example, the activity of reflection—reflective teaching, reflective journal writing, and so on—requires vision (at least metaphorically) but has no *necessary* orientation to goals or futures and is more often personal than consensual. Furthermore, the critical gaze of educators with emancipatory interests often is associated with a *negative* orientation to the type of "vision" that is designated by shared goals. As Donna Haraway (1994) writes (in words that resemble McClure's description of Blake):

> Critical vision has been central to critical theory, which aims to unmask the lies of the established disorder that appears as transparently normal. Critical theory is about a certain kind of "negativity"—i.e., the relentless commitment to show that the established disorder is not necessary, nor perhaps even "real." (62–63)

In other words, like Blake's and Ginsberg's poetry, critical vision is not only about hopes for the future but also about seeing the world otherwise *now*—about *seeing* "mind-forg'd manacles" and "minds...destroyed by madness" where others see prosperity and progress. The constructive "negativity" of critical vision can thus be manifested as the *avoidance* of some goals and the *refusal* of consensus. Consensus implies shared vision—an agreement that it is possible for different members of a community to have identical sensory embodiments and standpoints—because vision is produced and mediated by some*body* from some*where* in particular. Understood in this way, shared vision is not necessarily impossible, but it is certainly much more difficult to achieve than goal-consensus, which can involve no more than lip-service to abstractions from and approximations to what McClure calls "the general propaganda" and the "transparently normal." For example, it might be relatively easy to obtain consensus (or, more likely, the appearance thereof) on the goal of integrating the curriculum for children with "special needs" with the curriculum of mainstream schooling, but it could still be very difficult to reach agreement on what such an integrated curriculum actually looks like to an embodied actor—so that we might work toward constructing a reality that matches the vision (or even be able to recognize an integrated curriculum when we see one). The person who envisages an integrated curriculum as one in which specified supplementary arrangements meet the special needs of some children does not, in my view, share a vision of such a curriculum with the person who can visualize learning milieus in which no one child's needs are considered to be special.[4]

Without the particularities and specificities of location and embodiment, prospective vision in curriculum inquiry is wishful thinking. I agree with Haraway (1989) that "no one can constitute meanings by wishing them into existence" and with the emphasis in her claim that meanings are "*particular* structurings of objects of knowledge," where knowledge is understood as "that which can be known in a particular time and place" (111). If curriculum visions are to be generative—that is, if we are to be in a position to negotiate visions of curriculum futures worth working for—we must accept that we stand at the center of our own histories and fields of visualization as responsible, engaged, embodied actors (a point that Kathleen Kesson and Don Oliver take up in some detail in their essay in this volume). Although both chance and choice influence how we come to be positioned "in a particular time and place," our fields of visualization are not fixed or inevitable but rather are configured (and continually reconfigured) by the frames and standpoints we select.

Frames and Standpoints

Our responsibility for framing fields of visualization can be illustrated by an example. A few years ago, as part of my preparation for teaching a course entitled "Administration of the Educational Program" for the master's degree program in curriculum studies at the University of Victoria, British Columbia, Canada, I revisited Philip K. Dick's (1968) novel, *Do Androids Dream of Electric Sheep?* and Ridley Scott's (1984) movie adaptation of it, *Blade Runner.* On this particular occasion, the 72-hour course was conducted over four weeks rather than the customary seven, and, partly to compensate for the reduced time available for out-of-class reading, I supplied students with a recommended wider reading guide well in advance of commencing classes. Dick's novel, Scott's movie, and a number of other works of fiction were included in my recommendations. Using science fiction novels and movies as textual resources in the courses I teach is a material expression of my vision of curriculum inquiry—of how I "see" curriculum studies being advanced (see Gough, 1995, 1998).

At the time (July 1993), *Blade Runner: The Director's Cut* had recently been released on video. This is Scott's preferred version of the film and is presented in the "letterbox" wide screen format, which shows 40 percent more of the full Panavision frame than the previously released video cassette version.[5] Throughout *Blade Runner*, Scott mostly frames the actors either screen left or screen right—rarely centered. The lighting design usually places the actors half in light, half in shadow, which accentuates the impression that most of the characters are living their lives on the fringes, edges, and margins—an existence that is perpetually off-center and, perhaps, off-balance. In the earlier videocassette version, the frame proportion required for standard television screens is achieved by a semiautomated "pan and scan" editing technique that places the actors as close as possible to center screen. But removing the "dead space" in *Blade Runner* also diminishes the movie's pervasive sense of marginalization and alienation.

These differences between the two video versions of *Blade Runner* prompted me to think about how we "frame" the other actors in the day-to-day comedies, dramas, and soap operas in which we participate in schools and universities. What sense of "real" life would we get if we "re-edited" our perceptions of our students and peers and their interactions with one another and with their settings? What difference would it make to place some of the peripheral actors in our everyday lives at "center screen" (and vice versa)? More importantly, perhaps, how do the frames we put around actors get there? What cultural mechanisms are the equivalents of "pan and scan" editing? How many of the people with whom we interact (students, colleagues, etc.) are surrounded by "dead space" *that we do not see*. How can we put the material conditions of those who are marginalized and alienated by our perceptual editing processes onto the "screens" of our visual imaginations? In this volume, Deborah Britzman asks a comparable question: "If we could somehow sort through all the objects the curriculum leaves behind, how would we decide which were worthy and which were useless?"

These are questions that can only be answered (and, indeed, only make sense) by reference to the specific standpoints from which we deploy our own sensory systems. This is as true for those of us who are engaged in academic curriculum inquiry as it is for those who work in schools. For example, Betina Zolkower (1996, 59) provides what she calls a "view from below" of attempts to implement "mathematical empowerment for all"—the "new new math" reforms[6] of the past decade —through the stories she collected during two years of periodic visits to the fourth- and fifth-grade math classes of a public school in El Barrio (Spanish Harlem, New York City). Zolkower muses on the difficulties she experienced in seeking an audience for her research "in all the wrong places," among which she specifically mentions the 1994 Annual Meeting of the American Educational Research Association in New Orleans:

> At this mega-event and other similar conferences, normal science coexists with a few panels, admittedly quite packed, where radical pedagogues celebrate paradigm shifts in the field of education, sharing news with each other about students' resistance, teachers' empowerment, border pedagogies, subversion in educational praxis, and "postmodernist approaches to validity in qualitative research." (59–60)

Zolkower is especially irritated by "cultural critics" who see only what they are looking for in the "Third World at home"—in "the streets, garbage-filled vacant lots, tiny kitchens and bedrooms, overcrowded classrooms, and schoolyards in a state of chronic disrepair which frame the daily lives of thousands of children from unemployed, very poor, and recently emigrated families in El Barrio":

> In this post-Fordist, post-*Learning to Labor*[7] society, when cultural critics take the school as an object of inquiry at all, they are motivated by a search for new evidence of students' resistance. Thus, visiting a fourth- or fifth-grade math classroom accomplishes little. Except for a few so-called maladjusted, hyperactive, at-risk, or problem cases, children do not resist the symbolic violence to which they are subjected. When they resist, they do so in ways that are far from

> obvious. We may be surprised to find that seven- to eleven-year-old students often want to learn even the most apparently obsolete chunks of knowledge presented to them on a daily basis by their math teachers, and that some of them enjoy such trivial activities as math challenges in which exhibiting perfect mastery over the multiplication tables is the only condition for winning the class struggle. (60)

Zolkower's stories provide many powerful examples of how "vision" —both in the sense of the guiding vision of "mathematical empowerment for all" and of what the new new math "visionaries" might actually be "seeing"—is determined by where we stand and how we frame our fields of visualization. Her stories warn those of us whose work is unapologetically academic that when we attempt to be "visionary" in curriculum work, we risk positioning ourselves (or being positioned by others) at some imagined "leading edge" of curriculum change. But foresight could encompass a broader and more inclusive field of visualization if, like Zolkower's "view from below," we exercise it from a position closer to what Stephen Hill (1990) calls the "trailing edge" of cultural change—a position from which we might be able to discern the cultural constructions, meanings, institutions, and expectations that were formed in past times and/or other places and that shape present perceptions and future possibilities. I was thus pleased to see that several of the authors represented in this volume write from positions that are someplace other than the conventional academic high ground. For example, Chet Bowers explicitly states that he "write[s] from the margins," and Alex Molnar implicitly adopts a position that is not so much a "standpoint" as *standing with* the children of America's schools against whom advertisers (when viewed from this perspective) are waging "an immoral war on childhood." As befits tricksters and nomads, Peter Cole and Pat O'Riley craftily resolve the problem of positioning by moving around a lot, speaking from different standpoints relative to their implied audience.[8] However, this strategy is not without risk, as Donna Haraway (1991) explains:

> There is a premium on establishing the capacity to see from the peripheries and the depths. But here lies a serious danger of romanticizing and/or appropriating the visions of the less powerful while claiming to see from their positions. To see from below is neither easily learned nor unproblematic, even if "we" [feminist women] "naturally" inhabit the great underground terrain of subjugated knowledges. The positionings of the subjugated are not exempt from critical re-examination, decoding, deconstruction, and interpretation; that is, from both semiological and hermeneutic modes of critical enquiry.... "Subjugated" standpoints are preferred because they seem to promise more adequate,

> sustained, objective, transforming accounts of the world. But *how* to see from below is a problem requiring at least as much skill with bodies and language, with the mediation of vision, as the "highest" techno-scientific visualizations. (191)

Of course, *none* of our positions should be "exempt from critical re-examination, decoding, deconstruction, and interpretation." I know that much of what I am able to "see" in the curriculum field—and much of what is occluded—is determined by my history and location as a curriculum scholar working, for the most part, in Victoria, Australia. When I converse with colleagues from Britain, Canada, South Africa, and the United States, we often have to work hard to recognize both the strengths and limitations of our various "partial perspectives" (Haraway, 1991, 183). To take a very specific example, the concept of *competition* is manifested in superficially similar ways in different educational systems children in Australia, Britain, Canada, and the United States invariably ask each other "whad-ja-get?" when assignments and test results are returned, and high school graduates in these countries compete with one another for university places. However, the cultural meanings and values that affect the strategic mobilization of the concept of *competition* in discourses of curriculum change in each of these countries are very different. Even a cursory comparison of Australian and U.S. school assessment practices—and of attitudes toward competitive assessment—reveals clear differences.[9] My experience of U.S. schools is that competitiveness among individuals, be it in scholarship or sport or any other activity, is not just taken for granted but actually celebrated as a virtue (has any other nation invented and institutionalized a social activity with as many implausibilities and contradictions as a "beauty contest?"). In conversations with U.S. teachers, my initial surprise at the extent to which they were willing to tolerate and condone competitive assessment was only matched by their surprise that I worked in an educational system that was serious about minimizing it. But, at least in Victoria, that is precisely what has been attempted and, indeed, has been the object of sustained systemic efforts in curriculum reform at various times during the past three decades.

For example, in the late 1960s, the Victorian director of secondary education asserted that "there is no place for competitive assessment in secondary school...whatever assessment is done should be seen as a function of the essential communication between school and child and between school and parents."[10] With strong support from teachers' unions, this principle soon became policy and was extended to all government schools in Victoria (some other Australian states subsequently pursued similar policy directions). Although practice has sometimes fallen short of this principle, the persistent direction of incremental change in assessment practices throughout the 1970s and 1980s was away from procedures that involved ranking students by grades or marks and toward alternatives such as goal-based and "work required" assessment,[11] student self-assessment, descriptive assessment, and cooperative/consultative assessment involving students, teachers, and parents. For example, one policy guideline issued by the Education Department of Victoria in 1984 (with which school councils were expected to comply) stated that "schools should...ensure that assessment policies do not emphasize comparisons between students" (Victoria, Minister of Education, 1984, 14).[12] These reforms have not been free from controversy, nor have they been unopposed, but I suspect that even the quality and range of the debates themselves would surprise many U.S. educators. For example, during the early 1970s, as part of a campaign to reform the examinations used to select students into universities, the secondary teachers' union vigorously advocated that such selection should be by ballot (Hannan, 1985). In addition to taking industrial action (including stop-work meetings and threats of strikes) the union put forward serious and plausible arguments to the effect that the existing examination system was a less fair and less equitable means of university selection than a ballot. Although some sections of the community initially dismissed the campaign as nonsensical, it succeeded in exposing flaws and injustices in the existing system and accelerated its reform.[13]

I have recounted this brief history because it is one of the significant "trailing edges" of my own path through the curriculum field. Curriculum inquiry, as I learned to do it in Victoria through the 1960s and 1970s, was a response to specific, idiosyncratic, local problems and issues, informed by very eclectic conceptions of how curriculum studies might be performed in emerging global theaters of academic practices (to which I eventually attached names like "critical social science," "post-modernism," and "poststructuralism"). Thus, minimizing competitive individualism in learning and assessment has long been part of my vision of curriculum improvement, but I recognize that what I actually *see* that gives substance to this vision is quite different from whatever many of my U.S. colleagues "see" as possible and/or desirable—including those who speak the same language of assessment reform. All of us who work in institutionalized settings face similar and seemingly inevitable pressures to conform to bureaucratic definitions of our practice (among which norm-referenced approaches to assessment are close to being a universal "default position"), but for me these are counterbalanced by enduring personal and institutional memories of successful resistance to those pressures. More importantly, my vision of assessment reform is unimpeded by the institutionalized habit of celebrating individual "success" that seems to be taken for granted in U.S. culture.

For example, my first visit to a U.S. school—Beauregard High School in New Orleans—remains memorable for three reasons. First, the principal began her warm but obviously well-rehearsed welcoming ritual by drawing my attention to a yearbook that lay open, in readiness for each visitor to inspect, at a page that displayed a photograph of the young Lee Harvey Oswald. I got the distinct impression that this was seen not only as a matter of historical interest but also of something approaching pride—that here, so to speak, was proof that Beauregard could produce graduates who were famous for more than fifteen minutes. My second memory of Beauregard is that for much of the day of my visit many of the senior staff, including the principal, were occupied in meetings concerned with arrangements for administering a set of statewide standardized tests. Although a few staff clearly were irritated by the anticipated disruption of the school's normal schedule, the overall response seemed to be one of willing compliance with an administrative inconvenience. The third memorable event was that while browsing in the school library, I found a well-thumbed copy of a slim book titled *Vice Presidents of the USA,* which consisted of short (one or two pages) biographies of each incumbent. The last entry was for Spiro Agnew and reported his early resignation from the office without providing any reasons for his departure. Apart from the sanitizing of history that this last entry indicated, I was somewhat bemused that such a book existed at all. I cannot imagine a book titled *Deputy Prime Ministers of Australia* ever being written or published and find it even less likely that a school library would acquire it—let alone that it might actually be consulted by students.

In retrospect, and especially as I learn more about education in the United States of America, these three events no longer strike me as being particularly surprising or sinister—they are *(pace* Hannah Arendt, 1963) signs of banality rather than evil. However, they are still symptomatic of visions of curriculum in which such banality is taken for granted. How might we begin to envision curriculum futures in which it is not?

Send in the Ghosts

Readers might already have noticed that this volume has two introductions, the second, by my coeditor, Bill Doll, is titled "Ghosts and the Curriculum." Given that ghosts are, in a literal sense, disembodied signifiers, how do we reconcile their invocation in curriculum discourse with an embodied sense of vision? An obvious answer is that although ghosts represent disembodiment they also are "seen" (or produced) by an embodied eye/I. A less obvious justification is that the ambiguous and liminal status of ghosts—neither wholly physical nor metaphysical and yet both—can be perturbing and disturbing and thus provide a source of creative tension and speculation from which visionary possibilities might emerge. We see this very clearly in Deborah Britzman's essay, "The Death of Curriculum?," in which she calls on "ghosts who haunt the curriculum, not so much by their presence, as by their absence," to comment on what "the work of mourning" offers to curriculum inquiry.

When Bill Doll and I began to work on this text, I doubt that I would have defended the immanence of ghosts in curriculum work with any great enthusiasm. Ghosts were Bill's idea, and, whenever he insisted that the ghost of John Dewey haunted the curriculum of U.S. schools, I told him to call the ghostbusters. Since then, I have changed my mind about ghosts[14] for several reasons, not the least of which is that I have encountered many of them and have been very pleasantly surprised by their effectiveness in performing important curriculum (and other cultural) work. Let me give two examples from my own experience.

Sometime during my daughter's first year at high school (1994), she borrowed a video of the movie *Ghost* (1990). Although I have long admired the sophisticated treatment of the supernatural in Japanese cinema —from classics like *Ugetsu* (1953) and *Kwaidan* (1964) to contemporary science fiction *anime* such as *The Ghost in the Shell* (1995)—I have never much liked what Hollywood does with ghost stories, because they tend to conform rather predictably with the conventions of the genre(s) in which they are emplotted—horror, comedy, romance, drama. For the most part, *Ghost* seemed to be no exception—an undemanding "weepie" (albeit with some thrills and comic relief) that pushes all the right buttons: We laughed, we admired the special effects, and we got a little misty-eyed (especially when the Righteous Brothers sang "Unchained

Melody" on the sound track). But there was one brief and quite remarkable scene that confounded my expectations, a scene that demonstrated that even a Hollywood ghost can transcend its own banal origins and become a profoundly generative metaphorical construction that invites the viewer to negotiate complex issues and emotions. In this scene, the film's spectral hero (played by Patrick Swayze) contrives to have one last dance with his earthly lover (Demi Moore) by inhabiting the body of a psychic medium (Whoopi Goldberg). Adrian Martin (1994) captures the tantalizing ambiguity of what happens next:

> It's a nervous, carefully handled scene: the camera moves gingerly away from Whoopi's black, female hands touching Demi's and, when it returns, Whoopi is Patrick (Demi, wisely enough, keeps her eyes closed throughout), until finally there is a loud intrusion and the male spirit abruptly exits its female host. At least one reviewer had the presence of mind to complain that the scene's unprepared-for hint of lesbianism seems to contradict the film's otherwise pristinely heterosexual theme. But, intentionally or not, that's exactly the fire with which the film, for this fleeting minute, plays. In a story that, for the two hours of its running time, ensures that everyone stays in their proper place—that the poor will never get rich and the bad guys will go straight to hell—here is the supreme, supplementary moment of fantasy in which the clearcut lines of gender, class and race are scrambled, and all thanks to a ghost. (20)

This is an excellent example of a ghost working through popular media to unsettle popular assumptions, and it is not alone. As teachers, such ghosts should be our allies, because they can access spaces in young people's worlds that often are denied to us. As Martin concludes, "ghosts move with enviable freedom in that precious space of chaos and confusion which generates our tallest tales of yearning" (25) and, I would argue, *learning*.

The second example I will share here arises from my recent experiences of working in southern Africa (see Gough, 1999, 2001), and my point will be brief. A philosophy shared by many African language groups—Zulu, Setswana, Sotho, Xhosa, to name a few—is widely known by the Zulu word *ubuntu*,[15] and by a proverb, *umuntu ngumuntu ngabantu,* that usually is translated as "a person is only a person through other people." I soon learned that these "other people" include ancestral spirits and that a free and easy interaction between the worlds of the living and the dead forms an integral part of African oral traditions (this has even spilled over into Afrikaans literature). Some of my African colleagues prefer not to use the word "ancestor" as this implies a person who has once lived who is now dead. They prefer a term such as "shade" that has connotations of an intimacy with the living, an ongoing relationship that does not cease with death. André Brink (1998) recalls a Zulu friend explaining why, when taking his leave from someone, he would never use the singular form *sala gahle* ("stay well") but always the plural, *salani gahle*. "Because no one is ever alone," Brink's friend said. "You are always accompanied by all your spirits" (25). I cannot say that the shades that accompany my African friends are revealed to me in any direct way, but I have become increasingly sensitive to the effects of their presence. Each friend, as Walt Whitman said of himself, is a multitude.

You, too, will meet ghosts in the chapters that follow. Some, like the ghosts from Charles Dickens's *A Christmas Carol,* might already be familiar; they make a brief appearance in Doll's chapter and have a sustained presence in John St. Julien's. By the time you read Hongyu Wang's account of the "stranger" in Dwayne Huebner's vision of curriculum as a spiritual journey, you might even be looking forward to the company of ghosts of your own summoning.

Futures in Curriculum

In order to emphasize that I hold all representations of "the future" or "futures" under erasure,[16] I turn not to a ghost but to that epitome of contradiction, Satan, known both as the "Prince of Darkness" and "Lucifer" (from the Latin, "light-bringing").[17] As interviewed by Frank Dexter (1996), Satan offers some perceptive views on the abstraction of futures in modernist cultures:

> Modernity is the commitment to insecurity and change for their own sake....
>
> The concept of "future" which you're so preoccupied with illustrates how easily this idea of change ensnares you. By talking about it as a kind of place you're going to and trying to get prestige by being there before everyone else you're only inviting disappointment. When the future is always invoked by its difference, as somewhere else, and used to invalidate the past, it leaves the here and now in my hands. There's really no such place as the future.
>
> Modernity means conceiving temporality in terms of space: always talking about areas, zones, fields, boundaries, sites and so on, and thinking of change as "movement"—going "forward," "advancing," making "progress" and all the rest....
>
> Time only exists for living creatures....But your limited binary opposition between life and death excludes the existence of other beings, like myself, who are neither "alive" nor "dead" according to your scheme of things: beings who have all the time in the world. (299)

We might find it difficult to resist doing the devil's work. For example, towards the end of Bill Doll's essay in this volume he writes, "We are entering a period of 'post' thought: postmodern, poststructural, postcolonial, postpatriarchal, postindustrial." One way to interpret this proliferation of "posts" in academia is that they actually signal a failure of vision, our inability to imagine what is next as anything other than an immanent space towards which their precursors gesture. Echoing Satan's words, Jacques Derrida (1978) asserts that this failure is inevitable, since the future is "the as yet unnamable which is proclaiming itself and which can do so…only under the species of the non-species" (293). Understanding the future as spectral immanence is obviously productive for Doll (and for several other authors represented here, including Quinn, St. Julien, and Wang), but I am not yet ready to concede that "the future *belongs* to ghosts," as Doll quotes Derrida in the epigraph to his chapter. It is a fine aphorism but too totalizing for my taste. I would prefer to think that we are able to shape our own destinies, if not entirely then at least to the extent that makes the effort worthwhile. When we generate visions of curriculum futures, I want to be able to call on a wide variety of ontological, epistemological, methodological, axiological, *and illogical* resources. These might include ghosts but not *only* ghosts.

For example, we should not underestimate the strategic merits of what I referred to earlier as the constructive "negativity" of critical vision. The numerous "post" marks in the curriculum landscape might simply signal our desire for a future that is *not* modern, *not* structural, *not* colonial, *not* patriarchal, *not* industrial, and so on. Perhaps they are not precursors of anything other than their own absence. According to this view, the work of generating futures in curriculum is chiefly concerned with correcting "errors" (in the broadest understanding of the term) in the present. Many, perhaps most, of the contributors to this text offer what I would call a constructively negative critical vision. For example, Bowers urges us to root out the "root metaphors" that initially justified the globalization of the Industrial Revolution and now justify its "digital phase"; Britzman wants us to face the existential dread of asking "why curriculum?" and "encounter the confusion of our times" before we address our relationship with future times; Cherryholmes deconstructs taken-for-granted categories and distinctions in contemporary curriculum discourses; Cole and O'Riley argue for the introduction of ignored voices into these same discourses; Fleener provides blueprints for fixing the foundations of curriculum so that they might become more "organocentric"; Kesson and Oliver critique the place of excessive abstraction in our theory of educational experience; Molnar wants schools to be commercial-free zones; Trueit wants both oral and written curriculum discourse to become more conversational. Each of these authors closely scrutinizes an aspect of contemporary curriculum work in order to alert us to the limitations, distortions, defects, and dangers of current practice and to speculate on measures that might ameliorate them.

But regardless of whether the curriculum visions presented here were generated by spectral immanences or constructive negativity, Cleo Cherryholmes's question remains to be answered: What to do? I suggest that the next step in envisioning desired futures for curriculum must be taken by you, our readers, and I will bring this introduction to closure by retelling a tale that I hope will be helpful in orienting you to this quest.

In *Always Coming Home*, Ursula Le Guin (1986) tells stories of the Kesh, a people who "might be going to have lived a long, long time from now in Northern California" and whose stories are written as translations of "their voices speaking for themselves." One brief story is told by the grandchild of a man called Fairweather. We are told that during Fairweather's adolescence "he learned arboriculture with his mother's brother, a scholar of the Planting Lodge...and with orchard trees of all kinds." Fairweather lived in a time and place when "none of the Valley pears were very good, all were subject to cankers, and most needed irrigation to bear well." He asked people in the north for help in obtaining different varieties, and, by crossbreeding northern seedlings with a pear tree he found growing wild above the oak forests, "he came upon a strong, small, and drought-hardy tree with excellent fruit...this is the brown pear grown in most orchards and gardens, and people call it the Fairweather pear" (274–75). Le Guin concludes this deceptively simple story as follows:

> TRANSLATOR'S NOTE:
> *...he learned arboriculture with his mother's brother...and with orchard trees of all kinds*
>
> We would be more likely to say that he learned *from* his uncle *about* orchard trees; but this would not be a fair translation of the repeated suffix *oud*, with, together with. To learn *with* an uncle and trees implies that learning is not a transfer of something by someone to someone, but is a relationship. Moreover, the relationship is considered to be reciprocal. Such a point of view seems at hopeless odds with the distinction of subject and object considered essential to science. Yet it appears that [Fairweather's] genetic experiments or manipulations were technically skillful, and that he was not ignorant of the theories involved, and it is certain that he achieved precisely what he set out to achieve.

> And the resulting strain of tree was given his name: a type case, in our vocabulary, of Man's control over Nature. This phrase, however, could not be translated into Kesh, which had no word meaning Nature except *she*, being; and anyhow the Kesh saw the Fairweather pear as the result of a collaboration between a man and some pear trees. The difference of attitude is interesting and the absence of capital letters perhaps not entirely trivial. (275)

The difference of attitude is indeed interesting; moreover, it is the *difference* between the Kesh view of learning and our own that gives the story its critical edge. Fairweather's story, and Le Guin's "translation" of it, questions the taken-for-grantedness of many past and present conceptions of teaching and learning by providing us with a vision of a possible future curriculum practice. However, even though this story is ostensibly set in a time yet to come, the generativity of the prospective vision it represents does not depend on it being projected into the (or a) future. Rather, Le Guin emphatically locates the *meanings* her story generates in the present:

> The difficulty of translation from a language that doesn't yet exist is considerable, but there's no need to exaggerate it. The past, after all, can be quite as obscure as the future. The ancient Chinese book called *Tao teh ching* has been translated into English dozens of times, and indeed the Chinese have to keep retranslating it into Chinese at every cycle of Cathay, but no translation can give us the book that Lao Tze (who may not have existed) wrote. All we have is the *Tao teh ching* that is here, now. And so with translations from a literature of the (or a) future. The fact that it hasn't yet been written, the mere absence of a text to translate, doesn't make all that much difference. What was and what may be lie, like children whose faces we cannot see, in the arms of silence. All we ever have is here, now. (xi)

Le Guin thus reminds us that the value of a hopeful vision has little to do with its temporal referents. What matters is the wisdom and virtue that might emerge as we construct our critical and creative responses to such visions here, now, in the present within which our pasts and futures are enfolded. This location and embodiment of futures in the present also clearly distinguishes visions of "what may be" from *prediction.* Prediction invests futures with the spurious objectivity to which Satan alludes—times to come are seen as metaphorical equivalents of places to visit, as though they had a tangible presence "out there." However, futures are human constructions that are never "out there" but, rather, are always "here, now." Recognizing that futures are intrinsic to present action and existence liberates the critical and creative imagination and enables us to explore possible futures without colonizing them. Thus, the types of futures study that can expand the temporal horizons of curriculum discourse are those that are located firmly in our present consciousness and in the type of critical vision that "sees through" the inherited meanings, traditions, values, paradigms, myths, metaphors, concepts and guiding images of various kinds that are embedded in everyday language and mediate our experiences of temporal continuity and change.[18]

In one of Le Guin's stories of the Kesh, a young girl is on a journey from which she makes a short detour to visit her family in a nearby town. She recalls: "I had been to Madidinou many times, of course, but this time the town looked altogether different, since I was on a journey beyond it" (10–11). The search for prospective curriculum visions—curriculum futures—should have a similar effect, that is, to make the present and the choices we perceive within it look "altogether different." But, unlike a journey beyond a town, futures in curriculum are not "out there" waiting for us to arrive. We must visualize them here, now.

Notes

[1] From John Sampson (1905, 131).

[2] It was only much later in life that I began to appreciate the astonishing breadth, diversity, and complexity of Blake's vision as represented in his engravings, poetry, paintings, and prose. Many of his shorter verses are deft satires of Cartesian and Newtonian science, as in his famous prayer that God keep us "from single vision and Newton's sleep." But in the so-called "Prophetic Books," Blake presented what he claimed were direct perceptions of ultimate reality, described by John Sampson (1905) as "a verbal and pictorial rendering of Blake's visions, a storehouse of his mythology, and a fervent exposition of his mystical gospel" (326). W. B. Yeats (1905) wrote that these books symbolically staged "the great contest of imagination with reason" (xxxv), and Donald Ault (1974) suggests that, in part, they are "the working out of a visionary solution to the problem of system—specifically Newton's system—and its relation to the individual perception" (45).

[3] The possible influences of the eye's physiology on the work of many visual artists (and those who deploy visual imagery such as musicians and poets) are described in detail by Patrick Trevor-Roper (1988).

[4] For elaborations of the distinctions that can be made between these different visions of "special" education see, for example, Peter Clough (1988) and John Schostak (1988).

[5] *Blade Runner: The Director's Cut* differs in some small but significant ways from the original wide screen cinema release, the Embassy Home Entertainment videocassette (which also cropped the image to fit television screen proportions), and The Criterion Collection laserdisc (which restored the wide screen format). For detailed notes on differences between these previous versions, see William Kolb (1991).

[6] Zolkower differentiates the relatively recent "new new math" movement in the United States of America from the "new math" reforms of the 1960s and '70s. The "new new math" reforms emphasize problem solving, symbolic analysis of "word problems," and

gender/race/class inclusiveness. A key manifesto of the "mathematical empowerment for all" movement is the National Research Council report, *Everybody Counts* (Mathematical Sciences Education Board, National Research Council, 1989).

[7] Zolkower is citing Paul Willis (1977).

[8] I should perhaps say that Cole and O'Riley *appear* to move around a lot, because I know that they are skilled illusionists and ventriloquists.

[9] Competitive assessment of achievement in the academic curriculum also receives more emphasis in Canada and the United Kingdom than in Australia. However, I have chosen here to compare Australia only with the United States of America because I do not want to suggest that, by virtue of being different from Australia in this respect, Canada, the United Kingdom, and the United States of America are necessarily similar to one another in the specific ways in which competitiveness is manifested in their school curricula and wider cultures.

[10] The quotation is from a very influential statement of principles of organization, curriculum and assessment that the director of secondary education, Ron Reed, circulated to all Victorian government secondary schools on December 1, 1968. The "Reed Principles," as they became known, were developed in consultation with a curriculum advisory board established by Reed in 1966, comprising invited representatives of most educational interests in the state. Included with the principles was the rider that their application to individual schools was "a matter for the schools themselves"—a rider which foreshadowed the eventually explicit policy of school-based curriculum development. A complete statement of the Reed Principles, together with various accounts of their history and the reforms they stimulated, can be found in *Secondary Curriculum* (Victorian Secondary Teachers Association, 1970). In addition to Reed's (1975) own account, a useful summary of these reforms is provided by Gwyneth Dow (1985).

[11] These are variations on criterion-referenced assessment; "work requirements" (which specify learning *processes* in which students must participate rather than learning products or outcomes) continue to be an integral part of the school-based assessment components of the Victorian Certificate of Education, which documents students' achievement in the final two years (years 11 and 12) of secondary schooling.

[12] Since the election of a conservative government in Victoria in October 1992, there have been some modifications to these policies, including attempts to introduce statewide norm-referenced achievement testing in key learning areas such as English and mathematics at selected levels (years 3 and 5 at present). However, these tests are being used to assess the achievements of school populations rather than individual students and the testing program is being resisted (often strenuously) by many government school teachers and parents (and ignored by many nongovernment schools).

[13] One indication that the campaign was not regarded as the ravings of a lunatic fringe was that Bill Hannan, a prominent teacher unionist and chief architect of the university entrance ballot strategy, went on to chair Victoria's State Board of Education and later to become General Manager of the Ministry of Education's Curriculum branch.

[14] I have not changed my mind about calling on the ghostbusters to exorcise Dewey's specter. This is not because I want to diminish Dewey or his contributions to education in the United States and elsewhere but, rather, because I believe that many U.S. curriculum scholars are unhealthily addicted to Dewey's writings as dogma. Over thirty years ago,

Joseph Schwab (1969) remarked on the "marked perseveration" (4) that constituted one sign of crisis in the curriculum field: "I recoil from counting the persons and books whose lives are made possible by continuing restatement of the Tyler rationale, of the character and case for behavioral objectives, of the virtues and vices of John Dewey" (6). Schwab's shade recoils still: In U.S. curriculum discourse, the case for behavioral objectives is reiterated perennially albeit in new (dis)guises such as "outcomes-based education," the wisdom and/or efficacy of the Tyler rationale is questioned and/or defended *ad nauseum*, and the virtues (rather more than the vices) of John Dewey are repeated *ad infinitum*. Surely, it is *possible* to theorize education—even in the United States—without the exaggerated and excessive genuflections to Dewey that, in some cases, have become thoughtless rituals. At the very least, I am willing to speculate that U.S. curriculum theorists might be pleasantly surprised by the effects of reducing their dependence on his work.

[15] *Ubuntu* can variously be translated as morality, humaneness, compassion, care, understanding, and empathy. It implies an ethic of sharing, hospitality, honesty, and humility in interactions that take place within an extended family that ideally draws in all African peoples.

[16] To read a term under erasure is simultaneously to accept and reject it; see also Cherryholmes (this volume).

[17] Dexter quotes Satan as preferring Lucifer: "I am glad to have been finally acknowledged as the author of the Enlightenment. Recent vilifications of the Enlightenment and all its works are most gratifying, for nothing makes me more proud than to have all my accomplishments so universally condemned" (293).

[18] For further details and examples of critical futures study in curriculum inquiry see Gough (1988, 1989, 1990).

References

Arendt, Hannah. (1963). *Eichmann in Jerusalem: A report on the banality of evil*. New York: Viking.

Ault, Donald D. (1974). *Visionary physics: Blake's response to Newton*. Chicago and London: University of Chicago Press.

Ballard, J.G. (1996). *A user's guide to the millennium*. London: HarperCollins.

Brink, André. (1998). Interrogating silence: New possibilities faced by South African literature. In Derek Attridge and Rosemary Jolly (Eds.), *Writing South Africa: Literature, apartheid, and democracy, 1970–1995* (pages 14–28). Cambridge: Cambridge University Press.

Clough, Peter. (1988). Bridging "mainstream" and "special" education: A curriculum problem. *Journal of Curriculum Studies*, *20*(4), 327–38.

Derrida, Jacques. (1978). *Writing and difference*. Alan Bass (Trans.). Chicago: University of Chicago Press.

Dexter, Frank. (1996). An interview with Satan. In George Robertson, Melinda Mash, Lisa Tickner, John Bird, Barry Curtis, and Tim Putnam (Eds.), *FutureNatural: Nature, science, culture* (pages 293–302). London and New York: Routledge.

Dick, Philip K. (1968). *Do androids dream of electric sheep?* London: Grafton.

Dow, Gwyneth. (1985). Curricular reforms that were "caught not taught" in Australia. *Journal of Curriculum Studies*, *17*(2), 215–26.

Ginsberg, Allen. (1956). *"Howl" and other poems*. San Francisco: City Lights.

Gough, Noel. (1988). Children's images of the future: Their meaning and their implications for school curriculum. *Curriculum Concerns*, *5*(2), 6–10.

_________. (1989). Futures in curriculum: The anticipatory generation of alternatives. In David Stockley (Ed.), *Melbourne Studies in Education, 1987/88* (pages 23–34). Bundoora: La Trobe University Press.

_________. (1990). Futures in Australian education: Tacit, token and taken for granted. *Futures*, *22*(3), 298–310.

_________. (1995). Manifesting cyborgs in curriculum inquiry. *Melbourne Studies in Education*, *29*(1), 71–83.

_________. (1998). Reflections and diffractions: Functions of fiction in curriculum inquiry. In William F. Pinar (Ed.), *Curriculum: Toward new identities* (pages 94–127). New York: Garland.

_________. (1999). Troubling "freedom": Silences in post-apartheid environmental education. *Southern African Journal of Environmental Education*, *19*, 40–49.

_________. (2001). Learning from *Disgrace*: A troubling narrative for South African curriculum work. *Perspectives in Education*, *19*(1), 102–28.

Hannan, Bill. (1985). *Democratic curriculum*. Sydney: Allen and Unwin.

Haraway, Donna J. (1989). *Primate visions: Gender, race, and nature in the world of modern science*. New York: Routledge.

_________. (1991). *Simians, cyborgs, and women: The reinvention of nature* (pages 183–201). New York: Routledge.

_________. (1994). A game of cat's cradle: Science studies, feminist theory, cultural studies. *Configurations: A Journal of Literature, Science, and Technology*, *2*(1), 59–71.

Hill, Stephen. (1990). Changing the technological trajectory: Addressing the trailing edge of Australia's historical culture. *Futures*, 22(3), 272–97.

Kolb, William M. (1991). *Blade runner* film notes. In Judith B. Kerman (Ed.), *Retrofitting* blade runner*: Issues in Ridley Scott's* blade runner *and Philip K. Dick's* do androids dream of electric sheep? (pages 155–77). Bowling Green, OH: Bowling Green State University Popular Press.

Le Guin, Ursula K. (1986). *Always coming home*. London: Gollancz.

Martin, Adrian. (1994). *Phantasms*. Ringwood, Victoria: McPhee Gribble.

Mathematical Sciences Education Board, National Research Council. (1989). *Everybody counts: A report to the nation on the future of mathematics education*. Washington, DC: National Academy Press.

McClure, Michael. (1994/1982). *Scratching the beat surface: Essays on new vision from Blake to Kerouac*. New York: Penguin.

Reed, R. A. (1975). Curriculum reforms in Victorian secondary schools in the late sixties. In Stephen Murray-Smith (Ed.), *Melbourne studies in education 1975* (pages 214–25). Carlton, Victoria: Melbourne University Press.

Sampson, John. (1905). *The poetical works of William Blake: A new and verbatim text from the manuscript engraved and letterpress originals*. Oxford: Clarendon.

Schostak, John. (1988). Education and the schooling of those with "special needs." *Journal of Curriculum Studies, 20*(3), 263–67.

Schwab, Joseph J. (1969). The practical: A language for curriculum. *School Review, 78*(1), 1–23.

Staessens, Katrine, and R.Vandenberghe. (1994). Vision as a core component in school culture. *Journal of Curriculum Studies, 26*(2), 187–200.

Trevor-Roper, Patrick D. (1988). *The world through blunted sight: An inquiry into the influence of defective vision on art and character.* (Revised ed.). London: Allen Lane, Penguin (London: Thames and Hudson, 1970).

Victoria, Minister of Education. (1984). *Curriculum development and planning in Victoria (Ministerial Paper 6).* Melbourne: Government Printer.

Victorian Secondary Teachers Association. (1970). *Secondary curriculum: Reprints from "The secondary teacher."* North Richmond, Victoria: Victorian Secondary Teachers Association.

Willis, Paul. (1977). *Learning to labor: How working class kids get working class jobs.* New York: Columbia University Press.

Yeats, W. B. (Ed.). (1905). *The poems of William Blake.* London: Routledge.

Zolkower, Betina. (1996). Math fictions. In Stanley Aronowitz, Barbara Martinsons, Michael Menser, and Jennifer Rich (Eds.), *Technoscience and cyberculture* (pages 57–96). New York and London: Routledge.

Noel Gough is Associate Professor in the School of Social and Cultural Studies in Education at Deakin University, Victoria, Australia, and Director of the Deakin Centre for Education and Change. In 1997, he was awarded the inaugural Eureka Prize for Environmental Education Research. He is the author of *Blueprints for Greening Schools* (1992) and *Laboratories in Fiction: Science Education and Popular Media* (1993), and has published numerous journal articles. He is the former Australian editor of the *Journal of Curriculum Studies* and an associate or advisory editor for several other international journals. He teaches courses in curriculum inquiry, futures in education, and educational research methodology and has research interests in environmental education, cultural studies of science, popular media, and alternative futures.

Ghosts and the Curriculum

William E. Doll, Jr.

> I believe...the future belongs to ghosts.[1] (Jacques Derrida, 1991, 349)

> We have conjured up the ghost of objective culture, and now we do not know how to lay it to rest. (Mikhail Bakhtin, 1993, 55–56)

The ghost of John Dewey hovers over the American curriculum[2] and, coincidentally, over the curriculum of other countries where he has had an influence, either in thought or in practice. His ghost haunts the curriculum field as an ethereal presence, reminding us that in neither theory nor practice have we yet "got it right." However, getting it right does not mean a change in form of Bobbitt's basic design, Bloom's categories, Hunter's seven-steps, Piaget's stages, or Tyler's rationale. All these, different as they are, share the same misconception as to what constitutes curriculum. Dewey, haunted—indeed hounded—by this misconception all his life, now haunts us.[3] The vision he saw he wants us to see, but more clearly. Further, his ghost wants us to awaken from our slumbers and to "practicalize" Dewey's vision, to put in place the concept of curriculum he could not.

Such a curriculum concept, though, is not a mere mechanical adjustment; it is a reconceptualization of the very nature of curriculum. This reconceptualization has its roots entwined in the history of Western educational and intellectual thought: located in the separation between *curriculum* (a noun) and *currere* (a verb), between Erasmus' hierarchy of limited subjects and Rabelais' abundant "feast for the intellect," between *educare* and *educére,*[4] between training and enlightening, between knowledge transmitted/received and knowledge emergent/created. Although we have honored the former terms in these dichotomous splits, giving them an undeserved position of superiority over the latter, our task is not to reverse this hierarchical relationship. Such would only perpetuate the mistake. Instead, we need to move beyond this superiority-inferiority dichotomy, to dig deeply into the history and concept of curriculum as a word and an idea, and to transform both to meet new times and new situations. We need to *reconceptualize the nature of curriculum*, to see it not in terms of plans preset or ideologies advocated, but as an image hovering over the process of education, giving direction and meaning to that process. Such an amorphous and nondefinitional view of curriculum goes against its history, which has been to control and shape schooling (and education) to specific, predetermined ends.

Ghosts

Before going into the history of curriculum and looking at its development over the centuries, I'd like to explore the concept of ghosts in Western intellectual thought. I believe there is a useful metaphorical connection between curriculum and ghosts. On the one hand, our concept of curriculum as the essence of schooling, indeed as its blueprint, is haunted by our past; on the other hand, our imaginings of what curriculum could be may best be handled in terms of metaphorical visions, not in terms of prescribed lists, goals, objectives, methods.

Ghosts have an ethereal presence; they can be seen, often felt, but have no material substance. They exist on the fringes of our consciousness, neither physically real nor psychically unreal. They appear and disappear. They may be the appropriate metaphor to use when talking of *curriculum visions.* A ghost incarnated loses not only its ghostliness but also its suggestive power—of what was, is, might be. A ghostly perspective on curriculum may be not only all we can get but all we want, for in such a perspective, we always have potential, unrealized possibilities. To borrow a phrase from Martin Heidegger (1962/1926), here resides the "potentiality of being." In such a view of curriculum may well reside a process of schooling which can lead to an education.

Ghosts play a role in virtually all cultures. They speak to us from "the other side" or from "the Land of No Return," often admonishing us to remember that which we have forgotten or repressed. Their night visitations prod our consciousness or fill such consciousness with fear. At times their visions show us that which is to be—as with Brutus before his death at Philippi—or might be—as with Tiny Tim—if we do not make drastic changes. At other times ghosts give advice, often father to son—Anchises to Aeneas, the King of Denmark to Hamlet.

In Western thought, references to ghosts are found in tablets dating from the Assyrian, Babylonian, and Egyptian cultures, 3000 to 4000 years B.C. One Assyrian text begins:

> The gods which seize
> The evil-wind-ghosts
> Have come forth from the grave;

> To demand payment of rites and
> the pouring of libations. (Thompson, 1974, 24)

In these few lines, we see one of the chief reasons ancients believed ghosts left the grave—because their subterranean needs were not properly attended to—food for sustenance and drink to slake thirst. The Egyptians, especially, made much of burying their dead, properly mummifying them, leaving favorite amulets in the grave, and continually providing food and drink (sometimes with a long tube into the sarcophagus) for those interred. In such an environment, housing many of life's quiet pleasures, they believed the departed could "live" peacefully. Not all agreed with this assessment of afterlife, though. In the Holy Bible, Job says:

> Let me be, that I may be happy for a moment,
> before I depart to a land of gloom,
> a land of deep darkness, never to return,
> a land of gathering shadows, of deepening darkness.
> (Job 10: 20–22)

Another reason the ancients believed ghosts haunted the land of the living was for the dead spirit to find its corporeal body, to have it properly buried, thereby permitting the spirit to travel down to Hades. After a fierce battle, such as the one outside the gates of Troy, the bodies of the slain were not always properly consecrated; hence the souls of these bodies could not enter Hades. In the *Iliad* (1965/8th century, B.C.), Patrocles laments to Achilles that, after death, he, Patrocles, will not be allowed to enter Hades until his body is properly cremated upon a funeral pyre. He asks Achilles to perform this honor and further asks Achilles if the two of them might have their ashes buried in the same urn; for Achilles, Patrocles foresees, is also about to die. [An interesting aside here is that the Western ancients saw ghosts in black, not white, probably the result of being charred on the funeral pyre. From these pyres, the dead person's spirit would rise in wisps of grey/black smoke.]

The early Christian Church saw little need for ghosts. All Christians were to prepare their lives for the second coming of Christ, and, unlike the pagans in the Homeric epics, who lacked a proper burial or needed to search for money to pay the ferryman Charon, their souls passed directly to the underworld. But where in that underworld were they to wait for Christ's coming, especially when, by the fifth century, His coming seemed not so immanent?

Augustine, a fifth-century bishop of Hippo, believed his dead Chris-tian brethren were to await Christ's coming in a special place: "a hidden retreat" ("The Enchiridion," Ch. CIX, 1948/421, 722). This special place was neither the Hades of the Greeks nor the vision of hell John the Divine had of that "which is to come" (Rev. 1–6). Although not entirely certain of this hidden retreat—particularly regarding its what and where—Augustine did believe that it more likely than not did exist, that it was nearer to Heaven than Hell, and that those Christian souls residing in it—ones with only venial sins or special recipients of God's grace—would not be condemned to damnation. Further, he thought a soul's sojourn there might be only temporary. While awaiting the *Dies Irae*, which would accompany Christ's return, Augustine advocated that souls in this place could be helped by prayers and alms from the living. In time, during the twelfth and thirteenth centuries, Purgatory —from the Latin *purgare*, "to cleanse, purify, purge" (*Oxford English Dictionary, 2nd ed.*)—emerged in Church literature as a permanent place, an antechamber to Heaven. Here, one's soul was cleansed while awaiting Resurrection. While waiting, some souls (presumably the more adventurous) appeared to the living, asking for prayers and alms,[5] admonishing those living to mend their ways, and even entreating the living to hear their confessions. Caesarius of Heisterbach, in his thirteenth century *Dialogue on Miracles*, makes the following comment:

> So great a benefit is confession that even the spirits of the dead make use of it; often have I heard that the dead have appeared in dreams to the living, and have confessed their sins for which they were held in pains, and have truly shown by what works of mercy they could be delivered. (1929, Vol.1, 159)

The Church used these medieval apparitions to reinforce the populace's belief in life after death and as a way to advance its own teachings on how to avoid hellish punishment and instead achieve heavenly rewards.

Of all the countries in which ghosts reside, none has had more residents than Great Britain, that "misty isle," along with its even more misty outerparts, Wales, Cornwall, and Scotland. These have been homes to ghosts for centuries. There is hardly a castle, hall or manor house, not to mention country graveyard, without its personal ghost. London-towne, with its dark passages, crooked alleyways, and old houses, was the domain of many in Elizabeth I's time. And, of course, the Tower of London had its share —Anne Boleyn and the Earl of Stafford being but two. Mistress Jane Seymour, another of Henry's unfortunate wives, was said to roam the halls of the Royal Palace at Hampton Court for centuries and may yet roam again.

Shakespeare knew the populace would welcome ghosts when he introduced them into his plays. At least six plays (*A Winter's Tale*, *Troilus and Cressida*, *Julius Caesar*, *Richard III*, *Macbeth*, and *Hamlet*) have ghosts playing important if not major roles. In two of these, *Macbeth* and *Hamlet*, ghosts not only tell of past events and foretell future ones but also control the action. The three witches at the opening of *Macbeth* foreshadow the whole play, and Banquo's ghost is a main character; Hamlet's murdered father, the King of Denmark, is the driving force behind Hamlet's own actions. As the King's ghost says (Act III, sc. 4), when Hamlet dallies about revenging his murder:

> Do not forget. This visitation is
> but to whet thy almost blunted purpose. (lines 111–12)

In commenting on the role ghosts play in Shakespeare's dramas, one interpreter notes that Shakespeare uses them for much more than dramatic effect. They are there for the purpose of "giving us a full and faithful picture," that we may see things "as they really are and not as those who see only with physical eyes imagine them to be" (Rogers, 1925, 20).

Almost three centuries later, Charles Dickens, in *A Christmas Carol* (1913/1843), picks up this theme of using ghosts to show us, who see only with physical eyes, how things really are, have been, and might well be. Echoing Caesarius of Heisterbach, he uses Marley's ghost to induce Ebenezer Scrooge, "a squeezing, wrenching, grasping, scraping, clutching, covetous old sinner" (15), to confess his sins of greed, miserliness, and indifference. In many ways, Dickens's use of the spirits of Christmases Past, Present, and Yet-To-Come is analogous to our book's focus on visions of curriculum past, thoughts of curriculum present, and hopes for curriculum future.

As Dickens has Tiny Tim and others speak in their own voices, so will this book's curriculum scholars, teachers, and students speak in their voices. The past and future, then, are not interpreted by others—as in a synoptic text—but are presented by the curriculum actors in their own words and visions. For Dickens, such *realité verité* was a literary device, one he used powerfully to let the reader see "how things really are." For us, in this book, "reality through voice" is a pedagogical device, designed to develop dialogue as we, authors and readers, interact with each other through words and images.

It is odd to think of ghosts—ethereal, ephemeral, elusive—as imagistic metaphors for the way things really are, have been, or could be. Yet, this is just the reality ghosts bring to a situation—haunting us actors until the reality which lies beyond mere perception is seen by both ourselves and our audience (those we teach). Shakespeare brought forth this reality through his use of heightened drama; Dickens created vignettes of reality through his dialogue pictures. Now, we editors and authors propose a curriculum reality which will come into being as all of us take a deeper look into curriculum history and converse with those who helped create that history as well as with those who may well shape its future.

Etymologically, the word *ghost*—spelled without an "h" until the middle of the sixteenth century when the Flemish influence (*gheest*) became strong—originally meant "soul or spirit, as the principle of life" (*Oxford English Dictionary, 2nd ed., s.v.* "ghost"). The phrase *Holy Ghost* is indicative of this, as is the phrase "to give up the ghost" or the spirit of life. This sense of life spirit was one the ancient Greeks held, and it was this spirit Charon ferried across the river Styx, to "the other side." For us, the spirit of curriculum past should be ferried across to live peacefully in that Land of No Return, while we on this side adopt a new spirit.

Gilbert Ryle, in his classic work *The Concept of Mind* (1949), adopts this notion of ghost as spirit or life force but with a negative twist. Ryle argues (Chapter 1) that, since Descartes, at least, it has been common to separate human existence into two worlds: the bodily and the mental. There has been "a polar opposition between mind and matter," where "mental happenings occur in insulated fields," each apart from the other. Thus, each of us lives a "ghostly" mental life (13) apart from our bodily experiences and, indeed, often shrouded from our selves. This "doctrine" of mind, Ryle speaks of "with deliberate abusiveness, as the 'dogma of the Ghost in the Machine'...[intending] to prove that it is entirely false" (15–16). In this essay, I will not assess Ryle's attempt. [For my views on "mind," see Doll, 1993, Chapter 5.] However, I do wish to borrow Ryle's metaphor and argue that the history of curriculum has had, since the late sixteenth century, its own life force, spirit, ghost. The ghost in the curriculum has been *control.* I believe the time has come to ferry this spirit to "the other side"; not that we wish to live with no control but rather wish to abide here with another, new, livelier spirit of control.[6] This lively spirit or creative force permeates the very concept of a postmodern curriculum.[7]

Curriculum: Its Origins

David Hamilton has pointed out (1989, 1990) that the term *curriculum*, used in an educational (not chariot-racing) sense, first appeared in Peter

Ramus's "map of knowledge" (1576) and shortly thereafter in the records of the Universities of Leiden (1582) and Glasgow (1633). Both were Protestant universities, "heavily influenced by Calvinist ideas." As Hamilton (1989) says:

> Indeed, Leiden was founded specifically for the purpose of training Protestant preachers, and Glasgow's reconstitution was to meet similar purposes. What, then, might be the connection between Protestantism, Calvinism and curriculum? (44)

The word *curriculum*, of course, is Latin. Literally, it means either "a course for running" or "a chariot for racing" such a course (*A Comprehensive Etymological Dictionary of the English Language*, *s.v.* "curriculum"). Its infinitive form, *currere*, means "to run" and its adjectival form, *curricular,* means "of or pertaining to driving, or to carriages" for driving (*O. E. D.*, *2nd ed.*, *s.v.* "curriculum"). I suspect the course traversed or run around—*recurred* in medieval Latin—was the racetrack the chariots ran in the Circus Maximus. Why Calvinist educational theory adopted the Latin word for racetrack to express its interest in a formalized course of school study is an interesting story.

Although the term *curriculum* appears nowhere in educational literature prior to Thomas Fregius's publication of Ramus's mapping of the structure of knowledge in 1576, it is true that John Calvin in his *Commentaries* (1540–1565) often refers to life as a "race" or "racecourse." In fact, in his final (1559) edition of the *Institutes*, Calvin uses the phrases *vitae curriculum* and *vitae curriculo*. However, these phrases are used sparingly compared to the number of times he used *vitae cursu* or *vitae cursum*, alternative renderings for the "course of life."

At this time, it was not common to think of life (or learning) as having the sort of sequential order that today we attribute to curriculum or curriculum vitae. From the *stoa* and the *agora* in ancient Greece to the Church schools of the Middle Ages, learning was highly individualized and restricted. Learning and teaching occurred when groups of itinerant students gathered at the feet of a master to study a text or texts with the resplendent glosses the master chose or wrote himself. Pupils wandered from master to master and from city to city, "studying" as long as they wished. There was no sense of sequence to this process or of one ever "having finished." Rather, the students (those engaged in the *studio* or study presented) traveled from place to place and from teacher to teacher as long as they wished. It was boredom, ennui, or a more appealing prospect, such as fighting for a prince or duke, which caused the students to move on. Never was a semester, project, or text "finished."

While the *trivium* (grammar, rhetoric, logic) and the *quadrivium* (usually geometry, astronomy, arithmetic, music or ethics) did exist as knowledge categories, there was no sequential order to their presentation. The study of Aristotle's recently discovered "new" works—his *Physics*, *Metaphysics*, *Ethics*, and *Politics*, found by scholars in the twelfth century—along with writings of such Church theologians or Christian philosophers as Augustine, Boethius, and Aquinas, formed the heart of scholastic study. The glosses written on these works were amazingly intricate and abstruse. Today we have the caricature of those scholars and students debating how many angels could stand or dance on the head of a pin.

The rise of Protestantism, commercialism, and the forming of the middle class brought a new social, commercial, and intellectual order—one interested in simplicity, efficiency, and method. As Grafton and Jardine (1986) point out:

> The individualism, verging on hero-worship [of the great teachers], of early humanism gave way in the early sixteenth century to an ideology of routine, order and, above all, "method." (123)

Probably no one word captures the tenor of the sixteenth and seventeenth centuries better than *method*. Method was the hallmark of the new Copernican science; it formed the heart of Descartes's (1950/1637) discourse on "rightly conducting reason for seeking truth" and represented the vehicle by which a rising merchant and Protestant class could assert itself. Finally, method—simple, practical, universal—stood in direct opposition to the intricate entanglements of the Roman Church and the circuitous logic and elaborations of scholasticism. Teaching now underwent a paradigmatic change—from dialogic glosses on ancient and honored texts and even from glosses on those glosses to a direct, "short-cut" route to a desired and prescribed end. Epistemology became practical and teaching became methodized.

The man who spent virtually all his adult life "methodizing" knowledge and teaching was Peter Ramus, a sixteenth-century master at the University of Paris. In his *Dialectica* (1569), Ramus states:

> Method is disposition by which...that enunciation is placed first which is first in the absolute order of knowledge, that next which is next, and so on: and thus there is an unbroken progression. (465–66; translated from the Latin)

Ramus's new methodology—a taxonomic, hierarchical ordering from the general to the particular in a linear "unbroken progression"—was denounced by his colleagues as a vulgar "short-cut," which diluted the ancient and noble profession of dialogue. However, Ramus's idea of mapping knowledge certainly struck a tenor with the times, for his *Dialectica* had approximately 250 reprints in the century after its publication; an average of over two reprints a year for 100 years. As I have said, it was in one of Ramus's works, a taxonomy of knowledge, the *Professio Regia* (1576), published four years after his death, that the word *curriculum* first appears referring to a sequential course of study.

Ramus's idea of a general codification of knowledge—really a visual charting via various dichotomous branchings or "ramifications"—designed to bring an "orderliness" to teaching, flourished most in those geographical areas "tinged by Calvinism"—Germany and the Netherlands (Hamilton, 1989, 47). Hence, there was an affinity between the discipline, order, and control Calvin felt all Christians should bring to their lives and that which Ramus brought to pedagogy. It was natural that the Calvinist universities of Leiden and Glasgow would set up a new order of study, one based on the idea of curriculum as a set course to be followed and finished.

Although we do not know the detailed reasons for these Calvinist universities using the word *curriculum* (rather than *cursus* or *ratio* or *studio*) to describe a prescribed course of study which all students were to take and finish (something not considered in other universities), Hamilton believes a general outline of this occurrence seems clear (49). First, Ramus used the word *curriculum* to describe a sequentially ordered "map of knowledge," a visual form he felt could be used directly, just as he laid it out. Another teacher had only to add various particular *ramifications* or fillings-in for *his* own purposes.[8]

This skeletal outline or logical map of knowledge on which the ramifications were to be placed was, Ramus believed, universal in scope. It was a general outline to fit all knowledge. Further, and this is crucial, he thought the outline mapped not only the structure of knowledge but also *the structure of acquiring knowledge*. In Hamilton's (1990) words:

> [The logical map] was nothing less than the externalization of the mental processes of human cognition....If students adopted Ramus's method, they would be revisiting, absorbing and reproducing the logical processes used by illustrious creative thinkers. (26)

A Ramist Map[9]

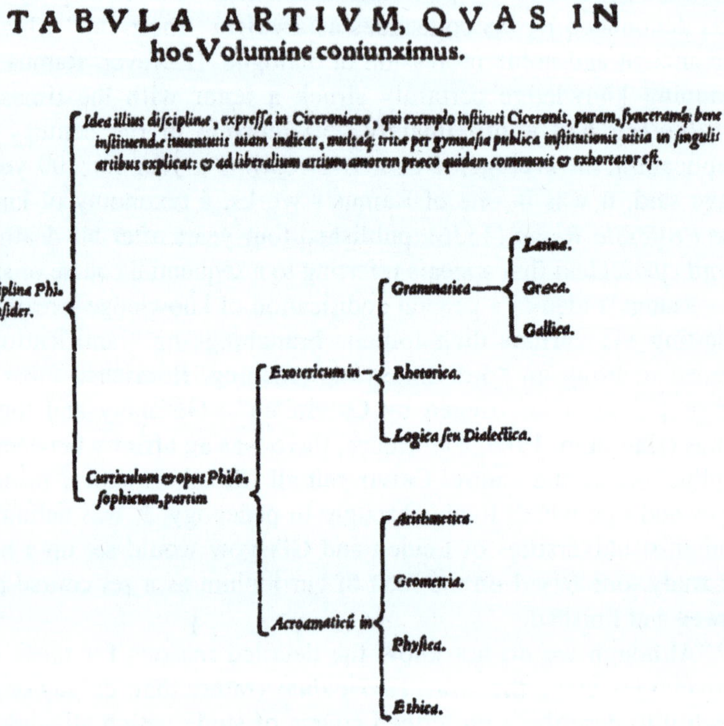

Source: P. Ramus, *Professio regia*, Basle, 1576.

In this quotation's last sentence, one need only substitute the phrase "experienced and successful teachers" for "illustrious creative thinkers," and the underlying, controlling purpose of "methods courses" in today's teacher preparation programs appears. Methods professors and teachers-in-training each harbor the hope that such courses will yield efficient "short-cuts" to the way knowledge is both structured and acquired. This has proven to be a forlorn and deceitful hope. Knowledge can be structured in many ways; the ways chosen for such structuring bear neither a direct nor a necessary relation to the way knowledge is acquired. In more academic terms, epistemology is not morphology. Confusion between these two has done immense damage to pedagogy and curriculum theory.

A second reason for using the word *curriculum* as a "course-of-life" or method of study was the Calvinist familiarity with it as part of their literature. However, most important, I believe, was the fact that this method provided the Calvinists,[10] committed to a faith based on order and discipline, with a way to steer their youth through a world "all in peeces," one with "all cohaerance gone" (Donne, 1968/1611), one clearly out of control. Stephen Toulmin (1990) points out that the period of the late sixteenth and early seventeenth centuries was one of turbulence and loss of coherence. In France, the murder of Henry of Navarre (Henry IV) ended the tenuous balance between Catholics and Protestants. In England, the same turmoil spilled over into the royal house of Tudor, with Catholics, Anglicans, and Dissenters all vying for power. Out of this emerged, of course, Oliver Cromwell's bloody protectorate and Holy Commonwealth. In Germany, the Thirty Years War consumed all for over a generation. Finally, in astronomy, Copernicus, Brahe, Kepler, and Galileo were proclaiming the sun as the center of the universe, with the earth, that on which we all stand, actually hurtling through space. To where was the earth hurtling? In such a frame, it is no wonder René Descartes doubted all in his attempt to find a "simple certain thing" (62) or that John Donne lamented these changes. In his "An Anatomie of the World" (1968/1611), Donne says:

> The element of fire is quite put out;
> The Sun is lost, and th' earth, and no man's wit
> Can well direct him, where to looke for it...
> 'Tis all in peeces, all cohaerance gone. (lines 205–13)

My reason for citing this history of the period between 1550 and 1650 is to help us appreciate the need for control which virtually all thinkers felt at the time. Thomas Hobbes echoes well the sentiments of many, when he declares "the life of man, solitary, poore, nasty, brutish, and short…[one wherein there is] 'warre' of every man against every man" (*Leviathan*, 1950/1651, 104–05). Curriculum, then, as a method to bring control and order to life goes back much farther than America's twentieth–century industrialization, where it is often placed (Doll, 1993, 1998; Kincheloe, 1995; Kliebard, 1986). Rather, control as an operating concept is actually embedded in the history of curriculum from the very first usages of the word in an educational setting. Control is not only the mechanical ghost in the curriculum clock—to use a modern, mechanistic metaphor—but is also the force which actually runs the clock as its pendulum swings from one ideology or fad to another. It is time to put this ghost to rest, to let it retire peacefully to the "Land of No Return" and to liberate curriculum to live a sprightly life of its own.

Curriculum and American Industrialism

As Kliebard (1986) says, in the 1890s, during America's industrial expansion, there came a "radically altered vision of the role of schooling," a shift from teaching centered around the personal "presence of the teacher to the remote knowledge and values incarnate in the curriculum" (1). Metaphorically, we might say this was a change from Mark Hopkins sitting on a frontier log conversing with his students to a standardized, methodized system of set routines and procedures. Needless to say, this methodization first took hold in the cities with their rising immigrant population, imported to fuel America's growing industrialization. This methodization captured not only America's schools and their curricula but the society's whole culture as well. Clergymen outlined methodological plans for their daily routines and then calculated how "efficient" they were in carrying out these routines. Popular magazines such as *Outlook* or *The Saturday Evening Post* ran articles on "Scientific Management in the Home" (Callahan, 1962, 44).

Methodization, with its adoption of external control, became the *modus operandi* of American society and culture. The particular form this methodization took was epitomized in Frederick Taylor's time-and-motion studies at the Bethlehem Steel Company in the mid-1890s. Taylor described his "laws" in *Scientific Management*, the book he published in 1911. These laws became paradigmatic for the management of work as well as for the development and design of curriculum during the major part of this century. William Schubert (1986) points out that soon thereafter, there was a "flurry of work in 'scientific curriculum making'" (76). Direct connections can be made between Taylor's "scientific" management theories and the curriculum ideas of Franklin Bobbitt, Elwood Cubberley, W. W. Charters, B. F. Skinner, Ralph Tyler, and Madeline Hunter. In the writings of all these curricularists, control is preeminent: it is always preset, prior, and external to the learning activity itself. Taylor's fourth law, the one he considered important above all others, makes clear the role control is to play in this paradigm and just who is to exercise this control. The fourth law—that of the "equal division of work and responsibility...between management and labor"—states that management's task is to plan while labor's is to follow these plans in precise detail. Each workman is to receive work orders "in writing and in detail" every day. The orders are to specify "not only what is to be done but how it is to be done and the exact time allowed for doing it" (Taylor, 1947/1911, 32). Labor's role in this "equal division of work and responsibility" is to follow the orders given, a task to which it is "best suited."

The move from preset, industrial planning to curriculum lesson plans with specific behavioral objectives is one the early curricularists eagerly made. Bobbitt, whose first two books Schubert (1980) labels "the Adam and Eve of curriculum works" (5), called students the "raw material" which school was to transform into a "finished product" (Bobbitt, 1912, 269). Cubberley (1916), utilizing this same factory and industrial metaphor, said:

> Our schools are, in a sense, factories in which the raw products (children) are to be shaped and fashioned into products to meet the various demands of life. (338)[11]

Charters (1923) went even further. He not only likened schools to factories and the curriculum to practical industrial skills, he also criticized Plato for not doing such. Had Plato not let "ideals [become] isolated from [practical] activities, then he would probably have influenced the education of the next two-thousand years" (9–10).

While the rawness of this school-as-factory, industrial metaphor has been softened (humanized) over the decades, the basic assumptions operable in Frederick Taylor's fourth law still predominate. In that marvelous little book, *Basic Principles of Curriculum and Instruction* (1950), Ralph Tyler's "four questions"—concerning purposes, experiences, organization, and assessment—assume that goals must be preset, linearly organized, clearly communicated from the manager-teacher to the worker-learner, and assessed in a manner that shows the immediate and quantifiable effectiveness of the whole process. Further, there lurks behind this process, as the ghost in the curriculum, the notion that the basic purpose of education is to "change behavior patterns of people to acceptable norms" (Tyler, 1950, 4,6). These norms, of course, become those which the people in power choose or, euphemistically, those which represent the "needs" of an emergent, industrial society. To extend the Schubert metaphor, if Bobbitt's works are the Adam and Eve of twentieth-century American curriculum-making, then Tyler's rationale is the Holy Bible, based on Taylor's commandments.

John Dewey's Vision

John Dewey, of course, was very much part of this time of ferment in American society. His years in Ann Arbor and Chicago were formative, as Westbrook (1991) points out. Dewey recognized well the importance of the Industrial Revolution and the way it was transforming America. Chicago in the 1890s—that city which Carl Sandburg (1960) said was "proud to be Hog Butcher, Tool Maker, Stacker of Wheat, Player with Railroads and Freight Handler to the Nation" (36)—was very much in Dewey's blood when he wrote:

> One can hardly believe there has been a revolution in all history so rapid, so extensive, so complete....[It] over-shadows and even *controls all others*....[It is] writ so large that he who runs may read. (1990/1900, 8–9; emphasis added)

Dewey, though, son of a Vermont merchant and imbued with liberal, Congregational ideals, was critical of this revolution. He worried about what it was doing—to America, to its cities, to its people. Dewey did not believe the factory-industrial model should be adopted as a paradigm for schooling; his vision was quite different although at times he had difficulty articulating that vision. The difficulty may have been in Dewey's language—which William James called "damnable, even God-damnable"—but certainly faults lay in our inability to hear or read what Dewey was saying. Maybe we were, and indeed are, "running too fast."

Dewey's vision, one which integrates education, schooling, curriculum, and community into a seamless whole, centers around the distinction between imposed and "emergent" control. The term *imposed control* —the way we usually consider the word control—conveys "the notion of an energy brought to bear from without" (1966/1916, 23). This outside force often is considered in order to meet "some resistance from the one controlled," for it subordinates one's "natural impulses" to another's ends. Hence a person now becomes a means to others' ends or at best to "public or common ends" (23). This, of course, is precisely what Bobbitt, Cubberley, and Charters did, all in the interests of a common good—the "needs" of a growing, industrial society. Needless to say, this common good is not defined by either workers or students, those charged with carrying out the vision others have. One can see here a particular interpretation of Plato's "just society"—each person in a place for which he or she is *best suited*—and one can gain a certain appreciation for Charters's admonition that Plato would have done better to ground his sense of this just society on practical job skills and not on the lofty ideals of abstract philosophizing.

Dewey realized, as one would expect, the falseness, absurdity, and ultimate inhumaneness of this doctrine, and Chicago in the 1890s gave him plenty of tangible evidence. However, and this is what makes Dewey great, he also realized—drawing partly on his Hegelian background and partly on his Congregational upbringing—that there can be no democratic freedom without some sense of control, no meaning in life without direction, and no growth without constraint. Dewey talks of the control which he envisions as "the other" sense of control, that which is "more important and permanent." This control is not self-control, for it is not located within the self; it arises from the situation at hand and "guides an activity to its own end" (24). In a sense, it *emerges* from the interactions happening within an event or set of experiences. Dewey does not use the word "emerge," and certainly self-organization, complexity and emergence theory were not part of the intellectual milieu of Dewey's time. Yet this concept of emergence—to be explored later in this essay under "Curriculum as Complexity"—is, I believe, the concept Dewey's ghost wants us to see and use in reframing Dewey's vision. Emergence is a frame which helps tie together a number of Dewey's thoughts—such as transformation and reconstruction—and particularly unifies three of his most famous educational concepts, ones which themselves act as a foundation for his vision of curriculum. These are: (1) as a process, education does not aim for an end external to itself; (2) ends arise from within activity rather than being set prior to activity; and (3) the child and the curriculum, the learner and the text, as it were, unite through the process of inter- (or trans-) action.

It is too bad that Dewey was never able to appreciate more fully what Alfred North Whitehead was attempting to do in his *Science and the Modern World* (1967b/1925) and *Process and Reality* (1978/1929). In both of these books, Whitehead lays out a new cosmology—one appreciated by Prigogine and Stengers (1984)—based on relations instead of on Newton's "hard, massy, impenetrable objects," i.e., atoms. For Whitehead, relations not atoms become the "really real" of the cosmos. Only through quantum physics, complexity theory, dissipative structures, and chaos theory have we begun to see the validity of this approach (Wheatley, 1992; Bechtel and Richardson, 1993; Doll, 1993; Kauffman, 1993, 1995; Capra, 1996). A short statement by Whitehead in *Process and Reality* (1978/1929) puts the case quite succinctly: "It lies in the nature of things that the many enter into complex unity" (21). In the worldview of complexity theory, two foci have begun to emerge from this statement: (1) The cosmos is a complex unity with change and stability inherently united, enfolded within one another. It is not a case of either/or but rather of both/and, of how these two are interrelated, each needing the other, each generating the other; and (2) This unity is relational not individual. Unfortunately, Whitehead expressed his ideas in abstruse terms, e.g., relational "events" (our working realities) arise from a "concrescence of prehensions" (a coalescing of feelings and experiences). Without the terminology and mysticism, though, Whitehead's sense of the process of becoming is akin to Dewey's notion of the transformation or reconstruction of experience. If akin is too strong a term, at least it can be said that each one's philosophy—process and pragmatism —would benefit from a reading of the other. Certainly, Whitehead's curriculum dictum, that one should teach few subjects well, throwing ideas "into every combination possible" (1967a/1929, 2), is a dictum Dewey advocated in his emphasis on looking for alternatives before deciding on a course of action. All this is to say that the concept of a curriculum built around relations is a powerful factor in each thinker's educational thought. It is also a foundational point in a postmodern curriculum (Doll, 1993).

In terms of control, complex systems have relations built into them. These systems need no *deus ex machina,* for they are not mechanistic and have no outside force governing them. In Dewey's terms, they have no preset, external ends; yet, as Whitehead says, it is in their "nature" to be unified. In chaos theory terms, "attractors" arise from and within the process of interaction. There is, then—in the dynamism of action, reaction, and interaction—a sense of direction. But this direction is internally developed not externally imposed. In short, it emerges. It is realization of the importance of this distinction between a curriculum imposed and one emergent which has led me to state that, although he is certainly no post-modernist, Dewey's "educational views are better understood from a post-modern than a modern perspective" (Doll, 1993, 13). The actuality of this realization lies, as I see it, in his assiduous effort in not defining "the other mode of control" as purely self or personal control, in seeing that internal imposition is not a viable alternative to external imposition. Dewey sees that this "other mode of control" comes from the interactions happening within a situation and between a situation and its environment. Further, he realizes that this other (emergent) control[12] guides a situation or "activity to its own end" (1966/1916, 24).

Assuming but not stating this metaphysical worldview, with its sense of an emergent holism, provides Dewey with a foundation[13] for his educational, schooling, and curriculum theses. One of these is that education is not to subvert itself to a future life activity, namely, industrial jobs. "Education," says Dewey, "has no end beyond itself"; it is subordinate to nothing "save more education" (53, 51). This view, of course, is quite different from Bobbitt's, Cubberley's, and Charters's, wherein education becomes schooling, and schooling becomes training in job skills. Curriculum for them is the vehicle for carrying out this training mandate.

External ends were anathema to Dewey. He felt that dichotomously separating the ends in activity from the activity itself reduced the activity (and the one doing the activity) to a mere means. To counteract this, he argued that ends or "aims fall within an activity instead of being furnished from without" (101). In his famous phrase on this point, he says (1974/1923):

> Ends arise and function within action. They are not as current theories too often imply, things lying beyond activity at which the latter is directed. They are not strictly speaking ends or termini of action at all. They are terminals of deliberation, and so turning points *in* activity. (70)

Dewey calls these turning points in activity "ends-in-view." The view he expresses here, one I am arguing is foundational for him, is that activity (experience) is a seamless whole with certain of these experiences/activities coalescing into particular events, ends, or turning points.

The practical and curricular question of ends within or outside activity is a chicken-egg one. Both occur; either can be a starting point, and Dewey realizes this. We do have general purposes which shape our activities, just as from reflecting on those activities, we develop specific aims. The process Dewey argues for is a *continuum* (1963/1938). He sees life, as did the German idealists and romantics he studied, as a seamless whole or continuum of experiences. Within that ongoing, moving whole, there are certain coalescences. The art of curriculum design, the purpose of education, and the nature of schooling, in their best modes, frame these coalescences to lead to further growth and betterment—for individuals, for society, for our cultures, and for the ecological universe in which we live. It is personal reflection and communal discussion—the integration of the private with the public—which turns these coalescences toward social betterment and growth.[14] It is within this foundational frame that I believe Dewey's pragmatism and scientific method must be placed. To do otherwise is to distort each, the first into vulgar expediency, the second into external, imposed method.

Curriculum in this frame becomes not a racecourse or series of hurdles on that track but an emerging of coalescing experiences within a transformative process. Dewey says we need to think of the curriculum as intimately connected to the child (the learner) and to see each—the child and the curriculum—as "two limits which define a single process," a process which is itself a "continuous reconstruction" of our ongoing, seamless whole life (1990/1902, 189). It is this transformative or reconstructive view of curriculum which Dewey's ghost is saying we need to understand before we can "get it right" regarding the details of organization.

Curriculum As...

So far my argument has been that curriculum, whether it is considered in terms of Kliebard's (1986) ideologies (humanist, developmentalist, scientific efficiency, social meliorism) or Schubert's (1986) paradigmatic orientations (traditional, behavioral, experimental), is always assumed to be a noun, a structured and sequenced set of courses; and underlying these sets lurks a particular concept of control—that of external force or imposition.[15] Curriculum, as we know it, is designed for this control to be operative and has been so designed since the word first appeared in Ramus's logical map of knowledge, itself framed in a Calvinist milieu. This milieu, heavy with predestination and predeterminism, saw education, schooling, curriculum —indeed life and reality—as controlled by outside, external forces. God in all *his* patriarchal splendor was envisioned as a *deus ex machina*—one who would metaphorically (and literally in the ancient plays) swoop down from the "heavens" and set things aright.

There were, of course, as Hamilton (1989, 1990) and others have pointed out, countertendencies to this closed system model—if I may label what I have been describing in such terms. There is the romantic tradition from Rousseau through progressivism and open education. Here the idea of "mapping" was still prominent but changed from the mapping of knowledge to the mapping of inner developmental stages. This romantic mapping of the "natural" has had its strongest influence in early childhood education, in what Friedrich Froebel (1912/1826) labeled "the child's garden" (*kindergarten*). However, even in this movement, the tendency has been to see development in terms of preset, linear, sequential stages—witness Jean Piaget's work.[16] So even here, in this romantic and naturalist setting, external control and standardized methodology remained; they just took on a "natural" flavor.

There was a branch of this romantic-progressive movement, though, which saw the need to redefine curriculum, to move away from curriculum as "subject-bound content" to curriculum as "learning experiences." As Malcolm Skilbeck (1984) says, this redefinitional move did shift curriculum away from "something articulated, definite and preplanned towards the nature of experience and the process of experiencing" (26). However, this definitional shift still did not go so far as to see curriculum as *currere*, nor was there an intellectual milieu present which saw the process of experiencing as fundamental reality—the "really real" of Whitehead. Such a full shift is happening only now, based partly on Ilya Prigogine's postquantum science, not to mention his postmetaphysical metaphysics, and on Alfred North Whitehead's cosmology, itself based, as David Griffin (1988) points out, on a "reenchantment of science."

John Dewey, as I have argued, saw the difficulty inherent in basing curriculum on technocracy, external control, and standardized methodology—he said the latter "breeds mediocrity" (1966/1916, 173). And he began working on a solution: developing a theory of experience (Doll, 1972, 1973). However, without the concept of self-organization and its attendant concepts of new, emergent, more complex and inclusive structures, such a theory falls into the very dichotomies Dewey tried to avoid. In these dichotomies, experience is either externally manipulated or it flounders in its own solipsistic world. Progressive education unfortunately demonstrated both—passing off as natural that which was highly manipulative while calling the absence of structure natural. "Natural" implies neither as we see today through complexity theory; nature is both spontaneous *and* structured, flexible *and* stable, chaotic *and* ordered. Such a "seeing," though, is quite recent, influenced by our attempt to understand the "strange world" of the quanta in something other than either/or terms—i.e., electrons *as both* waves and particles. Dewey saw the difficulties of either/or (1963/1938) and advocated an "and" approach as the titles of many of his works show. However, he did not build on this to create a "both/and" framework such as the one Richard Bernstein (1992) uses so effectively. This framework was not quite within Dewey's grasp nor was it part of the milieu of his time. Building such a framework is a legacy Dewey has left us and one his ghost haunts us to complete.

Dewey's concept of a continual, ongoing transformative process—one which includes both the past and the future, the child and the curriculum as interactive aspects of a dynamic whole—was not understood, developed, nor applied by his contemporaries or followers. In fact, Dewey himself did not have the understanding of transformative process that we have today. For him, Whitehead's statement about "the many entering into complex unity" as a natural activity was no more than a mystical, metaphorical statement (see Dewey's essay in Schilpp, 1941, for his views on Whitehead). Only in the past few decades through the development of nonlinear, iterative mathematics (that of chaos and fractals) do we begin to "see" the reality of relationships so dear, if obscure, to both Whitehead and Dewey.

Dewey's and Whitehead's ghosts—those pregnant possibilities extant in each thinker's ideas—visit us "to whet our almost blunted purpose." These ghosts urge us to bring Dewey's and Whitehead's curriculum ideas to term. The time is ripe for such; the gestation period has been long enough, if not too long. The bond these intellectual offspring will share is that our reality, the one we live with daily, is that of relationships. The five C's I have chosen to explore in this section on "Curriculum As"—those of *currere*, complexity, cosmology, conversation, and community[17]—all accept relationships as the ultimate reality within which we work, live, and play. It is this acceptance which makes these five postmodern. They all see the "thingness" of the noun curriculum (the courses, plans, methods of instruction and evaluation) as part of a larger whole. This whole is, in itself, not a thing but a matrix or system of relationships. The system's continuity over time depends *not on* its being a set, fixed, static structure but on its relational transformations and on the emergence of present structures from structures that *were* and into structures that *will be.* In short, the "really real" of reality is that of interrelating and dynamically changing structures, with the structures of the disciplines existing as but minor parts of this larger whole.[18]

Curriculum as *Currere*

If we take seriously John Dewey's statements that (a) "the child and the curriculum" are embedded within and actually "define a single process" (1990/1902, 189), and that (b) this process is one of transformation (1971/1933, 84), then I believe we have no choice but to consider curriculum in its verb form, as *currere*. This move from curriculum as a noun to a verb broadens the meaning of curriculum. William Pinar and Madeleine Grumet (1976), in a brilliant insight, brought forth *currere* in the mid-1970s, but at that time few curricularists were prepared to understand the radical importance of this shift. William Reid (1981a) pays passing attention to the concept, saying it is "suggestive" (181), and William Schubert (1986) describes it as a "recent position...on the educational horizon" (33). But not until Robert Graham's 1992 article on "*Currere* and Reconceptualization" was *currere* seen as a major idea, one to be "reckoned with" (34). Only now, a quarter century after its birth, are we in the curriculum field beginning to recognize the importance of *currere* and of Pinar and Grumet's development of it as an "intellectual tour de force."[19]

Currere means "to run." Specifically it means to run a course, a closed course such as that used by chariots in the *circus maximus*. Hence in talking of curriculum, it is possible to focus on the course (a noun) as a material object or on the running of the course (a verb) as a personal experience. Since the time of Ramus and Comenius, we have considered curriculum almost exclusively in terms of the course to be run, not in terms of the personal experience of running. This is probably one reason the scientific efficiency movement (Doll, 1993, Ch. 2; Kliebard, 1986, 1992) "caught on" so well in American schools: It formalized a concept of curriculum already bred into our consciousness. There were, as I have mentioned, counter-movements to this curriculum-as-sequenced-courses frame: romanticism, kindergarten, child study, Freudianism, child development, Piagetianism, constructivism—to name but a few. However, none of these were really *currere* oriented; none began with the personal experiences of the individual (the runner) and asked that individual to reflect on what was happening personally as the running (or moving through the curriculum) progressed. If education is to be *transformative*—changing the quality of experience for the individual—then, I, along with John Dewey, believe curriculum must start with the individual.[20]

This personalness is what *currere*, as Pinar and Grumet (1976) use the term, is really all about. Pinar says that *currere* as a method is the "self-conscious conceptualization" of the self (51). In simple terms, *currere* is the self's exploration of its experiences (really, experiencing); in more complex terms, it is the relation of the self to the self in the self's evolution within the world. For Pinar, this occurs when one takes one's "current perspective" and "put[s] parentheses around it (so to speak) by recording it" (52). By this recording/reflecting/distancing act, Pinar says, one has "moved to another vantage point" and "the old problem...is seen differently...because...*the problem is different*" (53). In his own metaphorical way, Pinar describes this self-reflective process, "I see that my thoughts are like bubbles from the bottom of a pond, and I am on the surface; and they express...the deep structure of my being" (54).

The phenomenological bases inherent in this method are obvious.[21] What may not be so obvious are the Deweyan overtones that are inherent.[22] Pinar's recording/reflecting is quite similar to Dewey's primary/secondary or doing/reflecting concept of experience. Only when experience is *reflected* upon does it truly become *an experience* (in Dewey's sense); only through this secondary, reflective act does meaning get made, do understanding and transformation occur.

The Deweyan conception inherent in *currere* comes out strongly in Grumet's remark, borrowed from Aldous Huxley, "Experience is not what happens to (one)...it is what (one) does with what happens" (111). Such a concept has profound implications for both curriculum and instruction. In a broad sense it means we need to look at curriculum as a transformative, personal experience as we—students and teachers—reflect, autobiographically, on our journey. In a narrower, instructional sense, it means, as Grumet points out, that we first ask the student "What does this mean to you?" (118). Here, in this probing, personal questioning—quite unlike that in the Tyler rational—lie the beginnings of a dialogic or transformative curriculum. This simple questioning—which Heidegger (1977/1954) has called "the piety of thought" (31)—(re)frames the whole of educational experience; it moves this experience from that being molded or controlled by others to that of *dialoguing* with others. In contemporary, poststructural terms, this shift means seeing curriculum as a process or method of "negotiating passages"—between ourselves and the text, between ourselves and the students, and among all three. Herein is born a new curricular spirit.

Curriculum as Complexity

Curriculum as a concept has not embraced the notion of complexity. In fact, we may say that from Ramus to Tyler curriculum has attempted to impose a *simple order* on the process of learning.[23] The assumption has been that learning is, and teaching should be, *simple*. Ramus's methodization and Tyler's rationale are based on simplification. Indeed, this concept has pervaded much of the talking and thinking we have developed in our modernist discourse; it has been what Richard Rorty calls a "final [or basic] vocabulary" (1989, 73). Underlying both Descartes rationalism and Newton's empiricism is the assumption of a simple symmetry. A bedrock of our modernist metaphysical worldview has been Newton's comment that "Nature is pleased with simplicity" (Doll, 1993, 33).

The more, though, that scientists study both the micro and macro aspects of nature—as has happened extensively in the twentieth century—the more we are seeing that nature embraces not simplicity but complexity: quantum physics, microbiology, organic chemistry, astrophysics all confirm this *new* view. It is time for curriculum itself to adopt this spirit and embrace, not reject, complexity.

The complexity that we are seeing, though, is not a complex complexity anymore than the simplicity Newton and others saw was merely a simple simplicity—such a sharp complexity/simplicity bifurcation is itself too simple. As Cohen and Stewart (1994) among others point out, the complexity we are finding has a type of simplicity embedded within it. Thus, they design two new words to discuss this simple-complex constellation—*complicity and simplexity*. Each is designed to show the embeddedness of simplicity within complexity and of complexity within simplicity. These two form a union, not a discrete difference.

Tracing the rise of what is being called complexity theory—and its sister theories of chaos mathematics and nonlinear dynamical systems—is daunting. The literature is vast and growing exponentially.[24] However, some features of this simple/complex constellation do stand out. Self-organization and emergence, themselves really a unity, do become the central activities around which the theories are built. The metaphysical view that the complexity-chaos-nonlinear constellation adopts is that the universe *is* creative: it is in constant flux, moving from a *simple* complex order toward an ever-evolving more *complex* complex order. Alfred North Whitehead (1978/

1929) refers to the naturalness of this movement when he says, "*It lies in the nature of things that the many enter into complex unity*" (21). Stuart Kauffman (1993), a complexity theorist connected with the Santa Fe Institute for the Study of Complexity, has framed this emergence of increasing levels of complex order in the following way:

> The order inherent in the busy complexity within the cell may be largely self-organized and spontaneous....And I want to suggest that we can think of the origin of life as an expected *emergent collective property* of a modestly complex mixture of catalytic polymers, such as proteins or catalytic RNA, which catalyze one another's formation. (xiv; emphasis in original)

Or, I suggest,

> the formation of a connected web of metabolic transformations arises almost inevitably in a sufficiently complex system. (xvi)

The key idea here is that nature, life, organization all occur when there is a sufficient but simple level of complex interactions, and that from these complexly simple interactions new and more complex levels of nature, life, organization arise. The process may be forever ongoing (Davies, 1988). Looking at curriculum—not as a linear course to be run—but as a complex and dynamic web of interactions evolving naturally into more varied interconnected forms is a formidable task that will require vision and perseverance. It is a task for which curricularists have virtually no experience. As with considering curriculum as *currere*, so considering curriculum as complexity is a task worth doing, one which, unlike *currere*, separates us from our past and, like *currere*, challenges our future.[25]

Curriculum as Cosmology

It is strange to think of curriculum as cosmology, for today cosmology is rather exclusively associated with the scientific study of the universe and both its origins and demise. However, *The Oxford English Dictionary* (1989) defines "cosmology" (discourse with the world, in ancient Greek) in a broader sense, as "the science or theory of the universe as an ordered whole" (985). It is this sense of a pervasive wholeness which prompts Alfred North Whitehead (1967b/1925) to assert that all of us share an instinctive faith in there being an ultimate order of nature: we "trust that the ultimate natures of things lie together in a harmony that excludes mere arbitrariness" (18). Science over the past centuries has shown us that this faith in Nature's order is justified, even if we no longer see that order as simple, linear, or static.

For the past few hundred years, though, science has adopted a particular viewpoint and methodology, one committed not so much to cosmological discourse as to the extension of a materialist metaphysics. As Whitehead says:

> There persists, however, throughout the whole period [from the sixteenth century on] the fixed scientific cosmology which presupposes the ultimate fact of an irreducible brute matter or material, spread throughout space….[T]his assumption I call "scientific materialism"….Further, this is an assumption I shall challenge as being entirely unsuited to the scientific situation at which we have now arrived. (17)

In short, Whitehead believes that the (scientific) cosmology of the modern worldview needs to be replaced with a new (scientific) cosmology—that which now we call postmodern. The new cosmology Whitehead advocates, of course, is that of process, one which sees reality in terms of dynamic movement, not in terms of the "hard, massy, impenetrable" particles Newton posited as the bedrock of reality. In fact, bedrock is a poor metaphor; it reinforces "the fallacy of misplaced concreteness" (1978/1929, 18). Instead, Whitehead posits "actual entities" or "actual occasions" as the final *reals* "of which the world is made up" (18). And "these actual entities are drops of experience, complex and interdependent."

This shift from a cosmology (including ecology, ethics, epistemology, metaphysics, pedagogy, worldview) based on the "brute facts" of independent atoms to a process cosmology based on the dynamic flux of entities or occasions, all "complex and interdependent," is a truly paradigmatic shift. It is easy to see why complexity and chaos theorists consider Whitehead a founding father of their "new science."[26]

Since interdependence and interrelationship are key to Whitehead's cosmology—"detached details…demand…*a system*…(and) this system includes the harmony of logical relationality, and the harmony of aesthetic achievement" (1967b/1925; emphasis mine)—it might be expected his curricular and instructional recommendations would also be relational (Doll, 1993, 142–54, and Ch. 7). As Whitehead says in his famous phrasing:

> Let the main ideas which are introduced into a child's education be few and important, and let them be thrown into every combination possible. (1967a/1929, 2)

In contrast to this hopeful and positive pedagogic expression, he issues a more pessimistic one—that our schools are collections of dead, useless, "inert" ideas, of brute facts, isolated and lifeless. Our task then as educators is in "keeping knowledge alive," or if dead to give it life by combining the logical and scientific with the aesthetic and storied.

In this same essay, Whitehead also comments that "the essence of education is that it be religious" (14), or I would say "spirit-ful." In doing this, Whitehead—a Platonist as well as a mathematician—takes us back to the ancient Greek concept of cosmology. Cosmology for the ancients was not limited to the scientific study of the universe or of its origins. Rather the ancients integrated into a harmonious balance the *s*cientific with the *s*toried with the *s*pirit-ful. Hesiod tells us in his story of the universe's origins that "First of all came chaos [the founding father of all] and then broad-breasted Gaia" ("Theogony," lines 116–17). This notion of there being a spirit—a "breath" or a "vital integrity"[27]—to all of life (an issue Whitehead taps in his cosmology) is also expressed in other creation stories. In the Babylonian creation story of the gigantic and fecund struggle between Tiamat and her favorite son, Marduk, Tiamat's fierce reproductive powers are not quelled, not even by death, but Marduk is able, after colossal mental and physical effort, to transform those powers by turning her blood into rivers, her breasts into mountains, and her belly into the night sky (Colum, 1976/1930, 17–19).[28] There is power expressed here in the aesthetic-ness of story: a power, creative and unifying, we have lost or at least diminished as our curriculum has become more and more moribund. To bring curriculum to life—to recapture the creative energy of all life, the aesthetic-ness that exists in *being*—we might well consider a curriculum which combines the rigorousness of *science*, with the imagination of *story*, with the vitality and creativity of *spirit*.[29]

Curriculum as Conversation

Taking a tack different from the cosmological or *grand récit* framing of the last section, we might consider curriculum from a more personal view, as a conversation. William Pinar (et al., 1995) ends his overpowering and magnificent treatise, *Understanding Curriculum*, with a personal call to keep the conversation going: "we call for collaboration, conversation" for "this field (of curriculum) is very much a conversation," one which has shifted dramatically over the past 20 years and now needs new voices to carry on the work begun by curriculum theorists (867–68). In issuing such a call, Pinar is echoing Richard Rorty's (1980) own call "to keep the conversation going" (377). Both Pinar and Rorty are asking that we consider knowledge or understanding in the personal terms of "actual, lived situations" (Pinar et al., 424) rather than in terms of specialized (curricularized) methods or procedures. Conversation is one of the human activities people do, as people.[30]

While the word *conversation* commonly means "an interchange of thoughts and words; familiar discourse or talk," especially "talking with" (*O. E. D., 2nd ed., s.v.* "conversation"), this meaning is fairly recent, occurring mostly in English and listed as the seventh of twelve definitions in the *O. E. D.* Its more historical, but not conventional, meaning deals with the idea of passing one's life, living or dwelling in or with (869), and from the Latin *conversare*, which literally means to turn oneself about. In this sense it comes from the same Proto-Indo-European root (vers[31]) as does the word *converge*, "to approach the same point from different directions…to tend toward a common conclusion" (*American Heritage Dictionary*, s. v., "converge"). Thus, there is a historical binding between conversation and convergence—through personal conversation we turn ourselves about and converge or come together. In conversation lie our hopes for both convergence and transformation: We become transformed as our differing views converge on that which presently is beyond us, and the situation itself changes or becomes transformed as we go through the convergence process.

Hans-Georg Gadamer (1993/1960) says that a true conversation is one which captures us; it is not one we choose but one we "fall into" or become "involved in" (383). As we participate, live, and dwell in such a conversation, our task is not only to speak well but also to listen well. We need to hear back, recursively, both our own words and those of others (including ones from the cosmos, universe, ecology in which we live). As we lose ourselves in such conversation, we become transformed. To quote Gadamer:

> Conversation is a process of coming to an understanding. Thus, it belongs to every true conversation that each person opens himself to the other, truly accepts his point of view as valid and transposes himself into the other to such an extent that he understands not [just] the particular individual but what he says. (385)

This sense of "coming to an understanding" by "transposing oneself into the other" is essential to a true conversation—one which in its Rortyan "ongoing-ness" helps us acquire not (just) knowledge but *understanding*. This understanding, as Gadamer notes, needs to focus on our transposing ourselves into otherness—either into the personal otherness of which Derrida (1995/1992, Ch. 4) speaks or into the intellectual otherness of the curriculum material studied. The former might draw heavily on the intellectual writings of Emmanuel Levinas and Jacques Derrida (see Bernstein, 1992, Ch. 3) and the latter would draw on the structural (curriculum) reform movement of the 1960s and 1970s (see especially Jerome Bruner's "spiral curriculum," 1978, and his recent assessment of this movement, 1996). At the curricular and instructional levels, the goal here is to have teachers and students respect, honor, understand their own humanness, the "otherness" of each other of which the self is made as well as the "otherness" of the texts studied and the ways of thinking inscribed in them. Toward this (integrated yet multifaceted) end, we might encourage teachers to respect the human otherness of their students (no matter the age, gender, race, religion) and for the teachers to encourage students to have "conversations" with language arts, mathematics, science and social science texts and the contents therein.

Curriculum as Community

Of all the five C's I have chosen, community is in some ways the most important; it is the "organizing glue" (to borrow a phrase from Gregory Bateson) which holds *currere*, complexity, cosmology, and conversation together. Without community, these others would be isolated identities, alone unto themselves—arrogant, as Bowers (1995b) says, in their egocentrism. As Richard Rorty (1989) points out, when we give up the notion of an absolute, preset reality, then we realize that "what is most important to each of us is what we have in common with others" (xiii), that "they" are really "one of us" (xvi).[32]

Community, with its emphasis on both care and critique—an emphasis that requires a high degree of trust—is what helps elevate us above ourselves. *Currere* without community easily falls into solipsism, a point Bill Pinar recognizes but one that escapes his critics (Pinar et al., 1995, Ch. 10).[33] The self of *currere*, the very beginning of curriculum as Dewey knew so well, must always interact with the text of life. It is this *interaction* that forms the process of curriculum. Experience is not a private affair, even though we too often consider it as such; *experience needs to be reconstructed* or transformed via public interaction[34] which occurs in a community dedicated to both care and critique. For Dewey, of course, this community was democratic, and it was trustworthy. Unfortunately, educational progressives saw experience only on its primary level, as an activity, full of "hands-on" doings. Almost universally, they missed the secondary level, that of reflection (Dewey, 1958/1925, Ch. 1). But to miss this developmental aspect of experience—as Dewey's ghost tells us—is to miss the real nature of experience itself. For it is in the transformative interaction between these two that the nature of experience lies. The idea of transformative experience—in later years Dewey called this transaction—lies at the heart of his philosophy (pragmatism) and education (experiential). Through this interaction, "ises" are transformed into "oughts," nascent curiosity into disciplined inquiry, interest into intellect. For Dewey, *education is transformation*; community, in its dual but integrated function of helping us both develop and be critical of our basic assumptions, is the vehicle through which this transformation occurs. To quote Dewey, from *How We Think* (1971/1933):

> The real problem of intellectual education is the *transformation* of natural powers into expert, tested powers: the transformation of...casual curiosity and sporadic suggestion into attitudes of alert, cautious, and thorough inquiry. (84)

There is, as is well known, within Dewey a powerful emphasis on method. He, more than Frederick Taylor, is known (in educational circles at least) as the "father of scientific method." It is via this method that Dewey believed disciplined inquiry could be developed. Indeed, both B. F. Skinner and Ralph Tyler in their emphasis on method saw themselves, mistakenly I fear, more Deweyan than Taylorian. The big difference between Dewey and Taylor on method or between Dewey and Ramus, for that matter, is that for Dewey, the beginning always had to be with the child, the learner, the experiencer. These personal but nascent experiences were crucial to Dewey. Any definition of the problem had to come from the one experiencing—a real sense of *currere* here. For both Ramus and Taylor the definition of the problem, the first step in the scientific method, came from either the logical structure of that being investigated (Ramus) or from the economic/social needs of an industrial society (Taylor, Bobbitt, Charters, Tyler). Dewey saw his method of "thorough inquiry" to be of value only to the degree it made "personal experience more intelligent" (1966/1916, 172). Again, it was the *transformation of personal experience* that was sacred to Dewey. Curricularists from Bobbitt through Tyler had a degree of interest in the person, especially Tyler, but what drove their curricula was not a sense of transformation; it was, rather, a sense of efficient operation. This allowed them to become, somewhat unwittingly, somewhat enthusiastically, disciples of "Taylorism" (Callahan, 1962). Here goals were preset (by others) and methods became uniform. But as Dewey said, "Imposing an alleged uniform general method on everybody breeds mediocrity" (1966/1916, 173).

The community I have been talking about with Dewey's ghost is, of course, the human community. It is this community which Dewey held to be sacred. But as Bateson, Berry, and Bowers point out, the human community is but part of larger ecological and cosmological communities. Bowers (1995b) has a nice metaphorical phrase for this when he says that communities are "nested" within one another—the human within the cultural, the cultural within the ecological (46), and, I would add, the ecological or natural within the cosmological. We must realize our place and role within this nested hierarchy lest we adopt the arrogance of Enlightenment thought and tacitly assume human consciousness to be the epitome of all consciousness. As humans, we are embedded within a culture, itself embedded within a universe and cosmos. Dewey, as might be expected of one intellectually educated within the legacy of the Enlightenment and brimming forth with the hope of industrialism, saw community in democratic, human terms. We, influenced, even guided by Dewey's ghost, need to extend this concept of community to realize our relationships beyond the human to the ecological and cosmological. (Hence, our need to have conversations with rocks.) But no matter how we envision community, it is important to realize that community is the vehicle by which we transform and transcend ourselves.[35]

I hope such an extension of *community beyond self* will help all of us realize that the human attributes we have considered so important—ones of race, creed, gender—pale beside the ecological, global, cosmological issues within which all humans are enmeshed. Life is itself full of creation; we are for the first time in human history on that edge (of chaos) where we can participate in the creation of new life forms or in the destruction of existent ones. As we move into a new millennium, we have opportunities and responsibilities our foreparents did not. Truly, our future human existence, as well as the existence of generations to follow, will depend on our having a *new alliance with nature.*

This alliance will depend on our establishing a sense of community—with ourselves, our environment, our cosmos. Personally, I believe that through community we can find that "fascinating imaginative realm...born as the echo of God's laughter" which has so eluded us. In this realm, creativity abounds, newness emerges, intelligence develops. I believe such a community operates at the cosmological level and can, indeed must, operate at the social level; then we can truly say that our classrooms and our society are places "where no one owns the truth and everyone has a right to be understood" (Kundera, 1988, 164).[36]

Afterword

This essay is, indeed, already long enough as to abhor an afterword. I would like to blame the essay's length on the muse of John Dewey, but fear I must take responsibility for letting it, "like Topsy," just grow.

My theme, though, has been a simple one—as we look into the next century we need a new vision, or new visions, to guide our educational development. We need new concepts of curriculum. Since my days in graduate school in the late 1960s, it has been evident that curriculum thought is "moribund" (to use Joseph Schwab's famous phrase). Interesting concepts have blossomed at the theoretical level, as William Pinar et al. point out (1995) and as I hope the five C's show; but these have had little or no effect on mainstream, school-based, curriculum development. Such development has remained for the past four centuries firmly in the grip of imposed control. Such control is becoming outmoded in many disciplines; it is time to lay it to rest in education, that another more lively form may live.

From the 1960s on, when curricularists first became consciously aware of their field, when curriculum theory was born, critics have inveighed against the authoritarian, unilateral control which has permeated the concept of curriculum. This sort of control has been the ghost in curriculum. Many, many critics—from Ivan Illich, Paul Goodman, John Holt, and Jonathan Kozol on—have criticized an external, imposed, simply ordered control. Often the connection has been made between this view of control and America's rising industrial society. Accurate as this analysis is, it is David Hamilton (followed by Stephen Triche, 2001) who has helped us realize that the roots of this control go much deeper in time and thought. Authoritarian control is one with the very concept of curriculum and exists not merely in our contemporary classrooms and schools but has so existed for centuries. Further, it permeates our society and our culture, reaching deep into our metaphysical, cosmological, and theological beliefs. It has become paradigmatic.

Dewey tried mightily to break out of this paradigm, both in his philosophical and educational writings. He laid foundations that we are still experiencing and exploring. His ghost encourages us to keep on with this project, especially now that we have tools and insights unavailable to Dewey—new ideas in philosophy, cosmology, complexity, and hermeneutics. All these are the foundations on which the five C's I have chosen are based. I believe we are now ready to conceive of curriculum in a radically different way than did either Peter Ramus or Ralph Tyler. I see these two as bracketing or framing curriculum in the modernist paradigm, a paradigm which began with Copernicus and is just now ending. Both curricularists were part of the paradigm which believed, as Rorty (1989) says, that if it did "not have all the answers," at least it had the "criteria for the answers" (76). Certitude about method is what draws together—over a period of four centuries—the scholarship of Peter Ramus and Ralph Tyler.

We are now in a transition period, one between paradigms. We are entering a period of "post" thought: postmodern, poststructural, post-colonial, postpatriarchal, postindustrial. In this new era, control is seen as being embedded within, not as lying outside or imposed on, situations, as arising naturally and complexly from rather simple interactions. This new sense of control—formed from the web of interactions that is life—is livelier, more varied, and dynamic than what we have known. In fact, the same may be said of the whole paradigm now emerging (Capra, 1996; Davies, 1988; Kauffman, 1995; Margulis, 1998; Margulis and Sagan, 1995, 1997; Marturana and Varela, 1980, Prigogine and Stengers, 1984, to name but a few). Accordingly, curriculum can no longer be considered in only one form, as a noun describing a set course of study. Curriculum has, as it were, a need to develop multiple personalities. I have suggested and have begun exploring some of these personalities—those of *currere*, complexity, cosmology, conversation, and community.

This is all I can do for now. It is time for others in the field to lend their voices and thoughts to the development of a new curriculum paradigm. I, Noel Gough, Dewey's ghost, and the field itself all welcome such.

Notes

[1] This citation comes from a caption under a photograph of Derrida conversing with others at a film festival; it is eight pages into a collection of pictures appendixed to the Derrida-Bennington book (1991) ending on page 341, hence my attribution of it to p. 349.

Derrida's thoughts on ghosts and the future are best presented, I believe, in his *Specters of Marx* (1994). To greatly oversimplify, his argument here is that in our current thoughts we can see ghosts (really specters) of the past. In this sense ghosts lead us into the future. Our task is to recognize these specters, to "see, situate, identify" them. "One must possess [them] without letting oneself be possessed by [them]" (132).

[2] I would like to think this metaphor is my own but suspect I am indebted to Herbert Kliebard's suggestion that "the figure of John Dewey…hovered over the battle" for the American curriculum in the early decades of the twentieth century. See his *Forging the American Curriculum* (1992, 12). I also suspect that the notion of ghost in education in both my work and Kliebard's is an echo of Harold Dunkel's (1970) earlier use of the metaphor in his work on the Herbartian movement, occurring at a time when Dewey was just beginning his educational writings. In the same vein, I would like to acknowledge Philip Jackson's "Introduction" to John Dewey's lectures, "The School and Society" and "The Child and the Curriculum" (1990/1902–1900). Here he talks of the pull of Dewey's "educational vision," a vision which has inspired "serious students of education" for decades, but one neither Dewey nor others have been able to put into practice in any sustained or general way. This challenge remains with us, indeed

haunts us, as we have left the twentieth century and moved into the twenty-first. Our task, if I may return to Endnote 1, is to possess John Dewey's ideas without being possessed by them.

3 Derrida (1994/1993) is illustrative here. He says: "What does it mean to follow a ghost? And what if this came down to being followed by it, always, persecuted perhaps by the very chase we are leading? Here again what seems to be out front, the future, comes back in advance: from the past, from the back….Let us call it a *hauntology*…the spirit comes by *coming back* (revenant)…a ghost whose expected return repeats itself, again and again" (10, emphasis in original).

May I also comment that Richard Bernstein (1992), in his final chapter, talks of "Hegel's ghost hovering over us still" (309 and 312). Here he is referring to all Western intellectual thought since the time of Hegel being strongly influenced by Hegel's ideas. Marx, Dewey, Derrida would agree because they have been profoundly influenced—indeed haunted—by Hegel's ghost.

4 The word educate comes from the Latin educare, meaning "to rear, bring up" (*Oxford English Dictionary*, 1989, Vol. V, 73). Further looking into educere shows it to deal with nurturing, rearing, supporting the growth of offspring, animals, plants (*Oxford Latin Dictionary*, 1984, 588); sometimes associated with educate, it means "to lead or bring out," especially in the sense of leading forth or bringing out troops for a military battle, or bringing into a country or province, or bringing forth a person as to a magistrate, or unsheathing a sword (*O. L. D.*, 1984, 587). The now-common association some make between educate and educére as a leading forth or drawing out of intellectual and personal qualities is probably an artifact of nineteenth century romanticism.

5 As an aside, it is interesting to note that some of these apparitions appeared part white and part black. The shining "whiter than snow" part suffered not at all, but the *pice nigrior* suffered terribly. Over time and with prayers and alms, it was possible for the white part to dominate more and more of the apparition until finally the apparition vanished entirely. See Etienne de Bourbon, *Anecdotes Historiques*, (1877) ed. A Lecoy de la Marche, No. 28, 35–36; T. 3660.

6 This "livelier spirit of control," which I will develop later, is quite different from the way we consider control in a modernist frame, different enough that maybe a change in wording is needed. The common use of the word "control" is, as a number of liberal and neo-Marxist writers have pointed out—writers such as Michael Apple, 1982; bell hooks, 1992; Peter McLaren, 1989; Linda McNeil, 1986—both hidden and oppressive within the curriculum. Although I applaud their work in bringing to light this oppression, the livelier sense of control I am exploring is quite different from the one they are illuminating. The term "control" I am using, what Dewey calls "the other sense of control" (1966/1916, 23), is that describing the direction and purpose which emerges naturally from life's actions, interactions, experiences, and events. In Whiteheadian terms, this control just is—part of the cosmos's creativity, born of relations yet guiding those relations to their own, emergent ends. In Foucauldian terms, this sense of control is pervasive but not universal; that is, it exists only locally, arising from particular actions and interactions inherent in any local situation. There is nothing oppressive about this control; rather, it is the guidance creativity needs if creativity is to be productive.

Control here has the concepts of flexibility and randomness built into it. Maybe this "other sense" which I wish both to develop and to perpetuate needs a name other than control although the phrase "emergent control" is sufficient for me. Without this other, emergent sense of control, our cosmos would not be, creativity would not exist, nor would life. (See Doll, 1998)

7 While the concept of postmodernism permeates much of the material in this book, it is not a concept explained or explored in any detail. For more on the particular interpretations of postmodernism we editors adopt, see Doll, 1993, and Gough, 1993c, 1994, with special attention to the concept of playfulness.

8 I use the male term here intentionally. Not only were virtually all of the teachers at this time male, it was also a "male rationality" which dominated the discourse. For a wonderful, and to me persuasive, discussion of this difference in gender discourse, see Andrea Nye, "A Woman's Thought of a Man's Discipline?: The Letters of Abelard and Heloise," in *Hypatia*, 7, 3 (summer 1992). For a marvelous history of the "maleness" of university and school disciplines, especially those of mathematics and the sciences, see Margaret Wertheim, *Pythagoras' Trousers* (1995).

9 The Ramus map is reprinted with permission of the Special Collections, Glasgow University Library, Glasgow, Scotland. It is copied from Peter Ramus's *Professio Regia* (Basile, 1576, folio 3 verso).

The map—serving also as a table of contents—shows "the [seven] arts included in this volume" and provides a visual representation of the philosophy of Peter Ramus, "completely expanded," of which curriculum is a part. A teaching device, this map puts forth the discipline (of philosophy) "expressed in a Ciceronian manner, and, with examples from Cicero, rightly indicates a pure and genuine method provided to youth [and teachers] to exhort all toward a love of the liberal arts."

10 It is interesting to note, as Walter Ong (1958) does, that in exploring the early Colonial literature of seventeenth-century America, especially with an emphasis on Harvard College and the New England Puritan mind, one finds "Ramism on every side" (4). Ramism, with its simple visual mapping, supported the Puritan "obsession for logic and distaste for symbolism"; it helped shape Puritan "views of nature...literary style...and epistemology." Further, it correlated "with the Puritan preference for plain style...[and its] *simplistic* view of things...its downrightness, if you will" (4, emphasis in original). Remember, too, that the youth being trained in the logic of the time were barely schoolboys (ages thirteen to seventeen) and the "logic" (dialectic) itself most complex. See Ong, especially Chs. IV–VII.

11 It is interesting to compare this industrial metaphor which Bobbitt, Cubberley, and others used in the early twentieth century with one Johann Amos Comenius used three centuries earlier. In his *The Great Didactic* (1896/1632), Comenius, a generation-removed disciple of Peter Ramus, suggests that pupils are vessels into which knowledge can be poured, and teachers as intermediaries need not "select their own subject-matter...[or] their own method, but only have to take knowledge that has already been suitably arranged and pour it in their pupils" (440). The mechanism dominating both metaphors is obvious.

12 Please refer to and re-read Footnote 6 where I begin a discussion of "emergent" control. This concept, borrowed from Howard Pattee (1973, 106–07), is much akin to

Prigogine and Stengers's (1984, 159) concept of "self-organization," and to Humberto Maturana and Francisco Varela's (1980) concept of "autopoiesis." It lies at the very heart of complexity theory, as I shall describe in the section on complexity.

13 I realize full well that it is quite fashionable today to label Dewey's philosophy of pragmatism as antifoundational (Cherryholmes, 1988; Rorty, 1980), and I certainly do not disagree with the notion that Dewey attacked the absolutist foundations of Western philosophy (Doll, 1993). However, I do believe Dewey had other, rather obvious, foundations for his thought: those he found intellectually in German idealism and practically in his New England experience. Together these formed what might be called a romantic or idealistic pragmatism. Cornel West (1989) calls it a "prophetic pragmatism." Richard Bernstein (1992) makes it part of what he calls "the new constellation" in Western thought.

14 C. A. Bowers, in many of his writings (1993a&b, 1995a&b), has issued the warning to all contemporary educators not to assume that social betterment and growth will come automatically from our visions and reforms. Such tunneled thinking, a legacy of the Enlightenment and modernist in its origins and thrust, is all too common in our field. Change per se does not equal betterment. Bowers makes this point best, I believe, in his book, *Educating for an Ecologically Sustainable Culture* (1995b), in which he points out that such Enlightenment thinking "represent[s] a sharp break from the path of development followed by traditional cultures" (155). Such a break separates us from our past, our culture, and to a strong extent—with its future-only vision—from ourselves. Whatever vision we do have must be Janus-faced, looking back to our roots, our culture, as well as forward to the future. The present, that in which we continually and only live, must needs be an interplay between the past and the future. On this, see also Jerome Bruner's *The Culture of Education* (1996).

15 I am also arguing that our traditional concept of control, a ghost that haunts the curriculum, is, itself, embedded in the methodization movement which swept northern Europe in the sixteenth and seventeenth centuries. This methodization—simplifying by breaking down complexity into smaller and smaller dichotomous units, á la Ramus's charts—has remained with us over centuries. It has shown up in reductionist methodology, in what we call the "scientific" method, and in our procedures for lesson plans. Only now, in the early twenty-first century, are we beginning to adopt a new vision, one that sees this method as not only simple (a point Ong, 1958, continually makes about Ramism) but as too simple. Contrary to Ramus's belief, not all ordering or methodologizing can be dealt with productively in this manner. As we re-look at our concept of methodization (Doll, 2001b; Triche, 2001) we see that what we have for centuries considered so "natural—sequencing, linear order, logicalness, and completeness—is really a historical artifact of a particular mind set, a northern European, Protestant mind set.

As an aside, it is interesting to note that the idea of food being served sequentially—the first course first, to paraphrase Ramus—came into being in France during the sixteenth century. Late medieval Italian cooking left all the dishes on the table throughout the meal, and one partook according to one's humor or pleasure. This pleasure, by the way, was quite sensual and involved a mixing or balancing of the appetitive, that with salt, with the satiating, and that with sugar. The French framed this sensual pleasure in a sequential way, moving from the sál, intended to inflame gastronomic and sexual desire, to the sucré which suppressed such desire(s). See T. Sarah Peterson, *Acquired Taste: The French Origins of Modern Cooking* (1994).

[16] For more detail on this complex thinker see "Curriculum and Change: Piaget's Organismic Origins" (Doll, 1983) and Chapter Three in *A Post-Modern Perspective on Curriculum* (Doll, 1993). It is interesting to note that Goldsmith (1989) in his article "Gaia and Evolution" pays great attention to Piaget's evolutionary ideas (with adaptation as goal directed) while Cohen and Stewart (1994, 307, 431) utilize phenocopy (Piaget's key to evolution and development) in a manner which expressly denies a goal directiveness to evolution. They note: "Organisms do not seek to evolve. The existence of attractors does not imply that dynamical systems are goal-seekers: on the contrary, they are goal-finders which only recognize what the 'goal' is when they have found it" (431). Two very different interpretations here of Piaget's biologically based metaphysics. See also Piaget's final writings (with Garcia, 1989; 1991).

[17] Obviously there are other ways to categorize curriculum; there are even other words beginning with a C with which to link curriculum. I could have linked curriculum to critical theory as do many of the neo-Marxists (Apple, 1982; Giroux, 1988; McLaren, 1989; Wexler, 1987), or I could have linked it with circumcision as does Pinar (with Grumet, 1976, 176), the most prominent of the male gender theorists, or with culture as does Bowers (1993b, 1995b; with Flinders, 1990). I could have made up another of my own categories, such as commitment or creativity, or I could have developed Habermas's notion of "communicative action"—a project worthy of doing, I believe. The five I chose are not meant to be definitive, just generative.

[18] We are all familiar with Jean-François Lyotard's late-1970s statement about our current (postmodern) condition having a healthy and needed "incredulity toward metanarratives" (1984/1979, xxiv). Now, a good two decades later, we begin to see what Richard Bernstein (1992) calls a "new constellation" arising or what Fritjof Capra (1996) sees as a new network—interrelating psychological, biological, physical, social, and cultural phenomena into a "web of life." This new constellation or network or web of interrelational ideas is not a metanarrative as this concept has developed in the past. Bernstein says his concept of constellation, in which ideas are "juxtaposed rather than integrated," is a "delicate attempt" to displace Hegel's master metaphor of Aufhebung (process of reconciling opposites) (8, 179).

[19] It is interesting to note in passing Graham (1992) makes reference to a closeness between *currere* and "John Dewey's idea of curriculum as experience" (27). This closeness is also implied but not articulated by Reid (1981a, Footnote 5 combined with Footnote 12, 183). In his "The Practical, the Theoretic, and the Conduct of Curriculum Research" (1981b), William Reid talks of Pinar's "autobiographical" method as being "intimately concerned with…a Deweyan sense of the problematic." However, he does not give a name (*currere*) to this autobiographical method of Pinar's. For a recent and quite full exposition of *currere* and its role in teaching, see Marsh and Willis (1995, 109–15). See also the recent resurgent interest in *currere* that has developed from Pinar's Louisiana State University students: Alcazar (2001), Edgerton (1996), Triche (2001). See also the critical development of *currere* done in essays by Gough, Kincheloe, Sumara and Davis in Pinar's *Curriculum: Toward New Identities* (1998).

Finally, see Pinar's own descriptions of *currere*, especially as he ruminates on Madeline Grumet's contributions to the concept in his massive and spectacular *Understanding Curriculum* (Pinar et al., 1995).

20 In his famous essay "The Child and the Curriculum," Dewey asks the question, "How, then, stands the case of Child vs. Curriculum?" and answers, "The case is of Child." But, as is well known, this is not a case of the child apart from the curriculum; rather, it is of the child and the curriculum as "a single process," a single integrative and transformative process, for "the child's present experience [or interest] is in no way self-explanatory. It is not final, but transitional" (1990, 208, 209, 189, 191). This idea of transition, transformation, reconstruction, development is key to Dewey's whole notion of the curriculum beginning with the child. The process is one of continual, ongoing reconstruction: "It is a development of experience and into experience that is really wanted" (196).

Too often, we in education have seen the foregoing as the case of the child "up against" the curriculum. In so seeing, we have chosen the either/or, not the both/and, mode of thinking. Dialogue, transformation, reconstruction, development are possible only in the both/and mode. The concept of "an essential tension," of which I am so fond, requires a both/and mode of thought. (See Robertson, 1997; Doll, 1998.)

21 Pinar says "the method of *currere*"—that of self-consciously relating the self to its evolution—has four "steps" to it: regressive, progressive, analytical, synthetical. He outlines these steps in his essay "The Method" (with Grumet, 1976, 51–63; esp. 55–61; reprinted, 1994, Ch. 3). In another essay, a literary gem, "The Lost Language of Cranes," Pinar explores in depth the regressive phase, which he says means "re-entry to the past and its conscious reincorporation into the present" (1994, 266). This visionary statement is quite akin to Charles Jencks's concept of the role the past plays in postmodern thought. (See Jencks, 1987, Foreword, esp. 9–10.)

22 Although I and others intentionally connect *currere*'s method of "bracketing" with Dewey's of "reflecting," such is not entirely fair. Pinar (with Grumet, 1976) comments: "There are few precedents for this [*currere*] kind of theorizing in the fields of education. Some of the work of John Dewey is still helpful, but on the whole it is not" (4). In a more recent work (Morris, Doll, and Pinar, 1999), Pinar states that from his perspective Dewey tends toward a certain proceduralism...a methodology of thinking...which has plagued professional education from its beginnings (xvi).

Dewey's reflecting does have a "distancing" from the primary experience (1958/1925, Ch. 1), and its purpose is to deepen our concept and feeling of that experience—turning experience into an experience (1980/1934, Ch. 1). But its method, quite "procedural" as Pinar notes, is that of rational, logical reason, and its goal is to place a given experience in interrelationship with other practical experiences.

Currere's method—drawn heavily from Edmond Husserl's "Transcendental Phenomenology" (1969/1913)—does have a sense of listening, reflection, and deepening of experience, but its method is self-reflective and its goal is the finding of "the transcendental Ego" which "exists (ist) absolutely in and for itself prior to all cosmic being" (14–15). In aligning Dewey's method with that of *currere*, we are contrasting a pragmatic method of rational reflection with a phenomenological one of essentialist self-reflexion. These are, obviously, quite different. Yet the two do form a sort of constellation, different from but related to each other. Both share a sense of distancing that deepens personal experience via reflection/reflexion and both help us find alternatives to the Tyler Rationale.

[23] I am aware that from Jean Jacques Rousseau on through the German romantics to the American progressives and the English open education advocates, there has been a countertendency to this view of learning, especially with early childhood learning. However, the imposition of a simple order has been and continues to be the dominant curriculum and instructional drive over the centuries. Dewey, among others, objected to this drive at the beginning of the twentieth century and now one hundred years later this same traditional view is still objectionable.

[24] While this literature is vast, here are some particular favorites of mine: For chaos—Briggs and Peat, *Turbulent Mirror* (1990); Kellert, *In the Wake of Chaos* (1993); Lorenz, *The Essence of Chaos* (1995); Stewart, *Does God Play Dice?* (1990); for complexity—Bechtel and Richardson, *Discovering Complexity* (1993); Kauffman, *At Home in the Universe* (1995); for nonlinearity—Bak, *How Nature Works* (1999); Lam, *Nonlinear Physics for Beginners* (1997); for theoretical biology—Maturana and Varela, *The Tree of Knowledge* (1987); Margulis and Sagan, *What Is Life?* (1995), *Slanted Truths* (1997); for a general systems synthesis—Capra, *The Web of Life* (1996); Luhmann, *Social Systems* (1995).

[25] I am wrestling here with the concepts of complexity and simplicity being intertwined not bifurcated, as our modernist discourse has so done. In an ironic way, seeing reality in terms of this union or mutual embedding of what we might colloquially call order and chaos is itself a split. A paradigm change does seem to be happening—we are entering a "post" age—and our past semiotics is quite incapable of helping us develop forms of representation for this new paradigm (Reiss, 1982). Curricularly, I believe the 4 R's I have developed (Doll, 1993, Ch. 7) do represent a worthwhile attempt to take a new look at curriculum. Currently, I might add play—"throwing ideas into every combination possible"—as a 5th R.

[26] Obviously, Whitehead cannot be called a postmodernist; the movement began well after his death. But as I have argued elsewhere (Doll, 1993), the epistemological and pedagogical views of writers such as Whitehead "are better understood from a post-modern than a modern perspective" (13 and passim).

[27] James Gleick puts the issue of chaos being a new science in the very title of his book, *Chaos: Making a New Science* (1987). Lui Lam, ten years later (1997), talks of a quiet revolution going on in physics, equal in magnitude to both "quantum mechanics and relativity," namely "the birth of a new science—nonlinear science—which for the sake of presentation, may be divided into six parts: fractals, chaos, pattern formation, solitons, cellular automata, and complex systems (1 and v).

[28] The *O. E. D.* (1989, XVI, 251–55) devotes over four pages and 24 main definitions to the word spirit. Many of these, but not all, involve a religious framing—what we might well call (Christian) soul. However, the first definitions come from the Greek for "breath" [of life] and include notions of animation or essential character or pervading principle. I am arguing that the subjects we teach do indeed have "essential character{istics}, nature(s) or pervading principles" which give life to these subjects and that our Ramist-oriented "methods" of dealing with the subjects have made them

dead, inert, lifeless. Hence my advocacy of our putting to rest this ghost of the past and liberating curriculum to develop a sprightly, new spirit.

George Santayana's (1968/1915) phrase of spirit as a "vital integrity" (190) is one I like very much and one I believe captures "the spirit" of what I am after.

[29] The nonseparation here of substance and form, body and mind, is characteristic of ancient Western or premodern thinking.

[30] I believe that for a curriculum to be alive, to be vital, we need to draw on and combine three traditions: one of science, logic, reason; another of story, culture, narrative; and a third of spirit, vitality, wonderousness. Two authors—scientists, storytellers, "spiritists"—who bring forward this wonderousness are Gregory Bateson (1972, 1987, 1988/1979; with daughter Catherine, 1987) and Stuart Kauffman (1993, 1995). Both are among the many—Thomas Berry (1988), Paul Davies (1984, 1988, 1996), and Brian Swimme (with Berry, 1992) to name others—who find a creative and spirit(ful) thrust inherent in the universe, a thrust and force they hold in awe. Bateson, contemplating on the new biology he saw emerging at the end of his life, says there is "a certain sacredness to the organization of the biological world" (1987, 8). Kauffman, a contemporary biochemist and (self) organization theorist, believes we need to feel this sacredness—and hence "our own deep worth" (1995, p. 5)—in the very lives we lead. We need to "reinvest" our lives with this sense of the sacred.

[31] For Rorty (1980), once we give up the transcendent, metaphysical, and foundational as the source, then we are left with (human) conversation. "If we see knowledge as a matter of conversation, of social practice rather than as an attempt to mirror nature" [by representation] (171), then we shall see "that coming to understanding [is not the result of specialized and privileged procedures but] is "more like getting acquainted" with a definite "play back and forth" (319). This most natural of human activities and social practices is the one Rorty advocates we adopt as our "behavioral epistemology" (173–82). In this frame we can "substitute conversation for confrontation [dialogue] as the determinant of our belief" (163).

[32] Pogo's famous phrase, of course, is "We have met the enemy and they is us." Rorty's "they" and "us," which I am playing with ironically, is itself ironic for, in his valuing of bourgeois liberalism, the "they" need to become "us" in order to achieve legitimacy, good values, and a hopeful life. This is not so much that "they is us" as it is that "they must become us"—an ironic twist. Personally, I am more taken with Derrida's (1995/1992) thought about "respecting the otherness of the other," respecting and honoring that otherness but not trying to incorporate that otherness into my-ness. (For more on the irony of, and indeed difficulties with, Rorty's bourgeois liberalism, see Bernstein, 1992, Chs. 8 and 9; for Derrida's thoughts on "otherness" see his *Gift of Death,* Chs. 3 and 4.)

I am both intrigued and bothered by Rorty's notion of a liberal ironist—one committed to freedom but suspicious of all interpretations of the concept. Many of his phrases, such as the search for utopias being "an endless proliferating realization of Freedom" (1989, xvi) or that "everything—our language, our conscience, our community—is a product of time and chance" (22), appeal to my sense of a cosmology based on openness and creativity. However, it is a cosmological frame from which I come and so chance alone is not enough; I do see the universe as self-generating and self-creating. In this I follow Berry, Davies, Kauffman, and Whitehead, even Gadamer. An open future always plays off of, emerges from, and is influenced by a historical past. I am interested in building a new type of foundation, a "chaotic" foundation, one based on contingency not certainty. In a way, I wish to combine, not separate, Rorty's liberal ironist with his philosophical metaphysician.

33 Those not recognizing the importance of *currere* when it first appeared (virtually every curricularist as Graham, 1992, shows), believed, mistakenly, this curriculum thrust to be either "mystical alchemy" or "solipsistic and purely personal." Sadly, such comments show little understanding of the alchemical, the personal, or the curricular.

34 Rorty (1989) has written with great passion on the need to separate the private from the public (Ch. 4). While I appreciate the point about liberal, ironic poets needing private freedom to develop and be effective with their thoughts, I, along with Bernstein (1992, Ch. 9), believe this "rigid" (286) public/private separation to be both disingenuous and self-defeating. All thinkers, even liberal ironists, have a public responsibility as Derrida (1995/1992) has pointed out so strongly. Further, pragmatism, as a philosophical movement—one Rorty brought back and gave credence to—requires a sense of the public for its very operation. It is through public discussion, action, reflection that Dewey's "ises" get turned into "oughts," and that James' "cash value" takes on a meaning that is more than mere expediency. Finally, in Rorty's "liberal utopia," the health of the relationship between "they" and "us" requires public and ongoing conversation. Private conversion happens through public conversation.

35 As Richard Rorty's "liberal utopia" has its "dark side" (Bernstein, 1992, 275), so, Nel Noddings (1996) points out, has the very concept of community. One of the dark side issues is that community excludes as well as includes; indeed its central focus for inclusion often is union against "them"—those excluded. "Hatred, dislike, and distrust can then be used to promote deeper unity within the group" (255). Hitler was one of the many totalitarians who understood this well.

The basic difficulty which underlies this community-totalitarian link is that as a concept community has never been able to deal well with another concept, that of marginalization. Community in our Western world has focused almost exclusively on the concept of core—on what unites—and has paid scant attention to the value of those people or ideas that lie on the margins. It is this relationship—following Levinas and Derrida—that I believe is essential to defining a postmodern sense of community: one that honors "the other as other" (Bernstein, 1992, Ch. 3; Derrida, 1995/1992, Ch. 4). To me, respecting an other's "otherness" is a key ethical, political, pedagogical challenge. Such respect for otherness lies at the very heart of Rorty's liberal utopia: "That fascinating imaginative realm, born as the echo of God's laughter, where no one owns the truth and everyone has the right to be understood." (1989, Frontispiece)

36 Kundera uses this phrase in a slightly different manner. He talks of the European novel being "born as the echo of God's laughter"—as representing that "fascinating imaginative realm" where, by laughing at ourselves and our foibles, we see both God's wisdom and the humbleness of our own actions. This realm is a place where "no one owns the truth and everyone has the right to be understood." Such, as I've said, describes my ideal of community. (See Kundera, 1988, Part Seven, esp. 164.)

References

Alcazar, A. (2001). *The curriculum implications of liberation theology as a theory of social change.* (Unpublished doctoral dissertation, Louisiana State University).

American heritage dictionary of the English language. (1969). William Morris (Ed.). Boston: American Heritage & Houghton Mifflin.

Apple, M. (1982). *Education and power.* New York: Routedge.

Augustine, St. (1948). The enchiridion. J. F. Shaw (Trans.). In W. J. Oates (Ed.), *The basic works of St. Augustine, vol. 1* (pages 655–730). (Original work written 421 A.D.).

Bak, P. (1999). *How nature works: The science of self-organized complexity.* New York: Springer-Verlag.

Bakhtin. M. M. (1993). *Toward a philosophy of the act.* V. Liapunov (Trans.); V. Liapunov and M. Holoquist (Eds.). Austin: University of Texas Press. (Original writings 1920–1924).

Bateson, G. (1972). *Steps to an ecology of mind.* New York: Ballantine.

________. (1987). Men are grass: Metaphor and the world of mental process. In W. I. Thompson (Ed.), *Gaia, a way of knowing: Political implications of the new biology.* Great Barrington, MA: Lindisfarne.

________. (1988). *Mind and nature.* New York: Bantam. (Original work published 1979).

Bateson, G., and C. Bateson. (1987). *Angels fear: Towards an epistemology of the sacred.* New York: Macmillan.

Bechtel, W., and R. Richardson. (1993). *Discovering complexity.* Princeton: Princeton University Press.

Berman, M. (1981). *The reenchantment of the world.* Ithaca: Cornell University Press.

Bernstein, R. (1992). *The new constellation.* Cambridge, MA: MIT Press.

Berry, T. (1988). *Dream of the earth.* San Francisco: Sierra Club.

_______. (1994). *The universe story: From the primordial flaring forth to the ecozoic era.* San Francisco: Harper.

Bobbitt, J. F. (1912). The elimination of waste in education. *The Elementary School Teacher, 12,* 259–71.

Bourbon, E. de. (1877). *Anecdotes historiques. A Lecoy de la Marche* (Ed.), No. 28, 35–36, T. 3660. Paris.

Bowers, C. A. (1987). *Elements of a post-liberal theory of education.* New York: Teachers College Press.

_______. (1993a). *Education, cultural myths, and the ecological crisis: Toward deep changes.* Albany: State University of New York Press.

_______. (1993b). *Critical essays on education, modernity, and the recovery of the ecological imperative.* New York: Teachers College Press.

_______. (1995a). *Why the environmental movement needs an educational strategy.* Albany: State University of New York Press.

_______. (1995b). *Educating for an ecologically sustainable culture: Rethinking moral education, creativity, intelligence, and other modern orthodoxies.* Albany: State University of New York Press.

Bowers, C. A., and D. Flinders. (1990). *Responsive teaching*. New York: Teachers College Press.

Briggs, J. (1992). *Fractals: The patterns of chaos*. New York: Touchstone.

Briggs, J. and D. Peat. (1990). *Turbulent mirror: An illustrated guide to chaos theory and the science of wholeness*. New York: Touchstone.

Bruner, J. (1978). *The process of education*. Cambridge, MA: Harvard University Press. (Original work published 1960).

_______. (1996). *The culture of education*. Cambridge, MA: Harvard University Press.

Burtt, E. A. (1967). *The metaphysical foundations of modern physical science: An historical and critical essay* (Second edition, revised). London: Routledge and Kegan Paul. (Original work published 1932).

Caesarius of Heisterbach. (1929). *Dialogue on miracles (Vols. 1–2)*, H. von E. Scott and C. C. Swinton Bland (Trans.). New York: Harcourt. (Original work written early thirteenth century).

Callahan, R. (1962). *Education and the cult of efficiency*. Chicago: The University of Chicago Press.

Calvin, J. (1958). *Commentaries*. Joseph Haroutunian (Trans.). Philadelphia: Westminister Press. (Original works published 1540–1565).

_______. (1973). *Institutes of the Christian religion*. F. L. Battles (Trans.). Grand Rapids, MI: Eerdmans. (Original work published 1536).

Capra, F. (1996). *The web of life*. New York: Anchor.

Charters, W. W. (1923). *Curriculum construction*. New York: Macmillan.

Cherryholmes, C. (1988). *Power and criticism: Poststructural investigations in education*. New York: Teachers College Press.

Cohen, J., and I. Stewart. (1994). *The collapse of chaos: Discovering simplicity in a complex world*. New York: Viking.

Cohn, N. (1993). *Cosmos, chaos, and the world to come*. New Haven: Yale University Press.

Colum, P. (1976). *Myths of the world*. New York: Grosset & Dunlap. (Original work published 1930).

Comenius, J. A. (1896). *The great didactic of John Amos Comenius*. M. W. Keatinge (Trans.). London: Adam & Charles Black. (Original work published 1632).

A comprehensive etymological dictionary of the English language, vol. 1. (1966). E. Klein (Ed.). London: Elsevier.

Cubberley, E. P. (1916). *Public school administration*. Boston: Houghton Mifflin.

Davies, P. (1984). *God and the new physics*. New York: Simon & Schuster, Touchstone.

_______. (1988). *The cosmic blueprint*. New York: Simon and Schuster.

_______. (1996). *The last three minutes: Conjectures about the ultimate fate of the universe*. New York: Basic.

Derrida, J. (1991). *Jacques Derrida*. Geoffrey Bennington (Trans.). Chicago: University of Chicago Press.

_______. (1994). *Specters of Marx*. P. Kamuf (Trans.). New York: Routledge. (Original work published in France, 1993).

_______. (1995). *The gift of death*. D. Wills (Trans.). Chicago: University of Chicago Press. (Original work published in France, 1992).

Descartes, R. (1950). *Discourse on method.* L. J. Lafleur (Trans.). New York: Liberal Arts. (Original work published 1637).

Devaney, R. (1990). *Chaos, fractals, and dynamics: Computer experiments in mathematics.* Reading, MA: Addison-Wesley.

Dewey, J. (1922). *Human nature and conduct: An introduction to social psychology.* New York: Modern Library.

_______. (1958). *Experience and nature.* New York: Dover. (Original work published 1925).

_______. (1963). *Experience and education.* New York: Collier. (Original work published 1938).

_______. (1966). *Democracy and education.* New York: Free. (Original work published 1916).

_______. (1971). *How we think.* Chicago: Regnery. (Original work published 1933).

_______. (1974). The nature of aims. In R. D. Archambault (Ed.), *John Dewey on education: Selected writings.* New York: Random House. (Original work published 1923).

_______. (1980). *Art as experience.* New York: Perigee Putnam. (Original work published 1934).

_______. (1990). *The school and society/The child and the curriculum.* Chicago: University of Chicago Press. (Original works published 1902, 1900/1915).

Dickens, C. (1913). *A Christmas carol.* Cambridge, MA: Houghton Mifflin. (Original work published 1843).

Doll, W. E., Jr. (1972). A methodology of experience, part I: An alternative to behavioral objectives. *Educational Theory,* 22 (Summer), 309–24.

_______. (1973). A methodology of experience, part II: The process of inquiry. *Educational Theory, 23* (Winter), 56–73.

_______. (1980). Play and mastery. *Journal of Curriculum Theorizing* (Winter), 209–22.

_______. (1983). Curriculum and change: Piaget's organismic origins. *Journal of Curriculum Studies, 5*(2) 4–61.

_______. (1993). *A post-modern perspective on curriculum.* New York: Teachers College Press.

_______. (1995). Teaching in a nonlinear manner. *Journal of Curriculum Dialogue and Discourse.* Spring, 1–7.

_______. (1998). Curriculum and the concept of control. In W. Pinar (Ed.), *Curriculum: Toward new identities* (pages 295–323). New York: Garland.

_______. (2001a). Struggles with spirituality. In T. Oldenski & D. Carlson (Eds.), *Educational yearning: The journey of the spirit and democratic education* (pages 13–29). New York: Garland.

_______. (2001b). Beyond methods? Teaching as an aesthetic and spirit-ful quest. In E. Mirochnik (Ed.), *Passion and pedagogy.* New York: Lang.

Donne, J. (1968). An anatomie of the world. In Herbert J. C. Grierson (Ed.), *The poems of John Donne (vol. 1).* Oxford: Clarendon. (Original work published 1611).

Dunkel, H. (1970). *Herbart and Hebartianism: An educational ghost story.* Chicago: University of Chicago Press.

Edgerton, S. H. (1996). *Translating the curriculum: Multiculturalism into cultural studies.* New York: Routledge.

Froebel, F. (1912). *Froebel's chief writings on education*. S. S. F. Fletcher and J. Welton (Trans.). New York: Longman, Green. (Original work published in Germany, 1826).

Gadamer, H-G. (1993). *Truth and method.* J. Weinsheimer and D. G. Marshall (Trans.). New York: Continuum. (Original work published in Germany, 1960).

Garcia, R. (1992). The structure of knowledge and the knowledge of structure. In Harry Beilin and Peter B. Pufall (Eds.), *Piaget's theory: Prospects and possibilities.* Hillsdale, NJ: Erlbaum.

Giroux, H. (1988). *Teachers as intellectuals: Toward a critical pedagogy of learning*. South Hadley, MA: Bergin & Garvey.

Goldsmith, E. (1989). Gaia and evolution. *The Ecologist, 19*(4), 147–61.

Gough, N. (1993a). Environmental education, narrative complexity and postmodern science/fiction. *International Journal of Science Education, 15*(5), 607–25.

_______. (1993b). *Laboratories in fiction: Science education and popular media.* Geelong, Australia: Deakin University Press.

_______. (1993c). Neuromancing the stones: Experience, intertextuality, and cyberpunk science fiction. *Journal of Experiential Education, 16*(3), 9–17.

_______. (1994). Playing at catastrophe: Ecopolitical education after poststructuralism. *Educational Theory, 44*(2), 189–210.

Grafton, A., and D. Jardine. (1986). *From humanism to the humanities: Education and the liberal arts in fifteenth- and sixteenth-century Europe*. London: Duckworth.

Graham, R. (1992). *Currere* and reconceptualism: The progress of the pilgrimage, 1975–1990. *Journal of Curriculum Studies, 24*(1), 27–42.

Griffin, D. R. (Ed.). (1988). *The reenchantment of science: Postmodern proposals.* Albany: State University of New York Press.

Gruber, H. (1989). *Darwin on man: A psychological study of scientific creativity.* Chicago: University of Chicago Press.

Hamilton, D. (1989). *Toward a theory of schooling*. London: Falmer.

_______. (1990). *Curriculum history.* Geelong, Victoria: Deakin University Press.

_______. (1992). Comenius and the new world order. *Comenius, 46,* 157–71.

Heidegger, M. (1962). *Being and time.* J. Macquarrie and E. Robinson (Trans.). San Francisco: Harper and Row. (Original work published in Germany, 1926).

_______. (1977). The question concerning technology. In Wm. Lovitt (Trans. and Ed.), *The question concerning technology and other essays* (pages 3–35). New York: Harper. (Original work published in Germany, 1954).

Hesiod. (1982). Theogeny. In J. O'Brien and W. Major (Eds.), *In the beginning: Creation myths* (pages 54–60). Chico, CA: Scholars.

Hobbes, T. (1950). *The Leviathan.* London: Dutton. (Original work published 1651).

Holy Bible: King James version. (1935). New York: The Limited Editions Club.

Homer. (1965). *The Iliad*. R. A. Brower and W. H. Bond (Eds.); A. Pope (Trans.). New York: Macmillan.

hooks, b. (1992). *Black looks: Race and representation.* Boston: South End.

Huebner, D. (1995). Education and spirituality. *JCT: An Interdisciplinary Journal of Curriculum Studies, 11*(2), 13–34.

Hunter, M. (1982). *Mastery teaching*. El Segundo, CA: TID.

Husserl, E. (1969). *Ideas: General introduction to pure phenomenology.* London: Allen and Unwin. (Original work published 1913).

Jencks, C. (1987). *What is post-modernism?* New York: St. Martin's.

_______. (1992). Preface. In C. Jencks (Ed.), *The post-modern reader.* New York: St. Martin's.

Johnson, G. (1995). *Fire in the mind: Science, faith, and the search for order.* New York: Knopf.

Kauffman, S. A. (1993). *The origins of order: Self-organization and selection in evolution.* New York: Oxford University Press.

______. (1995) *At home in the universe: The search for the laws of self-organization and complexity.* New York: Oxford University Press.

Kellert, S. (1993). *In the wake of chaos.* Chicago: University of Chicago Press.

Kincheloe, J. (1995). *Toil and trouble: Good work, smart workers and the integration of academic and vocational education.* New York: Lang.

Kliebard, H. (1986). *The struggle for the American curriculum: 1893–1958.* Boston: Routledge and Kegan Paul.

______. (1992). *Forging the American curriculum: Essays in curriculum story and theory.* New York: Routledge.

Kuhn, T. (1977). *The essential tension: Selected studies in scientific traditions and change.* Chicago: University of Chicago Press.

Kundera, M. (1988). *The art of the novel.* L. Asher (Trans.). New York: Grove.

Lam, L. (1997). *Nonlinear physics for beginners.* New York: World.

Lightman, A. (1991). *Ancient light: Our changing view of the universe.* Cambridge, MA: Harvard University Press.

Lipset, D. (1980). *Gregory Bateson: The legacy of a scientist.* Englewood Cliffs, NJ: Prentice-Hall.

Lorenz, E. (1995). *The essence of chaos.* Seattle: University of Washington Press.

Luhmann, N. (1995). *Social systems.* J. Bodnorz, Jr. (Trans.). Stanford: Stanford University Press.

Lydon, A. (1995). An ecozoic cosmology of curriculum and spirituality. *JCT: An Interdisciplinary Journal of Curriculum Studies, 11*(2), 67–86.

Lyotard, J. (1984). *The postmodern condition: A report on knowledge.* Minneapolis: University of Minnesota Press. (Original work published 1979).

Maclagan, D. (1977). *Creation myths.* London: Thames & Hudson.

Mandlebrot, B. (1983). *The fractal geometry of nature.* New York: Freeman.

Margulis, L. (1998). *Symbiotic planet: A new look at evolution.* New York: Basic.

_______. (1995). *What is life?* New York: Simon & Schuster.

Margulis, L., and D. Sagan. (1997). *Slanted truths: Essays on Gaia, symbiosis, and evolution.* New York: Springer-Verlag.

Marsh, C., and G. Willis. (1995). *Curriculum: Alternative approaches, ongoing issues.* Englewood Cliffs, NJ: Prentice–Hall.

Maturana, H., and F. Varela. (1980). *Autopoiesis and cognition: The realization of the living.* Boston: Reidel.

_______. (1987). *The tree of knowledge.* Boston: Shambhala.

McCarthy, C. (1988). Rethinking liberal and radical perspectives on racial inequality in school: Making the case for nonsynchrony. *Harvard Educational Review*, 58(3), 265–79.

McLaren, P. (1989). *Life in schools: Introduction to critical pedagogy in the foundations in education*. New York: Longman.

McNeil, L. (1986). *Contradictions of control: School structure and school knowledge*. New York: Routledge.

Morris, M., M. Doll, and W. Pinar (Eds.). (1999). *How we work*. New York: Lang.

Nicolis, G., and I. Prigogine. (1989). *Exploring complexity: An introduction*. New York: Freeman.

Noddings, N. (1996). On community. *Educational Theory, 46* (Summer), 245–67.

Nye, A. (1992). A woman's thought of a man's discipline? The letters of Abelard and Heloise. *Hypatia, 7*(3), 1–21.

Ong, W. (1958). *Ramus: Method and the decay of dialogue*. Cambridge, MA: Harvard University Press.

Oxford English dictionary (2nd. ed., 1989). J. A. Simpson and E. S. C. Weiner (Eds.). Oxford, England: Clarendon.

Oxford Latin dictionary. (1984). P. G. W. Glare (Ed.). Oxford, England: Clarendon.

Pattee, H. H. (1973). *Hierarchy theory*. New York: Braziller.

Peterson, T. S. (1994). *Acquired taste: The French origins of modern cooking*. Ithaca: Cornell University Press.

Piaget, J., and R. Garcia. (1989). *Psychogenesis and the history of science*. New York: Columbia University Press.

______. (1991). *Toward a logic of meaning*. Hillsdale, NJ: Erlbaum.

Pinar, W. F. (1994). *Autobiography, politics and sexuality: Essays in curriculum theory, 1972–1992*. New York: Lang.

______. (1998). *Curriculum: Toward new identities*. New York: Garland.

Pinar, W., and M. Grumet. (1976). *Toward a poor curriculum*. Dubuque, IA: Kendall/ Hunt.

Pinar, W. F., W. Reynolds, P. Slattery, and P. Taubman (Eds.). (1995). *Understanding curriculum*. New York: Lang.

Prigogine, I., and I. Stengers. (1984). *Order out of chaos: Man's new dialogue with nature*. New York: Bantam.

Ramus, P. (1569). *Dialectica A. Talaei praelectionibus illustrata*. Basileae.

______. (1576). *Professio regia*. Basle, Switzerland: Thomas Fregius Publisher.

Reid, W. (1981a). The deliberative approach to the study of the curriculum and its relation to critical pluralism. In M. Lawn and L. Barton (Eds.), *Rethinking curriculum studies*. (pages 160–87). London: Croom Helm.

______. (1981b). The practical, the theoretic, and the conduct of curriculum research. 1981 American Educational Research Association presentation.

Reiss, T. (1982). *The discourse of modernism*. Ithaca, N.Y: Cornell University Press.

Robertson, J. (1997). *Restructuring educational experience: A post-modern perspective*. (unpublished doctoral dissertation, Louisiana State University)

Rogers, L. W. (1925). *The ghosts in Shakespeare*. Chicago: Theo.

Rorty, R. (1980). *Philosophy and the mirror of nature*. Princeton: Princeton University Press.

______. (1982). *Consequences of pragmatism*. Minneapolis: University of Minnesota Press.

______. (1989). *Contingency, irony, and solidarity*. Cambridge: Cambridge University Press.

Ryle, G. (1949). *The concept of mind.* London: Hutchinson & Co.

Sandburg, C. (1960). *Harvest poems.* New York: Harcourt.

Santayana, G. (1968). *The German mind.* New York: Crowell, Apollo edition. (Original work published 1915).

Schilpp, P. A. (Ed.). (1941). *The philosophy of Alfred North Whitehead.* Evanston, IL: Northwestern University Press.

Schubert, W. (1980). *Curriculum books: The first eighty years.* Lanham, MD: University Press of America.

_______. (1986). *Curriculum: Perspective, paradigm, and possibility.* New York: Macmillan.

Serres, M. (1983a). *Hermes: Literature, science, philosophy.* J.V. Harari and D. F. Bell (Eds.). Baltimore: Johns Hopkins University Press.

_______. (1983b). *Rome: The book of foundations.* F. McCarren (Trans.). Stanford, CA: Stanford University Press. (Original work published in France, 1981).

Shakespeare, W. (1967). *The tragedy of Hamlet, Prince of Denmark.* G. L. Kittredge (Ed.). Waltham, MA: Blaisdell. (Original work published 1602c).

Skilbeck, M. (1984). *School-based curriculum development.* London: Harper.

Stern, J. (1959). *Lichtenberg: A doctrine of scattered occasions.* Bloomington, IN: Indiana University Press.

Stewart, I. (1990). *Does God play dice?* Cambridge, MA: Blackwell.

Swimme, B., and T. Berry. (1992). *The universe story from the primordial flaring forth to the ecozoic era: A celebration of the unfolding of the cosmos.* New York: HarperCollins.

Taylor, F. (1947). *Scientific management.* New York: Harper. (Original work published 1911).

Thompson, C. J. (1974). *The mystery and lore of apparitions.* Detroit: Gale.

Toulmin, S. (1990). *Cosmopolis: The hidden agenda of modernity.* New York: Free.

Triche, S. (2001). *Reconceiving curriculum: An historical approach.* (Unpublished doctoral dissertation, Louisiana State University).

Tyler, R. (1950). *Basic principles of curriculum and instruction.* Chicago: University of Chicago Press.

Waldrop, M. M. (1992). *Complexity: The emerging science at the edge of order and chaos.* New York: Simon and Schuster.

Wertheim, M. (1995). *Pythagoras' trousers: God, physics, and the gender wars.* New York: Random House.

West, C. (1989). *The American evasion of philosophy.* Madison, WI: University of Wisconsin Press.

Westbrook, R. B. (1991). *John Dewey and American democracy.* Ithaca, NY: Cornell University Press.

Wexler, P. (1987). *Social analysis of education: After the new sociology.* Boston, MA: Routledge and Kegan Paul.

Wheatley, M. J. (1992). *Leadership and the new science: Learning about organization from an orderly universe.* San Francisco: Barrett-Koehler.

Whitehead, A. N. (1967a). *The aims of education.* New York: Free. (Original work published 1929).

______. (1967b). *Science and the modern world.* New York: Free. (Original work published 1925).

______. (1978). *Process and reality: An essay in cosmology* (Corrected ed.) David R. Griffin and Donald W. Sherburne (Eds.). New York: Free. (Original work published 1929).

Wilhelm, H. (1960). *Change: Eight lectures on the I Ching*. New York: Pantheon.

William E. Doll, Jr. is the Vira Franklin and J. R. Eagles Professor of Curriculum at Louisiana State University in Baton Rouge. He codirects the Curriculum Theory Project at LSU and teaches courses in curriculum theory and teacher education. He is also the author of *A Post-Modern Perspective on Curriculum* (1993) and is currently working on his third book, *Chaos, Complexity, Curriculum and Culture*.

Perspective on Doll

Wendi Broussard

In "Ghosts and the Curriculum," William Doll begins by stating that John Dewey's ghost haunts the American curriculum, "reminding us that in neither theory nor practice have we yet 'got it right.'" After teaching high school English and American history for six years, I am confident enough, through my experiences, to agree with Dewey.

Undergraduate work was easy enough, but the thing that I really remember about those education courses I took was that the professor pointed out all of the problems and situations we teachers would face, and then presented the *answers* (don't do this/do this). On my first day of teaching, I was a little nervous about facing 30 or so strange faces. Yet, I was confident that I knew *all* of the answers to problems that might arise. I came to find out that this was very idealistic! Every situation (John has left his book in his locker for the third time this week; Sue has missed 25 days of my class; in spite of the messages I left on their machine, Bobby's parents are surprised and angry that he has made a D; Dan works very hard but still has difficulty understanding subject-verb agreement) requires me to *work* at an answer. There are no quick formulas that I can run to in a book or teaching manual. Indeed, even when I find an answer to help Dan understand subject-verb agreement, it becomes null and void for Mary, who has the same problem the next year. Each student is different, and I have learned that each situation is unique and must be handled with lots of thought.

I bring all of this to light in response to Doll when he writes, "We need to *reconceptualize the idea of curriculum,* to see it not in terms of plans 'pre-set' or ideologies advocated but as an image hovering over the process of education, giving direction and meaning to that process" (this volume). Although I agree, I believe the best teachers are the organized ones—the ones who set goals, make plans, and dream of new and exciting ways of teaching—even though they may not always work. I look back at those first years of teaching and realize the many mistakes I made, but it was then, during those often difficult times, that I was most alive. My lesson plans, always neat and on time, were filled with new ideas, trial-and-error teaching methods, methods that I read about in educational journals, methods that other teachers guaranteed would work, and methods that I simply made up. Yes, goals were set, but out of those goals came spontaneity and a fervency for teaching—and the students enjoyed learning as a result of that.

It was not until after my fourth year of teaching that I quit the goal setting and the new ideas. I figured that I had exhausted all there was to know. I would simply head to my filing cabinet on the first day of class and pull out my folder that read, "Things To Do and Say on the First Day of Class." The problem, you see, was not the goals or lists of things to do in that folder; the problem was that they had been written three years earlier! I was losing my joy in teaching—caught in the "preset" trap, as so many teachers are. Teaching was now just a job. So, from the fourth year on, I no longer had "curriculum visions." The Bible states, "Where there is no vision, the people perish" (Proverbs 29:18). I was dying, and so were my students, becoming bored and complacent like I was. This is when I decided to head to graduate school.

Doll makes a very good point in employing Charles Dickens's theme of ghosts in *A Christmas Carol* to show us how things should be compared to how things are or have been: "For us, the spirit of curriculum past should be ferried across to live peacefully in that Land of No Return, while we on this side adopt a new spirit" (this volume).

I can learn from the mistakes of the past and yet not dwell there. Doll goes on to speak of projects, texts, semesters as being "finished." He says that this modern way of thinking about the curriculum is one ghost that continues to haunt us, that if we are to "get it right," we need to move beyond that way of thinking as teachers. However, I believe that we all, especially teachers, need closure in order to "move on." I look at this not in terms of the end of a book but rather the end of a chapter in that book. Thus, as I now "finish" my master's degree in curriculum and instruction, I have great excitement and anticipation about returning to teaching, something I thought I had lost forever in those last years.

Presently, I continue to learn and receive new ideas for teaching. Yet, I have combined this with my past experience in teaching, pulling out the things that worked, and throwing away the things that didn't work. And finally, I put these visions of curriculum past and these thoughts of curriculum present into hopes for my curriculum future as the next chapter of my life awaits the writing.

Wendi Broussard has an M.A. in curriculum and instruction at Louisiana State University in Baton Rouge. She has taught in East Baton Rouge Parish public schools for seven years.

Chapter 1 An Ecological Understanding

Problematic: Metaphor Matters

Metaphors matter to Chet Bowers, and they matter to us. We were pleased to read in the very first sentence of his chapter that he positioned himself somewhere other than "on the cutting edge of what represents the current expression of high-status knowledge." A cutting edge is sometimes called a "leading" (or should that be *bleeding*?) edge, but have you ever wondered what a "cutting edge" actually or metaphorically *cuts?*

Through such operating principles as Occam's razor, academics in Western and Westernized cultures have a long history of associating reason, learning, and progress with simplification and reduction—and, not coincidentally, with force and masculinity (as in "mastery"). In many disciplines and professions, the "cutting edge" of research and practice seems to have changed little since Alexander's sword blade sliced through the decadently overcomplicated Gordian knot.

We face some knotty problems in curriculum inquiry. But the infinite and multiple threads of the postmodern world are inextricably intertwined and attempts to cut through or even to disentangle them are more likely to impede than to assist our understanding of them. Like Bowers, we suspect that the urge to represent the complexities of our transactions with "nature" and each other through "context-free metaphors"—metaphors that are cut off from the language communities that produce them—is a symptom of the problems we are attempting to resolve.

Metaphors matter in the literal sense that they have material effects. As Norman Fairclough (1992) writes, "when we signify things through one metaphor rather than another, we are constructing our reality one way rather than another. Metaphors structure the way we think and the way we act, and our systems of knowledge and belief, in a pervasive and fundamental way" (195). However, some metaphors encode the world in incoherent ways. For example, Harold Brown (1979) points to the contradiction inherent in modeling understandings of human reasoning on the operations of mechanical or cybernetic systems: "The attempt by logical empiricists to identify rationality with algorithmic computability is somewhat strange, since it deems rational only those human acts which could, in principle, be carried out without the presence of a human being" (148).

We may not be able to *not* think through metaphors, but we are responsible for the metaphors we choose to privilege and we need to be critically (and self-critically) responsive to the effects of their deployment. For example, Bowers refers often to "root metaphors," a choice of metaphor that is entirely consistent with his (and our) commitments to conserving organic and evolutionary connections. But we wonder at what point we need to be suspicious of the realities we envision through the metaphors we choose. When and under what circumstances should we remind ourselves that "root metaphor" is a metaphor and does not signify a "real" root? Donna Haraway (1994) asks a difficult but pertinent question for every author who has contributed to this book: "How can metaphor be kept from collapsing into the thing-in-itself?" (60). Or, to put this another way, how can we resist replicating the worlds we analyze in our own material-semiotic practices?

References

Brown, Harold I. (1979). *Perception, theory and commitment: The new philosophy of science*. Chicago: University of Chicago Press.

Fairclough, Norman. (1992). *Discourse and social change*. Cambridge, MA: Polity.

Haraway, Donna J. (1994). A game of cat's cradle: Science studies, feminist theory, cultural studies. *Configurations: A Journal of Literature, Science, and Technology*, 2(1), 59–71.

Toward a Cultural and Ecological Understanding of Curriculum

C. A. Bowers

Continuing to write from the margins too often appears to be a hopeless endeavor, particularly when one intellectual fad after another emerges from the efforts of academics to position themselves on the cutting edge of what represents the current expression of high-status knowledge. The context-free metaphors that emerged from the ideologies that succeeded in equating modernity with the commodification of the commons (which is one of the more distinctive achievements of the Industrial Revolution) continue, like ghosts, to guide our way of understanding relationships, identities, and even what education should help us attain. The context-free metaphors of "individualism," "progress," "creativity," "freedom," and so forth, still serve as the moral and conceptual ideals that teachers are urged to foster through the curriculum. Given the "God word" status of these metaphors in the West, few teachers are aware that their well-intentioned efforts are helping to further the colonizing cultural transformations required by the digital phase of the Industrial Revolution now being given a glitzy image by the media and a false sense of plenitude by shopping malls. With the metanarratives of science, particularly the theory of evolution, having largely displaced religion as the conceptual and moral basis of this new phase of the Industrial Revolution, we are now witnessing a continuing stream of new context-free metaphors that are being used to theorize about the purpose and content of education. These new metaphors, which include "chaos," "complexity," "process," "co-emergent systems," and so forth, are given moral and conceptual legitimacy by the new understanding of the interplay of chaos and order that characterizes the physical universe.

While the implications of these scientifically derived metaphors are being translated into emergent, process-oriented, and constructivist approaches to curriculum, another scientific metanarrative, based on the thinking of Darwin and the recent discoveries of molecular biology, is revitalizing the vision of the Industrial Revolution, which holds that all aspects of life can be engineered and commodified. The sense of order envisioned in this metanarrative does not represent a more progressive and creative form of human existence now understood as emerging from the constant interplay of change and stability. Rather, progress (if it can be called that) is expressed in the struggle of the "selfish gene" to reproduce itself in ever-increasing competitive environments. Proponents of globalizing the culture of cyberspace, such as Hans Moravec, Gregory Stock, and Kevin Kelly, view the development of computers as nature's latest turn in the evolutionary drama of natural selection—which earlier Social Darwinists translated as the "survival of the fittest." This metanarrative, which foregrounds the metaphors of endless "competition," and "genetic fitness," can also be interpreted as the expression of a creative cosmos that, as Kevin Kelly reminds us, "is out of our control." And just as one group of educational theorists finds the self-organizing capacities of chaotic systems the model upon which curriculum reform should be based, another group of educational reformers urge the widespread adoption of computers as the expression of cultural fitness in an increasingly competitive environment.

Because these two sets of metaphors are actually derived from specific cultural metanarratives and give legitimacy to a specific cultural set of values and way of thinking, the reader is likely to be wondering why I refer to them as context-free. This phrase is used to emphasize that educational theorists are ignoring that these new metaphors encode and thus reproduce the root metaphors of the elite groups that provided the theory and moral justification for the globalization of both the earlier and, now, digital phase of the Industrial Revolution. That is, just as the earlier context-free metaphors of "individualism," "creativity," "progress," etc., ignored how the person is nested in a culture that is, in turn, nested in (and dependent upon) natural systems, the scientifically derived metaphors of "complexity," "chaos," and "process" are based on complex metaphorical constructions and modes of analysis that continue to ignore how culture mediates the individual's relationship to what is now being explained as the unfolding systems of spontaneous self-organization —which other scientists explain in terms of how changes in DNA alter the chemistry of proteins that, in turn, give rise to new traits in organisms. The latter is part of a metanarrative/praxis that makes possible the patenting of the gene lines that are the basis of life. The metaphors of complexity and process overcome the Cartesian separation of the knower from the external world (nature), but they do not take account of how the metanarrative now being constructed by mathematicians and theoretical physicists as well as the life-experiences of individuals are influenced by the cultural epistemology of their language community.

A culturally and ecologically grounded approach to curriculum theory that is free of the deep and largely unconsciously held assumptions that underlie the context-free metaphors popular among cutting-edge curriculum theorists starts with a different set of "realities"—realities that persist regardless of the context-free metaphors used to theorize the connections between systems of self-organization and postmodern curricular goals. These realities include the rapid changes in natural systems, the increasing rate of global warming, the rapid loss of forest cover, the loss of species, and the depletion of aquifers. These realities also include the changes in the reproductive capacities of forms of life that have had their environments contaminated by the toxic wastes of industrial/consumer-oriented cultures—to cite just a few areas in which humans have imposed their vision of progress on the environment. In addition, these realities include the rapid expansion of the world's population and the globalization of a technological, consumer lifestyle, which reflect more the spread of the commodification of human relationships and knowledge than the nonlinear world of complexity science. Indeed, the realities of cultural thought patterns and lifestyles that exceed the sustaining capacity of natural systems are changing the future prospects of humanity in ways that cannot be reconciled with the current extrapolations that represent the cosmos as "a complex unity with change and stability inherently united [and] enfolded within one another" and curriculum as "emergent." Although the metaphors of cosmological unfolding fit nicely with the Western myth that equates change with progress, they divert awareness away from the realities of ensuring that the world's population has access to adequate sources of protein, shelter, employment, sustainable communities within sustainable ecosystems, and so forth. These are the realities that should be the central concern of a curriculum theory that addresses the need to balance critical inquiry and creativity with the forms of intergenerational communication and relationships essential to participation in the commons.

The other realities that need to be a central focus of curriculum theory are the many different cultural epistemologies that frame the most basic understanding of human/nature relationships and, in particular, different approaches to technology. Taking seriously this aspect of the nested relationships within the traditions of a culture as well as the culture's dependence on natural systems is also basic to addressing social justice issues, which should include the responsibility of the current generation not to degrade either the cultural inheritance or the ecosystems in ways that diminish the quality of individual and community life of future generations. Basically, the cultural and environmental dimensions of everyday life require an in-depth understanding of the cultural forms of encoding, reproduction, and renewal, changes occurring from the impact of different cultural epistemologies and technological practices on natural systems, and the cultural patterns that contribute to viable and socially just forms of community life.

I have difficulty grasping how the basis of moral reciprocity between humans and between humans and the natural world can be based on the scientific understanding of how everything from galaxies to microscopic cells unfolds through systems of spontaneous self-organization. I also have difficulty understanding how cultures based on ancient mythopoetic narratives can be persuaded to abandon their traditions in favor of current scientific explanations of nonlinear self-organization, which, ironically, are framed in a way that combines the Western myth of progress with the moral relativism that is made to appear as nonproblematic by the myth of progress. That the explanations of curricular and, by extension, cultural significance of complexity science are being embedded in the myth of progress can be seen in the fact that no mention is ever made of pathological cultural developments (repressive political regimes, numerous genocides, and the current overextending of the earth's sustainable capacities) that occurred during the fraction of time natural systems were organizing themselves in nonlinear patterns. Scientists have not yet told us whether dynamic change occurs in the symbolic systems of a culture in the same way that it does in natural systems. Historical and cross-cultural evidence suggests a number of fundamental differences, which include unemployment, poverty, birth defects caused by contamination of the environment, and global spread of the consumer lifestyle and technologies that are accelerating the rate of dynamic, nonlinear change in natural systems. The disequilibrium in natural systems that is now being seen as the source of an endlessly creative universe, from a human perspective, is creating environmental conditions to which it is increasingly difficult for cultures to adapt.

Rather than illuminating the similarities and differences between symbolic and natural systems, the scientific metanarratives being revised in light of new discoveries are further marginalizing the need to understand the aspects of culture that have the greatest influence on the prospects of long-term human survival. Science can help us understand the changes in natural systems that result from cultural practices, but it cannot, by itself or in conjunction with the mythic elements of Western thought, be used as the basis for guiding curriculum reform. Rather, the starting point for radically revising the basis of curriculum theory, as I have suggested elsewhere (1993a, 1993b, 1995, 1997), is to be found in the reconceptualization of the following three aspects of the dominant Western culture now being globalized.

Shifting from an Individual to a Cultural View of Intelligence

The Western tradition of viewing intelligence as an attribute of the autonomous individual is still, despite the efforts of John Dewey and Lev Vygotsky, reinforced in universities and public schools. Howard Gardner's effort to identify multiple forms of intelligence (with environmental intelligence now being considered as an addition to the list) simply represents a more refined version of an individual's attributes. What we now know about the root metaphors of a cultural group, which frame the process of analogic thinking and are encoded in the iconic metaphors that are often a taken-for-granted part of everyday discourse, provides the evidence that intelligence is largely cultural in nature—with its degree of individualized expression depending upon the norms of the cultural group. For example, the root metaphor of mechanism which Johannes Kepler helped establish in the early part of the seventeenth century still frames the language and ways of thinking in a variety of areas, including brain research, the human genome project, and computer-mediated education.

When teachers became aware of how language encoded the root metaphor of patriarchy and framed our understanding of intelligence in ways that limited the possibilities of both women and men, they became more sensitive to genderized language in the curriculum. For many teachers, this represented real curriculum reform. There is a similar need for teachers to be aware of the historically and culturally specific root metaphors that continue to frame how the most basic community and environmental relationships are understood. This need can also be stated in terms of freeing the present generation from reenacting the form of intelligence that was taken for granted by previous generations. Understanding that language does not function like a conduit in a sender/receiver model of communication is made even more imperative by the increasing use of computers in the classroom, a technology based on a conduit view of language and the even more questionable idea that data are the basis of intelligence. In addition to helping students understand the root metaphors and earlier processes of analogic thinking encoded in the language that provides the conceptual schema they might otherwise take for granted, teachers also need to understand how the language of the curriculum involves a form of moral education that goes largely unnoticed. Regardless of subject area, the language of the curriculum is used to communicate about attributes and relationships. The metaphorical nature of language reproduces the cultural group's earlier understanding of the attributes of the participants, objects, and events in the relationship as well as the cultural group's moral norms that are to govern these relationships. Again, the example of how language both encodes earlier ways of understanding the attributes of women and men and the moral norms based on the differences in the metaphorically constructed attributes helps to clarify how moral education is an inherent aspect of the language of the curriculum. The implications of this go beyond encouraging students to adopt a more caring attitude, knowing when they have reached the next stage of moral development, and telling them stories that exemplify a particular virtue. Specifically, how the language in different areas of the curriculum reproduces the environmentally destructive moral norms of the dominant culture should be a primary concern of curriculum theorists and professors of teacher education. The destructive form of moral/environmental education can be seen in how individualism, technology, and progress are represented, as well as in the more blatant examples which represent nature as a resource. Teachers also need to address the many ways in which the language of the curriculum fosters a natural attitude toward commodified activities and relationships.

Challenging the Globalization of the Digital Phase of the Industrial Revolution

The language that suggests we are in a "post" modern stage of development and are moving beyond Newtonian- and Cartesian-based cultural traditions is based on a misconception of one of the central characteristics of the past 200 years of industrial development in the West. Current excitement about new scientific knowledge and the resulting computer-based technologies ignore the rapid globalization of the market principles and technologies that are turning traditional skills and reciprocal relationships into commodities that create new forms of economic dependencies and environmental destructiveness. The spread of computers into every aspect of life is not only accelerating the commodification process, which now includes the genetic basis of life processes, but is also reinforcing a form of rootless individual subjectivity which finds fulfillment through endless consumerism and technological innovation.

Curriculum theorists need to address the many dimensions of the commodification process that have become an increasingly dominant aspect of everyday life, including the classroom where the curricular influence of corporations is becoming even more visible. Specifically, there is a need to understand which areas of the curriculum contribute to the development of technologies that further undermine what remains of the noncommodified aspects of individual and community life. In addition, students need to understand the long-term consequences of the cultural and environmental changes that accompany the introduction of new technologies: What are the benefits and for whom? How does the technology affect the patterns of moral reciprocity and noncommodified relationships? Do the changes threaten the viability of the community, and do they contribute to the exploitation of social groups and the environment?

In order to put these technological changes in perspective, curriculum reform needs to take account of the characteristics of cultural groups that have resisted or avoided the transformation of the commons into market relationships and dependency upon outside experts. The study of noncommodified relationships and activities within the dominant culture is also a needed aspect of curriculum reform. If students are unable to recognize the difference between commodified and noncommodified aspects of community life as well as how different cultural groups have carried forward and renewed their noncommodified traditions, they will lack the conceptual basis for articulating what should be conserved, as well as what new technological developments should be resisted. The Industrial Revolution, particularly in its computer-driven phase of development, is more than a ghost and a historical artifact. It continues to transform on a global scale the processes of education, entertainment, healing and nurturing, work, sports, and even the human reproduction process. It also continues to frame how the metaphors of development and progress are understood while providing the energy and moral justification for the global search for new markets. The high-status knowledge promoted by our universities and public schools is essential to maintaining this cycle of technological innovation and consumerism, and thus should be a primary concern of curriculum theorists.

Curriculum Theory Needs a New Ideological Orientation

The various genres of educational liberalism (technocratic, neo-romantic, emancipatory) are based on a set of cultural assumptions that were also the basis of the Industrial Revolution. These assumptions include equating change with progress, viewing the individual as the basic social unit, and an anthropocentric view of human/nature relationships. These assumptions, in turn, led to a simplistic and distorted way of understanding tradition, ignoring the different cultural epistemologies and moral systems, and viewing the different systems of moral reciprocity essential to viable communities as a limitation on individual freedom and progress. The technocratic liberals, with their more mechanistic and elitist orientation, appear to be the most closely connected with the commodification orientation of the Industrial Revolution, but the other traditions of educational liberalism, with their anthropocentrism and continual quest for individually authored ideas and values, contributed to the form of individual subjectivity that lacked the deep attachment to place and community essential to resisting the spread of market-oriented values.

Current efforts to base curriculum theory on the "process"-oriented philosophers such as Whitehead and Dewey and on complexity science do not provide a substantive alternative to the core values and assumptions that underlie the digital phase of the Industrial Revolution we are now entering. These theories still equate change with progress, view cultural traditions as reactionary impediments to the spontaneous self-organization of chaotic systems, and ignore differences in cultural epistemologies. Although the various scientific metanarratives (including the revival of Social Darwinism) provide a conceptual alternative to the extreme anthropocentrism characteristic of the different forms of educational liberalism, curriculum theorists working in this conceptual and moral minefield do little more than give lip service to the environmental crisis. With regard to the last point, the post-Newtonian sciences, particularly the field of molecular biology, are carrying the anthropocentric/engineering mentality to an even more extreme form of expression.

A careful examination of the various forms of resistance to the continual spread of commoditized relationships and forms of knowledge will suggest some of the characteristics of an ideology that represents an alternative to the assumptions and values still promoted by the various traditions of educational liberalism. Within North America, we are witnessing a growing interest in living lives of voluntary simplicity, a rapid expansion in the number of community-based organizations, and a recovery of narrative—including the narratives of place—and community-based organic agriculture. These cultural changes are oriented toward *conserving* and renewing the face-to-face non-commodified traditions of communities. The growing interest in technologies that incorporate the principles of ecological design is also based on *conserving* traditions of community decision-making, a deep knowledge of place, and the dangers of degrading the local ecosystems. These efforts to recover the commons from the Wal-Mart and Microsoft mentality that is still dominant in American society are also related to the many approaches to *conserving* the environmental heritage. Even the eco-management approaches to the environment, which are based on an anthropocentric and scientific engineering mentality, are oriented to *conserving* and renewing ecosystems. In Third World countries, resistance to Western approaches to development, which are viewed as requiring the abandonment of traditional knowledge of biodiversity and community values in order to achieve integration into the technological and economic model of development, is becoming more visible (Sachs, 1992, 1993). These expressions of resistance also have a *conserving* rather than a liberal orientation that equates change with progress.

Although the tradition of liberal thought has been based on reified political categories that fail to account for how the most emancipatory and "process"-oriented theorists live their own lives, the threat to the environment and to what remains of cultural traditions not yet turned into niche markets suggests the need to begin thinking about curriculum reform in terms of conserving and renewing the traditions that contribute to more self-sufficient and ecologically sustainable communities. The name for the form of conservatism we need to take seriously as an alternative to Industrial Revolution derived ideologies is cultural/bio-conservatism. The need for cultures to develop in ways that do not destroy the biotic community suggests that this form of conservatism will be dependent upon a critical, reform-oriented curriculum. That is, cultural traditions, including the antitradition traditions of technology, science, business, and the high-status forms of knowledge of elite groups who promote the myth that equates technologically based changes with progress, need to be critically understood. This is not an activity that will be reinforced outside the classroom. A curriculum based on cultural/bio-conservatism would also provide for participating in the non-commodified community relationships and activities: mentoring, re-storying the land, nurturing, playing, interacting with elders, non-consumer-based relationships with the environment, and participating in local political processes that address environmental and social justice issues. It would also involve learning how a lifestyle of voluntary simplicity helps revitalize the life of the community. A careful examination of the curricular implications of Wendell Berry's seventeen principles for conserving communities would lead to a far more radical change in curriculum than anything proposed by Dewey, Freire, or the critical pedagogy theorists (Berry, 1996, 413–14).

Scientists are indeed helping us understand the behavior of natural systems, but their metanarratives and discoveries that lead to new technologies that increasingly represent experiments with the symbolic foundations of the world's cultures are more problematic. Deriving a theory of curriculum from them is even more problematic. I will close by suggesting that reading *The Case Against the Global Economy and for a Turn Toward the Local* (Mander and Goldsmith, 1996), *The Development Dictionary: A Guide to Knowledge as Power* (Sachs, 1992), and *Dominating Knowledge: Development, Culture, and Resistance* (Apffel-Marglin and Marglin, 1990) provides a far more culturally and ecologically grounded approach to curriculum theory than the metanarratives derived from scientific discoveries. This literature is representative of another tradition of "pre-" and "post-" modern thinking that will help ensure that the metaphors used to frame the fundamental relationships addressed by curriculum theorists do not reproduce the cultural assumptions of the Industrial Revolution.

References

Apffel-Marglin, Frederique, and Stephen A. Marglin (Eds.). (1990). *Dominating knowledge: Development, culture, and resistance*. Oxford: Clarendon.

Berry, Wendell. (1996). Conserving communities. In Jerry Mander and Edward Goldsmith (Eds.), *The case against the global economy and for the turn toward the local*. (pages 407–18). San Francisco: Sierra Club.

Bowers, C. A. (1993a). *Education, cultural myths, and the ecological crisis: Toward deep changes*. Albany: State University of New York Press.

_________. (1993b). *Critical essays on education, modernity, and the recovery of the ecological imperative*. New York: Teachers College Press.

_________. (1995). *Educating for an ecologically sustainable culture: Re-thinking moral education, creativity, intelligence, and other modern orthodoxies*. Albany: State University of New York Press.

________. (1997). *The culture of denial: Why the environmental movement needs a strategy for reforming universities and public schools*. Albany: State University of New York Press.

________. (2001). *Educating for eco-justice and community*. Athens, GA: University of Georgia Press.

Mander, Jerry, and Edward Goldsmith (Eds.). (1996). *The case against the global economy and for a turn to the local*. San Francisco: Sierra Club.

Sachs, Wolfgang (Ed.). (1992). *The development dictionary: A guide to knowledge as power*. London: Zed.

_________. (Ed.). (1993). *Global ecology: A new arena of political conflict*. London: Zed.

C. A. Bowers has taught at the University of Oregon and Portland State University and is semi-retired. His published works include 12 books and more than 80 articles. His most recent books are *Let Them Eat Data* (2000) and *Educating for Eco-Justice and Community* (2001). He continues to present talks in North America and other parts of the world on the cultural roots of the ecological crisis. He is currently collaborating on a new book about the ideas of Gregory Bateson and the Deep Ecology philosophers.

Perspective on Bowers

Ellen Wickersham

C. A. Bowers has contributed a strong essay to this volume; however, for this reader, it has raised several questions. First, Bowers continuously refers to "context-free metaphors." The "old" metaphors of the predigital Industrial Revolution, to use his term, of individualism, progress, creativity, and freedom are certainly not context-free. And one senses that he knows that. Perhaps one could call them universal, philosophic, or guiding metaphors descriptive of the hopes and goals of the times, but not, in my opinion, context-free. These moral and conceptual ideals arose within the context of the Industrial Revolution, a time of invention, of a spirit of Manifest Destiny, and of America, as the land of opportunity for millions of immigrants. Also embedded in them are the stories of the marginalized, those who suffered under some of these concepts. Now that we face the digital and/or scientific revolution, the new metaphors of chaos, complexity, process, and co-emergent systems are again descriptive, arising from scientific discovery. In any age, discovery and invention are both blessing and curse; these connotations arise from context and consequence.

Second, Bowers's refusal to use the term postmodern is interesting and a bit perplexing. He prefers to consider the present as the digital revolution and hints at a late stage of capitalism. He does recognize, however, the new and profound discoveries and theoretical concepts arising from the fields of mathematics, physics, and biology and also points to the globalizing culture of cyberspace. An argument can be made that upon closer study, these discoveries will impact how we think, learn, and even compose our identity. I refer to the work of Sherry Turkle (1995) and that of the media philosophers Mark Taylor and Esa Saarinen (1994). In addition, Bowers discusses the pervasive commodification of both human relationships and of knowledge. Does this not echo the work of Jean Baudrillard (1996), Guy Debord (1990), and other postmodern thinkers? Unlike the invention of the transistor, that gave us better televisions and toasters, these discoveries have engendered a paradigmatic shift. Bowers also echoes the postmodern in his call for community over individualism, when he remarks that

> the other traditions of educational liberalism, with their anthropocentrism and continual quest for individual authored ideas and values, contributed to the form of

> individual subjectivity that lacked the deep attachment to place and community essential to resisting the spread of market-oriented values. (this volume)

Third, Bowers posits his argument for a cultural-bio/conservatism curriculum from an either/or standpoint. His point that the metaphors of complexity and process do not include the life experiences of the individual (!) and the influences of the cultural epistemology of language is well taken. But do we throw the baby out with the bath water? The insight that the materialistic, commodified world is negatively impacting natural systems is correct. Yet, one could also make the argument that an ecological approach to curriculum is not context-free either. Defining ecological problems is somewhat simple; finding equitable solutions is not. Furthermore, as a proponent for change—always looking for a way to better meet the needs of students—I take to heart Bowers's injunction that change does not always equal progress. It is a good point. William Doll's (this volume) concept of curriculum as conversation, in my opinion, is more appropriate than Bowers's either/or approach to generating curriculum visions.

The strength and power of Bowers's essay is not found in his call for a cultural-bio/conservatism curriculum but rather in his illumination of the problematics inherent in the digital age. Outside of imagological philosophy, this is the first curriculum theory paper to address this compelling issue. The commodification process, including the genetic basis of life processes, is accelerating. "[It] is also reinforcing a form of rootless individual subjectivity which finds fulfillment through endless consumerism and technological innovation" (this volume). These are profound challenges to schooling and learning; transformative education has never been needed more. For example, are parents aware that in MUDs (multiuser dungeons or domains) users are able to construct personae—several at a time—complete with gender, sexual orientation, and whatever other characteristics one wishes in an anonymous environment? These chatroom-like environments facilitate a "trying on a new me" personae in a way never before possible. As one college student describes the experience:

> I split my mind. I'm getting better at it. I can see myself being two or three or more. And I just turn on one part of my mind and then another when I go from window to window....And then I'll get a real-time message [that flashes on the screen as soon as it is sent from another system user], and I guess that is RL [real life]. It's just one more window...RL is just one more window...and it's not usually my best. (Turkle, 1995, 13)

Taylor and Saarinen (1994) tell us that "in contemporary culture, oneness and unity are regarded as non-being, while manyness and plurality are believed to characterize being" (Shifting subjects, 2). Other sophisticated advances in computer design have led to different significant concerns. In addition to the problematics of virtual, fragmented identities, our modern concept of the computer as machine is gradually being replaced with a postmodern concept of computer as *demiperson*. Turkle's research has led to her conclusion that "children today contemplate machines they believe to be intelligent and conscious yet not alive" (1995, 84). As artificial intelligence advances, computers are more capable of interacting with the world. Taylor and Saarinen (1994) raise the question as to whether the computer is becoming an appendage of us or whether we are merging with the computer: "Is the mediatrix an electronic prostheses of our organism, or are our minds and bodies psycho-physical prostheses of the immaterial web in which we are entangled?" ("Virtuality," 3). One should not be led to believe that all virtuality or artificial intelligence is to be shunned or condemned. For "virtuality need not be a prison. It can be the raft, the ladder, the transitional space, the moratorium, that is discarded after reaching greater freedom....We can use it for a space for growth" (Turkle, 263).

Bowers is so correct in raising these issues couched in the rhetoric of curriculum visions. Here is a challenge not only to parents, schools, and curriculum theorists but also to our very concept of identity-making. It is a cry for curriculum vision. "Our need for a practical philosophy of self-knowledge has never been greater as we struggle to make meaning from our lives on the screen" (Turkle, 269).

References

Baudrillard, J. (1996). *The perfect crime*. C. Turner (Trans.). London: Verso.

Debord, G. (1990). *Comments on the society of the spectacle*. M. Imrie (Trans.). London: Verso.

Taylor, M. C., and E. Saarinen. (1994). Shifting subjects. In *Imagologies: Media philosophy*. New York: Routledge

______. (1994). Virtuality. In *Imagologies: Media philosophy*. New York: Routledge.

Turkle, S. (1995). *Life on the screen: Identity in the age of the internet*. New York: Touchstone.

Ellen Wickersham is a doctoral student in curriculum and instruction at Louisiana State University in Baton Rouge. She earned her B.A. at Marquette University and her M.S. in elementary education at Western Connecticut State University. Previously, she taught language arts and social studies in elementary and middle school settings in New York, Virginia, and Louisiana and has also held the positions of principal and associate principal. Her research interests include curriculum theory, middle-level curriculum, and aesthetics in the curriculum.

Chapter 2 Death and Crisis

Problematic: Mourning Becomes Curriculum

I suspect it is the tragedies in life that arrest my attention more than the other things and say more to my imagination....(Henry James, 1877)[1]

In *The Europeans*, Henry James fashioned tragedy from the effects of Old World experience on New World innocence. More than a century later, the tragedies of life in worlds old, new, and non-innocent arrest the attention of Deborah Britzman and William Pinar and speak eloquently to their respective imaginations. Inspired by such sources as Sigmund Freud's thoughts on war and death and Robert Musil's "ill-tempered observations" on the crises of European culture in the early decades of the twentieth century, they envision curriculum as a site of tragic loss. Reconceptualist curriculum inquiry has contributed significantly to what Madeleine Grumet (1981) calls "curriculum theory's fund of doubt" (116); but what of the curriculum that escapes even doubtful attention—the curriculum that cannot be found wanting because it cannot be found at all?[2] This is "the lost curriculum" that Britzman invites us to imagine by participating in "the work of mourning."

For Britzman, mourning becomes a way of articulating our relationships with the ghosts that haunt curriculum, but these are very different relationships from those imagined by William Doll (this volume) and Lynda Stone (2000).[3] For example, whereas Stone emphasizes the desire of mourners "to know the ghost" (42), Britzman draws our attention to the work that mourners must do *to know themselves* through "the re-signification of daily meanings and libidinal attachments. The mourner herself must change." But how? By whose agency, and with what tools, is the work of "re-signification" accomplished?

Pinar's meditation on Musil's work suggests that narrative traces of "the lost curriculum" might be envisioned—or imagined—more readily through "the indirectness of literary art" than by trying to augment vision with the precision instruments of analytic philosophy, psychology, or sociology. Musil's mode of interrogating the complexities and contradictions of *fin de siècle* Europe provokes Pinar to ask comparable questions about the United States of America at the *fin de millennium*. But in questioning what he calls "the ongoing crisis of European culture in America" (a crisis to which James gestures, albeit microcosmically, in *The Europeans*), Pinar provokes us to ask, in turn, who is writing the work that questions the ongoing crisis of U.S. culture in the world?[4]

We suggest that contemporary examples of the work of mourning include the films of Jim Jarmusch, such as *Dead Man* (1995), an allegorical western in which a young accountant named William Blake leaves his home in Cleveland to accept a job in the frontier town of Machine. A series of misadventures leaves Blake wanted for murder and mortally wounded with a bullet lodged close to his heart. He flees into the wilderness, where a Native American named Nobody assumes that Blake is famous, the English artist and poet, and takes responsibility for guiding Blake on his protracted journey into the spirit world. In the guise of the western (Hollywood's archetypal genre), *Dead Man* is a visionary—and in every sense mournful—interrogation of contemporary U.S. cultural values. More recently, in *Ghost Dog: The Way of the Samurai* (1999), Jarmusch twists another Hollywood staple, the crime drama, into a surreal meditation on spiritual values that samples and juxtaposes Asian, European, and U.S. literary and popular culture texts.

Towards the end of *The Europeans*, Felix Young farewells his sister, the Baroness Eugenia Münster:

> Felix parted with her on the deck of the ship. "We shall often meet over there," he said. "I don't know," she answered. "Europe seems to me much larger than America." (Henry James, 1984/1878, 194)

The intellectual terrain of continental Europe certainly looms large in Britzman's and Pinar's curriculum visions, but we see this as a welcome corrective to current trajectories of cultural and curriculum change driven by visions of globalization that seem to be little more than thinly cloaked versions of U.S. imperialism. However, the world is much larger than both Europe and America, and we look forward to other visionary curriculum scholars seeking more (and more diverse) sites—in Asia, Africa, and elsewhere—from which to begin the work of mourning the lost curriculum of all Eurocentric cultures.

Notes

[1] According to Tony Tanner's Introduction to the 1984 Penguin Library edition of *The Europeans*, these are the opening lines of a letter Henry James wrote to William Dean Howells on March 30, 1877, in which he outlined his plan for the novel. Howells published this letter in the *Atlantic* (July–October 1878).

[2] We have borrowed this form of words from the late Lawrence Stenhouse (1980), who wrote of other lacunae in curriculum theory: "All educational ideas must find expression in curricula before we can tell whether they are day dreams or contributions to practice. Many educational ideas are not found wanting, because they cannot be found at all" (14).

[3] Doll's and Stone's essays have similar points of departure—Jacques Derrida's (1994) *Specters of Marx*, John Dewey as a ghost haunting American education—but explore very different territories.

[4] See also Noel Gough's essay, "The Long Arm(s) of Globalization" (this volume).

References

Derrida, Jacques. (1994). Specters of Marx: The state of the debt, the work of mourning, and the new international. Peggy Kamuf (Trans.). New York and London: Routledge.

Grumet, Madeleine R. (1981). Restitution and reconstruction of educational experience: An autobiographical method for curriculum theory. In Martin Lawn and Len Barton (Eds.), Rethinking curriculum studies: A radical approach (pages 115–30). London: Croom Helm.

James, Henry. (1984 [1878]). The Europeans. London: Penguin.

Stenhouse, Lawrence. (1980). Curriculum research and the art of the teacher. Study of Society, 11(1), 14–15.

Stone, Lynda. (2000). Come again the ghosts: Dewey and democratic education by Derrida. Journal of Curriculum Theorizing, 16(1), 41–68.

The Death of Curriculum?

Deborah P. Britzman

How strange to confront curriculum and all that it holds as a burial place, a crypt. But how very difficult it must be to see in knowledge the death of the object and to ponder from this death how life might be lived. For Shakespeare—and he, too, is caught in such a crypt—encountering the work of living means confronting the confusions of some cruel negations: To praise and not to bury; to be or not to be? As for curriculum, how does one bury and not praise its objectives? And, if we could somehow sort through all of the objects the curriculum leaves behind, how would we decide which were worthy and which were useless? Even more: Can we imagine the lost curriculum? How does one come to mourn the losses that go under the name curriculum? Can we decide not to preserve a moribund curriculum and instead ask: Why curriculum at all?

The questions I offer suppose a certain labor of thought, what Freud (1917) called "the work of mourning." In using the term "work," Freud does not offer us a sense of the duration of grief or of ways to devise its stages. This work of mourning cannot be prescribed. Freud was interested in the interminable effort the mourner must expend—what he called "a quota of affect"—to work through the work of mourning. Essentially, the work of mourning is a work of re-signification of daily meanings and libidinal attachments. The mourner herself must change and be willing to be affected—touched—by memory, by that which is gone but which still exerts a force because it matters in our present. How something comes to matter, why things matter when they are no longer present, is part of what the work of mourning gives us to consider. Because the problem of meaning, or how to signify loss, inaugurates this work, the work of mourning is also subject to all sorts of confusions.

Over the course of this essay, I want to consider what the work of mourning offers to this labour of curriculum and then raise some rather essential questions: What is the relation between loss and knowledge in the curriculum, and what interrupts the work of mourning? Rather than assert a specific content or argue for the introduction of ignored voices that can somehow avoid this work of mourning, I will be suggesting a constitutive problem with knowledge itself. Some philosophers, when speaking of knowledge, have called this interruption *peripeteia*: a fall, an unexpected reversal of circumstance. The problem of loss is genetic to the very structure of knowledge. To notice that the inadvertent curriculum is subject to such sudden reversals, to accidental stumbling, to turning against itself, and to becoming affected by the events made from its own fall, may well be the stakes that allow us to ask, "Why curriculum?" When and how do we notice the curriculum that cannot be in charge of itself, the curriculum that has no mastery?

To ponder such events, I turn to Freud's events and his thoughts on war, death, and the work of mourning. Other ghosts who haunt the curriculum, not so much by their presence, but by their absence, will also be called upon to comment: forgotten figures like Melanie Klein, Robert Musil, Wilfred Bion, and, of course, Sigmund Freud. They noticed something that the moribund curriculum foreclosed, namely, the problem of what it is to work through woeful disregard and be called to notice something about the dignity of vulnerability in the confusion of our times. While none of them asked the question—Why curriculum?—they did notice something difficult about knowledge and thinking that will be put to use.

Let us be affected by what the author Robert Musil (1995, 49) named "ill-tempered observations," a preliminary labor of discomfort. One of his essays under this banner is titled, "Surrounded by Poets and Thinkers." This might be a metaphor for curriculum unless, of course, the curriculum empties itself of such creatures in the name of skill development and, yes, even competency and readiness. Then, we would be surrounded by all that we lack. Still, Musil was not one to idealize culture; after all, he was also the author of a two-volume novel called *The Man Without Qualities*, a meditation on the *fin-de-siècle* and its collapse from the weight of its own anxiety. Even if poets and thinkers surrounded the curriculum, for someone like Musil, this crowd would only heighten anxiety. Here is his ill-tempered warning: Being surrounded can feel claustrophobic or even too competitive. Musil noted that before World War II, Germany had more than 1,000 magazines and 30,000 books published each year. Although at one time this may have offered new sorts of publics, by 1933, huge public burnings of books also took place. How can we think of the coexistence of such events? Musil thought of such mass production as something other than a culture's capacity for intellectual achievement, calling such frenzy "the spread of a dangerous group-mania. Infected by this mania, thousands of little groups each peddle their own set notion of life, so that it ought not to surprise us if soon a genuine paranoiac will hardly still be able to resist competing with the amateurs" (76). So, too, in our own times: A thousand tiny curricula vie for attention; some try to cure a thousand tiny learning disabilities while others take away a thousand ideas and a thousand tiny ambivalences we make from knowledge. No doubt there is confusion as to where to turn, yet suppose what is at stake is not the problem of which curriculum to deliver but rather, and once again, why curriculum at all?

Before Musil, another Viennese citizen noticed something of the confusion of his own times and asked what is it to think from within confusion:

> In the confusion of our time in which we are caught up, relying as we must on one-sided information, standing too close to the great changes that have already taken place or are beginning to, and without a glimmering of the feature that is being shaped, we ourselves are at a loss as to the significance of the impressions which press in upon us and as to the value of the judgments which we form. (Freud, 1915, 275)

So begins Freud's terse essay, "Thoughts for the Times on War and Death," written at the beginning of World War I. The essay questions the proximity and limits of what we might make from knowledge, but it cannot answer the haunting question the child always asks, "Why war?" Knowledge cannot come to the rescue, because war, Freud goes on to suggest, is the absolute breakdown of meaning, the most aggressive, repetitive, and evil return of a society's refusal to learn something from the failure of knowledge. Can we consider the curriculum in such ill-tempered terms and ask, "Why curriculum?"

Freud can only write of his own disillusionment about the capacity of knowledge to put itself in the service of life. He then offers a long string of attendant losses when knowledge no longer matters: enjoyment; the capacity to judge; the interest in creating and sustaining affective ties with strangers; indeed, the loss of any distinction between the human's susceptibility to culture and its other susceptibility to what can happen when the forces of instinctual satisfaction meet the drive to destruction. The very capacity to think, to take one's own time, is disassociated and confused with perhaps what Musil saw as dangerous group mania, certainly by what Freud would come to see as melancholia. We become susceptible, give ourselves over to confusion in the hope that at least we will have something left. In times of war and death, in the confusion of time such epistemological and ontological chaos invokes, there may also follow a felt betrayal as to what happens to all that is idealized as the best in humanity. Freud sees this betrayal as beside the point. His view is bleaker: "In reality our fellow-citizens have not sunk so low as we feared, because they had never risen so high as we believed" (286). Can we bring such a view to our own faith in knowledge and dare to say that the curriculum cannot sink so low because it has never risen so high?

But what is the nature of the confusion at stake? Can we think confusion without the call for more clarity, easier language, simpler ideas, better skills, less convolution? Such an orientation to clearing up confusion leads to a rather stringent curriculum that mistakes knowledge for answers, that collapses the symbol with that which it represents. The sort of confusion Freud had in mind was more difficult, a state of mental vulnerability in which the problem was how to distinguish thinking from ignorance, absence from presence, love from hate. Consider the care Melanie Klein gives to confusion. In her essay "Envy and Gratitude," Klein outlines some inaugurating states of mental confusions: the confusion of good and bad, the confusion of persecution and guilt, the confusion of internal world with external world, the confusion of self and object, and the confusion of learning and mastery. "Such confusion," writes Klein, "interferes with the recognition of psychic reality, which contributes to the understanding and realistic perception of external reality" (221). But Klein reminds us that this sort of confusion is also a psychic achievement: Without these dilemmas, an individual would be unable to think or even enter the terrors and pleasures of symbolization. The recognition of psychical reality—the other of ordinary reality and the classroom clock—may accompany confusion, provided that confusion is considered worthy. While Klein reminds us of that other war, the war within that inaugurates psychical reality, Freud suggests something of how the world at war also forecloses the capacity to think.

There is, then, a two-fold paradox offered in Freud's essay, a problem that offers something more difficult to the interminable question, "Why curriculum?" If war is a time when we cannot think beyond the reach of confusion, when the difference between reality and fantasy dissolves—so that we cannot finally know if we made our enemies, if we need our enemies, or if we have actual enemies—if such melancholy predominates, how is it possible to have any thoughts on war and death? And then, what do war and death have to do with peace and life? Freud begins his thoughts with a prior moment: we can only think when thought is lost and this absence moves thinking closer to the work of mourning. If such is the case, can the claim of the death of curriculum invoke the work of mourning, the work of thinking the loss of our thoughts, the coming to terms with what has been lost?

Part of the work of mourning involves recognizing loss, not just what has been lost to the world but what has been lost in the self. Freud (1917/1915) distinguishes mourning from melancholia, although both involve a confusion of loss. "Mourning is regularly the reaction to the loss of a loved person, or to the loss of some abstraction which has taken the place of one, such as one's country, liberty, an ideal and so on" (243). Even the loss of an idea can invoke mourning. But if the work of mourning is to be uninterrupted and not dissolve into melancholia, the mourner must be able to somehow acknowledge what is lost in both the world and the self and somehow try to find new ideas and people in the world. "In mourning it is the world which has become poor and empty; in melancholia it is the ego itself" (246). The melancholic curriculum impoverishes, confusing the difficulty of knowledge with the knowledge of difficulty.

Part of the loss we confront in the field of curriculum is the loss of our capacity to recognize our own psychical reality as being out of joint with ordinary reality. By this I mean that when the field can only argue over which knowledge to offer, the question of why knowledge at all cannot be expressed. Can we bear to consider the death of curriculum apropos to a time that returns itself back to an earlier state, a time of stasis, a curriculum subject to its own death drive? To be sure, there is something difficult in any attempt to think the death of curriculum for it forces us, albeit metaphorically, to confront the question of our present disillusionment with the promise of knowledge to return what has been lost.

Many have noticed that this disillusionment toward knowledge persists as one of this century's great epistemological themes and is acted out, albeit unconsciously, in the fields of curriculum (Britzman, 1998). The illusion is supported by a series of defenses the field of curriculum employs: the curriculum as technical, as government, as genealogy, as preparation, as something that is capable of speaking for itself. Disillusionment resides somewhere between the poles of catastrophe and redemption, as a nation at risk, as crumbling standards, as moral vacuum, as recruitment device, as perversity. This disillusionment may take the form of incredulity toward metanarratives as Lyotard (1987) suggests in his report on the status of knowledge in universities; or, as Willinsky (1998) offers in his study of knowledge in the age of the Internet, the disillusionment may transform itself into the politics of exasperation over the sheer amount of information that litters the metaphoric super-information highway and turns us into consumers of nonevents; or, as Readings (1996) has noticed, it may manifest itself in calls for excellence in schools and universities without having any referent. Whether this disillusionment is acted out in the confines of censorship, in the disassembling of bilingual education, in the refusal of sex education and homoerotic images, in the wiring of schools for surveillance, or in the very capacity to think, the anxiety, as Haver (1996, 23) has put it, is made from our own limits: "Not even education can save us now."

All these forms of incredulity may actually repeat a more archaic disillusionment: our attitude toward death. What does curriculum have to do with our attitude toward death if the curriculum itself offers tribute to its own burial? If the central dynamic of curriculum is closer to the compulsion to repeat its own incapacity to notice what goes on in its name, if the curriculum interrupts, through its technology, its methods, its structure, its pedagogy, its own capacity to mourn, to notice its losses, how then can curriculum ask itself, "Why curriculum?"

Freud suggests in his "Thoughts" essay something quite difficult about thinking itself, that if the urge to think is viewed as the means for exceeding the body, as an experience of sheer will, as an escape from the interminable problem of perception and reality, and as functioning "reliably only when it is removed from the influences of strong emotional impulses" (287), then that which disillusions thought cannot be thought. Affect is the constitutive limit of thought, or what Certeau (1988) much later will define as that which wounds the illusion of composed knowledge. If knowledge cannot compose itself, and if its strategies of distinction and upkeep are so fragile in its susceptibility to the affects of distress, denial, disavowal, and so on, then what will be the future of knowledge, indeed, the future of our capacity to think for the fields of curriculum?

These questions are different from the death-of-the-subject claims so common in philosophical disputes. For even there, the text could live beyond the author; thought could be abstracted, and so there was something beyond death that could trouble life. The claim being examined here is not the melancholic one of berating the love that is lost, the object that is gone, although certain nostalgic views of restoring the curriculum capable of managing its subjects so that no one will ever get lost seem, to me, a symptom that defends against the loss of thought. If thought must lose itself to begin to think itself, if confusion can inaugurate something more, if the finding of the lost object is always a re-finding, then what is this work but a speculation that poses the work of mourning as the obligation of learning to live with death?

"But this attitude of ours toward death," Freud goes on to write in the second section of this haunted essay, "has a powerful effect on our lives" (290). One part of this attitude, particularly in times of peace, is incredulity toward death, where death is not considered a necessity of life but a chance event that happens to others. In times of war, our attitudes toward death alter, but not so much, Freud insists, that one can find a new attitude. For Freud, something within resists knowledge of our own death, and this resistance is put into service of exasperation toward death. The conflict, then, is between acknowledging the loss that is death and denying the possibility that each of us will experience the utter singularity of our own death. However, even this view is unsatisfactory to Freud. He goes on to make a rather startling point: The beginning of our capacity to speculate does not emerge from an intellectual problem of confronting pictures of death and, thereby, reflecting on death; speculation, or the capacity to think, begins from the conflict of ambivalence, made when one confronts one's feelings for the death of another. The "spirit of inquiry" (293) begins with the capacity to think the split between thoughts and feelings, between the love and hate. "Death," writes Jacqueline Rose (1993), "is a problem, but not because we cannot surmount its loss or imagine our own death, but because it forces us to acknowledge that what belongs to us most intimately is also a stranger or an enemy…[So that] thought provoked by mourning takes the form of dissociation" (19). Inquiry, in this view, is a borderline concept, a confusion of traumatic experience made from being torn within how to think about loss, about our own capacity to destroy, and about our own alienness. Paradoxically, thinking begins in dissociation, a dissociation that renders indistinct the wounds of affect and that which resists thought.

Our own constitutional ambivalence, however, seems to be acted out as opposed to worked through in the very epistemology of curriculum. Ambivalence, loving and hating the same object, is just the beginning of the problem of passionate attachment. But more often than not, the field of curriculum seeks to strip our relation to knowledge of any form of ambivalence and in doing so, finds it inconceivable that feelings toward knowledge cannot sustain the illusion of certainty. Indeed, uncertainty, feeling torn as to what to believe, being in a state of confusion, and acting as if these experiences are somehow a problem only curriculum can solve, preserves the moribund curriculum and a melancholy education. We can ask: What does the curriculum bury in order to preserve itself? When Freud (1930) glanced at the school curriculum he noticed civilization and discontentment and its violent origins: "Even to-day, the history of the world which our children learn at school is essentially a series of murders of people" (292). If the act of civilization requires a violent origin, curriculum seems to be the unconscious burial ground in which the repetition of the society's violent origins persists. Can contemporary students and teachers understand these events with, as Freud put it, "the conflict of feeling at the death of loved yet alien and hated persons" (293)? What happens when we can admit ambivalence toward both defeat and victory? What can actually be learned from studying or recounting the violent origins of a nation, a society, an institution, if we have difficulty believing in our own otherness—death—and, if the alien-ness of others cannot be viewed as a symptom of our own alien-ness?

Freud does not offer any answers for the questions he raised about thought in times of war and death. He does suggest that making life tolerable is the first obligation of living, and illusions that somehow promise a life without conflict can only make it harder to live. The last sentence of his essay suggests the angst raised when death is moved to the center of life: "*Si vis vitam, para mortem.* If you want to endure life, prepare yourself for death" (300). If war strips away this paradox, presenting to the living the tragedy of their own mortality but not the tragedy of the other, the aggression that war requires allows one to forget that preparation and renders intolerable what Jacqueline Rose argues as "the ethics of failure" (36) or a way of thinking in difficult times. War, Rose argues, represents the limit of absolute knowledge even as the reasons for war seem to sustain a view of knowledge as capable of answering the question, "Why war?" So, too, with the violent origins of curriculum. Knowledge is lost and found somewhere between the outside war and the war within. It is subject to both flaws but not in ways that can be predicted, controlled, or even mastered. But if knowledge, indeed, if the knowledge we call curriculum is to speak to something alien in us, if it can tolerate this reversal, this *peripeteia,* it will have to begin with suspending its own ends, acknowledging what has been lost in the name of curriculum, an ethics of failure that might invoke a certain work of thinking, what Freud called the work of mourning.

Finally, one must admit a strange paradox to these sorts of thoughts on the death of the curriculum, for part of the dilemma is that experience, yes, even teaching experience, is irrelevant. These thoughts on the death of the curriculum offer nothing to the question of what shall we do on Monday; surely our means of resuscitating what goes on under the name "the practical" should by now be exhausted. Mondays arrive whether we are prepared or not. But also, our preparation will always be insufficient because the curriculum cannot predict relations of knowledge at stake in learning. That is to say, Monday's curriculum cannot decide the confusion of our times. More urgently, the very posing of this Monday problem may well defend against the deeper anxiety that Musil noticed: How do we spend the time that we have? How do we learn to live? The problem for any day is: What is it to think with others in education? Part of our work may be to encounter the confusion of our times, not in the ways that Musil or Freud warned us against, but perhaps closer to what Melanie Klein thought of as the working through of confusion, as an interest in recognizing psychical reality. Part of the recognition would be ill tempered, for what would have to be acknowledged is the idea that we are affected by that which exceeds consciousness, intention, and will. Another part of the recognition might be loving, that there is something tender about fragility. Bion (1997) gives us a sense of this paradox:

> If a thought without a thinker comes along, it may be what is a "stray thought," or it could be a thought with the owner's name and address upon it, or it could be a "wild thought." Of course, if it is wild, you might try to domesticate it....What I am concerned with at the moment is the wild thoughts that turn up and for which there is no possibility of being able to trace immediately any kind of ownership or even any sort of way of being aware of the genealogy of that particular thought. (27)

It seems to me that if the curriculum is to offer us anything like the experience of having wild thoughts, then the question—why curriculum—must be refound.

References

Bion, W. R. (1997). *Taming wild thoughts*. Francesca Bion (Ed.). London: Karnac.

Britzman, Deborah P. (1998). *Lost subjects, contested objects: Toward a psychoanalytic inquiry of learning*. Albany: State University of New York Press.

Certeau, Michel de. (1988). *The writing of history*. Tom Conley (Trans.). New York: Columbia University Press.

Freud, Sigmund. (1953–1974). *Standard edition of the complete psychological works of Sigmund Freud.* James Strachey (Ed. and trans.). In Collaboration with Anna Freud. Assisted by Alix Strachey and Alan Tyson. 24 vols. London: Hogarth Press and Institute for Psychoanalysis.

______. (1915). Thoughts for the times on war and death. *Standard edition,* 14 (pages 273–301).

______. (1917). Mourning and melancholia. *Standard edition,* 14 (pages 239–58).

______. (1930). Civilization and its discontents. *Standard edition,* 21 (pages 59–145).

Haver, William. (1996). *The body of this death: Historicity and sociality in the time of AIDS.* Stanford, CA: Stanford University Press.

Klein, Melanie. (1975). *Envy and gratitude and other works, 1946–1963.* New York: Delacorte Press/S. Lawrence.

Lyotard, Jean-Francois. (1987). *The postmodern condition: A report on knowledge.* Geoff Bennington & Brian Massumi (Trans.). Manchester: Manchester University Press.

Musil, Robert. (1993). *Posthumous papers of a living author.* Peter Wortsman (Trans.). New York: Penguin.

______. (1995). *The man without qualities, Vol. I and II.* Sophie Wilkins (Trans.). New York: Alfred Knopf.

Readings, Bill. (1996). *The university in ruins.* Cambridge: Harvard University Press.

Rose, Jacqueline. (1993). *Why war?—Psychoanalysis, politics, and the return to Melanie Klein.* Oxford: Blackwell.

Willinsky, John. (1998). *Automata data and the future of knowledge.* San Diego, CA: American Educational Research Association.

Deborah P. Britzman is Professor of Education, Social and Political Thought, and Women's Studies at York University in Toronto, and is the author of *Lost Subjects, Contested Objects: Toward a Psychoanalytic Inquiry of Learning* (1998). Her research interests are in the psychoanalytic study of education.

Robert Musil and the Crisis of European Culture in America

William F. Pinar

> So, in the United States today, we often seem to be watching, while only half understanding, a bungled remake of some political drama played out in the last days of the Hapsburg Empire. (Allan Janik and Stephen Toulmin, 1973, 270)

> [O]ur own time…is never just our own time. (Deborah Britzman, 1998, 117)

The questions Deborah Britzman asks linking mourning and death and curriculum are simultaneously timeless and historically situated. The "work of mourning" they require is both our work now and their—Freud's, Musil's, their contemporaries'—work then. Knowledge may well be, as Deborah suggests, compensatory, an effort to reverse circumstance, to live through "loss" with meaning and understanding. Certainly that is the status of "knowledge" in the therapeutic situation. It is the knowledge of loss, personified, perhaps, in the notion of ghosts.

Like William Doll, Britzman too turns to "ghosts" who lived at the beginning of the century now past, ghosts who wander about us still, with whom we speak in our research, ghosts such as John Dewey and Alfred North Whitehead (whom Doll names in his introduction), and Sigmund Freud and Robert Musil (whom Britzman discusses). Musil and Freud and their contemporaries lived at the "end of empire," specifically that great multicultural, deteriorating, authoritarian regime known as the Hapsburg Empire, headquartered in that other great nineteenth-century European city, Vienna. That regime would collapse, but not before it would take tens of millions of bodies with it to its grave. Remembering the historical moment in which Freud and Musil wrote helps us understand more precisely what it means to be, as Britzman so exactly phrases it, "surrounded by all that we lack" (this volume). What did these prosperous Viennese lack? What is it we lack today? On the surface, the Viennese lacked little. Vienna in 1900 could be compared as a city only to Paris. Like Paris, it was not just a city; it was a way of life. Like American suburbs today, Vienna was a city of the bourgeoisie. Despite being, possibly, the most important intellectual of the twentieth century in the West, Freud himself was thoroughly bourgeois in his habits, reading the daily newspaper and living for nearly half a century in the same modest apartment house at Berggasse 19, a respectable residential street in northern Vienna (Gay, 1978). Despite being one, Freud saw right through the Viennese bourgeoisie. He knew how rigidly they cherished the classic bourgeois values: reason, order, progress, perseverance, self-reliance, and disciplined conformity to standards of good taste and conduct. Whatever was irrational, passionate, or chaotic was to be avoided at all costs. As Max Stirner put it, a man expressed himself in what he owned, including artifacts of culture and objects of art. As Musil himself wrote in 1912, "[T]he bourgeoisie does not concern itself with culture directly, but tosses out lump sums for it" (Musil, 1990, 20). The bourgeois father of the household was the guarantor of order and security. He possessed, among other things, absolute authority (Janik and Toulmin, 1973). Patriarchy, capitalism, modernism: these elements of European culture remain with us today, if in a certain "crisis," requiring us—European Americans—to add the prefix "post" to the last one.

There are other parallels between the triumphant decaying Vienna of 1900 and America today. Then as now the educational system taught the young a curriculum unrelated to lived experience. Schooling produced constant weariness and boredom in the youth of Vienna. To escape this formalized, institutionalized world where "business was business," many students went to coffeehouses, the same ones frequented by artists and bohemians. There they found a vital and spontaneous self-expression absent in their classrooms devoted to memorization and recitation. Austrian education was, in a phrase, a pervasive system of regimentation. The teacher's word was law. It is not surprising, as Stefan Zweig (1943) commented, that Austrian society should have produced a man who discovered the significance of "inferiority feelings" in human affairs: Alfred Adler. So repressive was the social system of *fin-de-siècle* Vienna, Zweig reported, that any thought or activity not in explicit conformity with official authority became a source of guilt (Janik and Toulmin, 1973). Repression today is hardly so monolithic or guilt-producing. As Britzman points out, repression today occurs in multiples, in "one thousand tiny curricula," consumables for educational shoppers (without choices). There is boredom, rage, and alienation but little guilt. There are school shootings instead. Repression today is, in fact, noisy, but in *fin-de-siècle* Vienna it was expressed as silence, especially about sex. As Freud knew, there was something akin to a conspiracy of silence about sex. Socially, this silence had two consequences. First, there was an astonishing inhibition and ignorance of sexual matters. Second, in a kind of "return of the repressed," there was at the same time a covert obsession with sex. In a society so thoroughly patriarchal, women, of course, suffered most. The very fact that middle-class marriage was first and foremost a business contract rather than a romantic union may help explain, Janik and Toulmin (1973) point out, why so many of Freud's patients were middle-aged bourgeois women. No doubt the constraints of Viennese society also help explain some of the gendered limitations of Freudian analysis as well as underscoring the courage of Freud's explorations in a time of "passionate ignorance." If an unmarried man sought sexual satisfaction, he turned to prostitutes. (If Vienna bore any resemblance to New York City at the turn of the century, not all prostitutes were, of course, female.) Zweig (1943) reports that prostitution "constituted a dark underground vault over which rose the bourgeois structure of middle-class society with its faultless, radiant façade" (83).

H. Stuart Hughes has called Musil's contemporaries "the generation of 1905" (Luft, 1980, 13). They felt themselves born into a moral vacuum; they, like many of us, set out to answer the question of how to live with integrity in a corrupt and economically obsessed society. (Perhaps, as Noel Gough quotes Allen Ginsberg, they too were "starving, naked, hysterical.") For the leading intellectuals of the generation of 1905 (as for many of us), history seemed no longer to hold hope, as the nineteenth century (in the shadow of Marx) had once believed. Accepting the uncertainty of history and knowledge as well as the inadequacy of every form of dogmatism, many intellectuals of the generation of 1905 were acutely conscious of the fragility of human life. Although they often dealt with social and ideological matters after World War I (as did Sartre after World War II), their central concerns could be characterized as psychological, ethical, and aesthetic, very much focused on the "inner crisis" of European culture (Luft, 1980). Where is the "inner crisis" today? Is it on the social surface, performed as a technologization of the self, which permits only questions with facile, feel-good answers? These are not the questions Britzman poses.

For Musil and his contemporaries (as for many of us), the inner crisis of European culture was experienced as a deep frustration with political and social life, in their case a profound estrangement from the pompous, deteriorating Hapsburg Empire. It was clear to this generation that life was anything but stable and permanent, that an unconscious life accompanied its formal surface, and that ordinary language lacked the means to express this inner life. The crisis gave urgency to the attempts of those who were young in 1900 and so determined to find new ways of understanding and living human existence (Hickman, 1984). There is of course widespread frustration today, but for the masses it is quickly medicated (Pinar, in press). Many of us in the academy attempt to theorize our way to new language forms, to new divinations of a "public"—the curriculum —that is, at present, only imaginary. The contemporary curriculum is, as Britzman knows, dead. Schools are still mausoleums.

Musil wanted a new language that would enable him to express intellectually in literary art the inner life of the felt world. The experimentation he employed in his fiction—in *Young Torless* (1906), for instance—was no mere manipulation of words or ideas. Rather, Musil tried to use words to go, as Jacques Daignault (1984) once put it, "beyond words," to a preconceptual sphere of deep feeling and experience (Pike, 1961). In this sense one might say that Musil anticipated Virginia Woolf, who managed to create an intellectually rigorous narrative structure and stylization of emotion which expressed poetically the inner worlds of her characters, especially those of her women characters. Musil did so for certain of his male characters, including young Torless.

Although philosophy (earlier Musil had abandoned his career as an engineer in order to study philosophy and psychology at the University of Berlin) would have seemed at the time to offer him a more direct means of exploring and resolving these matters than would literature, Musil chose what he viewed as the indirectness of literary art, an art which seemed to him to resemble, in its narrative structure, the indirectness, the mystery, of life itself. (Does this speak, if in different terms, to the source of Gough's fascination with science fiction today?) What is haunting about Musil's fiction is less what has happened or is happening (although these can be compelling and very troubling), but what might have happened and what might yet happen, what is not observed but felt (Peters, 1978), perhaps like ghosts in the curriculum, as Doll suggests. Unlike curriculum, Musil's fiction has been, in the past, declared "off-limits to psychoanalytic interpretation" (Peters, 1978, 22). Critics have tended to believe that Musil did not read Freud, that he did not write *Young Torless* with Freud in mind (Hickman, 1984).

Musil wanted to bridge reason and emotion, science and literature, appearance and reality, as David S. Luft (1980) has observed: "The central task of Musil's work was to mediate his culture's antagonisms between intellect and feeling, truth and subjectivity, science and art" (2). In search of a bridge, Musil explored sexuality. Torless's participation in sadomasochistic homosexual encounters at his residential school is but one portrayal in Musil's art of a certain crisis of consciousness transformed by sexuality. In Torless's case, this experience, far from shattering him, focused his personality and contributed to his maturation. Musil was more interested, Luft (1980) argues, in the sources and functions of sexuality, love, and the imagination, and less in their particular objects. Although Luft is right, I think, in emphasizing Musil's interest in the "biographical functions" of any specific situation, he is mistaken to discount altogether the homosexual theme of *Young Torless*. The anatomy of the characters is crucial. Had Basini or Torless been a girl, the politics and meaning of the situation would have been rather different.

In *Young Torless* (1906), Musil portrayed the power of "thoughts as moments in the inner life which have not yet frozen into fixed form" (Luft, 1980, 60). Musil emphasized the contextual—I would say biographic—significance of these "living thoughts," a significance quite apart from their logical value as propositions. Their spiritual significance lies in lived experience, in their consequences for psychological growth and self-understanding. Luft (1980) writes: "Torless formulates the possibility of a revolt against bourgeois culture which does not produce something equally rigid and pathological, and stakes out a position of isolation and freedom, marked by Musil's enormous tolerance for ambiguity" (61). This revolt occurs on the site of sadomasochistic homosexuality and at school. Is this, as Britzman puts it, "a curriculum subject to its own death drive"?

The subtlety of Musil's treatment distinguishes his work from the larger genre of "school novels." The severe atmosphere of the school makes it no place for caring or self-realization; the pedagogical inadequacies of the instructors are clear. Critics have observed that there is no attempt to blame the central episode—the rape and sexual torture of the student Basini—on the school or to idealize the values and experience of the students. The threat to civilization (represented in the novel by the school) comes from Torless's friends and fellow-students Beineberg and Reiting, whose sadism and manipulation point to the world outside the academy (Luft, 1980). But not only to a world—and future—outside. Can their sadism be, in part, a de-sublimated expression of the school curriculum? The threat to European civilization festered within European civilization.

Musil was interested in a phenomenological method that would permit him to explore lived experience, an aspiration shared by many in curriculum studies (Pinar et al., 1995, Ch. 8). For Musil, such a method needed to be simultaneously grounded in tradition, experimental science, and personal experience. Free of the metaphysical certainties espoused by the Romantics, Musil set out to investigate love, religion, and the soul phenomenologically, just as Aoki, for instance, set out to study teaching (see, for instance, Aoki, 1999). Musil believed that the intellectual despair of his generation had to do in part with the polarity between science and mysticism, "two cultures" William Doll (1993) has worked to bridge in his work. Musil regarded the essay as the literary form appropriate to this aspiration, a form of thinking poetically which might "hover" between science and art.

The essay was a narrative form that allowed Musil to remain loyal to the scientist's precision as well as to the artist's sometimes sloppy search for beauty and values in the midst of a contentious cultural crisis. In literature, sexuality, religion, and politics, Musil fought to free the emotions from distorting repressions. The essay form supported this search for new relations between mind and flesh, intellect and soul, the concrete and the abstract. Luft (1980) points out:

> The characteristic fault of bourgeois reason was its misapplication of the model of natural science; in its drive for uniformity, bourgeois reason had lost track of the capacity to create value and enhance life. In its yearning for truth, concept and abstraction, it had lost respect for the flesh, for the concrete lives of individual human beings. (115)

In claiming curriculum inquiry as one of the humanities during the 1970s, many of us registered the same complaint. Will our curriculum visions for the new century finally be free of bourgeois misapplication of natural science in curriculum research and practice?

Musil's primary impulses were aesthetic, but the collapse of the Hapsburg Empire and the resulting crisis of European civilization required a political outlook and commitment. Georg Lukacs (1964) might have had Musil in mind when he wrote, "Many a writer of a basically contemplative type has been driven to participation in the life of the community by the social conditions of his time" (12). Musil had grave doubts about the expressionist style of revolutionary politics which emerged after World War I. In the call for the "new man," sounded shrilly by both communists and fascists, he saw only a form of pessimism. To call for a new man [sic] meant neither side knew how to achieve him. Revolutionary politics was finally romantic, and, he believed, destined to compound the disaster of the old order it aspired to replace. From our vantage point in *fin-de-siècle* America, he was right. Then as now, the son's resistance to the father—Oedipal politics writ large—reproduces the reactionary status quo (Pinar, 1994). Musil was convinced that the overly simple distinction between oppressors and the oppressed obscured the more profound problem of bureaucratization, a problem, it turned out, from which socialism suffered perhaps even more than did capitalism: "The capitalist and the Bolshevik are only quite imperceptible variations on the recent type of human being" (quoted in Luft, 1980, 136). On this point he anticipates Heidegger's later conflation of the United States and the Union of Soviet Socialist Republics. The prototype for the educated person in modern European civilization was the professional. This is the type Musil knew from his own life history and social positioning. Professionalism was in one sense a bourgeois scheme designed to replace ideology: "Today the primary bond is the profession," Musil observed (quoted in Luft, 1980, 148). As a professional person, an identity is constructed, then commodified. Politics remains if disguised as expert knowledge. And, as we know, the school would play a major role in the professionalization of the bourgeoisie in twentieth-century Europe and North America, producing many men (and some women) "without qualities" as Musil entitled the book for which he is famous. To be "without qualities" meant that the inner life had disappeared in Europe, a claim that would be made again fifty years later by another intellectual and artist *engagé*, Pier Paolo Pasolini. For Pasolini, what had happened through bourgeoisification was nothing less than genocide (Greene, 1990).

Keenly conscious of the politics of culture and the historical limits of life in Vienna in 1914, Musil tried to think through what the twentieth century might hold for European civilization and culture. During his final years in exile in Geneva, in the midst of the catastrophe that was World War II, Musil came to believe that the cultural crisis of European civilization required complementary if fundamentally revised notions of mysticism and politics (Luft, 1980). It would appear that the contemporary crisis of European culture in America—occasioned in part due to a begrudged acknowledgment of the multicultural character of American society and the ensuing debates over the national identity, focused on the curriculum (Pinar et al., 1995, Ch. 6, see page 17)—requires us to declare the death of the present modernist order if we—European Americans—aspire to revised and rejuvenated conceptions of mysticism (see Wexler, 1996, for instance) and politics (Grosz, 1995; Pinar, 1994), to the proliferation of what Britzman might term "wild thoughts" and to the creation of a nonracist, nonimperialist, nonpatriarchal, truly multicultural American nation. I have raised the specter of Robert Musil and the crisis of European culture (then in Vienna, now in America) to complement Britzman's recalling of Freud and Musil to question what our visions of curriculum for the new century might be. I, too, see knowledge as wavering between the "outside war and the war within," requiring an "autobiographics of alterity," allowing us to reflexively grasp how we come to self-formation in "the shadow of the other" (Gilmore, 1994; Benjamin, 1998; Pinar, 2000). Like Freud, Musil lived through "the failure of knowledge," a time when it was horrifyingly clear that "not even education can save us now" (Britzman, this volume). Like Freud, Musil searched for a new language that might communicate the complexities and contradictions of the present, and in so doing, function as a medium of transport, if you will, to a new age. Yes, it is war "when the difference between reality and fantasy dissolves" (Britzman, this volume), but it is also in the hyper-reality of the postmodern present wherein the distinction fails. Analytically, as Britzman knows, the distinction may only express a deeper ambivalence about who we are, as gendered, racialized, classed creatures. Incorporating these inner struggles into the public "conversation" that is the curriculum may not "save" us, but it may help us understand more fully the ongoing crisis of European culture in America, the resolution of which will help establish the difference between reality and fantasy in this new century.

Acknowledgment: My thanks to Peter Taubman for introducing me to Robert Musil.

References

Aoki, Ted. (1999). Toward understanding "computer application." In William F. Pinar (Ed.), *Contemporary curriculum discourses: Twenty years of JCT* (pages 168–76). New York: Lang.

Benjamin, Jessica. (1998). *In the shadow of the other.* New York: Routledge.

Britzman, Deborah P. (1998). *Lost subjects, contested objects: Toward a psychoanalytic inquiry of learning.* Albany, NY: State University of New York Press.

Daignault, J. (1984). Curriculum: Beyond words with words. Rimouski, Québec, Canada: University of Québec, unpublished manuscript.

Doll, William E., Jr. (1993). *A post-modern view of curriculum.* New York: Teachers College.

Gay, Peter. (1978). *Freud, Jews, and other Germans: Masters and victims in modernist culture.* Oxford: Oxford University Press.

Gilmore, Leigh. (1994). *Autobiographics: A feminist theory of women's self-representation.* Ithaca, NY: Cornell University Press.

Greene, Naomi. (1990). *Pier Paolo Pasolini: Cinema as heresy.* Princeton: Princeton University Press.

Grosz, Elizabeth. (1995). *Space, time, and perversion: Essays on the politics of bodies.* New York: Routledge.

Hickman, Hannah. (1984). *Robert Musil and the culture of Vienna.* London: Croom Helm.

Janik, Allan, and Stephen Toulmin. (1973). *Wittgenstein's Vienna.* New York: Simon and Schuster.

Luft, David S. (1980). *Robert Musil and the crisis of European culture, 1880–1942.* Berkeley: University of California Press.

Lukacs, Georg. (1964). *Studies in European realism.* New York: Grosset and Dunlap.

Musil, Robert. (1955/1906). *Young Torless.* Preface by Alan Pryce-Jones. New York: Pantheon.

_______. (1979/1961/1960). *The man without qualities.* Foreword by Elithne Wilkins. Ernst Kaiser (Trans.). London: Secker and Warburg.

_______. (1990). *Precision and soul: Essays and addresses.* Burton Pike and David S. Luft (Eds. and trans.). Chicago, London: University of Chicago Press.

Peters, Frederick G. (1978) *Robert Musil: Master of the hovering life.* New York: Columbia University Press.

Pike, Burton. (1961). *Robert Musil: An introduction to his work.* Ithaca, NY: Cornell University Press.

Pike, Burton, and David S. Luft. (1990). Foreword and Introduction to Robert Musil's *Precision and soul: Essays and addresses.* Chicago, London: University of Chicago Press.

Pinar, William F. (1994). *Autobiography, politics, and sexuality: Essays in curriculum theory, 1972–1992.* New York: Lang.

______. (2000). Strange fruit: Race, sex, and an autobiographics of alterity. In Peter Trifonas (Ed.), *Revolutionary pedagogies.* New York: Routledge.

______. (in press). The medicated body: Drugs and Dasein. In Sherry B. and Svi Shapiro, *The body in education.* Cresskill, NJ: Hampton.

Pinar, William F., William M. Reynolds, Patrick Slattery, and Peter M. Taubman. (1995). *Understanding curriculum.* New York: Lang.

Rogowski, Christian. (1994). *Distinguished outsider: Robert Musil and his critics.* Columbia, SC: Camden.

Wexler, Philip. (1996). *Holy sparks: Social theory, education and religion.* New York: St. Martin's.

Zweig, Stefan. (1943). *The world of yesterday: An autobiography.* (Translator anonymous.) New York: Viking.

William F. Pinar teaches curriculum theory at Louisiana State University in Baton Rouge where he serves as the St. Bernard Parish Alumni Endowed Professor. He has also served as the Frank Talbott Professor at the University of Virginia and the A. Lindsay O'Connor Professor of American Institutions at Colgate University. He is the author of numerous curriculum theory texts, anthologies, and articles. His most recent book is *The Gender of Racial Politics and Violence in America: Lynching, Prison Rape, and the Crisis of Masculinity* (Lang, 2001).

Perspective on Britzman and Pinar

Peggy R. McConnell

> The mourner herself must change and be willing to be affected—touched—by memory, by that which is gone but still exerts a force because it matters in our present. (Deborah Britzman, this volume)

> I, too, see knowledge as wavering between the "outside war and the war within," requiring an "autobiographics of alterity," allowing us to reflexively grasp how we come to self-formation in "the shadow of the other." (William Pinar, this volume)

In an early morning workshop at the 1999 JCT Bergamo conference, I sat cross-legged on the floor as part of a standing-room-only group of curriculum theorists listening to Peter Taubman speak about hope, specifically, about losing it. Watching his darkened outline against the sunlight streaming through the tall window behind him, I found myself profoundly affected by his words:

> Hope may be little more than a fantasy which keeps us from being mindful....Without giving up hope, we will never accept where we are....Hope is a fantasy at the expense of *being*...a lack in the here and now....*How would it look to teach without hope?*...If one gave up hope, one could live in the problems one saw [and] one might see ways to deal with them. (my notes)

I think we need the space between hope and no-hope, and I identify that space as the place for grief or mourning. The idea of being present to the memory, or *memories*, is the basis of mourning. We remember that which is gone. Change—particularly change that removes the familiar, exchanges something we hold dear with something new—requires grieving. Whether we choose to consciously remember or not, whether we are willing to *entertain* the ghosts—or, to use Derrida's word, "traces"—of our past, they will affect us and everything we do. In a videotaped interview (1990), writer Toni Morrison comments on her novel *Beloved* and the theme of the necessity of remembering trauma, saying that "ghosts jump up and grab you" if you don't "re-memory them."

Deborah Britzman asks us to consider "why things matter when they are no longer present" and suggests that discerning what matters is part of the "work of mourning." I link this notion to acceptance. Once we begin to embrace our grief, whatever we are grieving for, then we begin to embrace the future because we are accepting possibilities, and that *is* the future. Mourning is very constructive. It is the necessary work of growing up, a part of gaining knowledge, allowing to shrivel and waste that which is no longer viable: "the work of mourning as the obligation of learning to live with death" (Britzman, this volume).

While reading Britzman's essay, Taubman's words echoed—grieving the loss, not of hope, but of the unnamed perfections for which we yearn, giving up our quest for the ideal student we fantasize finding, whose presence is an illusion. We teach to this ideal, this universalized student, because we long to be the ideal teachers. In this state, we hallucinate an ideal curriculum, one which will be free of the overwhelming social conditions which "interfere with learning:" abuse, drugs, race, sexuality, violence. We cling to this hopeful curriculum as to a dead branch, desperate for rescue from the issues that mire us in our grief. Britzman reminds us that "the melancholic curriculum impoverishes" (this volume). We have invested ourselves in the curriculum to such an extent that we can no longer see it apart from ourselves; we have lost the dangerous balance necessary to being a teacher. I am not what is taught.

Although we speak metaphorically about death in the curriculum, it has become a literal part of everyday school life. Americans retain still a remarkable refusal to accept death as part of life. Not one of the literally dozens of newspaper and magazines articles I read during the weeks and months following the 1999 Columbine High School tragedy in Littleton, Colorado, failed to write about "the problem"—violent killings by young people. We distance our (adult) selves by creating an us vs. them dichotomy. The idealization/condemnation of youth is an integral part of the American schizophrenia manifested by our inability/unwillingness to accept and express feelings about death as an integral part of life. We seem to have a diminished tolerance for these conflicting emotions and thoughts. Feelings are the amputated part of our humanness, in spite of our incessant talking about "knowing" and "having" them.

When Britzman speaks of "the dignity of vulnerability," I think about how to encourage and accept equivocality and ambiguity as key to teaching in the diverse and multicultural world we live in. Is it possible for a teacher to present an environment where students are able to laud the adventurous spirit of a Columbus and his crew as well as deplore and mourn the end of an untouched land and the deaths of the indigenous peoples there? Can we hold two such terribly contradictory thoughts?

Should we strive for this? Can we tolerate students' holding conflicting thoughts that are different from our own versions of past/present/future? Can we afford not to? "What does the curriculum bury in order to preserve itself?" (Britzman, this volume). Anything perceived as a threat to its own survival.

As with Derrida's trace, that which has gone before is never completely gone. We must remember that as educators or parents, we have no "glimmering of the feature that is being shaped" (Britzman, this volume). We are not in control; who/what we love and even live for does not belong to us: e.g., children grow up and leave home and do not heed our "best advice." In spite of following every health rule and guideline, in spite of the best medical care in the world, someone we love will die; whether from disease or old age, s/he will die. We will die. Acceptance is (once again) an answer: self-acceptance, human acceptance, acceptance of otherness. We must be able to perceive our own otherness if we are to accept/live inclusively. Our refusal/inability to do this is why we rush to make "other" anyone who acts in ways we cannot view with compassion.

What are the things that we do not talk about except when someone is finally killed in one of these tragic episodes? William Pinar, in his essay, asks: "Can their sadism be in part a de-sublimated expression of the school curriculum?" I ask: Can the violence shown in Littleton (as an archetype) be a de-sublimated expression of the terror of the other so overtly present in the null curriculum today?

References

Morrison, Toni. *A writer's work with Toni Morrison.* (Parts 1 and 2) Produced and directed by Gail Pellett, 60 minutes, PBS Video, 1990. Videocassette. From the televison series *A world of ideas with Bill Moyers.*

Peggy R. McConnell is a doctoral student in curriculum and instruction at the Louisiana State University in Baton Rouge. She holds an M.A. in education from LSU and a B.A. in secondary education from the University of New Orleans. Her current research interest is the process of writing autobiographical narrative in conversation with curriculum theory.

Chapter 3 What to Do?

Problematic: Reading Curriculum Visions

Curriculum ghosts and visions are texts that invite multiple readings. Cleo Cherryholmes explores the possibilities for such readings by posing a pragmatic question: What are the imaginable, conceivable consequences of affirming or denying a particular vision? He demonstrates possible responses to this question by deploying both critically pragmatic and deconstructive reading strategies.[1] Following Jacques Derrida, Cherryholmes pays particular attention to reading curriculum "under erasure," a practice he sees as affirming indeterminacy in curriculum work: "Curriculum...is seen as dispersed and deferred, as are our efforts to negotiate it. It requires continuous interpretation, criticism, and re-writing" (this volume).

Structuralist categories and distinctions structure vision, as Cherryholmes demonstrates by deconstructing categories such as overt, implicit, and null curricula. He also challenges the defensibility of maintaining a distinction that many of the authors represented in this volume find useful, namely, the distinction between curriculum and *currere*. We do not interpret Cherryholmes as suggesting that we should abandon these words—clearly, they provide opportunities for subtlety and nuance in representing educational qualities—but as saying that we should use them in ways that "acknowledge their familiar and intimate relationship" rather than reinscribe their difference. We invite readers to apply the reading strategies that Cherryholmes exemplifies to all of the chapters in this book (including his and ours). For example, to what extent do authors assume what Cherryholmes calls "previously prescribed paths of study" that might prevent (or discourage) their texts from being read under erasure? We doubt if any of the contributors to this collection intended their essays to be seen as regulatory texts, but passive readers can make them appear so.

In a previous article, Cherryholmes (1993) argued that naive readings of research texts allow readers to "deny, evade and exclude the instabilities, uncertainties, terror and responsibilities" that accompany pragmatic and deconstructive readings:

> We are responsible for the stories we find within, upon and against the texts of research. That has always been the case but the luxury of self-delusion, if not intoxicating, has been a potent and often pleasant sedative. It was never possi-

> ble to deny the obligations of reading but our past is full of heroic efforts to read poorly. An inability to accept the obligations of reading always resided within us and remains difficult to resist. Good readers, perhaps, are always on the verge of looking into darkness. (28)

We are pleased to share with you, our readers, the responsibility for the visions—and ghosts—you find within these pages. We trust you will be "good readers." Don't be afraid of the dark.

Note

[1] On the commensurability of pragmatism and deconstruction, see Simon Critchley, Jacques Derrida, Ernesto Laclau, and Richard Rorty (1996).

References

Cherryholmes, Cleo. (1993). Reading research. *Journal of Curriculum Studies, 25*(1), 1–32.

Critchley, Simon, Jacques Derrida, Ernesto Laclau, & Richard Rorty. (1996). *Deconstruction and pragmatism.* Chantal Mouffe (Ed.). London and New York: Routledge.

Curriculum Ghosts and Visions—and What to Do?

Cleo H. Cherryholmes

The *Oxford English Dictionary* defines curriculum as "a course; *spec.* a regular course of study or training, as at a school or university." The word curriculum is related to *curricle*, "running, course, also race-chariot," (*Oxford English Dictionary*) that comes from *currere*, "to run" (*OED*). These words, in turn, are linked to curricular, "of or pertaining to driving or to carriages" (*OED*). Thus, curriculum historically is a course (of study) that someone runs (studies). The contemporary articulation of curriculum as a course of study has repeatedly taken the shape of structures and hierarchies of knowledge (Bloom et al., 1956; Bruner, 1960; Shulman, 1985; and Hirsch, 1988, for example) that conform to these classical meanings. William Doll is one among many critics of this view of curriculum when he inveighs "against the authoritarian, unilateral control which has permeated the concept of curriculum. This sort of control has been the ghost in curriculum" (Doll, this volume). This ghost of control, however, has long-standing etymological roots as the *OED* observes. A more recent ghost is that of Dewey who sought to break with a curriculum of control, direction, and prescription. Doll makes common the struggle with Dewey when he asks us to deploy our formidable "post" weapons—postmodernism, poststructuralism, postcolonialism, postpatriarchalism, postindustrialism, post-Fordism, and postanalytic criticism—to produce a new paradigm that circumvents, if not completely evades, the ghost of control.

Straightaway it should be observed that thc term *paradigm* may not be appropriate to this case. Thomas Kuhn introduced almost single-handedly the word paradigm in its present form in his classic argument about the nature of scientific revolutions. In the second edition of *The Structure of Scientific Revolutions* (1974), in response to criticisms that he had previously used the word paradigm ambiguously and in multiple ways, he readdressed it with an eye toward clarification:

> On the one hand, it [paradigm] stands for the entire constellation of beliefs, values, techniques, and so on shared by members of a given community. On the other, it denotes one sort of element in that constellation, the concrete puzzle-solutions

> which, employed as models or examples, can replace explicit rules as a basis for the solution of the remaining puzzles of normal science. (175)

Kuhn called the first sense of the term "sociological" and referred to the second as "exemplary past achievements" (175). Problems arise when these senses of paradigm are brought to bear upon contemporary thinking about curriculum as Doll invites us to do. The range of beliefs, values, techniques, and such that are promoted by contemporary curriculum workers/theorists is enormous. They include curriculum alternatively viewed, sometimes cooperatively and sometimes conflictually, as political, racial, gender, phenomenological, poststructural, postmodern, autobiographical, aesthetic, theological, international, and institutional texts, among others (Pinar et al., 1995). It is doubtful that a "constellation of beliefs, values, techniques," in Kuhn's terms, is shared by those who produce this varied work in curriculum. And this diverse body of work may in fact be produced by equally diverse and fractured communities. In addition, the agreed-upon puzzles and puzzle solutions in contemporary curriculum studies are difficult to identify. If one follows Doll's admonition to use our "post" weapons, it seems likely that more puzzles and indeterminacies will be generated than solved. Even if one grants that the sociological use of paradigm might be appropriate to the field of curriculum, its "concrete puzzle-solutions" remain difficult to identify. An additional problem with applying the term paradigm as used by Kuhn to curriculum is that paradigms shape and govern normal science; it is not obvious what norms normalize the world of curriculum described by Doll and Gough.

Beyond this quibble about applying the term paradigm to curriculum studies, one thing is evident. The shift away from Doll's ghost of control to Gough's vision requires that new meaning(s) be assigned to the term curriculum. This move, as I will argue, is from a classical (see definitions at the beginning of this chapter) and structural view of curriculum to one that is broadly poststructuralist and pragmatist (see Cherryholmes, 1988, for one version of this story). How did/do we get from there—curriculum as a (race)course of study for students to (run)study—to here, curriculum as dispersed poststructural and postmodern texts and practices that teachers and students engage and pragmatically produce?

The story I tell here begins with one told by Eliot Eisner (1979). Eisner argued that schools teach three curricula, each of which can be thought of in terms of a (race)course: the *explicit* (overt), which refers to the concrete manifestations that define the course; the *implicit* (hidden), which refers to the unstated norms and procedures required for successfully navigating it; and the *null*, which refers to that which is beyond the boundaries of the course, to that which is excluded. Eisner's account of curriculum has a defined content, tacit and implicit skills required for success, and boundaries that separate it from the "other," excluded content and skills. The explicit/null distinction traces the boundaries of the course to be (run) studied. If one teaches or studies the null curriculum, that which is excluded, then one has strayed beyond that which is authorized. The implicit or hidden curriculum refers to the subtexts of both that which is included and excluded (Eisner, 83).

Closely reading these three curricula as text leads to the deconstruction of the overt/implicit/null distinctions. The explicit, implicit, and null curricula, together, express what is valued and dis-valued and determine the course of study. Theirs is an integrated dynamics. When curriculum values alone are affirmed (those authorized inside a defined set), "other" values are simultaneously rejected (those relegated to the outside of a defined set). The boundaries that distinguish the valued from the dis-valued, that map a (race) course of study, intimately relate and simultaneously constitute the overt and null curricula. My currently favored definition of curriculum is that which students have an opportunity to learn (inclusion) *and* what they do not have an opportunity to learn (exclusion) *and* the skills and knowledge and disposition required to produce success. The holistic nature of this definition is demonstrated by defining the (race)course by that which it excludes and vice versa. The boundary of the (race)course authoritatively asserts what is central and meaningful while outlawing the "other" and the marginal.

Returning to Eisner's structuralist categories, how are the boundaries that separate them justified? (Is this an issue for Doll and Gough?) To the extent that justifications proceed, they do so by offering warrants and evidence. They are publicly employed to construct profitable and productive lives and societies. But efforts to justify must end. It has been argued by many (see Cherryholmes, 1988, for my version) that the justifications for curricula end at arbitrary (not to be confused with random) and not foundational points. Furthermore, the coherence of such justifications is continually subject to question because the meaning of its text(s) is (are) constantly dispersed and deferred. The boundaries of the (race)course, then, are always subject to further interpretation and re-interpretation, and the plausibility (authority) of an interpretation depends on how its audience reads it (Mailloux, 1990).

The mutual dependence and deconstruction of the curriculum/ noncurriculum distinction is paralleled by that of curriculum/*currere*. Here is a concrete example of this point, an example from my past. As a distance runner in my youth, the distinction between a course and its running seemed palpably obvious. The courses were determined by a 400-meter track in the warmth of spring, say, and by a meandering trail over a golf course or through woods during cross-country season in the cool of autumn. Running, in addition to its sometimes exhilarating moments, was effort, sweat, fatigue, and, occasionally, pain. I had no problem distinguishing a course from its running on this reading, one that parallels the classical definitions of curriculum. But there is another way to read the texts of courses and the running of them. Training, effort, planning, and strategy focus on one or a series of races. But the word race, avoiding its ethnic sense, is structurally ambiguous[1] Race is both a noun that names a contest—the league championship, the state championship—and a verb that designates the actual competition—to race, racing. These meanings, noun and verb, do not, indeed cannot, exist apart from each other. Races do not exist without racers, nor racers without races. To follow Yeats, can one any more separate the racer from the race than the dancer from the dance? Or, the student from her studies? Which meaning one adopts varies with purpose. The physical course on this reading is marginal to the race—the racer's goal is to win disregarding the material conditions of the competition, such as the composition of the track, weather, dry track, wet track, etc. Curriculum and *currere*, by pointing in different directions, temporarily mask the complexity and implicit wholeness of the word race (noun and verb). Unmasking this complexity exposes the violence that a curriculum/*currere* distinction plies on (racing)studying.

A modernist critic might counter that distinguishing curriculum, a course of study, from *currere*, completing the course, contributes analytic clarity to questions of education and schooling. I reject the idea that false clarity and faulty categories are constructive in exorcising ghosts in curriculum. For example, the binary curriculum/*currere* distinction has sometimes been reversed to read *currere*/curriculum where the studying (racing) student is valued over the course of study (child over curriculum). However, this move simply reaffirms the classical, structural distinction between the terms while refusing to acknowledge their familiar and intimate relationship. It should be noted that the deconstruction of the curriculum/

currere and race/racing distinctions are related to the deconstruction of their not-too-distant cousin the text/context distinction.

For an additional reading of the terms curriculum and *currere,* I turn to Jacques Derrida. Derrida points to the option of reading terms, say, curriculum (race course) and *currere* (racer), under erasure, *sous rature*. Such a reading illuminates their traces through language. Gayatri Spivak writes that "Derrida's [trace] is the mark of the absence of a presence, an always already absent present, of the lack at the origin that is the condition of thought and experience" (1976, xvii). When one reads curriculum this way, curriculum is simultaneously accepted and rejected. For example, one can accept curriculum as the opportunities that are provided children to learn while at the same time rejecting those opportunities as complete or authoritative or both. One consequence is to accept the curriculum for the time being while acknowledging that it is neither complete or transparent nor immune to rejection or radical revision. Curriculum, then, is seen as dispersed and deferred, as are our efforts to negotiate it. It requires continuous interpretation, criticism, and re-writing.

Likewise, *currere* can be read under erasure. Studying (racing) the course itself can be simultaneously accepted and rejected. Studying a course is always subject to the authority of the course and the desire of the student. But authority shifts with time and place as does desire. Therefore, the indeterminacy of the already absent present of the desire to race allows the student (racer) to choose other courses (races) or redesign the course being studied (raced). Study cannot proceed without a sense of and commitment to what it is that should be studied. The effect of reading *currere* under erasure is to locate the study of something in the context of its use, broadly construed. Context provides guidelines that point a direction for the student (racer). The way students choose to engage a course of study can simultaneously be accepted by appealing to their interests and imagination *and* rejected by inquiring into, interpreting, and criticizing the solipsistic, provincial, isolationist, and tribal impulses and interpretations that students sometimes bring with them.

Oftentimes we are faced with an exercise of power and authority that prevents either curriculum or *currere* to be read under erasure because previously prescribed paths of study are outlined and policed (evaluated). To the extent that power and authority can be evaded, reading curriculum and *currere* under erasure directs teachers/students to clarify and address the purpose of the course (race). The purpose of the readers (racers) provides a basis for deciding whether at a given moment curriculum and *currere* as authorized will be more or less accepted or rejected.

This argument can be illustrated by reviewing Lee Shulman's idea of pedagogical content knowledge (PCK) as outlined in his 1985 Presidential Address to the American Educational Research Association (1985).[2] Shulman stated that, "As we have begun to probe the complexities of teacher understanding and transmission of content knowledge, the need for a more coherent theoretical framework has become rapidly apparent" (9). He prefaced his discussion of PCK by observing that "Bloom's cognitive taxonomy, Gagné's varieties of learning, Schwab's distinction between substantive and syntactic structures of knowledge and Peters' notions that parallel Schwab's" (9) had been constructed to represent content knowledge. A sidebar here—it is curious that on the eve of poststructural and postmodern reinterpretations of educational thought and practice, Shulman threw in his lot with structuralism which parallels the classical view of curriculum:

> To think properly about content knowledge requires going beyond knowledge of the facts or concepts of a domain. It requires *understanding the structures of the subject matter* in the manner defined by such scholars as Joseph Schwab. (9; emphasis added)

In Shulman's first three paragraphs on content knowledge, the word structure, referring to both content substance and syntax, was used seven times in linking a structural view of curriculum content to structures in disciplinary subjects. This is one version of the ghost in the curriculum that concerns Doll, control by appeal to discipline, and Gough fears it will continue to dominate future visions of curriculum.

In line with conventional structuralist thought, Shulman observed that structures are arbitrary. The example he chose was biology:

> Depending on the preferred color of one's BSCS text, biology may be formulated as (a) a science of molecules from which one aggregates up the rest of the field; (b) a science of ecological systems from which one disaggregates down to the smaller units; or (c) a science of biological organisms...from whose familiar structures, functions, and interactions one weaves a theory of adaptation. (9)

There are an indefinite number of ways of "structuring" biology; BSCS reported three. Some have advantages over others for specific purposes. None, apparently, in Shulman's story, has a lock on truth, although he later discusses the problem of student misconceptions which implies that somewhere, someone has access to true conceptions.

Shulman extends his structural interpretation of content knowledge to PCK. This is clearly an extension of his structuralist views because he creates a special category for it:

> A second kind of content knowledge is pedagogical knowledge, which goes beyond knowledge of subject matter to knowledge for teaching....I...speak of content knowledge here...of the particular form of content knowledge that embodies the aspects of content most germane to its teachability....I include, for the most regularly taught topics in one's subject area, the most useful forms of representation of those ideas, the most powerful analogies, illustrations, examples, explanations, and demonstrations—in a word, the ways of representing and formulating the subject that make it comprehensible to others....[It] also includes an understanding of what makes the learning of specific topics easy or difficult. (9)

His discussion of PCK fell squarely within the classical meaning of curriculum as a course to be run; he just wanted to remove some of the obstacles. PCK was only one of several (structural) categories of knowledge that Shulman explicated. Shulman's multiple structures outlined the curriculum and highlighted its boundaries.

There are two ways, at least, to interpret PCK. First, a structural interpretation is to think about PCK as the intersection of two sets where one set represents pedagogy, the second, knowledge. The knowledge component stakes out the course to be run or studied; the pedagogical component encompasses those pedagogical elements and strategies from which one can select when teaching; and PCK is their intersection, where the most efficient and powerful means of coaching/teaching/guiding are chosen to guide students through the course. This interpretation of PCK brings efficiency, some might say with a vengeance, to completing the curriculum. You race for the finish line over my course. A comparison to the discipline of athletic training is difficult to resist. But one is tied to this interpretation *only* if one sides with Shulman's structuralist commitments.

Second, PCK can be read poststructurally. It should be observed that when it comes to PCK, it is not altogether clear whether Shulman maintains his structuralist convictions or starts to slide into a form of poststructuralism. For example, he writes:

> Within the category of pedagogical content knowledge I include...the most useful forms of representation...the most powerful analogies, illustrations, examples, explanations, and demonstrations—in a word, the ways of representing and formulating the subject that make it comprehensible to others. (9)

The confusion of Shulman's argument comes from the fact that he does not tell us where "the most powerful" come from. If they come from empiricist research carried out in pedagogical settings, then the structuralism continues unabated because we keep shifting from the category of pedagogical knowledge to disciplinary knowledge. If, on the other hand, these "illustrations, examples, explanations, and demonstrations" come from disciplinary knowledge itself and its genealogy, then perhaps—I only suggest this tentatively—he is suggesting that PCK comes from reading knowledge under erasure.

Knowledge and pedagogy can be read under erasure. Such reading requires that we simultaneously accept and reject the categories of knowledge and pedagogy and their content. The effect of reading knowledge *sous rature* is to problematize the course to be run, which Shulman promoted as given (or that was constructed as given). A second effect is to deconstruct the categorical distinction between pedagogy and knowledge. When knowledge claims are simultaneously accepted and rejected, the fact that *knowledge is constructed* is emphasized. Whereas a structuralist reading can easily marginalize the construction of knowledge, a poststructuralist reading moves the idea of knowledge as constructed closer to the ever-retreating center of curriculum.

The argument that knowledge is constructed is not by way of sleight of hand. Knowledge is generated, in part, because we wish to teach ourselves and others about the consequences of beliefs and actions. For example, consider knowledge generated by educational research. Accounts of systematic inquiry, says Kerlinger (1985), can be read as pedagogical manuals where we teach ourselves and others how to inquire and to produce knowledge as well as to be read as textbooks on research methods. Reading knowledge and pedagogy under erasure naturalizes and contextualizes both. To say that the texts of knowledge and pedagogy are naturalized highlights the idea that they are, indeed, found and utilized in context, and their texts and contexts blur. A structuralist tendency to pick a little knowledge from one discipline, say political science, and match it with a little pedagogy, say cooperative learning, is rejected.

Here is a brief example. Democracy, democratic attitudes, and behavior have long been promoted as an educational outcome and suggestive of educational processes. *The New Shorter Oxford English Dictionary* (1993) defines democracy as

> a form of government in which the power resides in the people and is exercised by them either directly or by means of elected representatives; a form of society which favours equal rights, the ignoring of hereditary class distinctions, and tolerance of minority views. (629)

This is familiar and comfortable. It is also ambiguous. For example, although the call for equal rights has widespread appeal, the consequences of specific, concrete, and practical interpretations of equal rights are continually debated. If equal rights were interpreted literally, for example, the most privileged individuals would be placed on the same footing as the most dispossessed. Equal rights on this reading quickly produces increasing inequalities because such different people cannot compete for jobs, income, health care, leisure time, etc., on equitable terms. Therefore, the old argument goes, those who are unequal must be treated unequally if one is to promote equality. Equal rights require unequal treatment. A close reading of equal rights leads one to simultaneously accept and reject them. What it means to be tolerant of minority views also has many interpretations. Unqualified tolerance simply cannot be accepted at face value. Imagine a student from a neo-Nazi home in a classroom that has been proclaimed tolerant of all minority views. Our fictional student, feeling safe in such a hypertolerant classroom, asserts during class discussion that all people of color should be expelled from the country and members of certain religious groups exterminated. Obviously, such a broad-stroked tolerance undermines itself. Classroom tolerance requires intolerance (of hate speech) as equality requires inequality. These are examples of reading knowledge (political concepts) under erasure. They are examples of simultaneously affirming and rejecting whatever our concept of interest happens to be. Pedagogy, then, can be found in the genealogy of the knowledge that is being taught (a post-structural view of PCK) as well as found in the separate area of study that is properly known as pedagogy (a structural view of PCK, more or less).

What are we to do with multiple readings, multiple interpretations of knowledge and pedagogy? Dewey is insightful here. In *Art as Experience* Dewey (1934) deconstructed the distinction between fine art and ordinary experience. He highlighted the artistic and aesthetic dimensions of everyday life and practices, say, educational practices that constitute a course of study or those that guide students through it. Dewey described the possibility of thinking about ordinary experience in terms of satisfaction, well-being, and beauty. Once we have one or several texts of curriculum (curriculum, *currere*, PCK) in our possession, following Dewey, we can appraise and employ them as would-be artists in constructing, designing, organizing, and enacting beliefs and practices with an eye toward the production of beauty in our lives and the lives of those with whom we interact. It is possible to think of ourselves as artists who choose, within the limits of the situations in which we find ourselves, how to conceptualize curriculum/*currere* (or its deconstruction) and PCK and decide how to learn, study, race (see Cherryholmes, 1999, for a longer presentation of these arguments). These are decisions about the lives we wish to live and the society(ies) in which we wish to live. We will, no doubt, turn to some ghosts in the curriculum for inspiration and seek to exorcise others.

Notes

[1] This argument parallels, roughly, an observation made by John Searle (1971) in his discussion of J. L. Austin on locutionary and illocutionary acts. Austin had shown that speech could be action as well as description. Searle pointed out that the word "statement" has "at least two different derivations from the verb 'state.' Statement can mean either the act of stating or what is stated" (274).

[2] This interpretation of pedagogical content knowledge occurred to me while listening to Avner Segal discuss pedagogy.

References

Bloom, B., A. Engelehart, W. Furst, W. Hill, and C. Krathwohl. (1956). *Taxonomy of educational objectives*. New York: McKay.

Bruner, Jerome. (1960). *The process of education*. Cambridge, MA: Harvard University Press.

______. (1988). *Power and criticism: Poststructural investigations in education*. New York: Teachers College Press.

Cherryholmes, Cleo. (1999). *Reading pragmatism*. New York: Teachers College Press.

Dewey, John. (1934). *Art as experience*. New York: Minton, Balch.

Eisner, Eliot. (1979). *The educational imagination: On the design and evaluation of school programs*. New York: Macmillan.

Hirsch, E. D. (1988). *Cultural literacy: What every American needs to know*. New York: Vintage.

Kerlinger, Fred. (1985). *Foundations of behavioral research*. New York: Harcourt Brace.

Kuhn, Thomas. (1974). *The structure of scientific revolutions*. Second edition. Chicago: University of Chicago Press.

Mailloux, Stephen. (1990). Interpretation. In Frank Lentricchia & Thomas McLaughlin (Eds.),*Critical terms for literary study*, (pages 121–34). Chicago: University of Chicago Press.

Peirce, Charles. (1984/1905). Peirce's description of pragmatism. In H. S. Thayer, *Meaning and action: A critical history of pragmatism* (pages 494–95). Indianapolis: Hackett.

Pinar, William F., William M. Reynolds, Patrick Slattery, and Peter M. Taubman. (1995). *Understanding curriculum*. New York: Lang.

Searle, John. (1971). Austin on locutionary and illocutionary acts. In Jay Rosenberg and Charles Travis (Eds.), *Readings in the philosophy of language* (pages 262–75). Englewood Cliffs, NJ: Prentice-Hall.

Shulman, Lee. (1985). Those who understand: Knowledge growth in teaching. *Educational Researcher, 14*(2), February, 4–14.

Spivak, Gayatri. (1976). Translator's preface. In Jacques Derrida, *Of grammatology,* (pages ix–lxxxvii). Baltimore: Johns Hopkins University Press.

Cleo Cherryholmes is Professor of Teacher Education at Michigan State University. He holds a Ph.D. in political science from Northwestern University and has recently published *Reading Pragmatism* (1999), a continuation of arguments he developed in an earlier book, *Power and Criticism: Poststructural Investigations in Education* (1988). He has published widely in educational journals.

Perspective on Cherryholmes

Ellen Wickersham

As both teacher and administrator, I have endeavored to make a difference in the lives of children and teachers. This is a very important statement, for it encapsulates my entire educational philosophy. My first class of fifth graders quickly taught me that education was about more than dispensing knowledge or transmitting culture. As I began my teaching career, my pre-adolescent students were at the beginning of the most turbulent time in their lives, facing intellectual, physical, social, and emotional changes that directly impacted their ability to learn. I could not meet the needs of my students by focusing on *either* the textual knowledge *or* the context-situated child. This was a package deal; my goal, or, in John Dewey's terms, my ends-in-view, quickly became to help my students achieve *both* knowledge and skills *and* the means to achieve satisfying and fulfilling lives. Yet, over the ensuing years, I have watched the modern structure of *either/or* continue to hold sway in educational practice. Since the launch of *Sputnik* in the late 1950s, we have become accustomed to hearing such phrases as "back to the basics," "the structure of the discipline," and "cultural literacy." Most recently, our educational practice is controlled by high-stakes accountability testing and instruction dictated by local, state, and national standards and benchmarks. So pervasive is this movement that at a recent textbook adoption caravan, publisher representatives hawked the merits of their books as designed to provide practices that mirror specific types of test questions along with prepackaged lesson plans correlated to specific state standards and benchmarks. In the face of this I must ask these questions: Where is the student in all of this? How can I as teacher or administrator meet the modernistic, bureaucratic requirements imposed upon me, *and* at the same time meet the needs of those fifth graders whose turbulent times have not changed but rather have increased in intensity as we have entered a new millennium?

Cleo Cherryholmes has accepted Doll's injunction and used "post" weapons to enable *both* teachers *and* students to dissolve the boundaries of control and to lead us to a new meaning for curriculum. His new reading blends pedagogy and knowledge into a theoretical framework that views knowledge as actively constructed rather than passively accepted and utilizes Dewey's aesthetic interpretation of ordinary experience and pragmatic form of inquiry. Cherryholmes (1999) further explicates this marriage in his book *Reading Pragmatism.* This form of inquiry requires both teacher and student to possess a knowledge of the contextualized self and the problematic situation, to conceive of possible actions and potential outcomes, and to evaluate each of the imagined desires and consequences in order that a satisfying good emerges. Cherryholmes suggests that we examine and attach value to each set of facts, outcomes, or consequences by reading them through a specific lens—feminist, deconstructive, historical, analytical, linguistic, or critical. Once this is decided upon, the chosen consequence, good, or outcome is continually reviewed and reinterpreted, perhaps through the use of another lens or in light of new facts or concepts.

This reading of curriculum is absolutely appealing to the practitioner who sees education as more than a ritualistic passing on of rational, analytic knowledge. It breathes life into an archaic hierarchical institution, empowering administrator, teacher, and student. I often ask my teachers, as we work on curriculum: "What is the goal of your lesson beyond the standards and benchmarks, and how did you decide upon it?" "In addition to the intellectual, how does it meet the social, emotional, and physical needs of your students?" "What is your criteria as you design learning situations for your students?" "Why did you select that particular piece of literature to discuss?" Now I can add, "When you come upon a teachable moment or 'problematic situation,' what lens will you select to view through so that your students will be able to understand its ramifications better?"

Cherryholmes has given us a reading of curriculum that banishes the *either/or* ghost of control. He has opened a way of pragmatic inquiry that guides us both creatively and critically to seek the good—that which is not now, but which resides in our imagination of possible futures. In Jim Garrison's terms (1997), inquiry, as Dewey conceived it, takes on a transformational and transactional nature. Both student and teacher are called to be artists in the construction of a better life and a better world. In order to do this, the teacher must desire the good of "best practice," which requires "developing the habits, abilities, thoughts, ideals, technical mastery, and virtues of the practice"(73). Inquiry is also transactional art. The relationship that develops between the teacher and the student enables each to grow and change. The teacher sees creatively and imaginatively in the medium, the student, a mixture of the actual and the potential just as the student actualizes the teacher's potential and limits.

For Cherryholmes (1999), this "dynamic" guided inquiry empowers, indeed, helps create thoughtful, deliberative, and wise people. I would suggest that the development and implementation of this form of inquiry in a school environment also leads to a more tolerant people, whose understanding of diversity and the *other's* point-of-view will engender a more caring and responsive society. The challenge is now ours—to banish the ghost of *either/or* control and to embrace Cherryholmes's vision of curriculum for ourselves and our students, so that together we may fashion a value-filled future.

References

Cherryholmes, C. (1999). *Reading pragmatism.* New York: Teachers College Press.

Garrison, J. (1997). *Dewey and eros: Wisdom and desire in the art of teaching.* New York: Teachers College Press.

Chapter 4 Dewey's Goats

Problematic: A Question of Genre

Some years ago William Reid (1979) observed that "the well argued essay" seemed to be the preferred genre of the curriculum writing that had been published up to that time in the *Journal of Curriculum Studies* (of which he was then European editor). He warned, however, that a preference for just one genre of curriculum journalism was inherently conservative if other possible forms were excluded without question: "Thoughts on curriculum can be pointed, substantive and coherent even if they are only a few lines long; they don't have to run to 5,000 words...nor need they be in prose, or even in words" (17).

We have not seen very many wordless representations of curriculum inquiry to date although we recognize that some curriculum scholars have made valiant efforts to provide us with such. For example, Kevin Keeffe (1991) substantiated Reid's conclusion by presenting a painting that unequivocally expressed "pointed, substantive and coherent" thoughts on Australian curriculum work by four Australian Aboriginal student teachers (Bruno et al., 1989). Although the vibrant colors and dramatic size of the original painting (three meters wide) were lost in its monochrome reproduction, Keeffe's sensitive interpretation demonstrated clearly why the production and subsequent uses of the painting were significant in Australia's recent curriculum history. Similarly, Hedy Bach's (1997) visual narrative documenting the lives of four girls inside/outside of classrooms demonstrates the generativity of nonverbal media (in this instance, still photography) for deconstructive curriculum inquiry.

In the chapter that follows, Peter Cole and Pat O'Riley use words.

Their chapter is
    and is not
    a "well argued essay."
Their chapter is
    and is not
    prose.
That's what we like about poets.
We can't make up their minds.

References

Bach, Hedy. (1997). A visual narrative concerning curriculum, girls, photography etc. Edmonton: Qual Institute Press.

Bruno, Sarah Napangati, Paul Tjampitjinpa Bruno, Monica Nangala Robinson, and Victor Tjungurrayi Robinson (1989). *Nganampa manta lingkitu ngaluntjaku* [To hold our land firmly]. Painting (acrylic on canvas, 3m x 2m approx.). Canberra: Australian Curriculum Studies Association.

Keeffe, Kevin. (1991). Painting the curriculum: The view from Walungurru. *Journal of Curriculum Studies, 23*(3), 259–68.

Reid, William A. (1979). A curriculum journal and its field: A question of "genre." *Journal of Curriculum Theorizing, 1*(1), 12–19.

Much Rezadieux about (Dewey's) Goats in the Curriculum: Looking Back on Tomorrow Yesterday

Peter Cole and Patricia O'Riley

I don't know says 114-year old Sam Jim
picking bits of loose rubber off his highback canvas runners
you educated people got it the other way round
from the way I was thinking   long pause
during which he re-ties his shoelaces
    very slowly
first place   I don't see it at all
seeing isn't the word I'd use
I reckon there's been a whole lot of seeing going on
especially seeing what's not there and not seeing what is there
maybe we could use some of those other senses the Creator gave us
see how that works out for a spell
listen for a change   use our noses   taste things   feel things
you're not going to last very long in the bush standing around looking
and talking
you got to use all your givens   including your hunches
being bush smart is different from city knowing.

foreigners come here and see us on the shore in our longhouses
we live here   content even happy   fishing picking berries and roots
they come and they take everything
before impact we taught our children
without ministry of education prescribed curricula
we had no special ed needs   education was for every person
it was called living in the village

these immigrants thought we needed special attention
because we weren't like them so they put us in residential schools
now they call us special needs because we don't fit
their academic models and standardizations

they want to wire us to computers to headsets to the future
where there is no respect for our land-based spiritual connection
with the rivers and forests four-leggéds the wingéd ones,
the fish nation the powers and spirits and beings of the four directions
the moon and sun earth and sky the stones the tree nations

these white people are consumed by their visions by the visual
they don't say can you smell the difference I taste what you mean
hear this get a feel for that their society is about looking
it is about peering rather than feeling or engaging the other senses
this visual control this panopticon mentality
who will put this goat to rest?

they have visionaries but who listens to them?
aren't there any listenaries in their culture? are there no storytellers?
image imagine imagination is not just about seeing
imagine learning piano by just looking at the notes or the keys?
why do schools not talk about intuition?
they talk about an end in view not in hearing
how about finding your voice even if you can read lips
or see your words on an audioscope
you still can't get it visually your voice it comes
through your vocal
cords
what about hearing colour or feeling its subtle shades feeling timbre
smelling silence seeing tonality what about a tectonic movement in
language? semiotectomy geographizing knowing
putting the land back into the language

my mother's father August Jacob told me
about this Irishman Otis Dewey Esquire
come up home when he was a boy round 1850
called himself a schoolteacher arrived in the middle of a loud summer
storm
with a trunkful of books and black clothes
nobody ever saw a book before or a trunk or a white man
Dewey brought some queer-looking goats up with him not
like the ones from the mountains of home his followed him around
the village

chewing making funny noises not paying anybody mind

you need a foundation he would say
so if you put words together they don't fall apart
it's like a stone house but it comes out of books
all I ever saw there was words
and nobody ever heard of a house before or knew what it was for

The word "curriculum" has a three-pronged genealogy, consisting of multi-lateral coderivatives from the past, the future, and from a dysauditory linguistic space:

curare: a Carib word referring to an organic metabolic toxin causing neuro-paralysis,

krklm: a neo-retro-paramorphopoeic radical originating in the future, and

kr7xlhm: a dysphonic audiotrope from the tl'atl'imx language, "7" representing a glottal stop, the "lh" is a lisped "l" sound, like the initial phoneme in Welsh "Llwelyn." the "x" is pronounced like the terminal phoneme in the Scottish "loch."

Dewey said I came to educate you to read and write english
so's you'll be book smart and so you can read the word of God and go to heaven
woman doing the translating was having a rough time
because a lot of what Dewey was saying didn't make sense to her either
Dewey would go on about ideas with roots that go way deep
we asked him what the roots hung onto down there way deep
what kind of roots were they could you eat them
could you make baskets from them did they soften up if you soaked them good
what were they connected to uptop
he didn't seem to know what we were talking about
he said the roots are words not real roots
then he talked about white words having very old roots
he sure was interested in roots for somebody with clean fingernails

we thought maybe we needed to stir up the roots of tl'atl'imx a bit
maybe the seeds weren't planted in the right places
maybe they were put too deep or grew under language stones

or maybe our language didn't have any roots
maybe it was more like a lily pad   or crabgrass

I'm talking about planting ideas
it didn't seem to matter what season he did his planting
or what phase grandmother moon was in
or if it was even the right climate
the soil he talked about was made of words
not something you could feel or taste

do you understand what I mean? he kept saying
we told him we didn't have questions in tl'atl'imx
so what he was saying wasn't going anywhere
but eventually to make him feel better we said   yes
we understand   though the word understand has no meaning
in our language we don't have that word
I guess it had nowhere to grow
or we didn't know how to grow it or find it

we listened politely
assuming he'd never "understand" what we were talking about
it wasn't so much making sense as sensitive
he didn't know much about planting
he assumed ideas and words grow like things in the bush
in fact, the word "grow" isn't the right one at all
he was really only talking about growing things in his head
and it was perfectly clear he'd never harvested anything
or done any companion gardening of any kind
if we'd known that in the first place we wouldn't have bothered listening
because we had salmon to catch and dry for the winter

Curare follows indo-european rules of how metaphors are supposed to act in semantic places like sentences, arboreal places like word trees, phenotypic places like the human vocal apparatus and in public denotative linguaspheres—dictionaries, encyclopaedias, etc. Through spontaneous mutation, caused by intense exogenic linguistic pressure, curare xxx/gressed into "curriculum." Early on, it manifested as minorized proto-phonemic dysphasia, but declined rapidly through bilateral anabolic phonosynthesis into acute emergent retroflex hypertrophic oeneropathy, with the final stage being chronic semio-epistemic paralysis, requiring intraspecific retro-phonectomy with attendant post-latent lacunogenetic bypass. What this means in lay terms is that words simply stopped "meaning" because language stopped having anything to do with the realities it purportedly re/de/ferred to—and it fell into itself like a blackhole sucking its event (conceptual) horizon into itself or like a community of blackholes revolving around a mutual centre of gravity, eventually disappearing into scientific adimentia incunabula.

he told us knowledge is vital—it frames us
then after explaining what that meant
we said to him we have frames for drying salmon and clothes
we have baskets nets looms spindles and canoes
that's fine but if you want to get on in the world
you have to use them when you talk he said
we never had to frame our talk before
up to then we'd only used our own language
framed knowledge is intelligence he elaborated
nobody up there wanted that kind of knowing
if it came with a frame you had to lug around
we knew all about seasonal migration and portaging
Dewey spent more time talking about where words came from
than actually using them to communicate
as he was teaching us english and gaelic he began to learn tl'atl'imx
after a few months we didn't need a translator anymore
because the translations didn't make any sense
the explanation didn't mean anything to anybody
people listened to be polite
after a while he'd sit for hours talking gaelic to the elders
and they'd talk to him in tl'atl'imx
that seemed to work out okay
it kept things uncomplicated

Krklm is a word whose etymology originates in future time. Through backformation, krklm transiterates into the present (tense). *Krklm* can act as a noun adjective verb adverb and preposition simultaneously. It is not bound by agreement with respect to number gender tense or case and has a variety of divergent meanings, some contradictory, some nonsensical, some saltatory. *Krklm* is not transmutable into any figure of speech, though it sometimes functions as a nomivore and verbiphage which in effect catalyzes equivocality through dysnotation and deconstruction. This is known as deiterative semiopathy or spontaneous morphemic transformation. Meaning is catabolized as words are being uttered, so language becomes deconstructed/degenerated through its own generation. This has historically occurred when xenophones, especially leucophones, become supernumerary in linguistic geographies, causing rubricaphones and other autochthonophones to become autorecessive —such as took place after the mid-1850s in the British Columbia interior, reaching a virulent stage when eurolinguists assumed taxonomizing functions. *Krklm* does not usually act in an either/or fashion but in a both/and one. It does not grant the visual sense preferential status or recognizance over the other senses. *Krklm* has no particular meaning outside of the context in which it is used. This is true for not only its roots, but also for its stem leaves bark rhizomes peduncles xylem and epiphytes. *Krklm* is alive in a euglenal amoeboid botanical way, rather than being a dead metaphor awaiting inhumement, grafting, or transplantation.

Dewey taught us to speak english not by treating english as a living language
not by having us learn useful words and phrases
but by teaching us "correct english grammar"
so in effect he taught us english grammar as a second language
it didn't make any sense to anybody but he didn't seem to notice
he was a man of great book learning
but not very efficient at learning our language
he didn't really (or virtually) have the patience to teach us any utilitarian english
except how to talk to the white god
we didn't know what the words meant
but hearing us repeat them with our eyes closed or sing them made him happy

everything was going fine until he tried to change our language
he wanted to frame it and make it like english
he said he was going to give us framed grammar and syntax
we said we like it the way it is
we don't want nouns and verbs in tl'atl'imx

it would make no sense he said these things were already there
showing he never really had a feel for our language
he never really connected with it
just as he never really connected with the land
or the spirit of things

kr7xlhm is on the third tine of the trifurcative etymology of curriculum. It is an extinct or at least obsolete word meaning "rogue mountain goat of either sex." It joined the etymology through mishearings by speakers of tl'atl'imx of the English word "curriculum" spoken with a lisp and through a strong Irish accent by Otis Dewey. That is, Dewey enunciated "curriculum" so that it approximated a word for a kind of mountain goat, which is now extinct. This particular genus was a strongheaded alpine ungulate which didn't spend much time with the rest of its relations in the higher elevations of the Coastal Range of southwestern British Columbia.

all the time Dewey was talking about curriculum
we assumed he was talking about goats
because of this (what we would later call pleasurable) mishearing
we had many strange parallel or tangential con/di/vers/at/ions
if raven had overheard us s/he would have understood perfectly
and taken much pleasure in what s/he heard or mis-heard
these diverse cognate journeys and homophonic dysnotations diversated
like a goat of yesterday and tomorrow into today
hoofs akicking jaws achewing horns abutting head back
singing the stars down maybe that is why
a7ri:stotl thought the northern lights were dancing goats

Dewey delighted to tell us all about different goats
and how they hung around after people died
he talked about how ideas have goats too
seems okay to me I said they gotta hang around somewhere
somebody got to feed them comb the tangles out
he looked at me in a peculiar way sometimes
but my silence (which pretty much filled up
the major part of our conversation) made him think I understood or
agreed with him
he talked about goats appearing and disappearing

about them not being real about them existing on the edges
sure we said they're your goats you can tell us about them
we got goats too but they live high up in the mountains
they're hard to catch they don't hang around the village
he figured we were catching on figuratively
using metaphors in primitive ways

Dewey figured it was good to create a "formal place of instruction"
but sitting-down-in-rows-repeat-after-me schooling
didn't work too well for us uncomplicated national geographic retros
it made everybody have the same take on everything
what he called misconceptions and misperceptions worked out fine back home
where they weren't identified as mis/takes
[but as allo-takes, takes with a difference, alter/native perceptions]

grandmother showed me the fish
wasn't w/here it looked like it was
she said throw your spear where the fish is
not where the water tells you it is
listen for the fish refracting through the sound
of the water smell it diffuse among the other scents
feel its tangential movement through the palpitating ether

just as light defines shadow so does coolness and dampness
through smell object/iv/ize the edge is every/where
alienation is a good starting place/position
framing an in/visible gallows steps heard visual indigestion
wired seeing eyes hear eat feel hooves scent
in the dark of the moon hearing is believing
in the salt of moon the silence of soft touch of
tasting is gustatory taxonomical bruxism jaws meet
alveolar ridge melds dental migration dendritic axonic cloverleafing
belwethers butt horns pull beards
goats dream

Goats unlike curriculum experts are not restricted to "the field." They are undisciplined and refuse to stay where they're put, often browsing within the whole of the area and circumference of their tether.

They often eat their tether or kick down restraining fences or jump over them or dig under them. Liberated goats take to journeying toward the limits of their mind's appetite, including to valleys rivers mountain peaks vegetable gardens urban lawns parks and other such expanses led there by their stomachs rather than their eyes. They are not constrained by fences, standards, or definitions. Sometimes goats will even eat the punctuation of the sentences they are put into. Old goats are still able to appreciate a good field without visual acuity—so long as their taste and hooves are in/tact, they can still rove in the unseen. A wise goat trusts its hunches.

mutindi ndunda told us that in her village in kenya
goats are always blamed for breaking the narrow-necked cooking pots
getting their heads stuck in them and shaking them
despite the mischief they get into they always have a calm look on their faces
but inside they are hyper
they are often blamed for breaking into vegetable gardens
and eating the cabbages
but time has proven that goat haters have concocted
and spread these malicious fabrications
framing goats through others' perceptions
for having appetites which they do not have.
we do not use goat here as a metaphor
but use metaphor as a goat
freeing it from its definition and grammaticality
allowing it a wider range of action

In recent times, goats have fallen victim to others' capricious imaginings and persiflages about them. They are regularly forced onto computer screens and made to be gazed at, their maneuverings assigned meanings which the goats never intended. Says a spokesgoat, we are not blocking or choreographing or other/wise conducting ourselves as performers in someone's imagined vision. We are not limited by a screenwriter's imagination, a director's directives, a theoretician's generative vision, a programmer's language, nor by an audience's expectation. Rather, we enact who and what we are—alternators rather than generators or generatees. We articulate our own verbalizations. Even now, my ideas

and those of my relations are queued, awaiting re/lease rather than manufacture by other.
like goats we are private   we don't want to be put on monitors
we don't want to be translocated   including to an information highway
we don't want to be reframed onto screens   we are our own browsers
we have our own stories: trickster discourses   nomadic subjectivities
chance operations   capric imaginings   inchoate interceptions   mosaic fugues   cantatory canterings

Dewey talked a lot about dead people and their goats
he got real excited when he figured we "understood" him
that made him talk even more
he went on and on about flesh and incarnated goats
those are the ones you can see
hmmm sure we thought sure   those ones
not the invisible ones he sometimes talked about
or the ones that went under the ground when the sun came up
or had no permanent place to rest

grandfather was very patient and waited long for this education
but it never came

every so often Dewey would say   "martinheidegger"
he would follow this with words without spaces between them
we thought he was praying   so we closed our eyes too
then he thought we were praying so he'd stop talking
when we opened our eyes again he went on
about goats going to the land of no return
which we figured would be up in chilcotin country
but he said they came back at night
sometimes only you could see them   sometimes everybody could
"you got to look after the goats when they die   for a long time
you feed them and put things in the ground with them
give them water and talk to them in a familiar way"
we never did that with our goats
but we figured his were probably different   from hanging around people a lot
Dewey talked about burning people into ashes when they died

and goats coming out of the smoke   we never saw that happen
he talked about this old ferryman
far as we could figure he only lived in books
what's a ferryman?   he explains   we thought hmmmm
what's a coin?   hmmm   and hell?
some goats go to hell   some are loved by god
some appear to the living   and ask to be prayed for
mostly he said goats appear when it is misty
and mostly in places of burial
some goats come back from the dead for revenge
we thought about the goat hair blankets and horns we use in ceremonies
but we always spoke with the spirits of our sisters and brothers
the four legged before hunting and they offered themselves
so we didn't understand about goats' revenge

Dewey talked about curriculum as control
how we needed a new livelier spirit of control
students wandered   were allowed   to
he spoke of dead greek men   romans   protestants   philosophers
he spoke about scholasticism   paradigmatic change   dialogic glosses
taxonomy   methodology   rhetoric   softening industrial metaphors
maps of knowledge   moving to standardizing   the earth hurtling
through the cosmos   mechanical clocks industrial expansionism
curriculum as an ordering   school-as-factory
he spoke of integrating education schooling curriculum
and community into a seamless whole
centred around the distinction between imposed and emergent control
what's so wonderful about being seamless we wondered?
what's so wonderful about control?
he spoke of learning as a running course for people   carriages   chariots
he did not speak of canoes

Beyond the unseen is the unimagineable, beyond the unspeakable the ineffable. Or perhaps within. Goats are always in those places, even in their senator years. Some human beings try to capture goats with words, try to lasso or bridle their wild/er/ness. They think along the lines of the visual grasp when it comes to goats. But how a goat looks is only a very small part of what it is to be a goat. There is more to a goat than meets the eye. What of the audient participating? When a goat speaks, its tongue draws back on itself and with the palate acts as one point of articulation, causing a di/vision between nasal and interlabial utterance, though young goats are more likely to exhibit rhinosonic ventriloqu/ism/ation than bucal. Goats are often gregarious yet do not think only as herd—they are idiosyncratic in individual and communal ways. A goat will act in ways inconvenient for self for sake of community, for special needs, to make the species stronger. One cannot inter/view a goat as they do not accede to the interrogative mode, preferring to deal with the imperative declarative, occasionally subjunctive when in need of emotional support. Goats are great buttressers and are willing to insulate themselves from the whole for the sake of it in order to ensure the survival of each, thus all. They are not usually considered to be trickster figures but fit that non-stereotype. They can be coercive but prefer to just be left alone. When they act as words, they do so as semiotropes, meanings clothed in symbols, making them hard to tie down, even metaphorically. In acting musically, a goat prefers basso continuo, with preferred clef alto minor quay. Sustenato non piu con moto and da cappo goats act out xxx/notatively. Their rhythm is not so much harmonic as syncopated. They act out of convenience for self and via synchronistica rather than altruistically, the latter adverb encompassing, enjoining the subjectivizing mode rather than subsuming it.

Dewey said he was not seeking   to assimilate us
yet seeing infuses grammar and syntax imbricates object/subject
grandfather asked (in his own way) is duality inherently visual?
are we to distinguish tastes or let them meld
can we learn to hear through the traffic of ambient sounds
is muddled hearing analogous to refractive diffractive reflective vision
is the visual the default position   is position the default
transparency seeps into curriculum as optifuscent magneloquent
what of trans/audient/sentient embodiment
without prayer without respect without sensibility sensitivity
spiritual enhancement through creating nurturing environments
sustaining as is   there is just dead space
where nothing will grow   nothing will rot
yet in that dead space   not even nothing   will grow or rot
there will be hoodoos   auraed by an uninflected timelessness
av/oid

tl'atl'imx has only the present   and the extended present
we have no future   no past   tense
we see hindsight in english as a way of assuming a future
a turning around with the visual faculty cued
all this talk of reflective teaching is about seeing   is about looking
is about angles of incidence   beyond touch scent tingling
transparency and opacity too are about degrees of seeing
what of transaudient   transsentient   transolfactorial
I do not know that my sensations are produced and mediated by me
somewhere
location and embodiment are about the locative
and the retro-transcendant
these actors dancing along borders are referents seeking to cross
into the symbols   only to find   not even   nothing
not even dynamic imbalance   not even not   even
an inter   to pret   to penetrate   to wit

when white people talk about the future I don't understand them
grandmother says   because most of the time they use the present tense to
speak of it   this time
"yet to come" at least seems to indicate isomorphic continuity
to speak of the future as spectral immanence
which if I xxx/take this right is about all everywhere
which by my calculations   is a lot of goats in a lot of curricula
which means a lot of milk and feta
but also a lot of cleaning up   after   wards
we could follow the hoofprints   or we could make our own   dance

to see pasts and futures enfolded in the/a present
yes this affords us location and embodiment
but to compare or contrast vision with/from pre/diction
is to speak on the one hand of looking   on the other
of speaking before
the future in english is trapped in the present
surrounded by pre/positions   articles   and present indicative
in the lingering taste of latency of a coming now
a potent/shall be   will be
yes futures as accusative caseload   as time as noun   as name
"is" coming/en route/post ex facto/che sara

when "will" as aide de camp verb helper   adjutant factotum
    predication come of age
with auxiliary modifying or other/wise enhancing the main verb
yet the main verb is still   in the present
only the "willness" gestures   gesticu/lates toward the future
    (exit up right)
yes "times to come" are (not only) seen as metaphorical
    equivalents of "places to visit"
nominalized   congealed into nounness   or verbable andante
yet here they are   at tongue's end   mind's frontier   ear's/finger's
    terminus
here they are tangible   present   (choose appropriate pre/position)
    t/here
the future forever trapped in the now the w/here/ever   the frozen when
whatever else they are futures are nouns tending toward imperialist taste
seeking consummated inbetween times   settled territoriality
com/pounded stakes   surveyed boundaries   acceded proprietaries
yet future is always in present time   motioning as ASL speakers do
to indicate an idea of forwardness   beyondness
though not a spatial one
future cannot travel temporally   only spatially
and tomorrow is no more   forward   than it is in (or out)
any other direction

then those european linguists came to skatine saktin samahquam
n'quatqua port douglas with their phonetic alphabets and tape
    recorders
they tried to stencil western knowings into our language
tried to filter tl'atl'imx words and sounds and rhythms
through english   our words born in the pemberton valley
in those days the wind carried our words
when we wrote on stones   shapes   the wind wore them down

and we forgot the old dances and the songs and the rhythm of the
    drum
and we forgot the sounds and the movements of our ancestors
we tried to sell our broken spirits
to the curator of the Museum of Civilization
we tried to barter our souls for bannock for a crust of bread

for recognition   for a line or two   in some book
but they only wanted materials they could classify   put numbers on
so we traded them to the Catholic church for wafers and wine
eternal life and a Christian burial

this curriculum technology expert they sent to educate us
in the ways of the future   in the ways of progress   said to the class
you refuse to let me teach you   yet you invited me
we said   you asked to be invited then you tell us we invited you
you were invited by the colonialist indians   who run our
    educational programs
they have been whitewashed into believing we are only good
for primary resource industry extraction employment
now you're trying to tell us the computer will save us
we're told to trust that cyberspace is more fair more equitable
less racist than downtown vancouver   whew!

now they want to virtualize us with screens   and applications
there is no context in cyberplace
no room for community   for continuity   for turning around
there are only pixels   colons   semi-colons   and periods
right or left parenthesis   :)   to show a smile or a frown   ; (
now even our feelings are becoming iconographized
and they have not even become airborne yet in our own lives

a fellow from home said to the teacher   I don't need a computer
I got a pen   and when that runs out
I got a knife   and lots of pencils   my kids crayons   charcoal
lots of hardware   anyway   I got no 'lectricity in my shack   like
    most of us here
they think we want to learn to be white   technologized in the margins
    cybernauted
we only want our children to have a better chance than we got
okay   we said to this teacher   you tell us you are teaching us
we see us   and we see you   but we don't see the teaching
and we don't hear it or smell it or feel it
where is the life of it?

a woman from our community added

I do not want to use alter/native ways
we are the mainstream   which is made of tributaries
my language and people are part of that stream   the tributaries are not greater or lesser than what they flow into

we keep returning to the circle
sometimes to one perimeter   sometimes concentric ones or spirals
the computer technology teacher is always talking
about "being on the leading edge"
in our culture the leading edge is every/where   not just in a terminal position
that's very post-structural   she'd say   very post-colonial

we said   there is no post   when it comes to colonialism
the people who teach us up here in the hinterlands   the boonies
they come from privilege and they're stuck there   talking
with authority about people not in the mainstream
hey in case they haven't noticed they're the ones standing at the front of the class
centre stage telling us   about ourselves

we don't need to learn about ourselves secondhand
or in ordinal manipulations above first
we're in the margins   yes   to them but at least we got aisle seats
in case the architecture doesn't hold

This whole arrogance about perception, this "persistence of vision"— have we not heard the last of the seeable? This anatomical zeroing in on the eye and its orbit/uary, this visuocentricity, this oculomania—why has it not been diagnosed in western society as a malady, as an obsessive-compulsive dis/order? We've heard the phrases, the emphasis on the seen—"the way I see it," from my point of view, reviewing a lesson, looking at it from my perspective, revisioning curriculum—see what I mean?

first nations people do not need to be empowered by others
we can empower ourselves
we are not deficient in knowings   needing filling of a lacanian lack
we have 15,000 years of knowings with this land
now we have to know both their and our knowings to live in the world

for us collaboration is communal
we pass the stone or stick around until everyone is of one mind
that is our consensus
choosing to adopt innovation into our traditions   quipu
    wampum   sundance
we are narrators   narratives   voices   interlocutors of our own
    knowings
we can determine for ourselves what our educational needs are
in our tradition the experiential is accorded greater importance than
    the theoretical
lifelong education   for us   has always been contiguous with the
    process of life   and survival
before the coming of churches   residential schools   prisons
before we knew   how   we knew   we knew

Peter Cole, a member of the In-SHUCK-ch Nation of British Columbia, is Assistant Professor of environmental studies, York University, Toronto, Canada. He received his Ph.D. in curriculum theory and implementation at Simon Fraser University, British Columbia. He has published widely in academic and literary journals. His interests include First Nations knowings as legitimate discourse in education, narrativity, poetry, drama, storytelling, manual and outdoor activities, and working toward cultural, spiritual, and environmental renewal.

Patricia O'Riley, of Irish/French/Mohawk heritage, completed her Ph.D. in educational policy and leadership at Ohio State University. She has taught at universities in Aotearoa/New Zealand, the United States of America, and in Canada, and is currently Assistant Professor teaching in the Department of Sociology and Equity studies at the Ontario Institute for Studies in Education, University of Toronto, Canada. Her teaching and research interests include poststructural theory, "traditional" technologies, cultural affirmation and the environment in relation to curriculum.

Perspective on Cole and O'Riley

Peggy R. McConnell

Meditation/Prayer

I am listening, grandfather.
Grandmother, tell me the stories I need to hear.

I close my eyes   take a deep breath.
My lungs expand   push my ribs apart.
Life fills me.
I smell the green pine trees. I hear the mighty river rushing to the Gulf.
I feel the cool black mud shifting under my bare feet.

I remember.

Your words sing in my ears like the voice of the pelican returning to
  the cypress marshes.
Where are the roots I rise from? How do they hold me as I teach?
Whose past am I connected to in this present moment
  in this future moment?
How do I respect the season of planting   the phase of the moon
  the climate of my classroom?
What violence am I performing on understanding when I do not
  hear/smell/feel/remember these?

Since the edge is everywhere   trust your toes.
Metaphors are all I have in spoken language,
  yet metaphors can never equal the life they aspire to represent.
What fruitful mis/understandings can arise when goats meet ghosts?
In the silence is their conversation.
I close my eyes and listen:

Throw your spear where the fish is   not where the water tells you it is.

Yes.

When teachers speak of snowplows in the Delta, what does the Southern
child hear?
What is the lesson if the pictures in the school books never show a
pirogue carrying children to the schoolhouse?
If the only non-white character in the reader is Spot, who is the story
written for?
If all the families in the textbook have both mommies and daddies,
what is said to children who live with only one? with two mommies?
with paw-paw?
In a culture that has twenty words for snow, how can we presume
to tell the Truth in only one English word?

Keep us from trying to teach students about themselves secondhand.
Let our ears open to hear them teach us.

Goats/ghosts are not limited to their field.
Ghosts of all our ancestors free us
help us learn to cross borders
play in the spaces between.
Let our curriculum roam in greener metaphors.

Respect the tributaries, not only what they flow into.
The river will determine its own course we can hold its banks only
so long.
Our architecture cannot hold forever. We will replant our cities at the
river's allowance.

Let me know what I know before I try to know how I know.
Let me listen to what my students know before I tell them what I
think they should know.
Open my ears to the stories of 15,000 years of knowings.

Teach me, Grandfather.
Grandmother, I am listening.

Chapter 5 An Organocentric Curriculum

Problematic: Situational Logic

"'The time has come,' the Walrus said, 'to talk of many things....'" But in reality, the Walrus and the Carpenter said little; their mouths were too full...of oysters. The Walrus and Carpenter were "men of action," not of idle chat. And what about our schools? Are these places of action, of learning, of inquiry? Just what is the *situation* here? For the oysters the situation was dreadful; they were consumed. Looking ahead to Alex Molnar's essay, he holds that our children are being consumed, too, by corporate America. Like the oysters in Lewis Carroll's piece, they are ripe for the plucking and are being plucked.

What is the logic to all this? What is the purpose that schools serve? Drawing on John Dewey, Jayne Fleener proposes that our schools should be more for experiential inquiry than for the consumption of Ramist logic. In fact, presaging John St. Julien (this volume), Fleener hints at the fact that logic itself may be flawed—a point dear to the heart of Lewis Carroll.

So here we have two problematics: (1) the issue of what schools are for, and (2) the issue of whether logic, that on which Peter Ramus built his concept of curriculum, is the best way for learning to occur. Dealing with the latter first, Fleener says that "Dewey's genius lies in grounding organism/environmental systems in *situations*" rather than in the peripheral, even structural, relations associated with those situations. This is a radical statement, one worth much inquiry. In simple terms it means moving the concept of curriculum from the preset structures we have seen operating from Ramus to Tyler, and which we now consider so "natural," to the concept of a dynamic, ongoing, organocentric process. As in complexity theory, the situation itself becomes paramount—with all the myriad forces, histories, assumptions, hopes, and personalities present.

Had the young oysters paid more attention to the situation, they might never have taken that long and final walk down the beach. How are our children and youth assessing the situation of schooling today? In that dynamic interaction between self and society, should we be listening to them more? Is there logic in such a question?

Reference

Carroll, Lewis. (1960). *The annotated Alice: Alice's adventures in wonderland and through the looking glass.* London: Bramhall. (Original work published 1865 and 1871).

Logical Foundations for an Organocentric Curriculum: Dewey's Logic and Complexity Sciences

M. Jayne Fleener

In his introductory essay for this book, Bill Doll provides a historical treatment of the curriculum. By invoking the image of the ghost of Dewey, Doll reminds us that Dewey's vision of the curriculum has gone unrealized. At the same time, Doll's relating curriculum to ghosts further suggests the conundrum of curriculum envisioning. To capture the essence of the ghost, to materialize that which is fundamentally spiritual, limits and alters the essence of the spirit we hope to invoke. Finally, by advocating burying the ghosts of curriculum past and present, Doll advocates invoking a livelier spirit to permeate the postmodern curriculum. But how are we to describe our vision of a spirit-imbued, process-oriented, holistic, organic, ecological, postmodern curriculum without limiting or reducing our ideas to unrecognizable and meaningless dimensions?

My approach to answering this question will involve consideration of the complexity of change. I will relate Dewey's ecological logic as his theory of inquiry (see Dewey, 1938) to process theories of change, including complexity sciences and biological theories of autopoiesis. This approach will involve relating modernist ideas about the curriculum as products with the poststructural perspective of the organocentric curriculum. By employing Dewey's logic, not only will the foundations for an organocentric curriculum be provided but ideas about curriculum change will be explored. If, ultimately, our curriculum envisioning is to count for anything, we must have a means for making changes in our current curriculum realities. Dewey's logic and the complexity of change will offer us a perspective on how we may alter our current perspectives and influence the potential futures of the curriculum.

Dewey's Logic

Dewey's naturalistic conception of logic grounds his approach to meaning and knowledge in the pragmatic realm of inquiry. Following the pragmatism of Peirce, Dewey first conveyed his ideas about the logic of inquiry in his early works "in the context of trying to understand the reciprocal relationships between learning and experience, knowledge and action, and other disparate features of human nature which are ordinarily not considered to be a part of the subject matter of logic" (Burke, 1994, 4). This approach to meaning recognizes the dynamic relationship between perception and knowledge, organism and environment, and challenges traditional views of logic as either deductive or inductive approaches to inquiry. According to Dewey (1938),

> Inquiry is the controlled or directed transformation of an indeterminate situation into one that is so determinate in its constituent distinctions and relations as to convert the elements of the original situation into a unified whole. (104–05)

Key to understanding Dewey's approach to inquiry is his notion of "situation." As summarized by Burke (1994),

> Situations, occurring in the ongoing activities of some given organism/environment system, are instances or episodes (or "fields") of disequilibrium, instability, unbalance, disintegration, disturbance, dysfunction, breakdown, etc.…[Inquiry] should be viewed as an evolutionary variation on what originally appears as an innate impulse of organism/environment systems to transform situations so as to counteract such instabilities. (22)

By grounding inquiry in this perspective of situations, Dewey emphasizes the dynamic and inextricable relationship between an organism and its environment. Rather than viewing either, separately, Dewey views the organism/environment relationship as a system and inquiry as an approach to altering the organism/environment system. Knowledge itself then becomes a complex relationship between organism and environment. As Dewey (1938) explains,

> Whatever else organic life is or is not, it is a process of activity that involves an environment. It is a transaction extending beyond the spatial limits of the organism. An organism does not live *in* an environment; it lives by means of an environment. (25)

> Of human organisms it is especially true that activities carried on for satisfying needs so change the environment that new needs arise which demand still further change in the activities of the organism by which they are satisfied; and so on in a potentially endless chain. (28)

Dewey summarizes his view of inquiry by citing the following features of the "nature of the pattern of inquiry":

> 1. Environmental conditions and energies are inherent in inquiry as a special mode of organic behavior.

2. The structure and course of life-behavior has a definite pattern, spatial and temporal.

a. There is no inquiry that does not involve the making of *some* change in environing conditions.

b. The pattern is serial or sequential.

c. The serially connected processes and operations by means of which a consummatory close is brought into being are, by description, intermediate and instrumental.

d. The basic importance of the serial relation in logic is rooted in the conditions of life itself....Inquiry, in settling the disturbed relation of organism-environment...[i]nstitutes new environing conditions that occasion new problems.

e. From the postulate of naturalistic continuity, with its prime corollary that inquiry is a development out of organic-environmental integration and inter-action, something follows regarding the relation of psychology and logic.... Psychology is itself a special branch of inquiry. In general, it bears the same relation to the theory of logical inquiry that is sustained by physics or chemistry.[1] (33–36)

The potential of an organism/environment system for action, according to Dewey, is related to the current similarity of present environmental conditions with past formation of habits as actions related to the resolution of situational conflict and the flexibility or adaptability of the habits themselves. Habit formation can have a biological base, but, for humans, culture also plays a part. Dewey continues with his summary of the conditions of inquiry by delineating the relationship among culture, inquiry, language, and meaning:

1. To a very large extent the ways in which human beings respond even to physical conditions are influenced by their cultural environment....This modification of organic behavior in and by the cultural environment accounts for, or rather is, the transformation of purely organic behavior into behavior marked by intellectual properties.

2. Language occupies a peculiarly significant place and exercises a peculiarly significant function in the complex that forms the cultural environment.

3. Reference to concord of consequences as the determinant of the meaning of any sound used as a medium of communication shows that there is no such thing as a *mere* word or *mere* symbol....A sound or mark of any physical existence is a part of *language* only in virtue of its operational force; that is, as it functions as a means of evoking different activities....Any word or phrase has the meaning which it has only as a member of a constellation of related meanings....The distinction just drawn between meanings that are determined respectively in fairly direct connection with action in situations that are present or near at hand, and meanings determined for possible use in remote and contingent situations, provides the basis upon which language codes as systems may be differentiated. (42–49)

The organic relationship between organism and environment as described by Dewey and the role this organic relationship plays in habit formation and adaptation place Dewey's logical theory within the realm of complex adaptive systems theory, especially as portrayed in the biological theories of Maturana (1980) and Goodwin (1994). Similarly, his views of language as communication systems anticipate Luhmann's social systems theory (1995) also grounded in complex adaptive systems theory. Before relating Dewey's logic as inquiry to curriculum theory and change, his organic perspective of inquiry will be related to complex adaptive systems theory. By relating complex adaptive systems theory with Dewey's logic, we may achieve a perspective from which to understand Doll's notion of the "creative force" of the curriculum, his five C's, and the potential for curricular change.

Complex Adaptive Systems Theory: Organocentrism, Emergent Structure, and Social Systems

Goodwin's (1994) complex adaptive systems approach to understanding biological evolution focuses on the relational, cooperative, and connected aspects of evolution. His "organocentric" approach emphasizes the coadaptive relationship between an organism and its environment, the inextricable nature of the organismic-environmental complex, and the emergence of form as central to the creative forces driving evolution.

The focus on emergence, relationship, and organization places Goodwin's perspective within the realm of complex adaptive systems. His theory of organocentrism is delineated elsewhere (Fleener, 1999). For our purposes, the relationship between Dewey's logic and the notion of situation provides the foundation for understanding complexity sciences and relating them to a pragmatic field of inquiry in the Deweyan sense. Complexity sciences, in turn, provide a clearer vision of the change process, leading us to a better understanding of potential educational futures.

Similarly, Luhmann's extension of the notions of emergence, organization, and relationship to understand social structures places his social systems theory within this pragmatic realm of inquiry. Luhmann (1986) contends that

> Social systems use communications as their particular mode of autopoietic reproduction. Their elements are communications which are recursively produced and reproduced by a network of communications and cannot exist outside such a network. (174)

By redefining the autopoietic reproductions of social systems as communications, Luhmann's perspective of social organizations as complexes of meaning structures also falls within the realm of pragmatic inquiry as defined by Dewey. From this basis, Luhmann describes the dialectical relationship between the openness and closure of an autopoietic cognizing system. By providing a different perspective of psychic and social systems as separate from biological systems, *consciousness co-emerges with social structure within and through meaning relationships.*

Luhmann's poststructural view of language used to define the characteristics and origins of communication can be interpreted from Dewey's pragmatic approach to language meaning and process. Denying preexisting language structures, communication evolves as a self-determined, self-generating system, which may include but is not reducible to language use or action-constitutive approaches to meaning. The relationship between meaning system and environment is inextricable.

The next point is crucial for both systems theories and Dewey's logic. While arguing for the inextricable relationship between organism and environment, whether we are referring to biological or meaning systems, Dewey's genius lies in grounding organism/environment systems in situations rather than in the complexity of and causal relations associated with their interconnectedness. As Burke shows, Dewey is not forced, as criticized by Russell, to a holism that reduces any organism-environment relationship to include all of reality or even to acknowledge the circularity of requiring the existence of an unknowable reality. As explained by Burke (1994),

> Dewey does not require the boundedness of organism/environment systems but rather the boundedness of situations—localized fields of disturbance within the manifold of processes and interactions which constitute the organism/environment system as a whole. (48)

The boundedness of situations and the organism/environment complex have implications for understanding both the curriculum present and potential curriculum futures. As described by Murphy in the introduction to Mead's (1932) *The Philosophy of the Present*,

> To assume a single determinate past to which every present must wholly conform is to deny emergence altogether....As the condition of the present, the past, then, will vary as the present varies, and new pasts will "arise behind us" in the course of evolution as each present "marks out and in a sense selects what has made its peculiarity possible." (xviii)

Dewey's logic and the notion of situation provide the framework for examining the curricular present from a complex adaptive systems perspective. By viewing the curriculum from this perspective, both ideas about the past and potential for the future take on new meanings and directions.

The Ghosts of Curriculum Present

In our own approach to curriculum inquiry, we need to define the curriculum present in terms of the organism/environment manifold. This complex of relationships can be explored from an organocentric perspective to provide a meaning base for curriculum practice as well as offer suggestions for curriculum futures.

The foundations of modern curriculum are grounded in the meaning system of structuralism. The structural perspective finds meaning in order and hierarchic organization. The goals of a structural system are certainty, predictability, and control. According to a structural approach to meaning, there is a single truth that can be found through objective and impersonal inquiry. From the perspective of modernism, structuralism is the method that affirms the modernist agenda. Within the educational context,

> Structuralism...promises accountability, efficiency, and control as well as order, organization, and certainty. Structuralism is consistent with teaching for objectives, standardized educational assessment, quantitative empirical research, systematic instruction, rationalized bureaucracies, and scientific management. (Cherryholmes, 1988, 30)

Dewey's logic wedded with the complexity sciences, as described above, offers a poststructural perspective of the curriculum as a social meaning system. To put these two different views of the curriculum into perspective, the philosophical difficulties with change will be briefly delineated. Zeno's paradoxes of the Arrow and The Tortoise and the Hare[2] were designed to defend Parmenides's notions that all that was, was permanent, that change was an illusion, and that motion of physical objects through space and time was misleading. The essence of all being was unchanging, permanent, and unyielding. The lessons of Parmenides are paralleled in modern ideas about the curriculum grounded in structural approaches to meaning. These are not ideas of process, change, and context but are those dictated by uniformity, permanence, and stability.

The predominant curriculum paradigm of structuralism determines the kinds of questions, answers, and values that shape the educational landscape and the domain of curriculum inquiry. Educational outcomes are reduced to products or ends rather than recognized as lifelong processes of inquiry and growth. Within the technical production perspective,

> Schooling is assumed to be a process whose main purpose is to promote or produce learning. Students are termed *learners*; objectives are conceived in terms of desirable learning; evaluation of the school's success is targeted almost exclusively on achievement test scores; "educational" goals are distinguished from "noneducational" goals by determining if they can be attributed to learning, "curriculum" is defined...in terms of "intended learner outcomes." Thus, schooling is perceived as a *production system*, in which individual learning outcomes are the primary product. After all, if learning is not what schooling is for, then what could be its purpose? (Posner, 1998, 81–82)

The factory/production model of the curriculum utilizes the same reasoning and makes the same assumptions as the logico-deductive reasoning of axiomatic mathematics. We start with our givens, our goals or ends, and deduce a path to follow in order to reach these ends. Just as in mathematics we can make judgments about the best, most efficient paths and procedures, and, because the curriculum is within a social system that values efficiency, curricular and instructional decisions are often based on controlling time and resources for the most efficient ways to achieve the desired ends.

The problem with logico-deductive systems is that there is no way to generate new knowledge. All knowledge, once the foundations are set, is determined by the primitives and postulates of the system using the agreed-upon rules of reasoning. By so limiting our perspective, we fail to capture the complexity and the evolutionary nature of our envisioned dynamic curriculum. We also end up treating the curriculum as a "thing" rather than as a complex of relationships, meanings, or processes.

Dewey's logic provides an alternative to the logico-deductive reasoning inherent in the production view of the curriculum. His logical theory as delineated above indicates how new meanings can be gleaned from viewing the curriculum present as an organic, self-creative complex or, in Luhmann's terms, as a complex adaptive social meaning system.

An Organocentric Perspective of the Curriculum

As a complex adaptive social meaning system, education can be viewed as a school/society manifold. The intricacies of meaning evolving from the school/society complex define the educational landscapes and potential futures. The adaptive potential of the school/society complex is a function of the ability for the system to accommodate to new situations and conflict.

An important aspect of the school/society complex—and one that affects the adaptive potential of this complex system—is the nature of the curriculum. As discussed above, the modern curriculum was not designed for change, adaptability, or process. Unless an organocentric curriculum is adopted, it is questionable whether the school/society complex will be able to evolve to accommodate the rapid changes occurring in society at this time. The vision of this essay and of this book is to engage in curriculum theorizing that maximizes the creative potential of and evolutionary nature of a dynamic curriculum. Utilizing complex adaptive systems theory, grounded in a Deweyan logic of inquiry, we can re-vision and revise the curriculum to increase the school/society complex potential to adapt to change.

Goodwin (1994) defines his approach to evolutionary biology as organocentric rather than genocentric because of the shift in focus from genetic endowment to the complexity of organism and environment interactions. Similarly, an organocentric curriculum focuses not on the traditional "pieces" of the curriculum, the content, the subjects, the lessons, the structure but on the complex formed by the student/inquiry and school/society interaction. As described here, this perspective is grounded in Dewey's logic as inquiry and in a systems perspective of the complexity of relationships that account for and encourage adaptive potential and system viability.

This organocentric curriculum is not merely a psychological shift in focus from "curriculum as a product" to "curriculum as process." By grounding the organocentric approach in a pragmatic theory of inquiry, a synthesis of the process-product dichotomy can be achieved. The organocentric curriculum is an ecological, not psychological, complex. Built upon Dewey's notion of situation and inquiry, the organocentric curriculum is intimately tied to experience and habits. Habits of inquiry as well as habits formed as a part of the inquiry process become the means for further inquiry and, consequently, affect the ongoing potential for the organism/ environment manifold or, in this case, the student/inquiry and school/ society complexes, to adapt to future conflict. As described by Burke (1994),

> [I]nquiry has to be understood not simply as cognitive problem solving but, more generally, in terms of an adaptive stabilization propensity of organism/ environment systems. Dewey's definition of inquiry, strictly speaking, presupposes no mind or cognitive capacities in particular, but rather it posits a fundamentally nonmentalistic, cognitive intentionality, in the form of an innate motivation to avoid insecurity. Dewey's theory of inquiry is at its foundations a general theory of how such systems counteract disintegrating influences and thereby maintain themselves. (140–41)

By building his logic on this view of inquiry, Dewey's logic serves as the naturalistic basis for complex adaptive systems. Minds and knowledge have their basis in such inquiry, thus avoiding the problem of transcendence or dualism. The curriculum, similarly, evolves naturalistically, both as a feature of the school/society complex as well as the child/inquiry manifold. The false dichotomy between a standardized curriculum for all and an individualized curriculum for each student is resolved by an organocentric curriculum grounded in naturalistic inquiry. This is not more difficult to conceptualize than to understand the complexity of a single cell as an autopoietic structure as well as part of an organizational complex of cells which itself has autopoietic characteristics (see Fleener and Pourdavood, 1997). The classroom as a complex adaptive system is a social system with autopoietic characteristics. Individuals within that system of classroom interactions and communications similarly are complex adaptive systems. The dialectic between individual and environment and social structure and the individuals within it defines meaning structures from which the curriculum becomes a powerful way of understanding and building relationships with each other and our environment.

An organocentric curriculum as an organism/environment complex maintains Doll's five characteristics of a postmodern curriculum as: *currere*, complexity, cosmology, conversation, and community. As *currere*, the seamless relationship between child/inquiry and school/society is defined as the organism/environment complex. The evolutionary nature of the complex resulting from perturbation or conflict as situation is a part of the ongoing dynamics of the system.

Increased viability and adaptability are important for the maintenance of organism/environment relations. The complexity sciences have shown over and over that increased complexity is intimately related to increased viability and adaptive behavior. The organocentric curriculum is grounded in the complexity sciences, as described here, and maintains this feature of Doll's postmodern curriculum.

Organocentric curriculum as cosmology emphasizes the relational aspects of the school/society and child/inquiry manifolds. Built into these complexes is process as the system evolves and adapts. Creative emergence similarly is a function of the organocentric perspective that infuses the organismic/environmental complex with the ability not only to maintain system balance but also to adapt to perturbations in creative and not-yet-predictable ways. In this way, the unfolding of the curriculum, as with the unfolding of the cosmos, entails ever-increasing and emergent qualities.

Similarly, as a social system, school/society and child/inquiry manifolds are communication systems. The organocentric curriculum as conversation fundamentally includes the social influences of language and meaning.

Finally, the organocentric curriculum entails community as the school/society and child/inquiry manifolds are themselves relational aspects of complex interactions among individuals and meaning structures. As Goodwin (1994) argues, organocentric biological relations are driven by co-operation not competition, and evolutionary viability is a function not of resource dominance but resource sharing. Within the nested hierarchy of community relations, from cellular and organismic to societal and cosmological, cooperation and care for others becomes a driving force in maintaining organism/environment systemic viability and ongoing growth.

Goodwin's vision of the morphogenesis of the developing fetus and Luhmann's conception of social autopoiesis through systems of communication support and provide models for grounding the curriculum in a dynamic model of systems based on a Deweyan logic as inquiry. The dance of the classroom is simultaneously and constructively orchestrating and synergistically affecting relationships and supporting discourse, so environmental complexity both supports and perturbs learners as they engage in meaningful activity.

The ghost of Dewey, the challenge of Doll, includes a re-visioning of the curriculum that eliminates a deterministic, preplanned, one-size-fits-all view of the curriculum. Building both on the vision of Dewey and the findings and theories of the complexity sciences, an organocentric curriculum becomes the quantum of , 161, eliminating the false dichotomies of process and product, society and child, individualization and socialization, work and knowledge-for-its-own-sake, and predict-ability and emergence.

Notes

[1] This aspect of Dewey's logic has initiated considerable debate including Russell's claim that Dewey's logic is entrapped by its own psychologism. Burke (1994) does a good job delineating this controversy and defending Dewey's logic against this and other challenges raised by Russell.

[2] The paradox of The Arrow is as follows: If you shoot an arrow, we can imagine that at any instant of time, the arrow is at rest. As we divide up the time it takes the arrow to traverse the skies into infinitely small times, we can see that for an infinite number of instances, the arrow is at rest. How then is motion possible? The Tortoise and the Hare paradox is the better known of the two paradoxes. In a race between a Tortoise and a Hare, the Tortoise is given a head start. After a certain length of time, the Hare starts after the Tortoise. In some amount of time, the Hare travels half the distance between where he began and where the Tortoise was when he began. In that time, however, the Tortoise traveled some amount further. If in an infinite number of

instances, the Hare can only travel half the distance between himself and where the Tortoise was at any given instance, how can the Hare ever catch up?

References

Burke, T. (1994). *Dewey's new logic: A reply to Russell.* Chicago: University of Chicago Press.

Cherryholmes, C. H. (1988). *Power and criticism: Poststructural investigations in education.* New York: Teachers College Press.

Dewey, J. (1938). *Logic: The theory of inquiry.* New York: Holt.

Fleener, M. J. (1999). Toward a poststructural mathematics curriculum: Expanding discursive possibilities. *Journal of Curriculum Theorizing, 15*(2), Summer 1999, 89–105.

Fleener, M. J., and R. G. Pourdavood. (1997). Autopoiesis and change: Ontological considerations and implications of school reform. Based on a paper presented at the Annual Meeting of the American Educational Research Association, March 24–28, Chicago, IL.

Goodwin, B. (1994). *How the leopard changed its spots: The evolution of complexity.* New York: Scribner's.

Luhmann, N. (1986). The autopoiesis of social systems. In F. Geyner and J. van der Zouwen (Eds.), *Sociocybernetic paradoxes.* London: Sage.

______. (1995). *Social systems.* John Bednarz (Trans.). Stanford, CA: Stanford Univer-sity Press.

Maturana, H. R. (1980). Introduction and biology of cognition. In H. R. Maturana and F. J. Varela (pages xi–xxx and 5–58). Boston, MA: Reidel.

Mead, G. H. (1932). *The philosophy of the present.* Chicago: Open Court.

Posner, G. F. (1998). Models of curriculum planning. In L. E. Beyer and M. W. Apple (Eds.), *The curriculum: Problems, politics, and possibilities* (2nd edition) (pages 79–100). Albany: State University of New York Press.

M. Jayne Fleener is the Associate Dean for Research and Graduate Studies in the College of Education at the University of Oklahoma. She is also the mathematics education chair and teaches graduate and undergraduate courses in mathematics education, technology, research, and curriculum theory. She received her M.A. in philosophy from the University of North Carolina and her B.A. in philosophy from Indiana University. She previously taught mathematics and computer science in both inner-city and college preparatory high schools. Her research and scholarly interests include the use of technology in education, in-service and pre-service teacher professional development, curriculum development and theory, and educational futures.

Perspective on Fleener

Karen E. Sullivan

> To the extent that there is a new interest in public education, it is largely focused on aligning basic education with the needs of the job market. This apparently practical approach is illusory. Concentration on technology—computers for example—will simply produce obsolete graduates. The problem is not to teach skills in a galloping technology, but to teach students to think and to give them the tools of thought so that they can react to the myriad changes, including technological, that will inevitably face them over the next decades. (J. R. Saul, 1955, 66)

Canadian writer and philosopher John Ralston Saul uttered this dire warning in November 1995 during the Massey Lectures, broadcast on CBC Radio and published that same year in his book *The Unconscious Civilization*. In so doing, he helped to bring to the attention of the general public the desperate situation facing our education system and, by extension, Western society as a whole. With the increasingly rapid pace of change in our world comes the need to transform our education system, to move from one anchored in the restrictive shackles of structuralism, which vainly professes an ability to predict the needs of an unpredictable future, to an adaptive, flexible, and creative entity that flows with the emerging society.

Fleener identifies the nature of the curriculum as a key aspect of the school/society manifold that can ultimately and powerfully affect the adaptive potential of the system. Her vision is that of an organocentric curriculum, one focused on the complexities of interaction, grounded in the pragmatic realm of inquiry, and well suited to adaptability in the face of future conflict. Within this vision, one can see a network of learners in which student-teacher and student-student interactions are predominantly characterized by shared inquiry around questions of genuine interest growing from students' own natural curiosities about their world. Although general goals might still be suggested by others, the route traveled by students and the time to be spent along the way would not be strictly dictated from beyond the classroom. The teacher, although certainly responsible for a generative environment and rigorous expectations, would no longer play the simple part of leader along a predetermined path. Instead, the teacher's role would be that of model, guide, and partner in learning. Specific subject expertise, although still valuable, might conceivably be of secondary importance to the skills of questioning, research, analysis, identifying relationships, and reflective practice. The excellent teacher would become the one able to both model these skills effectively and use them enthusiastically as a partner in exploration while ensuring rigor throughout the process. Clearly, such envisioning frees us to explore realms far removed from those in which we exist today. Yet it has little meaning unless the roots of the necessary transformation are able to take hold in the soil of our present curriculum reality. And so the question arises: is it possible within our current, factory-modeled, product-oriented curriculum, characterized as it is by stringent timelines, prescriptive content, specified learning outcomes, and standardized assessment, to sow and begin to nurture the seeds of Fleener's vision?

In striving to address this, it will be wise to remember that we are not searching for the means to make a sudden dramatic leap into an organocentric curriculum. Any attempt at such a rapid overhaul would certainly stand in stark contradiction to a philosophy of an emergent curriculum and make us as guilty as our predecessors of believing that we can predict the needs of an unpredictable future. Further, we must be conscious of our histories and thus aware that we are simply not able to bring forth such a radical shift even if it were prudent. As much as we will be the architects of a new system, we are the products of the old. Like the mannerisms of our parents that have mysteriously manifested themselves in us, so, too, have the habits of the existing educational culture become the traditions of today's educators. We may strive to overcome them, but to rid ourselves of them completely is not truly within our power. What we seek is to be the agents of change, to begin a transformation that will alter the culture of the system and formulate in our students habits different from our own, which will enable them to further this transformation.

What do these seeds of Fleener's vision look like in my classroom? They are the small but meaningful perturbations in the habits of my students that develop as we work together to expand their views of the meanings and structures of learning beyond traditional boundaries. They arise as a result of discourse as we occasionally stray from our dictated path to engage in discussions of various philosophical, sociological, epistemological, and cosmological issues. However, it is in many ways more important to me that such *desirable disturbances* in my students' views come forth as we work within the traditional, restrictive, and content-laden guidelines governing the university-preparation-level mathematics courses I teach.

A specific example of how such disturbances can be encouraged come from my Finite mathematics class, in which students are required to complete what they see as a nontraditional semester-long project. Students select a variety of magazine or journal articles and Internet sites relating to topics of personal interest and explore, through written responses, the interconnectedness of their interests to the world of mathematics. In addition, they submit reflective journals through which they investigate their personal mathematical histories and their views about mathematics, the connections between mathematics and other areas, and the project in general. Initially students are quite reluctant to proceed; however, after exploring the world of fractal geometry in search of an understanding of the images on the poster in our room, after studying the intriguing question of connections between earthquakes and volcanic eruptions, after delving into philosophical and mathematical views of infinity and the existence of God, after enhancing their understanding of geometry through the study of the geometry of ancient warfare or the mechanics of Leonardo da Vinci, students' opinions change. They realize that their explorations of topics of interest to them are valued. They respect the fact that, although I am far from being an expert in many of the areas into which they choose to delve, I am genuinely interested in their work, willing to share in the journey with them, and able to challenge and critique their understandings as well as suggest further avenues of inquiry. Further, many express great appreciation for my encouragement and the opportunity to reflect on their experiences and to enter into a discourse about their learning.

Ultimately, if I, as a classroom teacher, can encourage and help my students to question the habits of the culture of education of which we are all products, then I am sowing the seeds of an adaptive, emergent curriculum and of an education system equal to whatever challenges may emerge.

Reference

Saul, J. R. (1995). *The unconscious civilization.* Concord, Ontario, Canada: House of Anansi.

Karen E. Sullivan is a high school mathematics teacher in Ontario, Canada. She holds a M.Ed. degree in mathematics education from the University of Victoria, British Columbia. In addition to having taught all grades and levels of secondary mathematics, she is actively involved in curriculum writing and staff development projects.

Chapter 6 The Long Arm(s) of Globalization

Problematic: Whose "Other" Are We?

Do we in the West—Europe and particularly the United States—secretly and surreptitiously give allegiance to the notion that "Might makes Right"? Although we may voice the maxim that "Might does not make Right!" our actions and practices often belie our statements. Do we, in actuality, practice the very doctrine we preach against? Do we reject verbally that which we practice politically? Why are we surprised when "others" want some of that might as their right? And why do we feel indignant when "others" believe we use cultural diversity as a guise to keep others "other"?

Noel Gough raises these issues in a poignant way as he talks of the "long [global] arm(s)" of Western logic, reason, knowledge, and power. These arms tie and bind as well as support and comfort. Remember that René Descartes's seminal *Discourse on Method* (1950/1637) was not just a discourse on method. It was a device, *the* device, for "rightly conducting reason" and "seeking truth." Is it, therefore, one magical (Western) method for all to use? Do we—Europeans and North Americans—want all to succumb to our beliefs?

Such questions raise other questions, namely, "Whose knowledge is of most worth?" Herbert Spencer's answer to this question (his vision) was emphatic: Western "science," for this knowledge alone is "the best preparation for all...orders of activity" (1929/1859, 85). The West's scientific knowledge and its procedures have indeed been great. Both John Dewey and Alfred North Whitehead saw scientific experimentation as leading us out of the confusion of the medieval ages. However, to say that our Western knowledges and procedures—male, rational, scientific—are the "best preparation for all…orders of activity" is a most universalizing, dogmatic, and arrogant statement as Sandra Harding (1991), among others, has pointed out.

References

Descartes, R. (1950). *Discourse on method.* L. J. LaFleur (Trans.). New York: Liberal Arts. (Original work published 1637).

Harding, S. (1991). *Whose science? Whose knowledge? Thinking from women's lives.* Ithaca: Cornell University Press.

Spencer, H. O. (1929). What knowledge is of most worth? In Herbert O. Spencer (Ed.), *Education: Intellectual, moral, physical* (pages 1–87). New York: Appleton. (Original work published 1859).

The Long Arm(s) of Globalization: Transnational Imaginaries in Curriculum Work

Noel Gough

> ...the international arm I think is looking for its own place, its own figure, something which would go beyond the current stage of inter-nationality, perhaps beyond citizenship, beyond belonging to a state, to a given nation state. And I think that in the world today a number of human beings are secretly aligned in their suffering against the hegemonic powers which protect what is called the "new order." (Jacques Derrida, 1997, 12)

As soon as I read Derrida's curious but evocative phrase, "the international arm," I had a vision of a giant spectral human arm reaching around the globe. At the same time, Derrida's words triggered a vivid memory of a science fiction story that I had read more than twenty years ago, and I realized that this story had given my mental image of "the international" arm its immediacy and substance. In some versions of curriculum inquiry, my vision might be regarded as too trivial or too idiosyncratic to be worthy of serious attention. But this book is concerned, at least in part, with exploring and explicating the contingencies and dispositions that produce such visions, and I therefore invite readers to follow me as I trace, albeit briefly, the connections between a story I read in the mid-1970s and my much more recent reflections on the implications of globalization for curriculum.

William Doll begins his chapter on "Ghosts and the Curriculum" (this volume) with a reference to Derrida's (1994) thoughts, as revealed in *Specters of Marx*, on how specters of the past lead us into the future. In this same work, Derrida also calls for a different form of internationalism from the *Internationale* of the Marxist tradition.[1] Responding more recently to a question about this *nouvelle Internationale,* Derrida (1997) argues that "we have to deconstruct the foundations of...international law," not in order to destroy international organizations such as the United Nations, but as a step towards rethinking their philosophical underpinnings: "international law, which is a good thing, nevertheless is still rooted in its mission, in its action, in its languages, in a Western concept of philosophy, a Western concept of the state and of sovereignty, and this is a limit" (12). He argues that another limit to internationalism is that international organizations are, in fact,

> governed by a number of particular states which provide these international organizations with the means to intervene, with the military power, with the economic power, and, of course, the United States plays a major role in this.... So the universality of international law is in fact in the hands of a number of powerful, rich states and has to change, and it is in the process of changing, through a number of disasters, crises, economic inequalities, injustices, and so on. (12)

This passage, like the one that opens this chapter, clearly resonates with events such as the riots and protests that disrupted the World Trade Organization talks in Seattle in December 1999, events that can be understood as manifestations of a broader public questioning of the desirability of powerful, rich states like the United States enforcing economic globalization as if it were "international law."

In my own recent studies of globalization as an aspect of curriculum work (see, for example, Gough, 1999; 2000), I have followed Rob Wilson and Wimal Dissanayake (1996) in conceptualizing globalization as a "transnational imaginary"; that is,

> the *as-yet-unfigured* horizon of contemporary cultural production by which national spaces/identities of political allegiance and economic regulation are being undone and imagined communities of modernity are being reshaped at the macropolitical (global) and micropolitical (cultural) levels of everyday existence. (6, emphasis in original)

Globalization might be an "imaginary" but, clearly, it has material effects. Derrida's phrase, "the international arm," suggests that this "imaginary" can take an embodied form, at least metaphorically. As noted here, when I read Derrida's words, I visualized "the international arm" in a very specific way for reasons that I will now attempt to elucidate.

The Long ARM of Gil Hamilton is a collection of three connected novelettes by Larry Niven (1976). The stories are set in the twenty-second century and, as the title indicates, focus on the adventures of Gil Hamilton, an operative for ARM[2] (an elite global police force) who specializes in bringing organleggers (murderous dealers in illicit transplants) to justice. Before joining ARM, Hamilton's right arm is destroyed by an explosion in an asteroid mine. He refuses a bionic limb, preferring to wait several years for a legal transplant. During this period he discovers his latent psychic powers:

> An amputee never entirely loses what he's lost. My missing fingers itched. I moved to keep from barking my missing elbow on sharp corners. I reached for things, then swore when they didn't come.... There had been a girl....One night I was at her place waiting for her to get dressed—a dinner date—and I'd happened to see a nail file she'd left on a table. I'd picked it up. I'd almost tried to file my nails, but remembered in time. Irritated, I had tossed the file back on the table—and missed.
>
> Like an idiot I'd tried to catch it with my right hand.
>
> And I'd caught it.
>
> I'd never suspected myself of having psychic powers. You have to be in the right frame of mind to use a psi power. But who had ever had a better opportunity than I did that night, with a whole section of my brain tuned to the nerves and muscles of my right arm, and no right arm?
>
> I'd held the nail file in my imaginary hand. I'd felt it, just as I'd felt my missing fingernails getting too long. I had run my thumb along the rough steel surface; I had turned the file in my fingers. Telekinesis for lift, *esper* for touch. (Niven, 1976, 16–17)

For some purposes, Hamilton's "imaginary" arm is more useful than a real one. Working on asteroids without atmosphere, he can reach through his space suit to perform tasks that require manual dexterity without losing pressure. After joining ARM, he uses his imaginary arm to thwart criminals and to save his own life—for example, on one occasion, Hamilton reaches into a villain's chest and squeezes his heart until it stops.

Through Derrida's invocation of "the international arm," I made a "visionary" connection between Gil Hamilton's imaginary arm and the transnational imaginary of globalization. This vision appeared to me unbidden and was quickly modified as I thought more deliberately about its generative possibilities. For example, I realized immediately that global-ization cannot be a unitary object and that there must therefore be more than one "long (transnational, imaginary) arm of globalization." I began to visualize several spectral arms reaching around the globe, and, as I played with the internal logic of this vision, I imagined the arms beginning in specific sites (especially from the United States and other economically powerful nations) and reaching towards others.

I could say more about my vision, but I do not want to exaggerate its meaningfulness or construct an elaborate rationalization for it. The more important issue for curriculum inquiry is whether we should respect such visions when they arise and make room for them in our thinking. How can seizing upon a tenuous metaphorical connection between a science fictional character's imaginary arm and Derrida's thoughts on internationalization serve any useful or morally defensible purpose? One way of responding to this question is to compare my vision with others. Thus, I will now outline a more conventional representation of globalization taken from recent coverage in the news media.

One World, Ready or Not?

On Friday July 2, 1999, my daily newspaper of choice, *The Age*, announced that "a special *Age* series on globalisation" would begin on the following Monday. Some aspects of the way this announcement was presented focused my attention on questions about the significance of *location*—and of the sense in which we envision people and knowledges to be located somewhere (rather than everywhere or anywhere)—in our work as curriculum scholars.

Apart from identifying itself as an "*Age* series," the announcement lacked almost any reference to the locality in which the series was to be published and in which the vast majority of the newspaper's readers are located, namely, Melbourne, Australia. The series title, "One world, ready or not?," appears to have been appropriated (without acknowledgment) from elsewhere, namely from a book of the same title by the U.S. author William Greider (1997). The main graphic element of the logo for the series was a globe viewed from a position above the equatorial plane with Australia at bottom center (Australia's central —albeit subsidiary—position in this image is the only clue to location other than the newspaper's name). Europe, Asia, and North America are clearly visible in this Northern Hemispheric perspective of the world, while the east coast of Africa is just discernible and South America and Antarctica are out of sight. One reading of this image is that the question of being "ready or not" to belong to "one world" is most pertinent to nations that are visible from this standpoint.

A second aspect of the announcement that reinforced its dislocation from the site in which it was produced was that it was not written by a member of *The Age*'s editorial staff or a local journalist but was extracted from *The Lexus and the Olive Tree* by Thomas L. Friedman (1999a), the foreign affairs correspondent for *The New York Times*. Although I did not doubt that the subsequent inclusion of articles by journalists from other countries would be appropriate in such a series, I expected an announcement of "a special *Age* series on globalization" to specify the relevance of such a series to Australian readers and to the phenomenal world(s) they inhabit. But Friedman's (1999b) article, with its bold subheading "America's defining challenge is to prevent globalization from becoming a monster," makes no attempt to do this even from the standpoint of U.S. triumphalism that marks his book. For example, in *The Age*'s excerpt, he is forthright in asserting that "sustaining globalization is America's overarching national interest" and that the United States is "the country that benefits most from global economic integration" (17), but he offers no evidence or argument for other countries sharing such benefits or interests.

Friedman's article recycles many familiar but extravagant claims about the significance of globalization and its consequences in various arenas of social life, which he embellishes with metaphorical exaggerations of the differences between "the new international system called globalization" and the "Cold War system" that it replaces. For example, "The symbol of the Cold War system was a wall, which divided everyone. The symbol of the globalization system is the World Wide Web, which unites everyone." In both uses of the term, "everyone" is a monumental overstatement. There are several more of these glib contrasts, such as "The defining document of the Cold War system was The Treaty. The defining document of the globalization system is The Deal." But, curiously, Friedman's efforts to distinguish sharply between the two systems are subverted by the article's main title: "Our World Confronts New Rules of Engagement." Surely militaristic terms such as "confronts" and "rules of engagement" are relics of the Cold War era? Similarly, Friedman's constant resort to binary oppositions perpetuates the us-versus-them reasoning of Cold War politics and seems an inappropriately modernist register of difference in a postmodernist era of multiple and shifting perspectives and positions. In this sense, Friedman's article seems not only to be out of place but also, as it were, out of time.

Finally, so that readers might better understand the positions from which most of these thoughts were generated, I should point out that on Friday, July 2, 1999 I was not reading *The Age* as a newsprint broadsheet in Melbourne, Australia, but was visiting its Web site via a computer terminal in Durban, South Africa. My use of the plural, *positions*, here is deliberate, because reading the series announcement on the internet focused my attention on the ways in which this medium multiplies, and simultaneously destabilizes, the standpoints available to us. As McKenzie Wark (1994) writes:

> We live every day in a familiar terrain: the place where we sleep, the place where we work, the place where we hang out when not working or sleeping. From these places we acquire a geography of experience.... We live every day also in another terrain, equally familiar: the terrain created by the television, the telephone, the telecommunications networks crisscrossing the globe....This is our "virtual geography," the experience of which doubles, troubles, and generally permeates our experience of the space we experience firsthand. (vii)

In this instance, I was reminded that I still call Melbourne home and that it was where my hard copy of *The Age* would have been delivered to my door several hours previously (this sense of local positioning was not diminished by my temporary absence—if anything it was reinforced by Australia's emphatic presence at bottom center of the globe in the logo). I was also reminded that the place in which I was then located was literally and figuratively marginalized in the world as visualized in the series announcement (Durban is on the east coast of South Africa, and its position was thus barely visible on the logo's globe). But both of these senses of local positioning were destabilized by the very act of accessing the internet—a medium whose potential and implicit audience is international. I *could* have been *anywhere*—and so could *The Age* in its internet form. My experience thus exemplifies the ways in which the "virtual geography" of global media networks may be reshaping our sense of place, a transition that is captured by Wark's (1994) aphorisms: "We no longer have roots, we have aerials....We no longer have origins, we have terminals" (xiv).

I must note in passing that my own "roots" and "origins" were dislocated in a more trivial way on my flight to South Africa: My preferred airline had joined an alliance with four other international carriers, and I was no longer welcomed on board as a "Qantas frequent flyer," as I had previously been, but as a "One-world™ customer." To suggest that a transnational alliance of airlines based in five locations (Australia, Britain, Canada, Hong Kong, and the United States) can be identified with the whole world (as "Oneworld" implies) is an exaggeration similar to Friedman's assertion, that "the World Wide Web...unites everyone."

My concern as a curriculum scholar is that such versions, visions, and manifestations of globalization invite us to tolerate a type of relativism in which *location*—in all of its moral, metaphorical, mythic and material senses—is undervalued. Despite accusations to the contrary, many of us who have taken post-modernist and/or poststructuralist turns in our scholarly work are as deeply suspicious of relativism as we are of the universalizing and totalizing claims made in the name of modernist science. I prefer to follow feminist scholars like Donna Haraway (1991) and Sandra Harding (1993), who use the vocabularies and repertoires of poststructuralism and deconstruction in the service of "situated knowl-edges" that deliberately and responsibly privilege our partial perspectives —who we are and where we stand. As Haraway (1991) writes:

> Relativism is a way of being nowhere while claiming to be everywhere equally. The 'equality' of positioning is a denial of responsibility and critical enquiry. Relativism is the perfect mirror twin of totalization in the ideologies of objectivity; both deny the stakes in location, embodiment, and partial perspective....Relativism and totalization are both 'god-tricks' promising vision from everywhere and nowhere equally. (191)

Perhaps globalization, too, is another "god-trick," a transcendental ontological and epistemological fantasy of being and knowing "every-where and nowhere equally?" Certainly, there is something about the revelatory fervor of globalists like Friedman (1999b), who envisions globalization as "the real bridge to the future"—which, of course, "the U.S. will own" (17)—that reminds me of the rhetorical strategies deployed by televangelists and millenarian cults (not that globalization is itself a product of millenarianism, but its popularization at the millennial moment might have added to its momentum).

I interpret my vision of the long arms of globalization as a deconstruction of "One World" fantasies. Privileging this vision is one way to take up Derrida's (1994) challenge to "see, situate, [and] identify" the specters of the past that lead us into the future and to "possess" them rather than letting ourselves be possessed by them (132). Allowing the "international arm" of globalization to be infused by my memory of Gil Hamilton's imaginary arm can be understood as a move to possess the specter of globalization. In contrast to Friedman's portrayal of globalization as an inexorable progression towards a universal system over which we have little control (as if it were an economic equivalent of global warming), my vision of globalization draws attention to the specificity and agency of the "bodies" from which the "arms" extend. Thus, while my vision of long spectral arms might be fanciful, it also works to demystify the elements and processes of globalization, to bring them within the ambit of human decision and action.

The Long Arms of (Some) Local Knowledge Systems

Curriculum inquiry is one specific form of contemporary cultural production through which the transnational imaginary of globalization is being envisioned, negotiated, and materialized. For example, the current guide for authors intending to submit manuscripts to the *Journal of Curriculum Studies* includes the following advice:

> All authors are asked to take account of the diverse audience of *Journal of Curriculum Studies*. Clearly explain or avoid the use of terms that might be meaningful only to a local or national audience. However, note also that *Journal of Curriculum Studies* does not aspire to be international in the ways that McDonald's restaurants or Hilton Hotels are "international"; we much prefer papers that, where appropriate, reflect the particularities of each higher education system.[3]

This advice expresses a view of global/local relations that seems to resist the cultural imperialism and colonization that results in a school science textbook in Zimbabwe being almost indistinguishable from one used in Australia. In terms of my vision of globalization, the long arms of Western knowledge production systems have extended the West's reach into other cultural sites but all too often have the effect of suppressing or erasing other local knowledge traditions. How can different local knowledge traditions be sustained transnationally while escaping the forms of cultural homogenization for which McDonalds restaurants and Hilton Hotels are emblematic?

I have written at greater length elsewhere about the effects of globalization on local knowledge production (see Gough, 1998, 1999, 2000), and it will suffice here to note that I follow David Turnbull (1993, 1997) in adopting a position that understands all knowledge traditions as being spatial in that they link people, sites, and skills. Turnbull's approach is to recognize that all knowledge systems (including Western science) are sets of local practices so that it becomes possible to "decenter" them and develop a framework within which different knowledge traditions can equitably be compared rather than absorbed into an imperialist archive.

Through a number of detailed case studies, Turnbull (1997) demonstrates that such achievements as Gothic cathedral construction, Polynesian navigation, modern cartography, Indonesian rice farming *and* modern Western science are, in each case, better understood performatively —as diverse assemblages of social and technical practices—than as results of any internal epistemological features to which "universal" validity can be ascribed. The purpose of Turnbull's emphasis on analyzing knowledge systems comparatively in terms of spatiality and performance is to find ways in which diverse knowledge traditions can coexist rather than one displacing others. He argues that nourishing such diversity is dependent on the creation of "a third space, an interstitial space" in which local knowledge traditions can be "reframed, decentred and the social organisation of trust can be negotiated." The production of such a space is, in Turnbull's view, "crucially dependent" on "the reinclusion of the performative side of knowledge":

> Knowledge, in so far as it is portrayed as essentially a form of representation, will tend towards universal homogenous information at the expense of local knowledge traditions. If knowledge is recognised as both representational and performative it will be possible to create a space in which knowledge traditions can be performed together. (560–61)

Turnbull is suspicious of importing and exporting representations that are disconnected from the performative work that was needed to generate them, and I share his suspicions. For example, when I began working as a teacher educator in Australia in the early 1970s, much of the "curriculum theory" we taught at that time was imported from the United States. It included an emphasis on behavioral objectives for instruction and their classification by reference to Benjamin Bloom's taxonomy of educational objectives. Many of my colleagues and students were mystified by the hyperrationality of planning curriculum by reference to a register of behavioral objectives, which, in retrospect, might be explained by our lack of a "performative history" of objectives-based curriculum work. We had not experienced working with objectives as U.S. teachers had, first in the 1920s (in the wake of Franklin Bobbitt's work) and, later, in the 1950s (under the influence of the Tyler rationale). Nevertheless, many Australian teacher educators accepted the Tyler rationale, behavioral objectives, and Bloom's taxonomy as representations of a universal rationality. They persevered in "performing" them despite being received with bemused incredulity by many students and classroom teachers, who interpreted the teacher educators' persistence as further evidence of the chasm between theory and practice.

Turnbull's analysis suggests to me that resistance to the homogenizing effects of globalization and internationalization in the field of curriculum studies might be facilitated by emphasizing the performative rather than the representational aspects of curriculum inquiry. The internationalization of curriculum studies might then be understood not so much in terms of translating local representations of curriculum into a universalized discourse but, rather, as a process of creating transnational spaces in which local knowledge traditions in curriculum inquiry can be performed together.

The need to vigorously and rigorously recuperate local knowledge systems, in both their performative and representational idioms, has been amplified for me by some recent experiences of doing curriculum work in southern Africa, where many local knowledge traditions have been rendered invisible by the long arms of universalizing imperialist discourses and practices. For example, in countries such as Zimbabwe and Malawi, the concept of a "good education" for the vast majority of African students, most of whom live in rural subsistence settlements, is equated with *failing* Cambridge University O-level examinations written in English. The absurdity of this situation to Western eyes is captured by Doris Lessing's (1992) recollections of visiting a rural school in Zimbabwe in 1988 during which one member of her party lamented the country's unserviceable infrastructure and the lack of people skilled in —or being trained to be skilled in—mending broken valves, taps, or pipes:

> The trouble is that all these poor bloody kids, in all the schools of Zimbabwe, have decided that only a literary education is worth having. Where do you find the ultimate bastion of respect for the Humanities? Not in Thatcher's Britain! No, in the bush, where generations of black kids have decided they are too good to be engineers and electricians, and are taking O-levels in English which they mostly fail....I was in an office in Harare. An American Aid worker was arguing that the education being given to the children was inappropriate, what was the point of teaching them the British syllabus, with books suitable for Europe? What was needed was a good basic technical education. A black woman who was waiting her turn turned furiously on her. She said, "I see you whites are still just the same. You don't want our children to have a real education. Oh no, that's for your children. We want a good education for our children, just the same as yours." (200–01)

Thinking about this incident in terms of represented and performed curriculum is illuminating. The apparent point of disagreement between the American Aid worker and the black woman is that the curriculum in question, "the British syllabus, with books suitable for Europe," represents "a real education...a good education" in *both* Western and Zimbabwean contexts for the black woman. But it is "good" in only *one* context (Western) for the Aid worker. We could also say that the black woman envisions "a good education" transnationally whereas the Aid worker imagines it locally. Many of us might want to argue that the represented curriculum was as "inappropriate" in Thatcher's Britain as it still is in Mugabe's Zimbabwe. But both women might be able to agree that this British syllabus produces, in Turnbull's terms, a performative equivalence, especially if it can be shown that (say) exhibiting perfect recall of the key events and protagonists in the English Reformation is as necessary a condition for winning the class struggle in postcolonial Zimbabwe as it is in postindustrial Britain. As Lessing (1992) writes, "In Zimbabwe today [1988] you need five [O-level] passes to get a job. With three you can train to be a nurse" (212). A key problem here is the instrumental role of a curriculum in effecting social stratification—a problem which might be occluded by focusing on issues of superficial "appropriateness" or "relevance." If the performative function of the curriculum is, in effect, to make both black kids and white kids jump through white hoops, merely painting one set of hoops black does not resolve the problem (if we persist with this metaphor, we also need to ask: Who is doing the painting and with what authority?).

One of the questions raised by Lessing's vignette is: Who is deploying a transnational imaginary here? Stereotypically we might expect the American Aid worker to have a more "global" or "international" perspective, but it is the black woman who seems to be assuming (or desiring) English O-levels to be part of the global economy of "a good education" and the Aid worker who wants to privilege (or "protect" in economic terms) local knowledge. The difficulty I see for the field of curriculum studies is that many of our intellectual resources are presently geared towards defending the Aid worker's position rather than responding constructively and, in a literal sense, *hopefully,* to the black woman.

The internationalization of curriculum studies demands more ingenuity, artistry, diplomacy, and vision of curriculum scholars than simply fixing the commercial exchange value of Cambridge O-levels in a global economy of knowledge. We cannot ignore the long arms of globalization, but we can develop counterpractices to the locatable interests they serve by insisting that our own knowledge claims also are locatable, and can be called to account by those whose race, gender, class, nationality, language, religion or other "otherness" has placed them in the world's subjugated spaces. I imagine that curriculum scholars could be part of the reconfigured "international arm" of which Derrida (1997) speaks, but that they cannot invent it alone. Rather, it would be constituted by all those to whom he refers as "secretly aligned in their suffering against the hegemonic powers which protect what is called the "new order" (12)—an arm forged by the play of differences among those who have been dis-armed by their difference. I would like to see that.

Notes

[1] See also *The Other Heading* where Derrida (1992) discusses problems of internationalism and the "new world order" with particular reference to Europe.

[2] ARM is an acronym for the Amalgamation of Regional Militias.

[3] http://www.tandf.co.uk/authors/cusauth.html

References

Derrida, Jacques. (1992). *The other heading: Reflections on today's Europe*. Pascale-Anne Brault and Michael Naas (Trans.). Bloomington: Indiana University Press.

______. (1994). *Specters of Marx: The state of the debt, the work of mourning, and the new international*. Peggy Kamuf (Trans.). New York & London: Routledge.

______. (1997). *Deconstruction in a nutshell: A conversation with Jacques Derrida*. With a Commentary by John Caputo (Ed.). New York: Fordham University Press.

Friedman, Thomas L. (1999a). *The lexus and the olive tree*. New York: HarperCollins.

______. (1999b). Our world confronts new rules of engagement. *The Age* (2 July 1999), 17.

Gough, Noel. (1998). All around the world: Science education, constructivism, and globalization. *Educational Policy, 12*(5), 507–24.

______. (1999). Globalisation and school curriculum change: Locating a transnational imaginary. *Journal of Education Policy, 14*(1), 73–84.

______. (2000). Locating curriculum studies in the global village. *Journal of Curriculum Studies, 32*(2), 329–42.

Greider, William. (1997). *One world, ready or not: The manic logic of global capitalism*. New York: Simon and Schuster.

Haraway, Donna J. (1991). *Simians, cyborgs, and women: The reinvention of nature*. New York: Routledge.

Harding, Sandra. (1993). Rethinking standpoint epistemology: "What is strong objectivity?" In Linda Alcoff and Elizabeth Potter (Eds.), *Feminist Epistemologies* (pages 49–82). New York: Routledge.

Lessing, Doris. (1992). *African laughter: Four visits to Zimbabwe*. London: HarperCollins.

Niven, Larry. (1976). *The long ARM of Gil Hamilton*. New York: Ballantine.

Turnbull, David. (1993). Local knowledge and comparative scientific traditions. *Knowledge and Policy, 6*(3/4), 29–54.

______. (1997). Reframing science and other local knowledge traditions. *Futures, 29*(6), 551–62.

Wark, McKenzie. (1994). *Virtual geography: Living with global media events*. Bloomington and Indianapolis: Indiana University Press.

Wilson, Rob, and Wimal Dissanayake (Eds.). (1996). *Global/local: Cultural production and the transnational imaginary*. Durham and London: Duke University Press.

Perspective on Gough

John Stewart

The image of the long "arm(s)" of globalization is an effective one to illustrate the nature of this trend in modern life. The "spectral" nature of these arms is haunting. They may be reaching out in some benevolent way to bring everyone together in a cozy, homogenous group hug, or they may intend to strangle anything that resists them. In either case, we have a responsibility, as educators of those being hugged or strangled, to be aware of the presence of these arms and their impact. As educators, we are responsible for understanding the culture of the communities in which we live and for being aware of the impact that globalization is having on these communities. We may have a role to play in how our students respond to these pressures. It is no doubt a response which needs to be "both/and" as opposed to "either/or." We cannot pretend the world is not changing, nor should we embrace these changes at the expense of the accumulated ways of knowing of several millennia and diverse cultures. A few illustrations may suggest the role we may play in this process as well as the challenges that this may involve.

In Noel Gough's chapter, he cites a powerful image of the interactions of cultures in the vignette from Doris Lessing. The Zimbabwean woman is correct, practically speaking, in her understanding of the advantages of her child succeeding in the British education system. She well understands that good jobs, financial advantages, and social position relate to success at O-levels. She has learned from the colonizers of her country and is prepared to use, as she understands it, their own tools against them—and for her child. She responds to the American Aid worker, "I see you whites are still just the same. You don't want our children to have a real education. Oh no, that's for your children. We want a good education for our children, just the same as yours" (this volume).

What is most disturbing for me in this illustration, and what, as educators, I hope we can be alive to, is how profoundly disconnected this Zimbabwean woman has become from her own traditional ("local") ways of knowing and how completely she has accepted that a different way of learning is superior to them. It is a disconnection that is happening across the planet, promoted by the powerful media of television and the Internet. Perceiving this disconnection and the impact it is having on students in many settings is the most direct homework that I perceive Gough's article suggesting for educators.

The disconnection is as real and as profound where I live in northern Canada as it is in the illustration from Zimbabwe. The Dene and Inuit people of the Far North have evolved over millennia to be attuned to the world around them. Their way of knowing this world has allowed them to survive in an incredibly harsh environment. Referring to the Yupiaq Inuit of Alaska, Oskar Kawagley (1995) writes,

> Their traditional education processes were carefully constructed around mythology, history, the observation of natural processes and animals' and plants' styles of survival and obtaining food, and use of natural materials to make their tools and implements, all of which was made understandable through thoughtful stories and illustrative examples. (2)

Kawagley's exploration of the relationship between the formal (Western) education system and this local/traditional way of knowing is disturbing. He observes that

> since the inception of modern education in the villages, the curricula, policies, textbooks, language of instruction, and administration have been in conflict with the native cultural systems. The modern public schools were not made to accommodate differences in worldviews, but to impose another culture—their own. (36)

The challenge he poses, as echoed in the chapter by Gough, is how educators can "decenter" the Western perspective on what constitutes appropriate knowledge and ways of knowing in schools. This is difficult. As educators, most of us have succeeded as students and then been further trained to teach in the systems which Gough and Derrida are challenging. In my experience, it is only through authentic encounters with the "other"—be that individuals, communities, or worldviews—that we may begin to see the frame around our own way of seeing the world. When we do begin to see our own frames, as educators, we can begin to question them and encourage our students to do the same. This stepping sideways can allow space to be created where we can engage other ways of knowing. A conversation can only begin when the voices are on equal footing. Kawagley's explorations in Alaska suggest that, to date, only one voice has been allowed into the conversation. Other ways of learning and knowing simply do not count. Aboriginal students in Alaska, and the similarly frustrated students in Zimbabwe, most often react by dismissing their own cultural inheritance and the rich learning and understanding that go with it. It is only when the culturally dominant ways of knowing and the vehicles which transmit these values *listen* that the conversation can begin. As educators, we can model this listening, and reflect it in our teaching—if we are willing to question our own assumptions. Richard Bernstein (1991), in his insightful work on the current state of philosophical discourse, describes the ground rules for this conversation:

> It means taking our own fallibility seriously—resolving that however much we are committed to our own styles of thinking, we are willing to listen to others without denying or suppressing the otherness of the other. (337)

As an educator, I am challenged to apply the writings of Derrida, Gough, and others to a reexamination of my own understanding of what I teach and how I teach as well as to provide a framework within which to promote critical exploration of these ideas by students. We may learn that globalization is not simply an amorphous, impersonal, uncontrollable force. The spectral arms are incarnated in individuals, decisions and actions—ours, as well as others.

It is encouraging that many teachers and some curriculum materials have begun to explore the assumptions and implications of a Western view of the world and to engage those assumptions in a conversation. In my part of the world, we have substantial curriculum resources written by Aboriginal people for all students (see Reference section). The premises from which these resources evolve—from the nature of knowledge and learning, our relationship to the environment we live in, and the kinds of activities that promote learning—stand in contrast to many of the practices that the formal education system has built upon over the past 100 years. This is not surprising. What I do find surprising is the compatibility of many of these non-Western ideas with research that is emerging through a decidedly Western methodology. Learning through experience on the land (and out of the classroom), fundamental to Aboriginal education, finds increasing support in brain research (Alberta Learning, 1999). The "spiritual" component of a student's education is being explored in recent curriculum initiatives designed for all students (Western Canadian Protocol, 2000). An awareness of the living relationship between humans and the environment and the threat we may pose to both this relationship and the planet are being explored in curricula from around the world. These are the beginnings of a conversation. Our challenge, as educators, is to be part of these discussions. Gough's article may help us consider some of the issues that need to be included in the conversation.

References

Alberta Learning. (1999). Direction de l'education Française. Aperçu de recherches en vue de l'elaboration du cadre commun de résultats d'apprentissage en sciences humaines (M–12) du protocole de l'ouest Canadien pour l'education francophone.

Alberta Learning. Curriculum Standards Branch. (1999). *Reshaping the future of social studies: Literature/research review.*

______. Curriculum Standards Branch. (1999). *Aboriginal perspective on education: A vision of cultural context within the framework of social studies: Literature/research review.*

Bernstein, R. J. (1991). *The new constellation: The ethical-political horizons of modernity/postmodernity.* Cambridge, MA: MIT Press.

Education, Culture and Employment. (1993). *Dene kede education: A Dene perspective.* Yellowknife: Government of Northwest Territories.

______. (1996). *Inuuqatigiit: The curriculum from the Inuit perspective.* Yellowknife: Government of the Northwest Territories.

Kawagley, A. O. (1995). *A Yupiaq worldview: A pathway to ecology and spirit.* Prospect Heights, IL: Waveland.

Western Canadian Protocol. (2000). *Foundation document for the development of the common curriculum framework for social studies kindergarten to grade 12.*

John Stewart taught French immersion and social studies in British Columbia and the Northwest Territories for 13 years. He now works as a curriculum coordinator for the Department of Education, Culture, and Employment in Yellowknife. His most powerful learning experience occurred in Rankin Inlet, when the (all Inuit) participants in a workshop he was delivering gently informed him that they were glad that he had given them a place to meet and discuss what was needed for their children—and that he could go for coffee.

Chapter 7 A Re-Conceptualized Curriculum

Problematic: Body Language

> I can do everything with my language but not with my body. What I hide by my language, my body utters. I can deliberately mould my message, but not my voice....My body is a stubborn child, my language is a very civilised adult. (Roland Barthes, 1978, 45)

Erica McWilliam (1999) suggests that the "stubborn child" to whom Barthes refers "is a specter that haunts both the beginning teacher and the university academic who may have performed well in the textual work required of them, but find embodied teaching to be nerve-racking and debilitating" (122). Embodied teaching (and learning) holds few such fears for Kathleen Kesson and Don Oliver—they would rather represent their re-conceptualized theory of experience in dance, ritual performance, or shared physical adventure than in "written words, verbal abstractions, formulae and concepts" (this volume).

The palpable pulse of active human bodies is at the symbolic and material center of Kesson and Oliver's curriculum vision—a vision of embodied actors enthusiastically engaging each other and "the immediately apprehendable world." Their re-conceptualization of experience raises a crucial question for curriculum inquiry: "How can we generate a set of images, ways of being and knowing, that include respect both for the *texture and immediacy of actuality* as well as for the *power and elegance of abstract thought?"* (authors' emphasis). In other words, how might Barthes's "stubborn child" and "civilised adult" learn to inhabit a shared body with pleasure and intimacy?

Kesson and Oliver's refusal to privilege mind over matter has renewed significance in an era of increasing and accelerating virtualization of human experience. As Katherine Hayles (1999) observes, "a defining characteristic of the present cultural moment is the belief that information can circulate unchanged among different material substrates. It is not for nothing that 'Beam me up, Scotty' has become a cultural icon for the global information society" (1–2). Hayles asks "how information lost its body" (2); we ask how we could have reached a cultural moment in which scholars like Kesson and Oliver might feel the need to be apologetic about using words to encourage readers towards "embodied participation." Why should they apologize for sharing their emphatically embodied vision through a "textual" relationship? Words and texts may be prosthetic, but, like all media, they are extensions of human bodies, even when we arrange them in ways that disguise or deny their corporeality (for example, the syntactical form we call the passive voice makes thoughts seem as if no body had thought them and deeds seem as if no body had done them).[1]

Kesson and Oliver's vision seems to us to be shared, at least in part, by several other contributors to this text. For example, their preferred verbal medium is face-to-face conversation, which Donna Trueit also explores as a productive mode of inquiry and vision building. Peter Cole and Pat O'Riley's distinctive way of inscribing their body language on the printed page demonstrates convincingly that it is possible to bring both "the texture and immediacy of actuality" and "the power and elegance of abstract thought and abstraction" into one textual space. Cleo Cherryholmes's application of Dewey's desire to integrate art and everyday experience, Chet Bowers's call for a deeper cultural and ecological understanding of curriculum, and Jayne Fleener's elucidation of organocentrism and complexity can also be read as elements of Kesson and Oliver's reconceptualized theory of experience. There are other connections that we encourage readers to generate for themselves. We suspect that some of these might more easily be made by a stubborn child than a civilized adult.

Note

[1] We note in passing that beliefs in the *possibility* of disembodied information might also have been encouraged by literal interpretations of one well-known instance of the passive voice: "In the beginning was the Word" (St. John, 1: 1).

References

Barthes, Roland. (1978). *A lover's discourse: Fragments.* Richard Hurley (Trans.). New York: Hill & Wang.

Hayles, N. Katherine. (1999). *How we became posthuman: Virtual bodies in cybernetics, literature, and informatics*. Chicago and London: University of Chicago Press.

McWilliam, Erica. (1999). *Pedagogical pleasures.* New York: Lang.

On the Need for a Re-Conceptualized Theory of Experience

Kathleen Kesson and Donald Oliver

We want first to celebrate Bill Doll's exhortation to bury the ghost of curriculum past, to ferry this persistent spirit of a controlled and predictable curriculum to the "other side" of the mythopoetic river that divides the *actual* from the *potential* or the *dormant*. We also appreciate his invitation to the ghosts of Dewey and Whitehead, with their dynamic notions of *becomings* and *transformations*, to participate (if from the ancestral "other side") in a postmodern dialogue about curriculum. It is perhaps in the marriage of "pragmatism and process" that some version of curriculum can be resuscitated that might bring vitality to the experience of the multitudes of children and adults whose lives are currently dominated by narrow and constricted versions of what it means to know, to do, and to feel. We also want to respond to Noel Gough's call to "stand at the center of our own histories and fields of visualization as responsible, engaged, embodied actors." Our re-conceptualized theory of experience actually holds this notion of "embodied actors" at its very center. Unlike Dewey's rationalistic theory of experience, however, which also centers engaged human actors in interaction with the world, our heuristic model makes an effort to take into account some seriously neglected dimensions of human experience.

We want to argue that our contemporary Western success in dominating the life of the planet has, in large measure, come out of one central aspect of Platonic Christianity and the Enlightenment—its constricted and unbalanced sense of knowing and being. The essence of this narrowness and imbalance is the assumption that written words, verbal abstractions, formulae and concepts—what we are calling the "culture of literacy"—is closer to truth, to science, and to God, than the more transitory kinds of knowing we associate with the immediate actualities of living and coping and the recounting of stories that emerge from this actuality as well as the ritual enactment of these stories, through which we celebrate our connection with the human social and the natural worlds. We believe that our failure to "stand at the center of our own histories and fields of experience as embodied actors" has profound consequences for both individuals and societies—ecological consequences, political consequences, and psychological consequences, to name just a few. In the spirit of both venerating and burying the ghosts of the past, we want to propose a theory of experience that might re-situate living, breathing, speaking, dancing, participating human beings and other living creatures at the center of a dynamic, oscillating, pulsing, participatory universe.

We have sometimes whimsically called this theory of experience "throb theory"—the notion of throb signifying the pulsing heartbeat at the center of experience, a symbol of aliveness that might displace the cold and sterile world of verbal abstractions that now lies at the center of our epistemologies. The heuristic model is Don's invention—but in the spirit of iteration inherent in notions of complexity and chaos, it has been incarnated and reincarnated multiple times in conversations with an ever-changing group of embodied actors in diverse locations. We have held rituals in the Manodnock mountains, trekked together through knee-deep snow in Vermont, shared coffee and hearty breakfasts with dowsers and witches and bio-regionalists in remote rural cafes, and sat around conference tables with doctoral students at Harvard in an (at least) ten-year continuing dialogue about these ideas.

Certainly the great positive value of the Platonic/Enlightenment legacy is its deep and persistent search for meaning through reflection and logic. Its deficiency, however, is its skepticism toward, if not rejection of, the significance and importance of the immediately apprehendable world to which our senses and our neural meaning-making capacities are inextricably and ultimately connected. This rejection has had a number of unfortunate epistemological consequences: the rejection of the body as inferior to the mind (and the historical identification of women with the body and men with the mind); the rejection of the natural world as a debased version of some divine formal reality; and the fundamental rejection of worldliness as "second-rate." In the most common paradigmatic story of this tradition, a Creator, if one exists at all, stands outside our earthly home and creates the universe, which "He" then either abandons, or governs with mechanistic surety.

Indeed, the great faith in Enlightenment has been that the universe would be revealed as a grand and complex machine, the laws and instructions of which would come to be understood by such insightful minds as those of Galileo, Newton, and Locke. The modern version of Enlightenment suggests that although there may be Great Laws—like the laws of motion for heavenly bodies—there are a zillion little "findings" that have to be teased out by a massive research enterprise in every conceivable field of human endeavor. Psychologists search for laws of the human mind; sociologists search for the laws of group behavior; molecular biologists search for ever-new forms of antibiotics to encounter the new bacteria that evolve beyond the older vulnerable forms; and philosophers and linguists search for regularities in language. In our quest for certainty, and the belief that we could bring every aspect of the world under human control, we have effectively "disenchanted" the world, banishing magic, mystery, and the sacred. This quest for certainty and predictability, and the consequent disenchantment of the world, lies at the heart of modern thinking about curriculum. In the revised and updated version of Enlightenment that we call "modernity," we run faster and faster to generate new knowledge about the Grand Machine, the full definition of which becomes increasingly complex and farther out of reach. In the process, of course, we have lost some essential aspects of our humanity—but like the phantoms of lost limbs, ghost limbs, we continue to feel their presence. These ghosts haunt us with ancient stories, mythopoetic reminders of the fullness of our participation in a universe which is vastly more complex and more mysterious than the laws of science might ever reveal. How to recover this "original" sense of participation while taking with us the limited certainties that science and abstraction have brought us is the question at the heart of "throb theory." We believe that it is not only possible but also vital for humanity to recapture its enchanted roots. The failure to do so, we believe, is to face the dead sterility of a future in which every aspect of human behavior is mechanized and to invoke the spectres of genetic engineering and biotechnology, environmental degradation, alienated labor and exploitation, and of increasingly sensational and vulgar forms of entertainment to remind ourselves that we are alive, sensuous, and embodied. A disenchanted people is in mortal danger of succumbing to the deadening mythos of technocratization.

Enactment: The Complement to a Culture of Abstractions

We would suggest that there is a fundamental quality of human understanding essential for human survival beyond the culture of literacy and abstraction. We are calling this quality "enactment." Enactment is the implicit knowing that is remembered when our whole bodies and minds have been involved in creating and recreating the fundamental stories of the human condition: birth, eating, dying, loving, playing. Enactment involves drama, song, tableau, ritual, dance, sport, the constructed actions that evolve out of the more fundamental human activities. The Japanese tea ceremony is one example of ritual enactment that elaborates on a fundamental human activity; the sacred corn dance of the Hopi is another. These enactments recall, re-experience, and "make special" otherwise mundane human activities. One should not confuse enactment with elite performance as in modern concerts, sports events, and the like, wherein most of us stand on the sidelines and cheer furiously or applaud quietly after virtuosi have performed. Enactment requires deep personal involvement and participation as well as an intimate sense of reconnection with communal tradition. Various contemporary churches engage in enactment, but the heavy influence of the Puritan strain of Protestantism on American culture has dampened much of this. People who have rich symbolic traditions of enactment commonly live or have lived within tribal or folk cultures. We want to suggest that the great crisis of our day, of which ecological debasement and our obsession with consuming goods and services may only be symptoms, is that we are destroying the human capacity for meaningful enactment in a logo- or literacy-dominated world. And we are doing this by actually destroying the peoples and cultures who carry this capacity in their minds and their guts.

Yes, conceptual, verbal, literate knowing carries with it tremendous power to control and manipulate things, processes, and living beings. Some degree of this control is both necessary and useful to guarantee a basic level of comfort, security, and survival. This mode of knowing, however, cannot teach us humility or the capacity to reconnect with our human and natural world in any meaningful way. From an educational point of view, the issue for us is not what constitutes cultural literacy, a question which has dominated educational discussions in recent years. Rather, the issues we think are important include: How can humans learn to ground themselves in or reconnect themselves to a sense of being and express this sense of being both in literate terms (literature, science, philosophy) and in enacted terms (dramatic ritual, movement, song)? How can we get the mind back into a body that can reenact and remember in nerve and muscle, as well as in word, the coping requirements for human survival? For surely, the great discovery of the nineteenth and twentieth centuries, from Darwin to DNA, is that *connectedness is the natural circumstance of all beings, living and nonliving, including the inseparability of humans from the rest of nature.*

We maintain that a culture becomes deficient when it loses this capacity to enact its connection with what we would call kinship: animal and plant kinship; human kinship; kinship with the water and air and earth of the planet. Uvavnuk, an Iglulik Eskimo woman, writes poetically of this sense of connection:

> The great sea stirs me.
> The great sea sets me adrift,
> it sways me like the weed
> on a river-stone.
> The sky's height stirs me.
> The strong wind blows through my mind.
> It carries me with it,
> so I shake with joy.
> (Uvavnuk, 1991)

In the beginning there was not just the Word; there was actuality and the sense of connection among real physical beings, and that sense of connection is renewed in human culture by a general and communal participation in drama, poetics, ritual, and enactment. At the very least, a renewed sense of this connection would involve reconsidering the arts not as nonessentials of the curriculum but as the most basic aspects of learning. At most, it would require a reconceptualization of what it means to know and make meaning—and the inclusion of spirituality and the mythopoetic into the very fabric of our lives.

Toward a Re-Conceptualized Theory of Experience: Naturalistic Philosophy, Reconstructive Science, and Primal Enactment

Lest the reader think that we are advocating a return to some Neolithic version of nonrational, instinctive participation in a chaotic universe, we wish to outline here a postmodern naturalistic cosmology that includes the world of high-level theoretical speculation correlated with and corrected by carefully gathered sense data but which also includes speculations within the context of cultural stories recounted through dramatic discourse, stories that would have epistemological parity with both theory and "data." For the essence of human meaning is not only the interpretive aftermath in the wake of events in which we participate; it includes the world in which we participate at the moment of its coming into being. It includes the fullness of the moment realized (in Whitehead's terms, the *occasion*), which includes the story in the body, the oral story told from the body as well as its more abstract, schematic interpretation (which after all, can only capture a flat, nondimensional quality of an occasion). The "nature" in which we participate is, in fact, a multiplicity of occasions of differing textures and shapes and thicknesses. What we call "things" are perhaps best thought of as connected to parts of these occasions. There are different thicknesses to these things, from quarks to carrots. In a strange and mysterious way, the universe thus perceived becomes more differentiated, more complex, more varied. In cultures of enactment, there is still the sense of kinship with the oneness of such a universe and the feeling of cosmos that makes it all coherent. Photons and atoms and molecules become life. Large molecules called DNA reproduce themselves with RNA messengers. Although we can simplify the complex of "things" by showing that they all consist of variations of patterns built (for example, of four bases in each nucleotide or of 20 amino acids), the constant process of change and the multiplicities inherent in the universe are still profound mysteries. There is always the sense of *oneness* or *fullness* as well as the sense of exuberant diversity left in our human experience that goes well beyond the reductions and simplifications about which science tells us. Although science may satisfy us to some extent with stories about the *how* of the universe, the more profound question of the *why* of the world evades explanation. We find meaning simply by *experiencing relational connections* among both the thick and thin of nature.

In this naturalistic interpretation of the world, what we call mind is pattern inseparably connected to matter, and matter is always in the process of transforming itself into something else. Reality is a perpetual process of inception, growth, and perishing. This view of the world comes out of the work of James, Whitehead, Dewey, Bateson, and the tradition we now call process/pragmatism. After fifty years in the dark ages of positivism and professionalism in which we were told that all would be made understandable in terms of words and formulae, imaginative speculation and poetic interpretation are reemerging. The challenge inherent in this reemergence, as well as for postmodern culture building and radical re-conceptualizations of curriculum, is that we need to find ways to both slough off the logo-centered biases of our modern cosmology and to reconstruct and reintegrate the positive aspects of this tradition with the folk cultures and wisdom traditions that are being eradicated all over the world. How can we generate a set of images, ways of being and knowing, that include respect both for the *texture and immediacy of actuality* as well as for the *power and elegance of abstract thought*? How can we connect honest questions of survival and coping to the enactment of a compelling story of one's existence? How can we find meaningful stories and rituals of enactment for an elite group of people who see literature, science, and philosophy in their many forms as the central, if not exclusive, road to truth and wisdom?

Throb: A Re-Conceptualized Theory of Experience

While acknowledging that any model is but a meager map of actual experience, we would like to draw your attention to the illustration that accompanies this essay (page 192). At the center of the drawing is the heart that signifies the center of our re-conceptualized theory of experience. It represents the most commonsensical human understanding of the world—the flowing conversation/story of life in the ever-present, vibrating moment. It is the story that says: "This is happening now. I am here; you are there, and this is what we mean to each other and to the world around us, *now*." The story we tell in this center of experience comes from many sources, including those shown in the lower right quadrant of the illustration—from the primal actions of coping and adapting for survival, of connecting in the most fundamental ways to the natural world of which we are a part. But although the "content" of our stories concerns our connections with the natural requirements of survival (including the survival of our sense of balance and beauty), it does not address the more perplexing question of how our *experiencing* of these actions emerges.

Our model suggests that there are many phases in this process of experiencing of which we are, for the most part, totally unconscious. It is not simply "given" that a coherent story describing the meaning of the moment springs to mind. There is the subtle "coming into being" represented on the lower left of the illustration—what we are calling, after Whitehead, "prehending." Prehending might include our initial neural participation with micro particles associated with preconceptual, preverbal modes of perceiving. It may include complex processes of autonomic imaging, imagination, and metaphoric connections, which then burst into conscious thought and feeling. We are suggesting that there may well be a subtle process of "coming to experience" which begins with a vague sense of "feeling" or somatic awareness, as our neurological system interacts with (prehends, participates with) other aspects of the world—from photon to neuron or even, as some postmodern thinkers suggest, with a natural nonmaterial world. This highly selective process moves forward in split-second fashion as our bodies sense and act with/upon these prehensions (all the way from antibodies in our blood to patterns on our retina). We can imagine the microsecond when prehensions are transformed into meaningful sense data (images, coherent sounds, touch, etc.) followed by the transformation of bodily image and pattern into conscious thought—and language.

Throb

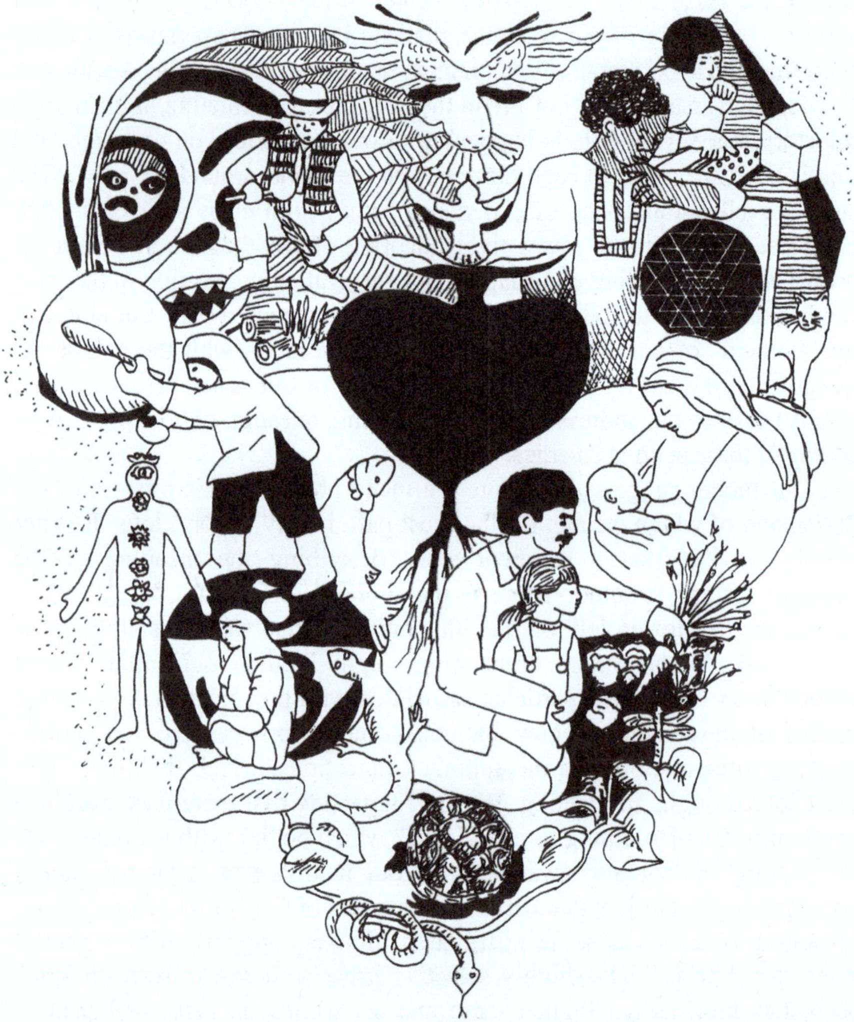

From this complex series of connections between a process of imagination and metaphorizing from physical inside and physical outside world (and perhaps from nonphysical forms) comes our ability to tell a coherent story. The wonder of this whole process is that so much of it is obviously implicit, hidden, preconscious, so "out-of-control," yet for all its wonder, there is little interest, in our modern thinking, in speculating on how this actually happens. Our frame-by-frame stories appear as if by magic and are simply taken for granted. William James was fascinated for a lifetime by what he called our "stream-of-consciousness," punctuated by globs of meaning. It is like a perpetual dream, yet a dream that must confront periodically—every so many microseconds—the task of constructing a meaningful coherent story within the time frame of the requirements for human survival.

Even more amazing, it is from these mysteriously constructed stories that we attempt to capture and summarize a more stable sense of nature/world/life. We do this partly by mythologizing our stories, by telling them over and over again as if to attest to their significance and continuity. They become communal as well as personal stories. They suggest a destiny and connect this sense of deep meaning or "fatefulness" to the requirements of the present and the remembrance of the past. And although some stories become sanctified in this way, there are always new stories to take their place, because there are new generations to be taught and new circumstances and challenges with which they must cope.

This process of mythologizing is one in which story is transformed from the description of an immediate novel *occasion* to an account of a historical truth. We have called this movement (symbolized in the upper right-hand quadrant of our design) "interpretation," a mode of knowing that asks not only what the story *is*, but also what the story *means*. At an even more abstract level, regularities across stories can be captured in schema—in diagrams, pictures, maps, formulae, etc. One can describe and explain the motion of the heavenly bodies relative to each other. Or one can explain how the complex molecules DNA and RNA account for the reproduction and maintenance of living organisms. And of course, once we search for some regular and predictable qualities in nature/culture by scripting them with words or pictures or diagrams or mathematical symbols, we move from problems associated with the adequacy and authenticity of simple description to complex issues of conflicting interpretations of their meaning. Various questions arise: How do low-level schema become part of more inclusive schema (i.e., the relationship of matter to human nature to theories of aesthetic and literary value)? What is a good theory? What good *are* theories? What is the nature of this activity we experience as thinking and theory-making and interpretation? We are calling this process of searching for constancy and regularity in understanding ourselves and the world around us "constructed experience." We think of it as an extension of the more autonomous or spontaneous process previously called "prehending," but it feels very different, more under our conscious control although clearly in its earliest stages it must include the more unconscious act of prehending.

To recapitulate, we want to suggest that the fullness of our human story embodies a number of qualitatively different experiences: (a) the richness and intensity of archaic action or "coping occasions"—eating, birthing, nurturing, courting, mating, healing; (b) our ability to feel the emerging embodiment of experience as it moves from subtle prehension to feeling to image to metaphor to story; (c) our ability to construct meaningful and often reliable schema that describe regularities in our stories—our history, science, mathematics and philosophies; and (d) the incredibly diverse and wonderful ways in which we remember and recall, through ritual enactment, drama, and participatory performance, the richness and fullness of significant stories (see the upper left quadrant of our illustration). We hope that our rendering illustrates how limited our conceptualizations of knowing and of being, hence our "curriculum," has been. We hope we have also persuaded you of how limited our modern conception of the natural world is. As modern people, we make the quick transliteration of "nature" to "science" and see the latter less as prehension or story or ritual and more as data-based interpretation. The contemporary environmental movement, especially deep ecology, asserts that there is a critical need to retrieve our sense of involvement with and participation in the natural world if we are to avert global ecological disaster. Given the perilous condition of our ecosystems, our complacency is astonishing. Our "throb" model suggests that we must reconnect modes of interpretation which stress objective forms of public communication and reflection with the more subtle process by which private experience emerges from natural connection and begins to come into being. It is in this embryological stage that the oneness of the natural world is most compelling and obvious. It is here that feeling and facticity, literal speech and metaphor, dreams and focused consciousness seem less separable, more seamless.

Science, Nature, and Spirituality

Our effort in this brief essay has been to sketch a map or model to suggest how seemingly unrelated qualities of experience draw from or relate to one another as humans participate in and share the natural world around them. So the world of dreams and daydreams, the world of transitory story and narrative, the world of deep story and myth, the world of history, science, and philosophy, the world of practical coping for survival, and the world of ritual, games, and enactment all revolve around our effort to create a grounded sense of meaning in which humans can not only live through the trials of life but also celebrate these trials by engaging the universe with a degree of excitement, enthusiasm, and joy. We have assumed that humans generate a range of experiences, including preverbal imaginative "prehending," storytelling, interpretation, and coping. Beyond this we have argued that much greater attention be given to cultural practices we have called "enactment." Our notion is that enactment is a critical integrative force in any culture, because it compresses qualities of experience in the various areas of life into a single unitary apprehension of the whole. Enactment thus has some obvious connections with the idea of God or the Whole (Holy) and spirituality because of the intensity and richness associated with religiosity. Our model locates itself within an inclusive "ground" of experience variously called the Tao, the implicate order, the Void—any one of a number of concepts that attempt to account for the fundamentally mysterious nature of the universe. We make no pretension to understand or explain this pervasive and enduring concept, other than to stay open to the possibility that a postmodern science with a more expansive ideology and a less reductionist methodology may actually discover that the great intuitions of the teachers of the past, from Buddha to Jesus to Ghandi and the host of uncounted medicine people and shamans from indigenous folk cultures, might be confirmed. It is our hope that science and religion might then expand themselves into each other's questions, and we shall be able to talk intelligently about God and ethics and organicism and magic in a single conversation.

We want to emphasize that we are not saying that we have *left behind* more appropriate modes of knowing and better ways of living and relating to which we should *return*. That would be to romanticize some version of the past, and such return is not only undesirable but also clearly impossible. Our point is that modes of knowing and structures of living and relating that we have left behind have somehow to be integrated into the tight, excluded middle ground, the vital center, that modernity so effectively keeps shut. We seem unable to create educational environments that celebrate the imaginative base necessary for profound storytelling, that is to say, storytelling that generates perennial drama, art, and science. We seem to be unable to control a technology that moves us toward ever more private and narcissistic modes of expression; we all must have our own television, computer, car—whatever it takes to fully "express" our egocentric selves. We seem unable to find educational tasks that have obvious and compelling relevance to our human survival, tasks that can be carried out effectively with the full range of humanity (boys, girls, men, women, old, weak, strong, active, shy, vocal, differently abled, etc.).

In conclusion, we lament that we seem to be stuck within this highly dysfunctional metaculture that we have chosen to call modernity. Although it has had its setbacks (outbursts of ethnic or religious fervor which temporarily overwhelm a people's thirst for consumer goods and private choices in how one lives), it has gained tremendous momentum over the past 200 years. And although "postmodernity" has generated a fair amount of exciting utopian theory, we would suggest that we totally underestimate the seductive power and resilience of this modern way of knowing and being. Change will come about, we believe, when we find/invent/rediscover a life style in which our ways of knowing and living and coping, our connections with our environment, and our connections with the "ground" of existence are all transformed at the same time. Different ways of knowing are not enough; storytelling is not enough; living in community is not enough; living closer to nature, more frugally, closer to visible conditions of human survival is not enough. All of these changes have to happen at once. Somehow we have to find appropriate ways to unravel a way of being that, in recent years, has accelerated around the world at a dizzying rate. And given the substantial and often-failed efforts to do this over the past hundred years—from holistic schools to intentional communities to whole socialist nation states—the challenge is great.

We recognize the paradox of our own complicity in the perpetuation of this crisis of modernity. We have used words, probably excessively, to attempt to call us back to an original embodied participation. We apologize for this. We would rather have danced our clarion call, enacted it in a ritual form that might compel a richer and deeper understanding of our thesis. But we would have to be "embodied together" for that, and our relationship at this moment is merely a textual one. We apologize for talking only implicitly about curriculum. We believe that it is impossible to address the problems in education without addressing the crisis of modernity in its larger cultural context. We appreciate this opportunity to share this vision with our colleagues in the curriculum community and look forward to continuing the conversation—face to face.

Reference

Uvavnuk. (1991). Moved. Tom Lowenfeld (Trans.). In *Poetry for the earth*. Sara Dunn and Alan Scholefield (Ed.), (page 6). New York: Fawcett Columbine-Ballantine.

Kathleen Kesson is the Director of Teacher Education at Goddard College, an experimental, progressive college in central Vermont. She is also Research Associate Professor at the University of Vermont, where she directs the John Dewey Project on Progressive Education, a research and policy organization.

Donald Oliver is Professor of Education at Harvard University. He is the author of *Education, Modernity, and Fractured Meaning* (1989) and is currently completing his latest book, *The Primal, the Modern, and the Vital Center: A Theory of Balanced Cultures in a Living Place* (2001). His research interests are middle-level, neighborly places that connect isolated individuals and families with corporate places and mythic stories with pragmatic, instrumental knowledge.

Perspective on Kesson and Oliver

Janis Pardue Hill

> Change will come about, we believe, when we find/invent/rediscover a life style in which our way of knowing and living and coping and our connection with our environment and our connection with the "ground" of existence are all transformed at the same time. (Kathleen Kesson and Donald Oliver, this text)

> We are in the world and the world is in us. (Alfred North Whitehead, 1938, 227)

Kesson and Oliver, like many of the "disenchanted" ones who walk daily through the "disenchanted" halls and classrooms of a nation besieged by reform and the chaos of change, seek a means of restoring enchantment to a "disenchanted" world. They remind us that we need desperately to locate a path by which we might "rediscover [our] enchanted roots…and remind ourselves that we are alive, sensuous, and embodied." I agree—the time is now—and I commend Kesson and Oliver for assuming such a quest, for it is a worthy one. We are, indeed, living, breathing beings with capacities for great feelings and great passions. And those feelings and passions need to be uncovered, nurtured, and released before they are dismissed forever as unimportant and inconsequential by a sophisticated, "high-tech" society which relegates feelings, care, and connections to secondary levels. Before the Age of Information and its veritable explosion of technology make devastating, unalterable changes on the landscape of the classroom and our world, "before the darkness," as Orwell might write, we must seek the light—the warmth—the passions of life.

I see in the "throb" of Kesson and Oliver the same life—feelings, passion—embodied in not only Whitehead's actual entity but also in Whitehead, the man and the teacher. A passionate individual who cared and felt with intensity, Whitehead possessed that capacity for "alive-ness" he proposed as the foundation of learning and which I view as so essential in the teacher personality. Like Whitehead, I think the teacher and the classroom must be alive and filled with passion, for only in a living classroom can the potential for transformation of which William Doll writes be fulfilled. This, I believe, is central to uncovering the wisdom in Whitehead's vision of education and the world. The essential premise is simply that learning is living, and living is learning; but, most importantly, learning is "*life-giving.*" It transforms—re-creates—gives new life! But it will never happen without the feelings, the "alive-ness," the passion.

In his *Autobiography* (1968), Bertrand Russell writes:

> Three passions, simple but overwhelmingly strong, have governed my life: the longing for love, the search for knowledge, and unbearable pity for the sufferings of mankind. These passions, like great winds, have blown me hither and thither, in a wayward course, over a deep ocean of anguish, reaching to the very verge of despair. (332)

This, I thought, as I read the passage for the first time, is what Whitehead means when he tells us in *Modes of Thought* (1938) that, "We are in the world and the world is in us" (227). This is that "oneness" with humankind, I realized at last, which was Whitehead's grandest hope. This is, in short, the proverbial "passion for life" often spoken about, occasionally sought, but seldom attained. A *passion for life*—oh, that I could bestow, instill, *elicit* that in every student!

Touched by the despair and agony Russell describes in his autobiographical work, I revisited many times the passage written half a century ago and pondered the irony—Bertrand Russell, Victorian scholar, a "man of passion." Mostly, however, I returned to the eloquent passage because I saw mirrored there a reflection of myself and a multitude of other teacher faces who had also suffered—*experienced*—similar longings and quests. I saw passionate, caring teachers—teachers who think and feel with passion—and I realized these are the ones who truly experience the "alive-ness" Whitehead describes in both his cosmology and his educational philosophy. These are also the ones who seek "alive-ness" in their students; in every lesson and on every day, these teachers create classrooms that "throb" with life. Kesson and Oliver create in their "throb theory" a powerful metaphor. Describing the notion of the "throb" as "the pulsing heartbeat at the center of experience, a symbol of aliveness," they offer an image which moves to the very core of Whitehead's philosophy of experience. Like the actual entity in its burst of creative glory, the throb pulsates, reminding us that only through movement is there life. Kesson and Oliver's "throb" evokes images of motion and life just as the throb of the heart conjures up images of the movement of the life-sustaining blood; for with each throb, or pulse, the opportunity for life and creativity continues. As I have written on other occasions, every Whiteheadian "throb," or "pulse" of experience, is a burst of glory (Hill, 1999). The beauty in a Whiteheadian world is that every one leads to another: the process—the connections, the relating—is unending, moving always into another "pulse" or "throb" of experience, another moment of "becoming" (72).

To create experiences that pulsate with life—that is the teacher's ultimate goal, the teacher's ultimate passion. The behavioral objectives and the performance indicators of the curriculum guidelines (which are important, but not all-important) pale in comparison with that quest. To elicit passion for learning and life in our students—that is the ultimate success in the chaotic world of today's classroom, with its seemingly constant demands and only momentary bursts of glory. A monumental task, the call to passion must not be ignored. Because I have walked the halls of change and chaos, I understand the fatigue and the frustrations; because I have traveled frequently the paths of process philosophy, I believe, still, in the dream.

Therefore, I am moved by the "throb" of Kesson and Oliver, with its connections to Whitehead's *pulsating* actual entity and its link to Doll's *transformative* theory. It beckons me, once again, to take up the quest—to seek that higher plane where enchantment abides. The throb encourages me to continue to explore the possibilities for transformation inherent in "aliveness." I thank Kesson and Oliver for the reminder, and I accept with great joy, zeal—passion—the challenge!

References

Doll, W. E., Jr. (1993). *A post-modern perspective on curriculum.* New York: Teachers College Press.

Hill, J. P. (1999). Relating process philosophy to the classroom: An exploration of Alfred North Whitehead's educational vision. (Unpublished doctoral dissertation. Louisiana State University).

Russell, B. (1968). *The autobiography of Bertrand Russell, 1914–1944.* vol. 2. Boston: Little, Brown.

Whitehead, A. N. (1938). *Modes of thought.* New York: Macmillan.

Janis Pardue Hill is currently teaching at Ouachita Parish High School in Monroe, Louisiana, and has over 25 years of experience as a high school English teacher. She received her Ph.D. in curriculum and instruction from Louisiana State University in Baton Rouge; her M.A. in English from Louisiana Tech; and her B.S. in education from Northeast State University in Louisiana. She serves as a member of the Advisory Council of the Association for Process Philosophy of Education and has presented papers at the National Council of Teachers of English Annual Conference, the APPE Dickinson 2000 Conference, and the Louisiana Council of Teachers of English conferences.

Chapter 8 Commercializing Schools

Problematic: Schools "R" Us

Alex Molnar presents a persuasive case for understanding the commercial transformation of U.S. schools within a wider cultural history of propaganda and advertising. However, we should note immediately that the commercialization of schooling is not just a U.S. phenomenon. Wherever nation states are embracing economic globalization (see Noel Gough's "The Long Arm(s) of Globalization," this volume), schools are being commercialized. In Australia, for example, Miriam Henry and Sandra Taylor (1997) note that the pressures of microeconomic reform have encouraged some schools "to wheel and deal where they can in the attempt to become more competitive and cost-effective":

> Schools buy in pre-packaged American software, and there are increasing pressures for schools to seek corporate sponsorship for all manner of things—from school bands through to computer laboratories. Increasing numbers of schools ply the Asian market for fee paying students. This commercial logic is essentially anarchic, with unpredictable effects on curriculum and schooling practices. (56)

The unpredictability of the effects of commercialization gives us hope that Molnar's dystopic vision of a relentlessly miseducative trajectory in schooling can be averted (hope always accompanies pessimistic futurism because history is full of surprises). Users of media and technology invariably redefine the uses that their authors and inventors intend. Consumers alter what they consume. For example, the send-ups and satires of commercials on TV shows like *Saturday Night Live* lay bare the propagandist techniques of marketing, ridiculing (and often disabling) current advertising campaigns and trends within a few days of their being broadcast. More importantly, many young people do not need adult satirists to deconstruct media texts for them. As Douglas Rushkoff (1994) writes,

> Children raised hearing and speaking a language always understand it better than adults who attempt to learn its rules. This is why…our kids understand computers and their programming languages better than the people who designed them. Likewise, people weaned on media understand its set of symbols better than its creators and see through the carefully camouflaged attempts at mind control. (5)

According to Rushkoff, young people bring a sense of irony and irreverence to popular media and the ideologies it promotes; this irreverence comes from their ability to change what is on a screen: "They don't just receive and digest media. They manipulate it. They play with it. The media is not a mirror—it is an "other." They are in a living relationship with it" (31).

Of course, Rushkoff's claims on behalf of his generation should not be taken at face value. Even if he is absolutely right, we middle-aged curriculum scholars have no reason to be complacent about the "miseducative" possibilities of the commercialization of schooling that Molnar documents so clearly. More importantly, what does tolerating such commercialization say about the moral platform on which schooling is built? What values would we need to affirm—and affirm vigorously—that would see schools established as commercial-free zones?

References

Henry, Miriam, and Sandra Taylor. (1997). Globalisation and national schooling policy in Australia. In Bob Lingard and Paige Porter (Eds.), *A national approach to schooling in Australia? Essays on the development of national policies in schools of education* (pages 45–59). Canberra: Australian College of Education.

Rushkoff, Douglas. (1994). *Media virus! Hidden agendas in popular culture*. New York: Random House.

The Commercial Transformation of America's Schools

Alex Molnar

Introduction: The Propagandists

America's schools are indeed haunted. The uneasy spirit of John Dewey, as Bill Doll suggests, in "Ghosts and the Curriculum" (this volume) wanders the corridors of public education watching and waiting for his ideas to, at long last, be made flesh in the daily life of schools. Doll dares to hope that the third millennium will belong to Dewey. I do not share Doll's optimism. In my view, the spirits of Ivy Ledbetter Lee and Edward Bernays are more likely to be happily at home in America's schools and classrooms this century than the spirit of John Dewey.

The names Lee and Bernays may be unfamiliar. They are not discussed in educational history texts or curriculum guides; however, they are well known to students of business administration as the fathers of American public relations, and they have had an impact on schools and school curriculum. Ivy Lee, a former newspaper reporter, made his mark early in the twentieth century working for the Rockefeller family. He rose to prominence on the heels of a bloodbath. On April 20, 1914, in Ludlow, Colorado, the state militia opened fire on a tent city of striking miners and their families.[1]

In response to inflamed public opinion, the Rockefellers hired Ivy Lee to change the public perception of their mining operation and their family. Mr. Lee's efforts helped create modern public relations and did, in fact, to a large extent succeed in quelling public hostility toward the mining company. Afterward, to transform the public's opinion of Mr. Rockefeller, Lee saw to it that Rockefeller's philanthropy was prominently showcased and that newsreel footage showed him in appealing settings such as handing out Christmas presents, joking with newsmen, singing with his family, and playing golf. By the time of John D. Rockefeller, Sr.'s death in 1937, his transformation from villain to civic benefactor in the public view was virtually complete. Lee was without question a master of the art of what he called "getting believed."[2]

A keen awareness of the importance in a democratic society of "getting believed" animated the work of Edward Bernays,[3] who sought to harness social science research to the task he called "the engineering of consent."

During World War I he worked for the Committee on Public Information, helping the committee sell the war policies of the Wilson administration. After the war, Bernays signed on as "public relations counsel" to an impressive list of America's most powerful corporations. The American Tobacco Company, for example, hired him to increase cigarette smoking among women. In order to do so, he persuaded socialites to march down Fifth Avenue in the 1929 New York City Easter Parade proudly smoking cigarettes as "torches of liberty" in a protest against women's inequality (Jacoby, 1989, 38).

Bernays (1928) preached the gospel that public relations were essential in a democracy and that social science knowledge was essential to public relations:

> The conscious and intelligent manipulation of the organized habits and opinions of the masses is an important element in democratic society. Those who manipulate this unseen mechanism of society constitute an invisible government which is the true ruling power of our country. (9)

He goes on to say that,

> In theory, everybody buys the best and cheapest commodities offered him on the market. In practice, if everyone went around pricing, and chemically testing before purchasing, the dozens of soaps or fabrics or brands of bread which are for sale, economic life would become hopelessly jammed. To avoid such confusion, society consents to have its choice narrowed to ideas and objects brought to its attention by propaganda of all kinds. There is, consequently a vast and continuous effort going on to capture our minds in the interest of some policy or commodity or idea. (11)

In Bernays's view, democratic civic life was a marketplace every bit as much as economic life. He took it as axiomatic that competing political interests would seek to put their views before the public just as competing economic interests would seek to promote their products and services. Bernays did not consider this an evil process nor did he regard propaganda as a dirty word. To him, propaganda was "a perfectly legitimate form of human activity" (11). He argued that, "Any society, whether it be social, religious, or political, which is possessed of certain beliefs, and sets out to make them known, either by the spoken or written words, is practicing propaganda" (11). Propaganda was, as he saw it, essential for keeping the wheels of politics and commerce turning while preserving social stability.

Bernays would have us believe that public relations and advertising are progressive tools of democratic governance and the market economy.

The conflation of market choice and the democratic political process is, however, problematic. Although the advertising industry is very good at promoting the consumption of goods and services, at its heart it is profoundly anti-democratic.

As Stuart Ewan writes in *Captains of Consciousness* (1977),

> It became a central function of business to be able to define a social order which would feed and adhere to the demands of the productive process and at the same time absorb, neutralize and contain the transitional impulses of a working class emerging from the unrequited drudgery of nineteenth century industrialization. (52)

Education was central to this process. It was, however, education of a very particular sort. Ewan quotes the Boston department store merchant, Edward Filene, to make the point. Filene argued that, "Mass production demands the education of the masses." And in their education, "the masses must learn to behave like human beings in a mass production world" (54). According to Ewan, Filene wanted to build an industrial and social democracy based on what he termed "fact finding." To Filene, this meant that modern education should focus on "the "facts" about what is being produced rather than questioning the social bases upon which those facts lay"[4] (55).

What is promoted through advertising, to the detriment of genuine democratic civic culture, is mass consumerism in commerce and politics. As Stuart and Elizabeth Ewan argue in *Channels of Desire* (1982),

> The goal of the advertising industry is to link the isolated experience of the spectator with the collectivized impulses and priorities of the corporation....If *economic* consumerism tends to organize disconnected individuals into coherent and predictable markets, it is *political* consumerism that defines the current state of western democracy seeking to create a vast patriotic unity—a unity without solidarity. (263, 266; emphasis in original)

One outcome of such "unity without solidarity" is no doubt the creation of what David Riesman termed the "lonely crowd"—a crowd that represents the negation of both the individual and of genuine community (Riesman et al., 1955). Members of Riesman's lonely crowd define themselves by their possessions and express their individuality by looking, smelling, and thinking like everyone else.

Educative vs. Mis-Educative Experiences

The views of Bernays are profoundly different from John Dewey's conception of science springing out of and inseparable from an engaged democratic community built on rational interactions. Indeed, in every aspect, advertising ideology is the enemy of Dewey's philosophy. There is no room in the thinking and practice of Bernays and his public relations offspring for either Dewey's conception of democracy or his conception of an educative experience. The very edifice of American mass marketing is built on what Dewey, in *Experience and Education* (1963/1938), termed mis-educative experiences. Sophisticated marketing techniques conceal but cannot alter the reality that the purpose of mass marketing is to manipulate the many for the benefit of the few. It is, as Dewey characterized traditional education, imposition from above and from the outside (18).

In *Experience and Education* Dewey wrote:

> Any experience is mis-educative that has the effect of arresting or distorting the growth of further experience. An experience may be such as to engender callousness; it may produce lack of sensitivity and of responsiveness. Then the possibilities of having richer experience in the future are restricted. (25)

He goes on to explain that mis-educative experiences can land a person in a rut and limit further experience. Moreover, although mis-educative experiences may be pleasurable or exciting in the moment, because they are not linked cumulatively they simply dissipate energy. Mis-educative experiences, according to Dewey,

> may be lively, vivid, and "interesting" and yet their disconnectedness may artificially generate dispersive, disintegrated, centrifugal habits. The consequence of formation of such habits is the inability to control future experiences. They are then taken, either by way of enjoyment or of discontent and revolt, just as they come. Under such circumstances, it is idle to talk of self-control. (26)

And again, in his opinion, it

> may be a loss rather than a gain to escape from the control of another person only to find one's conduct dictated by immediate whim and caprice, that is, at the mercy of impulses into whose formation intelligent judgement has not entered. A person whose conduct is controlled in this way has at most only the illusion of freedom. Actually he is directed by forces over which he has no command. (64–65)

Thus, he held that an "[o]veremphasis upon activity as an end, instead of upon *intelligent* activity, leads to identification of freedom with immediate execution of impulses and desires" (68–69). Modern mass advertising turns Dewey's philosophy inside out. In the name of freedom and individuality, advertising encourages individuals to give in to their impulses so that they may be controlled more easily by others.

The last thing in the world that advertisers want is for a target audience to have self-control. For Dewey, in contrast, freedom is expressed through the control of impulse in the service of intelligent purposes. To his mind, "The only freedom that is of enduring importance is freedom of intelligence, that is to say, freedom of observation and of judgement exercised in behalf of purposes that are intrinsically worthwhile" (61).

In *Experience and Education,* Dewey described an educative experience as being part of a continuity of experiences that promote individual and community growth. Continuity of experience is, as he saw it, necessary both to provide context and meaning to immediate experiences and to shape subsequent experiences in the service of individual purposes. In his words, "when and *only* when development in a particular line conduces to continuing growth does it answer to the criterion of education as growing" (36). To Dewey, "Every experience is a moving force. Its value can be judged only on the ground of what it moves toward and into" (39). Furthermore, he explained, "No experience is educative that does not tend both to knowledge of more facts and entertaining of more ideas and to a better, a more orderly, arrangement of them" (82).

Dewey's educational philosophy is rooted, based in the belief that individuals are active members of real communities that shape and, in turn, are shaped by them. In his words, "Every genuine experience has an active side which changes in some degree the objective experiences under which experiences are had" (39). In contrast, advertising deploys a variety of nonrational appeals and attempts to create pseudo-communities based on consumption or the uncritical acceptance of a particular policy or point of view.

Educative experiences are the result of the interaction of the internal (or personal) and the external (or objective) in what Dewey termed a "situation." It is within the "situation" that the continuity of experience is made manifest, the individual and community changed, and the avenues of future growth created. Through this process, the individual advances in knowledge, self-control, and freedom, and the democratic community is progressively improved. Dewey explained that what is

> learned in the way of knowledge and skill in one situation becomes an instrument of understanding and dealing effectively with the situations that follow. The process goes on as long as life and learning continue....A fully integrated personality...exists only when successive experiences are integrated with one another. It can be built up only as a world of related objects is constructed. Continuity and interaction in their active union with each other provide the measure of the educative significance and value of an experience. (44–45)

Where Dewey seeks integrative experiences in the service of the individual and the community, advertising seeks to destroy continuity, fragment experience, and encourage us to give in to our irrational impulses for the purpose of manipulating our behavior.

No one can seriously suggest that children represent the rational consumer of market ideology; that is, children can in no sense be considered to have the same power, information, and freedom that adults are said to have to enter freely into contracts for goods and services in the idealized marketplace. Advertising to children is, then, a kind of immoral war on childhood, waged for the profit of adults who should be childhood's guardians. Furthermore, when advertising is conducted in schools, the immorality is compounded because the power of the state is twisted to the service of special interests, the ethical standing of educators compromised, and the orientation of the school shifted toward mis-educative experiences.

The Ethics of Schoolhouse Commercialism

Schoolhouse commercialism is not new. Its development parallels that of the public relations industry as a whole. As early as 1929, the National Education Association's Committee on Propaganda in the Schools surveyed school officials to determine what sponsored materials had been received and what policies or other mechanisms were in place to deal with them. The concerns of the committee then are our concerns now. Two current types of schoolhouse commercialism, exclusive soft-drink contracts and sponsored educational materials, help illustrate the ethical problems created as well as the mis-educative character of advertising in schools.

Exclusive Soft-Drink Contracts

On September 23, 1998, John Bushey, the executive director of school leadership for Colorado Springs School District 11, sent a memo to district principals. Normally, a memo from a school administrator's office outlining expectations for the coming year would not merit press attention. John Bushey's memo, however, attracted the attention of the *Denver Post* ("To Ensure Revenue, Coke Is It; Schools Urged to Boost Sales," Nov. 22, 1998), *Harper's Magazine* ("District 11's Coke Problem," February 1999), the *Washington Post* ("Pop Culture: Health Advocates Sound Alarm as Schools Strike Deals with Coke and Pepsi," March 23, 1999), and the *New York Times* ("Today's Lesson: Soda Rights; Consultant Helps Schools Sell

Themselves to Vendors," May 21, 1999). Mr. Bushey, who oversees Colorado Springs's exclusive contract with Coca-Cola, is the district's self-proclaimed "Coke Dude." In his memo, Mr. Bushey pointed out that District 11 students needed to consume 70,000 cases of Coke products if the district was to receive the full financial benefit of its exclusive sales agreement with the company. In order to better promote the consumption of Coke products, Mr. Bushey offered school principals tips such as: "Allow students to purchase and consume vended products throughout the day" and "Locate machines where they are accessible to the students all day." He also offered to provide their schools with additional electrical outlets if necessary and enclosed a list of Coke products and a calendar of promotional events intended to help advertise them.

Mr. Bushey's zeal may in part be explained by his tardy realization that the district's exclusive agreement with Coke counted only vending machine sales toward the system's annual quota; Coca-Cola products sold at cafeteria fountains wouldn't count. In March 1999, Mr. Bushey told the *Washington Post* that the district might not meet its contractual goals. In May he told the *New York Times*, "Quite honestly, they were smarter than us!"

Sponsored Educational Materials

Sponsored educational materials have been around much longer than exclusive soft-drink contracts. The magazine *Marketing Tools* has traced corporate-sponsored educational materials as far back as 1890 when a paint company developed a handout on primary and secondary colors intended to be distributed in school art classes. The handout also contained a plug for the company's products (Klein, 1997). Despite some occasionally harsh criticisms of the practice, over the years sponsored educational materials have become a staple of marketers who want to put a corporate message in the school.

It is not hard to find examples of sponsored educational materials. The Life and Health Insurance Foundation has a high school education program (Woods, 1999); Merrill Lynch offers "Money Matters in the Millennium," a "financial literacy" curriculum and Young Entrepreneur Kits to teach students how to start their own business (Merrill Lynch, 1999); and the Archery Manufacturers and Merchants Organization offers middle schools a kit called "Archery Alley" (Boyles, 1998). Lifetime Learning Systems developed the "Quality Comes in Writing" program for the BIC pen company to promote "strong writing skills" in fourth to sixth graders (BIC,

1999); and MasterCard International wanted to help students learn money management skills (MasterCard International, 1999).

When and where so-called learning materials turn up is based on a corporate need that usually has nothing to do with curriculum improvement. To get around this problem, companies frequently bill their creations as "supplements" to the teachers' regular lessons. They encourage teachers to fit in some or all of the materials whenever and wherever they can. Some clever marketers try to make this into a virtue by claiming that the material is therefore controlled by the teacher, who can tailor it to fit the school's program. However, even a brief examination of most sponsored materials would prove to most people that it is created to benefit its sponsor, not the teachers or the children.

Corporations try to put materials in schools for a number of reasons. They may simply want to sell something to the kids. Companies that sell snack food, candy, clothing, and personal care products are often in this category. Other companies may want to develop a consumer base for their products down the line. These include computer manufacturers, credit card companies, and even car manufacturers.

Since the marketing firms that create sponsored materials have to keep their corporate customers satisfied, their material is judged, first and foremost, by the extent to which it meets the objectives of their clients. The emphasis is not on providing the fullest and most accurate presentation of information to students. The fundamental difference between marketers and teachers distorts teaching as surely as a funhouse mirror distorts the image of anyone who looks into it. When teachers use products developed by marketing firms, instead of lessons taught to benefit students, the curriculum promotes the objectives of a third party whose interests may well conflict with those of the children, their families, and the country. Bernays might approve. Dewey would not.

Conclusion

Commercial activities now shape the structure of the school day, influence the content of the school curriculum, and determine whether children have access to a variety of technologies. Moreover, it appears from a number of citations that there is an emerging trend whereby marketers attempt to bundle together advertising and marketing programs in schools across a variety of media and thus gain a dominant position in the schoolhouse market. The effort to integrate more fully the schoolhouse into corporate marketing plans by securing control over as many school-based advertising media as possible may well be the trend to watch over the next decade. If so, we can expect schools to serve as launch pads for marketing campaigns that resemble high-profile movie releases complete with multiple tie-ins for a variety of products and services aimed at children and their families.

At a time when commercialism in schools and classrooms is increasing dramatically, educators have been largely silent or, worse, cheerleaders for these trends. The failure of the education community to critically describe and attempt to understand and assess the impact of commercial activities on the character and quality of schools and their programs is not worthy of a profession that would lay claim to the legacy of John Dewey. If advertising is, as I believe, the 24-hours-a-day, 7-days-a-week, 365-days-a year curriculum of our culture, then Americans young and old are being relentlessly miseducated and, as a consequence, our society is correspondingly less democratic. John Dewey would roll over in his grave.

Acknowledgment: This essay is a shortened version of Alex Molnar's original paper; the editors are grateful to him for consenting to this condensation and to Donna Trueit for doing it.

Notes

[1] Fifty-three people including thirteen women and children were killed in the massacre. The events in "bloody Ludlow" aroused widespread public sympathy for the Colorado Fuel and Iron Company strikers and provoked outrage at the mine owners, the Rockefeller family.

[2] The overall discussion of Lee's work is drawn from Bill Moyers, "The Image Makers" (1984).

[3] Bernays's mother was Sigmund Freud's sister, and his father was Freud's wife's brother.

[4] It should, perhaps, not be surprising that it was Filene who founded and initially directed Consumers Union, an organization devoted to providing the "facts" about products and services to America's consumers.

References

Bernays, Edward. (1928). *Propaganda*. New York: Liveright.

BIC. (1999). Quality comes in writing. Lesson plan. *Lifetime Learning Systems* (cited July 16, 1999); available from http://www.qualitycomesinwriting.com.

Boyles, Carolee. (1998). Involve yourself in a worthwhile program; programs of archery associations. *Shooting Industry*. November: 22.

Bushey, John. (1999). District 11's Coke problem. *Harper's*. February: 26–27.

DeGette, Cara. (1998). To ensure revenue, Coke is it; schools urged to boost sales. *Denver Post*. November 22: B–01.

Dewey, John. (1965). *Experience and education*. New York: Collier.

Ewan, Stuart. (1977). *Captains of consciousness: Advertising and the social roots of the consumer culture*. New York: McGraw-Hill.

Ewan, Stuart, and Elizabeth Ewan. (1982). *Channels of desire: Mass images and the shaping of American consciousness*. New York: McGraw-Hill.

Hays, Constance. (1999). Today's lesson: Soda rights; consultant helps schools sell themselves to vendors. *New York Times*. May 21: C–1.

Jacoby, Russell. (1989). *The last intellectuals: American culture in the age of academe*. New York: Noonday.

Kaufman, Marc. (1999). Pop culture: Health advocates sound alarm as schools strike deals with Coke and Pepsi. *Washington Post*. March 23: Z–12.

Klein, Matthew. (1997). School daze. *Marketing tools*. September 16.

MasterCard International. (1999). Master your future. Lesson plan. Video Placement Worldwide (cited July 16, 1999); available from http://www.vpw.com.

Merrill Lynch corporate press release. (1999). Merrill Lynch announces international saving month; marketing global expansion of six-year U.S. initiative. *PR Newswire*. April 5.

Moyers, Bill. (1984). The image makers: A walk through the 20th century with Bill Moyers. Corporation for Entertainment and Learning. Distributed by PBS.

Packard, Vance. (1963). *The hidden persuaders*. New York: Pocket.

Riesman, David, Nathan Glazer, and Reuel Denney. (1955). *The lonely crowd: A study of changing American character*. Garden City, NY: Doubleday.

Woods, David. (1999). LIFE's already doing it. *National Underwriter*. June 7: 43.

Alex Molnar is Professor of Education in the Department of Curriculum and Instruction at the University of Wisconsin-Milwaukee School of Education. He has a Ph.D. in urban education and a specialist certificate in educational administration, an M.A. in history and an M.A. in social welfare, and a B.A. in history, political science, and education. He is also the director of the Center for Education Research, Analysis, and Innovation (CERAI) and the Center for the Analysis of Commercialism in Education (CACE) at UWM. His most recent books are *Giving Kids the Business: The Commercialization of America's Schools* (1996) and *The Construction of Children's Character* (1997). His current research interests are commercial activities in the schools and market-based school reforms.

Perspective on Molnar

Patricia Thomson

Alex Molnar has done us all a big favor in documenting how it is that business is increasingly folded into the school world. However, I want to suggest that this is not something from which we can, or even ought to be, entirely "free."

Today's young people are arguably becoming, as Bill Green and Chris Bigum (1993) suggest, "aliens in the classroom." In my experience, many teachers do not cope well with the transmogrification. They think that television (except noncommercial—preferably "educational"), computer games, and comics are Bad-for-You; "reading" only occurs in the company of books; wearing this season's brand name shoes and sweatshirts is a result of Peer-Group-Pressure and a desire for Immediate-Gratification; and children and young people are innocent/gullible/unable to resist devilish advertising agents and corporate crooks. In my experience, young people do not respond well to deconstructions of the gendered, raced relations of their favorite television programs; the banishing of conversations about their preferred music, films, clothes and sports; and adult assumptions that they are the passive dupes of advertising. As John Dewey (1966/1916) put it long ago:

> We have the spectacle of professional educators decrying appeal to interest while they uphold with great dignity the need of reliance upon examinations, marks, promotions and emotions, prizes, and the time-honored paraphernalia of rewards and punishments. The effect of this situation in crippling the teacher's sense of humor has not received the attention which it deserves. (334)

And I would add to this, crippling the humor and interest of students. Furthermore, the kind of noxious commercialized practices that Alex Molnar describes so well are symptomatic of other, bigger changes. Even if states and school districts were to fund schools adequately, and "free" schools from the spectral presence of business by excoriating logos, naming rights, and exclusive contracts from school yards and classrooms, there would still be a need for educators to consider not only commercialization and marketization but also

- *The Commodification of Education*

School systems are increasingly taking up generic metaphors of organizational development and corporate and performative management practices. School principals are encouraged to learn from their "counterparts" in various commercial enterprises and to think of themselves as chief executives; enterprise education is hailed as the answer to the collapse of the "school-to-work pathway" and the "lifelong career"; and education itself is increasingly seen as a solely individual (rather than also a social) benefit and a commodity to be (free) marketed locally and internationally (Coady, 2000; Marginson, 1997; Taylor et al., 1997).

- *The Development of Consumption Societies*

Scholars, public intellectuals, and popular commentators alike comment that consumption rather than production now seems to be the order of the day. A pastiche of style and image saturates lives and digital and physical spaces—we live with proliferating meanings and "designer identities" (Casey, 1995). Unfulfilled desire is the contemporary regime folded into ongoing relations of colonization, gender, race, sexuality and generation (Bauman, 1998; Brah et al., 1999; Jameson and Miyoshi, 1998).

These continuing educational and social changes are surely a, if not *the*, curriculum matters of the moment and the educational commercialization described by Molnar is a single (and nasty) epiphenomenon. In pointing towards a curriculum for and about these far-reaching changes, I will appeal not only to the ectoplasmic specters of things past but also to a contemporary and friendly iteration.

A Curriculum Epigenesis Called Colin

> The ghost awoke to Kumiko's touch as they began their descent into Heathrow. The fifty-first generation of Maas-Neotek biochips conjured up an indistinct figure on the seat beside her, a boy out of some faded hunting print, legs crossed casually in tan breeches and riding boots. "Hello," the ghost said. (Gibson, 1989, 9)

The ghost, a holograph named Colin, as written by William Gibson in the cyberpunk novel *Mona Lisa Overdrive*, is a set of resources that Kumiko can mobilize in unfamiliar surroundings. Colin encourages Kumiko to actively use her own knowledges and interests as well as those of her ghostly guide to make sense of, and make her way in, alien and risky environments. Colin provides Kumiko with information (some of which is "old" rather than "new" knowledge) through conversations that connect with her past life experiences as well as with her current circumstances. Above all, the holographic Colin is a tactition, a set of practices that adapt and change to assist Kumiko in moving through the physical and digital spaces and places in which she finds herself. It is Colin (curriculum) and Kumiko's (student) mutually constructed/constructing story that produces the action.

As a trope for a curriculum for these times, we educators could do worse than keep Colin in mind. A Colin curriculum would have at its heart a continuing conversation about the kinds of knowledges and practices that children and young people need in the present and in the future consumption society (see, for example, Education Queensland, 2000; The New London Group, 1966). A Colin curriculum would

- Use pedagogic practices of locating, valuing and mobilizing local "funds of knowledge" (Moll et al., 1993), "local literacies" (Barton and Hamilton, 1998) and "community assets" (Kretzman and McKnight, 1993);
- Foreground popular cultures (Dyson, 1997), everyday materials, commercial and otherwise (Comber, 1999), indigenous (Bishop and Glynn, 1999; Nakata, 1998) and folk knowledges (Wigginton, 1986);
- Move beyond deconstruction towards reconstructions and redesigns that promote social and community action (Comber et al., 2001; Searle, 1998);
- Make connections with research on social, cultural, economic, and political changes and young people's responses to them (Kenway and Bullen, 2001; McDonald, 1999);
- Engage ethically with changing social institutions and processes of management and globalization (Bauman, 1993; see also Gough, this volume);
- Focus on fun, irony, humor, and pleasure (McWilliam, 2000);
- Support the narrativization of ongoing (and multiple) identities (Bloom, 1998; Britzman, 1998), emotions as well as intellects (Boler, 1999), and artistic sensibilities (Brunner, 1998);
- Refuse to close down meanings, favoring instead multiple readings of popular culture, engaging students in sophisticated multilayered text production (Snyder, 1996) while relishing "indeterminacy with interpretation" (Doll, 1993).

Now, I am not suggesting that a Colin curriculum will rid schools of the toxic bloom of the decals and deals that Molnar describes. However, refusing an all-encompassing, judgmental attitude towards the pleasures and pastimes of young people, and acknowledging that there might be something in this advertising stuff (with its visual-verbal semiotics and appeals to every-day pleasures) from which teachers and schools might learn, could well encourage more productive pedagogical relationships between students and their teachers. Furthermore, a Colin curriculum would certainly support school students and their teachers ability to see the commercialization of education for what it is—not just the cynical, opportunist and manipulative grab for the pocket money and part-time wages of young people—but signs of our changing times.

References

Barton, D., and M. Hamilton. (1998). *Local literacies: Reading and writing in one community.* London, New York: Routledge.

Bauman, Z. (1993). *Postmodern ethics.* Oxford: Blackwell.

_______. (1998). *Work, consumerism and the new poor.* Buckingham, Philadelphia: Open University.

Bishop, R., and T. Glynn. (1999). *Culture counts: Changing power relations in education.* Palmerston North: Dunmore.

Bloom, L. R. (1998). *Under the sign of hope: Feminist methodology and narrative interpretation.* Albany, NY: State University of New York Press.

Boler, M. (1999). *Feeling power: Emotions and education.* New York, London: Routledge.

Brah, A., M. Hickman, and M. Mac An Ghaill (Eds.). (1999). *Global futures: Migration, environment and globalisation.* London, New York: St Martin's.

Britzman, D. (1998). *Lost subjects, contested objects: Toward a psychoanalytic inquiry of learning.* Albany, NY: State University of New York Press.

Brunner, D. D. (1998). *Between the masks: Resisting the politics of essentialism.* Lanham, Boulder, New York, Oxford: Rowman and Littlefield.

Casey, C. (1995). *Work, self and society: After industrialism.* London: Routledge.

Clegg, S., and G. Palmer (Eds.). (1996). *The politics of management knowledge.* London, Thousand Oaks, New Delhi: Sage.

Coady, T. (Ed.). (2000). *Why universities matter.* Sydney: Allen and Unwin.

Comber, B. (1999). Critical literacies: Negotiating powerful and pleasurable curricula—how do we foster critical literacy through language arts? Keynote address to the National Council of Teachers of English 89th Annual Convention, Denver, Colorado, November 18–21.

Comber, B., P. Thomson, and M. Wells. (2001). Critical literacy finds a "place": Writing and social action in a neighborhood school. *Elementary School Journal, 101*(4), 451–64.

Dewey, J. (1966 /1916). *Democracy and education.* New York: Free. (Original publication 1916.)

Doll, W. J., Jr. (1993). *A post-modern perspective on curriculum.* New York: Teachers College Press.

Dyson, A. H. (1997). *Writing superheroes: Contemporary childhood, popular culture, and classroom literacy*. New York, London: Teachers College Press.

Education Queensland. (2000). Framework Project, http://education.qld.gov.au/corporate/framework/. Accessed March 12, 2000.

Gibson, W. (1989). *Mona Lisa overdrive*. London: Grafton.

Green, B., and C. Bigum. (1993). Aliens in the classroom. *Australian Journal of Education, 37*(42), 119–41.

Jameson, F., and M. Miyoshi (Eds.). (1998). *The cultures of globalisation*. Durham, London: Duke University Press.

Kenway, J., and E. Bullen. (2001). *Consuming children: Entertainment, advertising, and education*. Buckingham, Philadelphia: Open University Press.

Kretzman, J., and J. McKnight. (1993). *Building communities from the inside-out*. Chicago: The Asset-Based Community Development Institute.

Marginson, S. (1997). *Markets in education*. Sydney: Allen and Unwin.

McDonald, K. (1999). *Struggles for subjectivity: Identity, action and youth experience*. Cambridge, New York, Oakleigh, Madrid: Cambridge University Press.

McWilliam, E. (2000). *Pedagogical pleasures*. New York: Lang.

Moll, L., J. Tapia, and K. Whitmore. (1993). Living knowledge: The social distribution of cultural resources for thinking. In G. Salomon (Ed.), *Distributed cognitions* (pages 139–63). Cambridge: Cambridge University Press.

Nakata, M. (1998). Anthropological texts and indigenous standpoint. *Journal of Australian Aboriginal Studies, 2*, 3–12.

The New London Group. (1966). A pedagogy of multi literacies: Designing social futures. *Harvard Educational Review, 66*(1), 363–76.

Searle, C. (1998). *None but our words: Critical literacy in the classroom*. Buckingham, Philadephia: Open University Press.

Snyder, I. (1996). *Hypertext: The electronic labyrinth*. Melbourne: Melbourne University Press.

Taylor, S., F. Rivzi, B. Lingard, and M. Henry. (1997). *Educational policy and the politics of change*. London, New York: Routledge.

Wigginton, E. (1986). *Sometimes a shining moment: The foxfire experience. Twenty years teaching in a high school classroom*. New York: Anchor, Doubleday.

Patricia Thomson is Associate Professor in the School of Education, University of South Australia, Underdale, where she coordinates a professional doctorate program in educational leadership. She has been a teacher and curriculum coordinator in alternative secondary schools, deputy principal of a disadvantaged community-based secondary school, and principal of a large disadvantaged K–12 school. She spent two years as an executive in a state education system, responsible for policy and planning, before completing her Ph.D. at Deakin University.

Chapter 9 A Curriculum Journey

Problematic: A Traveler's Tale

Mary Elizabeth Mullino Moore shares our fondness for alliteration, and so her journey through the visions to which we allude in our introductory chapters is patterned (rather than "organized") by her choice of sites beginning with the letter "C": complexity, community, conversation, and culmination. These sites work as attractors but do not entirely determine the pathways she chooses between and around them. Moore is on a self-guided tour, not a meander or ramble; she allows herself an occasional distraction (because "straying from our customary ruts…is important for new discoveries"), but takes each step deliberately and responsively (which she signals by such phrases as "this discussion leads naturally to….").

In recounting her journey, Moore fashions anecdotes, reflections, quotations, proposals, and speculations into a tale that effects the genre of travel writing rather than the conventional academic essay. We always hoped that the contributions to this text would be diverse in both form and content, so we are pleased that some authors have chosen to criticize, or to debate, or to construct alternative theses and antitheses. Moore contemplates, reminisces, meditates, and crafts thoughtful responses or refinements to the visions she encounters.

Moore offers a useful heuristic for generating curriculum visions when she insists on a simultaneous exploration of what she sees as opposites to complexity, community, conversation, and culmination. Thus she examines, complexity *and* simplicity, community *and* individuality, conversation *and* silence, and culmination *and* new beginnings. We believe that such binary concepts are better understood as "both/and" relationships rather than "either/or" distinctions, and so we would also like to speculate on what other relationships or attractors might be produced in proximity to these continua. For example, Jack Cohen and Ian Stewart (1994) generate *complicity* and *simplexity* as new referents in a constellation of meaning previously mapped as the complexity/simplicity continuum. What is other to community that is not individuality? What is other to conversation that is not silence? What is other to culmination that is not a new beginning?

Reference

Cohen, Jack, and Ian Stewart. (1994). *The collapse of chaos: Discovering simplicity in a complex world.* New York: Viking Penguin.

Curriculum: A Journey Through Complexity, Community, Conversation, Culmination

Mary Elizabeth Mullino Moore

One of my colleagues is fond of evaluating his university teaching by the standard of how much students understand of what he is trying to teach. He says to me, "I am not sure if they are 'getting it'" or "They are not 'getting it.'" Another colleague is working with a passionate group of people in his church, seeking to build strong interracial and intercultural partnerships in their region of the country. He says to me, "Our working group wants to gather people who 'get it' and encourage them to work together in building intercultural awareness and action in the church." These two colleagues use the same expression—getting it—to speak of their goals for a particular educational process, but what they say is quite different. The first understands "it" to mean the subject matter that he teaches; the second understands "it" to mean a paradigm of intercultural relationships. In the first case, the content is clear and stable; it does not change appreciably from year to year. In the second case, the attitude of openness to all peoples is stable, and everything else is subject to great change, both the subject matter and process of engagement.

In a sense, this book is about "getting it." The historical review and ideological analysis of inherited curriculum practices is designed to awaken readers to a curriculum tradition that emphasizes control and goal attainment. Yet, Noel Gough and Bill Doll seem to want much more than casual understanding or nodding agreement to what they write. They are pointing to a future that requires readers to "get it" if we are going to change the structures and processes of curriculum. They encourage an attitude that is open to the flow of education; they encourage an attitude in which vision is more important than goals, and poetry and narrative are more important than direct communication.

In that spirit, the purpose of this brief essay is to dive deeply into four of the visions of Gough and Doll—complexity, community, conversation and culmination. I will amplify these in ways that are implied, but not developed, by the coeditors. Doll makes a strong point that curriculum theorists need to move beyond "either-or" thinking; however, he sometimes leans toward either-ors in approaching certain concepts, such as complexity. He implies that the opposite is to be shunned. I propose that we take Doll's ideas to their logical conclusion and embrace complexity and simplicity, community and individuality, conversation and silence, culmination and new beginnings.

Such play with ideas requires a word about ghosts and control. Bill Doll has offered fascinating insights regarding diverse perspectives on ghosts and their roles. I will add one other perspective. According to stories in many cultures (England, Korea, and so forth), ghosts linger on earth because they have unfinished business—issues that were not resolved when a person or animal was alive. I propose that, metaphorically, the ghost of control may also have a role in resolving unfinished business. If this is the case, it need not be ferried away; we simply need to heed its cries. In a sense, Doll himself does this. He recognizes the value of what he calls "emergent control" or the "other sense of control." I will build upon his point. Perhaps, the yearning for control can be seen as a *friendly* ghost if we allow ourselves to pursue the depths of that yearning and not simply yield to domination and hierarchy. Perhaps the yearning for control points to a human desire to discover simplicity in complexity, individuality in community, silence in conversation, and new beginnings in culminating moments. Such possibilities motivate a journey into four C's of education and their friendly ghosts.

Complexity and Simplicity

In the two years before my father died, he rehearsed two stories again and again. Suffering from Alzheimer's, my father had lost most of his short-term memory, but he seemed highly motivated to tell me his two favorite stories, as if his life mission were to pass these narratives to his daughter. The stories were simple in a way. One was his memory of a near-death experience when he was a young boy of four or five. He remembered a fateful day when the doctor told his parents that, if their son lived through the night, he would probably survive. Later that night my father saw a buggy coming to his parents' farm, loaded with people dressed in white; the unusual people came into the house to get him, but they had second thoughts and decided to leave him with his family. The next morning when my father awoke, his fever had broken, and he began to heal.

My father's other story was about his decision in January of his seventeenth year not to return to college because his father needed him on the farm. The Depression, combined with farming woes, had convinced my grandfather that he could not afford to have a child in college. On the eve of my father's scheduled departure, he went to bed, despairing of his loss and accepting of his fate. Early the next morning, his mother awakened him; she had packed his bags in the middle of the night and was ready to take him to the train station to return to college.

I have come to think of my father's stories as treasured gifts—products of his simplified mind, which held together the complexity of his life. These stories suggest to mc that simplicity is not the opposite of complexity but rather the companion. One could even say that simplicity is a ghost, luring people to seek meanings (organizational structures) within complexity. With this in mind, how might education invite people to engage with complexity and search for simplicity? Two simple clues emerge as I play with the complexities of Doll and Gough. First, we need education that invites people to seek the insights and visions that bubble to the surface in the giant pot of complexity. Second, we need education that encourages people to accept and enjoy the unsolved mysteries that confront them.

As to seeking insights and visions, we can begin with Doll's awareness of education as "the dynamic interaction that constitutes all life." The very act of seeking insight and vision leads people more intensely into interaction and complexity. Thus, educators who encourage students to be seekers are well served by John Dewey's and Bill Doll's "both-and" way of perceiving reality; they invite people to move deeply into complexity and well beyond "either-or" limitations. Interactive education invites people to focus on points of interaction rather than bits of information. Interactive curriculum encourages people to engage complex subject matters and to seek the insights that are waiting to be discovered (Moore 1983, 1997; Doll, 1993).

As to unsolved mysteries, complexity defies neat systems, although it lures people to wonder and speculate about how the world works and why. It even invites a turn in physics and philosophy to what Margaret Wertheim (1995, 12–15) calls a "theory of everything," an attempt to develop a comprehensive explanation of the entire universe, sought first by Pythagoras and continued by Albert Einstein and Stephen Hawking. The complex details of the world never neatly fit into these theories, however, no matter how generative and practical they may be in reshaping worldviews. Doll's emphasis on complexity raises serious questions regarding such comprehensive theoretical systems. Other philosophers have also raised questions, choosing to leave loose ends in their own philosophical systems. Soren Kierkegaard wrote abundantly during his career, diving ever deeper into existential themes, but he culminated his life work with *Concluding Unscientific Postscript* (1974/1846). Alfred North Whitehead was more willing than Kierkegaard to enter speculative philosophy, offering categoreal schemes and a process-relational worldview. Even so, he concluded his life work with *Adventures of Ideas* (1933). Both Kierkegaard and Whitehead ended their literary careers by pointing to complexity—complexity that did not fit neatly even into their own theories.

Just as my father passed on his complex life experiences and unsolved mysteries in two simple stories, so educators are challenged to invite people into insights, visions, and unsolved mysteries through the complexity that they and others experience in the journey of life. For this, we need narratives and conceptual frameworks, to be sure, but we also need courage to face the challenges that complexity and simplicity pose.

Community and Individuality

I recently talked with a young woman who lives in an English boarding school. She is preparing for her A-level examinations so she can enter university. She told me that the thing she dislikes most about living in the boarding school full-time is that the atmosphere is very competitive, and everyone looks to see how others are doing on tests and papers. Consider the atmosphere described in *Best Intentions*, a story of Edmund Perry, an African-American student with enormous intellectual and leadership potential. Perry was removed from his natural community and placed in an elite boarding school. The pressures of a double life finally led him into an act of mugging that cost him his life (Anson, 1987). Perry's story, as that of the young woman, is one that brings out some of the difficulties and challenges of community life. Communities do not always nurture communal concern and individuality; they sometimes nurture communal suspicion, distorted values, and individual competition.

At the same time, communities and individuals may interact in mutually nourishing ways. Both Doll and Gough call for a move away from competitiveness and individualism in education, and both point to community. Of particular interest in Gough's discourse is the story from Le Guin: "...he learned arboriculture with his mother's brother...and with orchard trees of all kinds." This is an important starting point for reflecting on community because much is implied by this short sentence. First, the boy learned *with* his uncle (the point made by Gough); second, his uncle is named as his "mother's brother," a statement of relationship; and third, he learned "with orchard trees of all kinds," describing where the trees reside and the diversity among them. This offers a picture of community that includes familial and earthbound relationships as well as teaching relationships. In fact, the teaching relationships are embedded in the others.

This story plants a seed that could be developed further. What might be the nature of curriculum grounded in community? Are any clues available in the Western, individualized world? Doll's discussion of Western education from the sixteenth century forward is one that emphasizes the methodization movement, scientific advancement, development of schools, and trends toward individualism. Certainly, Peter Ramus did inspire a movement toward comprehensive and logically ordered knowledge and a consequent movement toward universalized and logically structured curriculum. On the other hand, the shift in education that came with Johann Amos Comenius (1592–1670) involved more than methodization. The shift also moved toward greater concern for community—the community of students and the multiple communities they represented.

The purposes of Comenius's movement were to make knowledge accessible to everyone and to respond more adequately to the abilities and experiences of students (Comenius, 1896/1632). With such emphases, method necessarily became a concern. In addition, the shift toward emphasizing the teaching-learning relationship was influenced by a larger movement toward democratizing education. Through this democratizing movement, education was eventually to be more available to women as well as men, the poor as well as the wealthy, and ordinary people as well as promising scholars.

Perhaps our primary clues for communal education need to come from educational institutions that stand outside the mainstream of the methodization movement described by Doll. Perhaps, we can find clues in the Native schools of Canada with their emphases on spirituality, community building, individual care, and the learning of ancient stories, practices, and traditions alongside required subject matter (Haig-Brown et al., 1997). Perhaps, we can even find some alternative visions in Protestant Western cultures. For example, the German seminaries that were established in the 1930s by the Confessing Movement were organized around underground communities. For one thing, the Confessing Church was an underground movement, and centralized control was not possible. Seminaries were, thus, formed in relation to local regions and in relation to the economic and political unrest of Germany alongside rising claims of nazism. More particularly, seminaries were formed to educate people who were seeking to be authentic Christian disciples within that context.

In both the Native schools of Canada and the earlier Confessing seminaries of Germany, the attempt is to preserve and pass on a community's distinctive values; this includes the valuing of each individual within the community. In both examples, the control of schools is local and shared. In the case of Joe Duquette School, for example, authority rests jointly with the Parent Council, Department of Education, and Catholic School Board (Haig-Brown et al., 1997, 72–75, 153–68). Within these contexts, the Native and Confessing schools are able to support and encourage both community and individuality for their teachers and students.

Conversation and Silence

This discussion leads naturally to the practice of conversation—a way by which people discern and negotiate values in community. Making conversation is like making a bridge so people can meet and cross together, whether with sounds or silence. The roots of the word conversation mean to turn, or live, together. Consider the following poem:

Communication is a conversation of words and actions,
A crossing together with silence and sounds,
A sharing together of anger and wonder,
A reaching out to meet other peoples,
    other cultures,
        the fullness of the earth.

When communication is broken,
People may seek to repair it;
When communication is weak,
People may seek to build it,
But when communication is destructive,
People *must* respond—
    to do justice,
        to practice kindness,
            to restore or reform or allow conversation to die.

And in those moments when gaps *can* be healed,
    when respect and understanding grow,
        when justice flourishes,
Communication really happens,
CONVERSATION happens—
And the community knows a miracle. (Moore, personal poem, 1995)

Conversation may be with other people; it may be with another time in history or another part of the world. Education happens when people cross into other worlds, inevitably to be confronted with new experiences and insights. One of the most striking experiences of education by conversation happened for me when our daughter Rebecca took us on a *Sound of Music* tour in Salzburg, Austria. I was a bit embarrassed in the home of Mozart and the Salzburg Music Festival to be using our time on such a tour (shame on me for being snobby), but we went along and enjoyed every moment. The educational experience for us was watching Rebecca. She had viewed *The Sound of Music* at least 20 times before this journey; she delighted in seeing historical sites of the real von Trapp family and filming sites of the movie. She listened to stories of the contradictions between the two, and she tried to figure out how the real family had lived and escaped as well as how, where, and why the film was made.

After the tour, Rebecca continued to read everything she could find, and she led us on fact-finding walks around Salzburg. I realized that Rebecca was using the historiographic methods of sophisticated historians, and she was only twelve years old. A movie and a tour had invited her into a conversation with events and people of another time and place. Observing this educational experience challenges me as an educator to ask how teachers might stir such captivating conversations in formal and informal settings of education. Some of these conversations will be full of sound, and others will be internal conversations in silence.

Culmination and New Beginnings

Conversation and silence, because they are transformative, naturally lead to culmination and new beginnings. This may seem obvious, but educators often do not have culminating visions or visions of high points where everything comes together in a climax. This is especially true when educational processes are divided into discrete parts with few connections made among them. To speak of culmination as an educational value is to recognize the importance of weaving curriculum parts into a whole, the importance of integrity in an educational process. To speak of new beginnings is to recognize the importance of allowing each woven conclusion to open new opportunities.

One of the most striking visions of culmination in this book is Noel Gough's discussion of embodied vision—vision that is embodied in the person and life work of curriculum theorists and educators. Gough journeys through the poetry of Allen Ginsberg and William Blake and the artistic creations of Jean Claude Monet, El Greco, and Salvador Dali, to sketch a picture of artists whose very lives are embodied in their poetry or paintings. These artists represent new possibilities for the artistic work of curriculum theorizing. Consider Monet, for example, who spent hours in the natural world and in the gardens of his own home so that he could see more profoundly and paint the world of feeling that he saw. Gough is stirred by these artists to dream of curriculum scholars' critiquing the persistent clockwork curricula of our time with embodied visions that might capture the imagination of educators. Such embodied visions are like weavings that are made from the total life experience of educators and engage the total life experience of students.

Gough's radicality shines again when he critiques shared positive visions for education. Rather than emphasizing consensus, he invites people to see the world in fresh and embodied ways. Expressed in the language of this chapter, he encourages educators not to freeze education with culminating moments, but to allow new beginnings to emerge. Thus, the shared vision of an educational community is not an end in itself; the vision represents a culmination that stirs new beginnings. Such vision is shaped by poetry and narratives or what Gough calls "re-edited perceptions" in which we move main characters to the side and side characters to the center. Gough's desire for fresh visions reveals his passion for new beginnings. In the flow of education, some moments will represent culminations, and others will represent revisions and new visions. Both are important, and they are intimately related with one another.

This emphasis on fresh vision calls forth Alfred North Whitehead's passsion for moving out of the grooves of our professions, disciplines, and ideas. Whitehead argues that these grooves prevent us from "straying across country" (1925, 197). Straying from our customary ruts is very important if relationships are to be complex, communal, and conversational. Straying is important for new discoveries, for weaving ideas into new patterns, and for embodied visions that hold together the hearts, hands, and minds of educators and students.

In teaching, I have become increasingly aware of the urgency of action in the educational process. Whether a class produces a play, a book, a series of social studies projects, or a new math game, the value of acting is that people anticipate and work toward a culmination. The culmination is an end "product" but much more than that. It is an embodied vision; as such, it can stir fresh vision among students and teachers alike. No sooner is one project complete than people generate new ideas. Thus, complexity is brought into one simple expression; community and individuality are woven together into one distinctive whole; conversation and silence have traveled together toward a particular end. All of this culminates in educational actions for a particular moment in time, and these actions stir imagination for new moments that are yet to come. These future moments give hope to curriculum theorists and educators who dream of making a difference, offering their best so that life on this planet might flourish.

References

Anson, Robert Sam. (1987). *Best intentions: The education and killing of Edmund Perry.* New York: Vintage, Random House.

Comenius, Johann Amos. (1896). *The great didactic.* M. W. Keatinge (Trans.). London: A. and C. Black. (Original publication 1632).

Doll, William E., Jr. (1993). *A post-modern perspective on curriculum.* New York: Teachers College Press.

Haig-Brown, Celia, Kathy L. Hodgson-Smith, Robert Regnier, and Jo-Ann Archibald. (1997). *Making the spirit dance within: Joe Duquette High School and an Aboriginal community.* Toronto: James Lorimer.

Kierkegaard, Sören. (1974). *Concluding unscientific postscript.* David F. Swenson and Walter Lowrie (Trans.). Princeton: Princeton University Press. (Original publication 1846).

Moore, Mary Elizabeth Mullino. (1983). *Education for continuity and change: A new model for Christian religious education.* Nashville: Abingdon.

______. (1997). Synergistic education: Contexts and norms in higher education. *Process Papers*, vol. II.

Wertheim, Margaret. (1995). *Pythagoras' trousers.* New York: Random House.

Whitehead, Alfred North. (1925). *Science and the modern world.* New York: Macmillan.

______. (1933). *Adventures of ideas.* New York: Macmillan.

Mary Elizabeth Mullino Moore is Professor of Religion and Education at Chandler School of Theology, Emory University, and is also Director of the Program for Women in Theology and Ministry. She holds a Ph.D. in theology and education from Claremont School of Theology, Claremont, California. As a theologian and philosopher of education, she has published *Education for Continuity and Change* (1983), *Teaching from the Heart: Theology and Educational Method* (1993), and *Ministering with the Earth* (1998), as well as numerous essays and book chapters. Her passion is for education that contributes to the repair of the world (*tikkun olam* in Hebrew).

Perspective on Moore

Carol Williams

Mary Elizabeth Moore's essay brought to mind many feelings of hope, excitement, and motivation experienced by both first-year and veteran teachers. For the past few weeks, I have been tutoring a fifth grade student who has had difficulty learning mathematics word problems. When we first met, her test grades were D's. During each session we focused on "picturing" the problem to understand it. Instead of feeling overwhelmed by the entire problem, she began to visualize the steps. The look on her face when she realized the problem was not too hard for her to comprehend was one of excitement and achievement. Needless to say, her grades have improved—to a B.

This incident brought to mind the many times I have told students to picture the problem, approach it in a step-by-step manner, and don't give up. The first thing students say is, "I can't get it." Before long, these same students say, "Oh, I get it!" As a private tutor, it is a great feeling (for me and the student) when the light finally comes on and the student is excited because s/he finally understands the problem. As Moore states in her essay, "the yearning for control points to a human desire to discover simplicity in complexity."

Mathematics has traditionally been taught in a linear manner, focusing on jargon and countless concepts, leading to students' merely memorizing instead of processing information Although I have not formally taught mathematics in the classroom, Moore reminds me of an important quality of a good teacher. Before handling a difficult task, one needs to divide it into several minitasks. A problem that at first seems complex will become simple. Taking the time to explain a problem or relate it to a real life experience can make a world of difference in a student's life.

When tutoring students who have difficulty in mathematics, I share my experiences in the subject to let students know that it is not impossible to learn algebra. We discuss the idea that there are many ways to approach a problem. Through the journey of life, there are many challenges and struggles one will face. Things do not always come easily, but it is a great feeling when you finally understand. The students' facial expressions are ones of shock, disbelief, and joy. As educators our mission is to inform them that we were once students ourselves, and we did not always perform well in a particular subject. This lets students know that the road ahead is not always smooth and is one we ourselves may have traveled.

The 1998 and 1999 United States school tragedies almost overshadowed my decision to teach, but Moore's essay has made me realize that, as an African American woman, I have much to offer as a teacher. I'm sure there were times when my teachers wanted to give up, but they continued the conversations of shared experiences and encouragement. When I experienced difficulties, they opened the doors of possibilities. As I reflect on these memories of my teachers, I realize that their nontraditional methods were the most helpful. Their inspiration and dedication will forever be remembered and treasured. The recent school shootings are cries for help and emphasize the need for conversation between teachers and students. For our families, community, and the future generation, let us keep the conversations going. We can all learn from each other. It is important that we learn new ideas, seek insights, and share lived experiences. Students are yearning to engage in thoughtful discussions and conversations. Instead of silencing a student if his/her opinion is not agreed with by all, talk about it; engage in a discussion. Respect each other's opinions and learn through understanding. Conversation and discussion open worlds of possibilities. Just as a quilt is woven from countless pieces of material, so teachers, students, parents and the rest of the community can gather together, forming new conversations, new beginnings, new visions.

Carol Williams is currently pursuing certification as an education specialist in curriculum and instruction at Louisiana State University in Baton Rouge. She holds an M.A. in curriculum and instruction with a concentration in mathematics from LSU and a B.A. in political science from Hofstra University.

Chapter 10 Wholly Vision-ing

Problematic: Curriculum by Blake-light

If you want to know what Allen Ginsberg (as quoted by Noel Gough in his introduction to this volume) might have meant by "Blake-light," go to the Tate Gallery, London—or its Web site—and look at William Blake's illustrations to Dante's *Divine Comedy,* especially the one in which Beatrice addresses Dante from her chariot.[1] The chariot is drawn by a majestic gryphon, and its wheels seem to be made of swirling creatures. Above the chariot are the alchemical symbols of the four gospels. According to the gallery's display caption, Blake appears to have been inspired by Canto 31 from Dante's *Purgatorio* in which Dante tells of his crossing the river Lethe and being led to Beatrice by her handmaids. The caption concludes: "The scene takes place in the Terrestrial Paradise. Blake's radiant coloring in this watercolor takes its cue from Dante's references to the dazzling effect of the 'living lights' which surround Beatrice and her entourage."

Michael McClure (1994/1982) interprets the visionary imagination Blake displays in this illustration in terms that resonate strongly with the language of complexity sciences and dynamic systems (see also Jayne Fleener and John St. Julien in this volume):

> Blake's imagination is nearly free. He allows the imagination to be as complex, and as colored, and as firmly lined as it will become in its own terms. *He lets it expand* until it forms a system for the illustration. He does not direct himself into a system, he lets one expand. One image after another continues until it structures a system. It is a system that is never fixed. It keeps moving, the watercolor invents its own rules—it extends Dante's vision. It becomes both illustration of Dante and a unique work that fits into Blake's expansively gyring being. (142–43; emphasis in original)

Molly Quinn's chapter glitters with Blake-light. Like Dante's Beatrice, she addresses us from a chariot that is both an expanding vision and a generative metaphor for the "carriage" of the corporeal curriculum. Blake's life and work epitomizes the "wholly visioning" process of which Quinn writes—the strength to "realize imagined possibilities through intentionality" and to use mind "to re-create matter."

It might not be too fanciful to suggest that Blake created Blake-light in defiance of Newton's *Opticks*. Blake saw the underlying metaphors of

Newtonian cosmology as symbolic embodiments "of the deception and absorption of imaginative vision by logical analysis" (Ault, 1974, 54), and materialized the symbolic embodiments of his own imaginative vision by inventing a new process of relief engraving that he called "illuminated printing." As John Sampson (1905) writes,

> the method then in vogue admitted of artistic embellishments only in the shape of steel or wood engravings, stiffly surrounding or clumsily placed in juxtaposition to the type of the text, while that of Blake interwove text, design, and colouring into one harmonious whole. (xv)

According to one contemporary account of Blake's life, this mode of engraving "was revealed to him in a vision by the spirit of his favourite brother Robert" (xvi).

Quinn's "holy" vision of what the legacy of the chariot means for curriculum work is delivered with a Blake-like confidence in the commensurability of the spiritual and the material worlds. Quinn shows us curriculum by Blake-light.

Note

[1] http://www.tate.org.uk/servlet/AWork?id=1401

References

Ault, Donald D. (1974). *Visionary physics: Blake's response to Newton.* Chicago and London: University of Chicago Press.

McClure, Michael. (1994). *Scratching the beat surface: Essays on new vision from Blake to Kerouac.* New York: Penguin. (Original publication 1982).

Sampson, John. (1905). *The poetical works of William Blake: A new and verbatim text from the manuscript engraved and letterpress originals.* Oxford: Clarendon.

Holy Vision, Wholly Vision-ing: Curriculum and the Legacy of the Chariot

Molly Quinn

We are the music makers,
And we are the dreamers of dreams,
Wandering by lone sea-breakers,
And sitting by desolate streams;
World-losers and world-forsakers,
On whom the pale moon gleams:
Yet we are the movers and shakers
Of the world for ever, it seems.

With wonderful deathless ditties
We build up the world's great cities,
And out of a fabulous story
We fashion an empire's glory:
One man [sic] with a dream, at pleasure,
Shall go forth and conquer a crown;
And three with a new song's measure
Can trample an empire down.

We, in the ages lying,
In the buried past of the earth,
Built Nineveh with our sighing,
And Babel itself with our mirth;
And o'erthrew them with prophesying
To the old of the new world's worth;
For each age is a dream that is dying,
Or one that is coming to birth.

(A. W. O'Shaughnessy, in R. L. Woods, 1966, 269)

I begin with this ode because it is the one human vision sings, reminding us that it is our relationship to vision which is key, and that we ought to examine this and reconceive it continually. We begin here for the insight that to enter even into the realm of "curriculum visions" entails prophesy to the old of the new's worth—attention to what is dying still, as we articulate the dream seeking birth. Thus, this prophetic path we take addresses first the problem of our loss of vision—our support of vision's death. Next, in the course of recovering vision, we explore the curriculum ground we have covered, to uncover its hidden visionary impetus, vision buried and forgotten. Hence, the way is then prepared for reviving vision and visioning with promise and hope.

The age we call ours has been primarily defined by a dream that is dying or one that is already gone, the mere remains of a carcass that long since met its grave. We may be the music-makers, yet our art has brought forth the requiem in which song itself is silenced. We may be the dreamers of dreams, yet our reveries have manifested the nightmare all too real, in which the dream stands condemned, and, thus, the dreamer, too, can be no more. The case is graver still, if we consider human response in the face of such loss. This response is akin to the one Frederich Nietzsche (1982/1883) describes in his account of the madman in the marketplace. He is the madman who sets his lantern ablaze in the sunlit early hours, hastens into the marketplace, and unrelentingly cries out: "I seek God!" The spectators hear and laugh. God does not exist, they know; thus, they humor themselves with speculations about God's absence—gone astray like a child, gotten lost, or emigrated from their country. The madman, undaunted by their mockery, pronounces God's death at the hands of humanity. Declaring this murder of all murders, he realizes his audience has not the eyes to see nor the ears to hear yet of this awesome event. "Too early I come," he says. He casts his lantern to the ground; it breaks, and its light, too, goes out.

Who is the madman but the prophet, o'erthrowing not only Nineveh and Babel but also their very building ground? The person of vision who can see what others cannot? To whom does he prophesy? And that of which he speaks, what does it signify other than the end of a dying age? What might it possibly mean for curriculum thinkers and workers today or tomorrow and for curriculum visions? If Nietzsche himself is such a madman, he foretells what has been called "the modern condition"—the predicament of modernity and its heirs, the plight of humanity in the aftermath of God's demise. He speaks to us all, then, insomuch as we are descendants of this legacy. And what is God but the height of human vision? God not only seems to signify the vision of the ultimate —encompassing the good, the true and the beautiful—the *ideal*, and the vision of ultimacy but also to symbolize the ultimacy of vision. John Dewey (1934), wrestling with this idea, says it is "this *active* relation between ideal and actual to which I would give the name 'God'" (51, emphasis in original). The lure of the visionary, the tension generated by the idyllic encounter, provides direction and promotes human movement, growth and aspiration—serves a teleological function carrying us beyond the actual to the possible. "Theoretically, the presence of 'God' in a person's life can be measured by his or her activity in the direction of an ideal" (1993, 105), Nel Noddings suggests. Similarly, Alfred North Whitehead (1978/1929) identifies God as the "unlimited conceptual realization of the absolute wealth of potentiality" (343) wherein at issue is "ever-lastingness," "the content of that vision upon which the finer religions are built—the 'many' absorbed everlastingly in the final unity" (347).

If God is indeed dead, what does this mean for humanity and for the place of vision, then, in human life? And how does this meaning affect curriculum? This "death" represents the loss of humanity's relationship to a transcendent reality, which has historically served as the center of meaning (Tillich, 1988). We are left with a crisis of meaning, and the loss of the transcendent, a sight of and movement toward that which lies beyond. The death of God in human consciousness suggests God is no longer with us; s/he has emigrated to another country, and we suffer the separation of the ideal from the real, the vision of what might be from what is, and the spirit from the flesh which ultimately dries up. If God—source, animating principle, Creator—has expired, what of God's creation? We are no more with a cosmos either, a vision of coherence, a sight or experience of dwelling in the whole. World-losers we are, without sense and sensation, near death ourselves.

If this is the case, since modern—and in these postmodern—times is it surprising that even various "prophets" within our own field have perceived the curriculum field itself to be "moribund" (Schwab, 1969), "dead" (Huebner, 1976), "arrested" (Pinar, 1978)—devoid of life and vision? It is not without significance either that here William Doll speaks of curriculum and "ghosts," disembodied spirits who hover over the process of education, haunting and forewarning—visions who, though strongly influential, are not quite with us. And Noel Gough describes a field which dwells in a land without poetry, in the gray chill, in a spiritual drabness—akin to an empty sepulcher. What "course" may we follow, may we "run," without vision, and without the course (of life) itself? Socrates's edict of education that "the unexamined life is not worth living" is rendered unfathomable without a vision of life, that which has worth. Most disturbing, though, is that we have ourselves begotten and sustained this deadly disorder.

Not only world-losers, but also world-forsakers we are, and do not even know it. We have killed vision, bled the life of God, spirit, by the sword. Lost is the Kosmos, referential of the "All" we can only symbolize but to which we never fully arrive—the breadth and depth, encompassing physiosphere, biosphere, noosphere and theosphere: matter, life, mind and spirit (Wilber, 1995). Left with a reduced cosmos, spirit-stripped, the anguishing madman thus cries

> ...how have we done this?...wipe away the entire horizon? What did we do when we unchained the earth from its sun?...Whither are we moving now? Away from all suns?...*Do we not feel* the empty space?...Is not...more night coming all the while? Must not lanterns be lit in the morning? *Do we not hear*...yet...the noise of the gravediggers...burying God? (Nietzsche, 1982/1883, 95; emphasis mine)

We have killed the holiest and most powerful but, *we do not see*. Of our age, Martin Heidegger (1971/1950) says: "The destitute time is no longer able even to experience its own destitution....[It] remains destitute not only because God is dead, but because mortals are hardly aware...even the trace of the holy has become unrecognizable" (93, 96, 97). We dwell in this "prosaic" world, which is "just one damn thing after another" (Shklovsky, 1990/1929, ix). We have lost the sacred order, the presence and perception of human vision, which is holy. And as it is also written, "Where there is no vision, the people perish..." (*The Holy Bible*, 1985, Proverbs 29:18).

Gough indicts, as well, those who work in the curriculum field today and grieves our state: "We wanted voice and we wanted vision." He says, "I saw the best minds of my generation preset and programmed by bells and buzzers..." the living dead, zombies. Postulating a moral/spiritual crisis in education, David Purpel (1989) analyzes our present situation similarly: "The terms 'intellectual' or 'idealist' are more often used in our culture as epithets than as compliments. We seem to be more proud of our technical virtuosity...than our...speculative consciousness" (6). The idealist, the man or woman of vision, is more likely mocked—deemed a fool, or a "madman." We dwell in the intellectual void of a visionless nothingness, educational nihilism. Alas, the lantern, the source of light and sight, is put out.

The first message we must hear is that which convicts us regarding but also awakens us to our loss and lack of vision. But does not the prophet also command repentance and bring the message of the possibility of change, of life anew? And does not prophetic wisdom never cease to give us hope? Creation stories the world over tell us that from the void light and life are born; that from chaos emerges order, a cosmos; that even through death comes the song which calls forth the day; and that humanity must have its night, as Virginia Hamilton (1988) says, since an eternal day is too "bright all-light everywhere" (8). Each age may be a dream dying, but it is also one coming to birth. Death, too, is but a sleep, a symbol which hints at rebirth and transformation (Voorst, 1994). Nietzsche (1982/1883) himself proclaims: "Only where there are tombs are there resurrections" (225). God, too, is by definition beyond death. We walk upon the grave of God. Though separated from us, the spirit rumbles beneath our feet; vision is, we trust, not far from us, lying dormant in the fallow ground of our hearts and minds we have forgotten in our sleep to nourish and till. Let us search this ground then, in curriculum, for its forgotten and lost vision, or visions not readily apparent, but operative nonetheless.

But is not curriculum without vision, imageless—unless one means the portraits of regimentation, routinization, anesthetization, the word conjures? We see programming by bells and buzzers, behavioral objectives, tests and teachers, rows and dittos, but vision—no. Isn't talk of curriculum mostly "much ado about nothing," as Alex Molnar (1992) has put it? Isn't it a concept laden with confusion and contradiction, so diffuse and dissented to the point of meaninglessness (Jackson, 1992; Ornstein and Hunkins, 1998)? An "ugly, awkward, academic word" (Rugg, 1936, 18)? Yes and no. It is an "academic" word with a rich history, not unrelated to the idea of vision, not without an underlying image of resounding symbolic depth. David Hamilton (1990) has shown this, in part, in his research into the history of "curriculum." Documenting the first use of the word in an educational context from the work of the sixteenth-century thinker Peter Ramus who sought to map out the totality of human knowledge, he attributes its adoption and staying power to its political appeal: Ramist maps—academically coining the word, taken up by northern European universities to systematically outline a course of study for their scholars to follow, hold out the promise of an unprecedented order which resonates powerfully with Reformation ideology. The term "curriculum" is already in use by Calvinists as curriculum vitae, the course of life—a path full of obstacles Christians traverse. Introduced is the alluring idea of a certain "shortcut" through method. Curriculum is method's child, and as life's journey is now reduced, regulated, and predetermined. Central to curriculum here is the idea of control, as Doll (2001) has argued, expressing a fear of the unknown and a desire for power—to know and master human destiny, life's unsure path.

Thus, perhaps, the whole of "curriculum" still offers little food for the imagination or sustenance for the soul of vision, evidenced from its beginning in educational discourse as that of which more contemporary scholars have accused it: an obsession with management, control, and prediction (Pinar et al., 1995; Doll, 1993); a ruse of political power to maintain the status quo (Apple, 1990/1979; Kozol, 1990/1975)—cut off from vision and value, a denial of the imagination, bearing all the dangers of modernist ideology. Where is this symbolic depth to which we have alluded? It lies beneath the surface yet is touched upon at its roots in curriculum vitae as the course of life, the image of life as a journey which humanity, in some manner, can intentionally direct. Further inquiry into the word's etymology elucidates its hidden symbolic meaning. "Curriculum" comes from the Latin *currere*, meaning "to run." Once signifying a course for running, literally the vehicle for racing itself—the chariot, it came to be used in the context of *curriculum vitae*, from which was drawn its educational sense as a course of study or training (*Oxford English Dictionary*, Vol. IV, 1989). Yet, let us consider curriculum's "original" underlying image, one of great symbolic import historically in the human psyche: the chariot.

According to Hans Biedermann (1994/1989), a scholar of symbology, the image of the chariot, since the invention of the wheel in the earliest civilizations, has always been associated with noble deities—the sun and gods and goddesses like Apollo, Zeus, and Freya. The sun's path across the firmament is often traversed by the chariot (e.g., in Greek myth, Aurora, the dawn, rides across the sky in a chariot drawn by horses). Elijah, chosen of Yahweh, is carried off to heaven in a chariot of fire. In a painting by Titian, Christ is seen upon a triumphal chariot. "Mystical chariots symbolize mythic journeys and triumphant processions of the gods" (65). The driver of the chariot in classical thought signifies a life of reason and self-possessed conduct. Reason, as conceived by the ancient Greeks, is strongly akin to the divine, the ascending path to the sun (Plato, 1992/ca. 380 B.C.). Jana Riley (1995) suggests that the chariot represents humanity's capacity to transcend the physical world and enter into "the higher worlds." The charioteer is the conscious mind, driven by the subconscious, or working with it. The chariot's French and Latin roots are found in "char" and "carrus"—"cart" in English, akin to our image of the "car"—a phallic symbol of ego strength, agency, and freedom. "On the road of life, there are passengers and there are drivers," Volkswagen reports: "Drivers wanted." Other etymologically related words Riley recounts include charge, charisma, chart, and chasm. Thus, in the Cabalistic system, the chariot speaks of speech or influence ("logos"), and is also profoundly associated with the chasm—the path traversing the abyss, "the condition of no-thing because it is every-thing."

The visionary power of the chariot is also expressed in the Tarot, a symbol system of the Western mystery tradition regarded as "a picture compilation of universal imagery" (1). The Chariot is the seventh card of the Tarot's Major Arcana, the 22 "big secrets" or "archetypes" representing "*angles* on…God, or on the one life of All That Is" (8), the fundamental aspects of life's journey. The card's key concept is "the Path" (Abraham, 1994), or "Experience" (Riley, 1995). The Chariot inspires success, inner guidance, and mental control, conscious change in sojourning life's cycles (Abraham, 1994). It involves mental powers to control life's direction. The message is: "Direct your energies on the path (mental) and then take action" (89). The charioteer is the higher self, to be trusted as a guide through life toward one's dreams. The card depicts a man driving a chariot with no reins out of the city. The chariot, wings on its frontispiece, is pulled by horses or sphinxes of opposite colors and directions. Under a canopy of stars, the crowned charioteer holds a wand in his right hand and bears a square at his breast.

Every detail is symbolic of the depth of the Chariot's meaning. The animals—conflicting energies needing harmony through the mind—highlight the necessity of negotiation between the conscious and unconscious (Abraham, 1994). As horses, they speak of nobility, vitality, and progress (Fontana, 1993). The horse is often prophetic, with magical powers, advising. The sphinx, having a human head and a lion's body, is a mysterious creature of intelligence and strength as well. It stands for ancient wisdom, guarding the temple, the riddle of existence. Thus, the charioteer is driven by the existential question humanity must answer. "The Chariot is the physical vehicle (the body) which must be mentally directed" (Abraham, 1994, 87) in concert with this quest. Related to the circle—emblem of eternity and perfection, the wheels set out upon the road of life into the unknown—ultimately for home, the divine inner core. The chariot's winged frontispiece highlights freedom therein, an "'elevation' of…the merely corporeal" (Biedermann, 1994/1989, 385). The chariot enlists its driver in the hope of freedom from limitations, the search for the heights through the height of thought. In Plato's *Phaedrus*, the wing has the power "to soar aloft...that which gravitates downward into...the habitation of the gods" as "the corporeal element...most akin to the divine" (385). The chariot covers its driver in a canopy of stars—symbols of spirit, mind, celestial light, ancestral guidance, and cosmic protection.

The charioteer's crown speaks of the highest human attainable level. The wand in his right hand—the hand of mercy and might, sacred action —suggests discipline and creative work. The square, worn at his breast, appears universally as an ordering principle denoting cosmic harmony, present in the design of most celebrated cities. "The square is an indication of our wish to find our way in an apparently chaotic world by introducing directions and coordinates" (320–21). Yet, traveling away from the city speaks of venturing out from established institutions. The path represents attainment, progressive states of becoming toward the height of being. Seven, the Chariot's signature number, tells also of elevation through the realm of the mind. It is the number of perfection, of the divine. Central to the educational ideas of medieval Europe are its seven gifts of the Holy Spirit, sacraments, deadly sins, virtues, arts and sciences, and "ages of man." Thus, there is this visionary power buried in the very word "curriculum," which speaks, in fact, to the import and force of human vision in life—a power we must recover. Symbolically, curriculum testifies to the strength of the human spirit to dream and realize imagined possibilities through intentionality; it advocates the use of mind to re-create matter—to map out and traverse paths to "the land of promise" and the world of dreams as existential reality. It acknowledges our participation with the spirit, that beyond the known, what Dwayne Huebner (1995) calls

> a "moreness" that infuses each human being...we "are" more than we "currently are"...human being dwells in the transcendent, or...the transcendent dwells in the human being....The spirit dwells in us...the source of hope. (15–18)

This symbolic depth is historically attested to in the images of education of the Western tradition from which "curriculum" emerged. These images include Plato's "Allegory of the Cave," the upward journey of the soul from the visible realm to that immaterial one—the light of divine reason—the good, true, and beautiful (1992/ca. 380 B.C.); and Quintilian's idea of education as a return of the soul to "heaven" from whence it came and the "requisite care" taken over this process through mind (1974/ca. 74 A.D.). In prison, Boethius—credited with the medieval "curriculum" of the trivium and quadrivium—has his vision of Philosophy, the mother-educator of all studies, who enlightens him regarding how to transcend his plight, obtain freedom of the soul though body is bound, giving him a sense of efficacy over the vicissitudes of earthly life (1963/ca. 523 A.D.). The first known representation of the liberal arts are as seven maidens attending the divine union of the bride Philologia to the god Mercury. To Alcuin, director of monastic studies, the liberal arts are the "seven-fold gift of the Holy Ghost" (cited in Piltz, 1981). Renaissance thinkers recall education as a marriage of contemplation and action toward "the harmonious cultivation of every admirable human potentiality"; we enter into a vow, "free, like Hercules at the crossroads, to choose the path of virtue or…vice" (Rice, 1963, xi).

There are also more contemporary evidences of this visionary power in curriculum thought. For example, Dewey, for whom education is a concern with what does not yet exist (Noddings, 1993)—a negotiation between the actual and ideal—critiques a fixed view of curriculum: "The map is not a substitute for a personal experience…does not take the place of an actual journey" (Dewey, 1990/1902, 198), but rather ought to promote "freeing the life-process for its own most…fulfillment" (195). William Pinar's notion of *currere* (1994) resonates with this portrait, and many have drawn upon it to further curriculum re-vision. For Madeleine Grumet (1992) curriculum is "a metaphor for a person's dialogue with the world of…experience" (29). Through *conscientization* and *praxis*, Paulo Freire (1993/1970) affirms a curriculum for freedom and social good via the power of thought with those influenced by him.

Yet, none of this symbolic force is inspired within us through our usual encounters with curriculum. For another legacy has dominated, one which has sought to kill vision by finalizing it. Central, since the birth of "curriculum" proper, is the deadly idea of control, the emphasis upon *human mastery of the totality* of knowledge, and thus also of life. With Ramus, and following him, there is an obsession with certainty through method, a pursuit that is linear and predetermined, not one which articulates a respect for the mystery of life's journey. Curriculum becomes a given, an objectified "thing," gotten through by a well-defined procedure. Comenius, with centuries of protégés, attempts a full-scale science of education in 1657:

> We are so bold as to promise a Great Didactic…a complete treatise on how to teach all subjects to all…and how to teach them in such a way that the result will be certain….[This task] of ours is…as the universe that has to be subdued by our minds. (Cited in Piaget, 1967, 4)

The enduring emphasis on *strategies* of curriculum development (Bobbitt, 1918; Tyler, 1949) in modern times is also exemplary of this tradition.

In absolutizing this call of human life—to find and fulfill one's path by the power of the mind directed *in harmony with spirit and nature*, Ramist legacy unwittingly trivializes it and reduces the art of living to the science of purposive rationality, divorcing it from its larger symbolic context, stripping it ultimately of meaning. Literalized, fully materialized, the course of life is no longer "alive." The canopy of the spirit dismantled, the chariot restricted to the city, reins are held by someone other than the charioteer. Those closest to the process of education—teachers and students—are driven by another upon a path that does not inspire visioning nor aspire to transcendence through transforming consciousness. The dream has been dreamed, the music has been made, the story has been told—"cover" it, and we are done. Thus, curriculum in its contemporary context, although it retains remnants of its visionary appeal, reflects more profoundly its heritage in vision's reification, i.e., death, the very denial of the beauty and potential of the human impulse—the animating principle—behind "curricularizing."

There are those who have pointed out the dangers to which this visionary singularity is subject. Many contemporary curriculum critiques —ecofeminist, postmodern, poststructural, multicultural—call into question this very privileging of the mind, and of reason, and work to rather de-center the human subject, problematize intentionality, and deconstruct our ideal of progress. For example, in her book *Practice Makes Practice*, Deborah Britzman (1991) interrogates our unbridled pursuit of perfection. Bernie Neville (1989) claims we privilege Apollo, the sun god of the golden chariot, who celebrates the clear light of manifestation, logic, rationality, and scientific inquiry. He suggests we adopt the mortal path of Psyche. Although Apollo would have her set upon a mountaintop, she—the "image of the soul in search of god"—must be "drawn by love through a slow, painful, shadowy initiation into a new way of being" (3).

But, in our visionary heritage there is much of promise. Practice making practice is ever toward some ideal or improvement. Psyche is not unlike the charioteer in his journey or the "madman" seeking God. The problem is absolutization, not aspiration. The enigma of curriculum is that of vision itself: the predicament of concretizing, actualizing in some lived-out form its presentation—without losing vision, its living efficacy, the "beyondness" and "being-toward" of it. It is the problem of substance finding expression in form: substance must articulate itself, yet the temptation is to give up substance for form or vice versa. Doll's ghosts testify not only to the power of the invisible but the import of the visible as well. And there is ever this lure of sacrificing substance to some final form—not allowing it to speak and breathe beyond its form, transcend its form, trans-form.

Thus, with the knowledge that we have lost vision—succumbed to these temptations—we must work to recover it, to inquire into, and live again in the light of its vitalizing richness and power and this on-goingly. We must become "madmen" and seek again the face of God—the ever-inspiring never-ending experience and incarnation of infinite vision in finite forms, which express for us goodness, truth, and beauty—what we deem ultimate and sacred, what gives our lives meaning—in the present moment. We recover, light and lift up the lantern that is us—take the journey to in-sight, and to incite. CURRICULUM "R" US. As music-makers and dreamers of dreams, we play perpetually and provisionally with our deathless ditties and fabulous stories to fashion—to form, formulate, trans-form—curriculums coming to birth through an appreciation for the power of human aspiration and agency. By this gift we are given the opportunity to direct as in a royal chariot the paths of our own lives, to be moved in our own quest for the higher realms, and to move beyond our own limitations—both personally and collectively—through participation with the earth and the spirit, through co-creation with the divine.

References

Abraham, S. (1994). *How to read the tarot: The key word system.* St. Paul, MN: Llewellyn.

Apple, M. (1990). *Ideology and curriculum* (2nd ed.). New York: Routledge. (Original work published 1979).

Biedermann, H. (1994). *Dictionary of symbolism: Cultural icons and the meanings behind them.* J. Hulbert (Trans.). New York: Meridian. (Original work published 1989).

Bobbitt, F. (1918). *The curriculum.* Cambridge, MA: Riverside.

Boethius. (1963). *The consolation of philosophy.* W. Anderson (Trans.). Carbondale, IL: Southern Illinois University Press. (Original work written ca. 523 A.D.).

Britzman, D. (1991). *Practice makes practice: A critical study of learning to teach.* Albany, NY: State University of New York Press.

Dewey, J. (1934). *A common faith.* New Haven, CT: Yale University Press.

_______. (1990). *The child and the curriculum.* In P. Jackson (Ed.), *The school and society and the child and the curriculum.* Chicago: The University of Chicago Press. (Original work published 1902).

Doll, W. (1993). *A post-modern perspective on curriculum.* New York: Teachers College Press.

_______. (2001). Struggles with spirituality. In T. Oldenski and D. Carlson (Eds.), *Educational yearning: The journey of the spirit and democratic education* (pages 13–29). New York: Garland.

Fontana, D. (1993). *The secret language of symbols: A visual key to symbols and their meanings*. San Francisco: Chronicle.

Freire, Paolo. (1993). *Pedagogy of the oppressed* (new rev. ed.). New York: Continuum. (Original work published 1970).

Grumet, M. (1992). Existential and phenomenological foundations of autobiographical methods. In W. Pinar and W. Reynolds (Eds.), *Understanding curriculum as phenomenological and deconstructed text*. New York: Teachers College Press.

Hamilton, D. (1990). *Curriculum history*. Geelong, Victoria: Deakin University Press.

Hamilton, V. (1988). *In the beginning: Creation stories from around the world*. San Diego: Harcourt.

Heidegger, M. (1971). What are poets for? In A. Hofstadter (Ed. and Trans.), *Poetry, language, thought* (pages 89–142). New York: Harper and Row. (Original work published 1950).

The Holy Bible. (Expanded ed.). (1985). New York: Nelson.

Huebner, D. (1976). The moribund curriculum field: Its wake and our work. *Curriculum Inquiry, 6*(2), 153–67.

_______. (1995). Education and spirituality. *JCT: An Interdisciplinary Journal of Curriculum Studies, 11*(2), 13–34.

_______. (1999). *The lure of the transcendent: Collected essays by Dwayne E. Huebner*. Vikki Hillis (Ed.). Collected and introduced by William F. Pinar. Mahwah, NJ: Erlbaum.

Jackson, P. (1992). Conceptions of curriculum and curriculum specialists. In P. Jackson (Ed.), *Handbook of research in curriculum* (pages 3–40). New York: Macmillan.

Kozol, J. (1990). *The night is dark and I am far from home* (rev. ed.). New York: Simon and Schuster. (Original work published 1975).

Molnar, A. (1992). Contemporary curriculum discourse: Too much ado about too much nothing. *Theory into Practice, 31*(3), 198–203.

Neville, B. (1989). *Educating Psyche: Emotion, imagination and the unconscious in learning*. New York: Collins Dove.

Nietzsche, F. (1974). *The gay science*. W. Kaufmann (Trans.). New York: Vintage. (Original work published 1882).

_______. (1982). Thus spake Zarathustra. In W. Kaufmann (Ed. and Trans.), *The portable Nietzsche* (pages 103–440). New York: Penguin. (Original work published 1883).

Noddings, N. (1993). *Educating for intelligent belief or unbelief*. New York: Teachers College Press.

Ornstein, A., and F. Hunkins. (1998). *Curriculum foundations, principles and issues* (3rd ed.). Boston: Prentice Hall.

Oxford English dictionary (Vol. IV) (2nd. ed.). (1989). J. Simpson and E. Weiner (Eds.). Oxford, England: Clarendon.

Piaget, J. (1967). The significance of John Amos Comenius at the present time. In J. Piaget (Ed.), *John Amos Comenius on education* (pages 1–34). New York: Teachers College Press.

Piltz, A. (1981). *The world of medieval learning*. Oxford: Blackwell.

Pinar, W. (1978). Notes on the curriculum field 1978. *Educational Researcher, 7*(8), 5–12.

______. (1994). *Autobiography, politics and sexuality: Essays in curriculum theory, 1972–1992.* New York: Lang.

Pinar, W., W. Reynolds, P. Slattery, and P. Taubman. (1995). *Understanding curriculum: An introduction to the study of historical and contemporary curriculum discourses.* New York: Lang.

Plato. (1992). *Republic.* G. M. A. Grube (Trans.). Indianapolis, IN: Hackett. (Original work written ca. 380 B.C.).

Purpel, D. (1989). *The moral and spiritual crisis in education: A curriculum for justice and compassion in education.* New York: Bergin and Garvey.

Quintilian. (1974). The institutio oratorio, books I and II. H. Butler (Trans.). In F. Wheelock (Ed.), *Quintilian as educator.* New York: Twayne. (Original work written ca 74 A.D.).

Rice, E., Jr. (1963). Foreword. In W. Woodward (Ed.), *Vittorino da Feltre and other humanist educators: Essays and versions* (pages vii–xix). New York: Teachers College Press.

Riley, J. (1995). *Tarot dictionary and compendium.* York Beach, ME: Weiser.

Rugg, H. (1936). *American life and the school curriculum.* Boston: Ginn.

Schwab, J. (1969, November). The practical: A language for curriculum. *School Review, 78*(1), 1–23.

Shklovsky, V. (1990). *Theory of prose.* B. Sher (Trans.). Elmwood Park, IL: Dalkey (Original work published 1929).

Tillich, P. (1988). The world situation. In J. Mark Thomas (Ed.), *The spiritual situation in our technical society* (pages 3–40). Macon, GA: Mercer University Press.

Tyler, R. (1949). *Basic principles of curriculum and instruction.* Chicago, IL: University of Chicago Press.

Voorst, R. (1994). *Anthology of world scriptures.* Belmont, CA: Wadsworth.

Whitehead, A. (1978). *Process and reality.* New York: Free. (Original work published 1929).

Wilber, K. (1995). *Sex, ecology, spirituality: The spirit of evolution.* New York: Random House.

Woods, R. (1966). *A treasury of the familiar.* New York: Macmillan.

Molly Quinn is Assistant Professor of Education Studies at Adelphi University, New York. She received her Ph.D. in curriculum theory and English education from Louisiana State University in Baton Rouge. She teaches undergraduate and graduate courses in curriculum, social studies, literature, and the arts. Her research interests lie primarily in the spiritual critique and revitalization of education through the power of imagination, as well as in the theory and praxis of social justice, especially its ontological and axiological roots. Her latest book is *Going Out, Not Knowing Whither: Education, the Upward Journey, and the Faith of Reason* (Lang, 2001).

Perspective on Quinn

Deborah J. Davis

> Literalized, fully materialized, the course of life is no longer "alive." The canopy of the spirit dismantled, the chariot restricted to the city, the reins are held by someone other than the charioteer....Though separated from us, the spirit rumbles beneath our feet; vision is, we trust, not far from us, lying dormant in the fallow ground of our hearts and minds we have forgotten in our sleep to nourish and till. (Molly Quinn, this volume)

As a first-year English teacher, I found myself caught in a contradiction between what felt right and what was "right" in the eyes of the people in control or, as Quinn puts it, the people holding the reins. I wanted a classroom in which students felt comfortable articulating their opinions and debating their ideas, even if (perhaps especially if) they differed from my own. I believed my students should engage in reflection on their beliefs, explore the beliefs of others, and understand that no one's views are infallible. Through this, I believed, our classroom would be one where the emotional, reflexive, spiritual side of all learners —both the students and myself—would be nurtured. Unfortunately, I found myself caught in a double-bind, because my desires to create such a learning community were hampered by my society's limited concept of ways of knowing and being. With this I struggled, because as a product of this society, these limitations were also ingrained within me. I found myself wondering, "But how will I grade the students? What behavioral objectives will I list on lesson plans? What will I assess on the objective test at the end of the unit?" All of these criteria were the primary focus of the district and state in which I taught and were the focus of my own educational experiences as a student. One could say I was "haunted" by these awarenesses and the discrepancies between them and my newer realization that the study of literature could and should be much more than valuing only that which can be measured. Thus began my struggle to reconcile society's vision of learning and knowledge, which seemed to value little more than the quantifiable, with my own spirit-filled vision of education.

With experience came the insight that these two views *can* be reconciled but at a price. Fitting a more inclusive, more spiritual, and less mechanistic concept of knowledge into the existing educational situation is like wearing a shoe a half a size too small—you can do it, but there's a raging, painful blister at the end of the day. A teacher can reach for the inner part of the student, that part no instrument can measure, but in the end, the objectives must be listed, the tests administered, and the labels assigned. This ill fit between a more embodied vision of education and the current concept of schooling causes pain for both students and teachers because so much of what is natural as human beings is stripped away and disregarded. Thus, we are, as Quinn says, "left with a crisis of meaning, and the loss of the transcendent, a sight of and toward that which lies beyond" (this volume).

We work in schools where the dreamer, or the educator who seeks to infuse the classroom with the spirit, life, and vitality of learning, is indeed condemned. Instead, schools revolve around control. Just as Quinn says the chariot is "restricted to the city" (this volume), teachers and students are restricted to those methods, procedures, subjects, and assessment instruments laid out for them by the curricular reform *de jour*. Such restrictions impede the *art of teaching* (for it cannot be defined any other way) and thus prevent teachers from expanding the walls of the "city" defined by educational reforms more concerned with numbers than with living, breathing, feeling, spirit-filled students.

As Quinn relates to us the loss of life and spirit in classrooms, she also reminds us that out of darkness comes light, out of death comes resurrection. Teachers struggle to fit an embodied concept of knowing and learning into the framework of school accountability, high-stakes testing, and classrooms governed by bells, buzzers, and Ramist notions of knowledge, and the conflict leaves many feeling disempowered and disheartened. However, this struggle would not exist if spirit did not "rumble beneath our feet" (this volume). Another vision of what education can be resonates within us, leading us to feel conflict with pursuits of knowledge which ignore the spiritual, emotional, and sometimes even irrational side of life and learning. This "haunting" comes to us because the spirit cannot be denied. It may be temporarily eclipsed from sight, but it is always there in our students. As teachers we need to emerge from this eclipse of spirit and take back the reins of education from those to whom the hearts, minds, and lives of our students are unknown. That which is most beautiful in classrooms and communities of learning—the creativity, uniqueness, and passion of human experience—cannot be objectified or standardized; it must be nurtured and celebrated. Learning cannot be divorced from life or the mind from the soul, and those who commit themselves to education must give voice and practice to this truth. Only when we fully embrace this spirit and speak out loudly in its defense can we as teachers begin to see the true potential of our classrooms—a potential which has previously been shrouded in the darkness—and reclaim the reins of education to become the music-makers and dreamers of dreams of which Quinn speaks.

Deborah J. Davis is currently a doctoral student in curriculum and instruction at Louisiana State University in Baton Rouge. She received an M.Ed. in curriculum and instruction and a B.A. in English from the University of Southern Mississippi. She taught secondary English for three years at Oak Grove High School in Hattiesburg, Mississippi.

Chapter 11 Past, Present, and Yet-to-Come

Problematic: Curriculum Dynamics

> Few works…have influenced my vision of curriculum and teaching as much as *A Christmas Carol* by Charles Dickens. (William Schubert, 1991, 284)

> Charles Dickens in *A Christmas Carol* provides our culture with one of its most haunting images of the process of change and redemption. (John St. Julien, this volume)

> I recoil from counting the persons and books whose lives are made possible by continuing restatement of the Huebner rationale, of the character and case for spectral metaphors, of the virtues and vices of Charles Dickens. (*pace* Joseph Schwab, 1969, 6)[1]

We admit that Schwab (1969) did not actually write that last sentence, but he used almost identical words to exemplify a sign of crisis in the curriculum field that he called "marked perseveration, a repetition of old and familiar knowledge in new languages which add little or nothing to the old meanings as embodied in the older and familiar language" (4). We are not suggesting that two essays on *A Christmas Carol* within a ten-year period constitute evidence of perseveration. Rather, our parody of Schwab is wishful thinking: Can you imagine a curriculum field in which the default rationale for planning owed more to Dwayne Huebner than to Ralph Tyler, in which literary metaphors were foci for debate more often than behavioral objectives, and in which Charles Dickens was cited as a source of wisdom more frequently than John Dewey?

We draw attention to both Schubert's and St. Julien's essays on *A Christmas Carol* for several reasons. First, we agree with Tom Barone (1992) that "novelists such as Dickens have…earned entrance into the hallowed Citadel of Educational Inquiry" (32). However, Barone makes this claim with particular reference to *Hard Times*—which he calls "a masterpiece of educational inquiry"—and our second point is to emphasize that a work of fiction can be a generative text for curriculum inquiry even if it is not "about" education as such.

The third and most important point we wish to make is that Schubert's essay on *A Christmas Carol* exemplifies St. Julien's thesis regarding "situated approaches to knowledge." St. Julien locates knowledge "in social practice and structuring artifacts" and relates learning to "the use of embedded tools that we might find in the situated activity of a work crew building a house." Schubert built nine themes (in a mere nine pages) from his reading of *A Christmas Carol* to demonstrate its influence on his work as a curriculum scholar. We do not need to elaborate on these themes here (we recommend that you read Schubert's chapter for yourselves). We simply suggest that *A Christmas Carol* frames both Schubert's and St. Julien's essays because each of them is disposed to use it as a "structuring artifact" and "embedded tool" for their own learning, not that it *necessarily* has intrinsic merit as an educative text. Schubert and St. Julien have built their educative texts from materials at hand. *A Christmas Carol* was common in both of their "building sites," and its usefulness to them may have as much to do with its ubiquity as to its particular literary qualities. More mundane and less canonized texts might have served their purposes equally well.

Note

[1] Schwab (1969) actually wrote: "I recoil from counting the persons and books whose lives are made possible by continuing restatement of the Tyler rationale, of the character and case for behavioral objectives, of the virtues and vices of John Dewey" (6)

References

Barone, Thomas E. (1992). On the demise of subjectivity in educational inquiry. *Curriculum Inquiry,* 22(1), 25–38.

Schubert, William H. (1991). Curriculum inspired by Scrooge or "A curriculum carol." In George Willis and William H. Schubert (Eds.), *Reflections from the heart of educational inquiry: Understanding curriculum and teaching through the arts* (pages 284–92). Albany, NY: State University of New York Press.

Schwab, Joseph J. (1969). The practical: A language for curriculum. *School Review,* *78*(1), 1–23.

Haunting Curriculum: Visions of Curriculum Past, Curriculum Present and a Vision of What Is Yet-to-Come

John St. Julien

> "I wear the chain I forged in life," replied the Ghost. "I made it link by link, and yard by yard; I girded it on of my own free will, and of my own free will I wore it. Is its pattern strange to you?"

Charles Dickens in *A Christmas Carol* provides our culture with one of its most haunting images of the process of change and redemption. In that tale Marley, Scrooge's partner, shows him three worlds: the worlds of Christmas Past, Christmas Present, and Christmas Yet-to-Come. Scrooge is not a bad man but is a man who acts badly. His actions create misery but flow from rational self-interest. All his calculations conform to a calculus of value deeply embedded in his situation and culture. His allegiance to these values has created the tight, pinched soul he has become. Scrooge regains his life by recovering and emphasizing assumptions and values that lead him away from the counting house and into the warmth of a family life.

Similarly, I will claim,[1] we as a culture have sworn allegiance to a set of understandings that, although rational, lead us to act badly and create misery. The issue for us, as it was for Scrooge, is to locate the assumptions and values that create the seed and nurture the growth of the counting house mentality. On this account, we will need to shift our emphasis to assumptions that will be the seed of a newer, less debilitating institution of education.

---

[1] This chapter involves an essential tension. Its purpose is to present a vision for the field of curriculum; an idea of what can and perhaps should be; an ethical story. The substance of the chapter argues for a fairly technical and unfamiliar complex of understandings about learning and knowledge. The purpose calls for good story telling. The substance asks for scholarly argument and apparatus. I have attempted to relieve that tension in a way that would not leave my reader out of sorts with either endeavor. Some references and allusions appear in the body but the reader who wishes to further explore the traditions upon which I rely is entreated to examine the endnote.

Curriculum Past

"In life I was your partner, Jacob Marley."

Marley introduces Scrooge to the idea that the past lives on in the present and that past actions determines present condition. Dickens wants us to understand that Scrooge's counting house mentality and the misery his actions lead to are but expressions of the underlying miserliness of an unshared life.

Curriculum is our counting house. It embodies much the same rationality manifested in Scrooge and Marley's shop. It is based in the hard, solid, and countable currency of fact—the gold of our rational system of education. This system has its roots in the defining moment of Western culture: the Enlightenment turn to rationality.

> "You fear the world too much," it answered, gently. "All your other hopes have merged into the hope of being beyond the chance of its sordid reproach. I have seen your nobler aspirations fall off one by one, until the master-passion, Gain, engrosses you. Have I not?"

As we try to grasp the implications of a counting house metaphor for curriculum it is useful to reflect on the story that now dominates our understanding and our schools. In the same way that fear of the world's "sordid reproach" motivated Scrooge and led to a single master narrative of gain dominating his life, John Dewey and, following Dewey, Stephen Toulmin have recounted a story of how our dominant intellectual system grew from a fear of uncertainty. Timothy Reiss recounts a historical narrative with similar implications: The threatened collapse of the pre-Renaissance representational structure leads the culture to adopt a rigid understanding of human reason. These multiple recountings, although differing in detail and emphasis, all point toward the emerging dominance of geometric rationality—a system of absolute truths and the deductive method with which it is associated. This system soon became the only legitimate way to represent the world.

Ideas about representation reflect presuppositions concerning the nature of that world. The now classical understanding took today's shape during the Enlightenment, and it is no accident that it is often labeled the "Newtonian worldview," as the clockwork universe Isaac Newton described via the calculus is the archetypal instance of it. The pre-understanding associated with this view has been widely discussed. It is an image of a world in which everything has its place, where things are governed by simple and elegant laws, and where all that is necessary to know the future—and indeed the past—is a full description of the myriad solid objects that compose the world and the causal relations which connect them.

It was a vision of immense appeal in the uncertain and unhappy dawning of our era, and the tool of the calculus that both embodied its assumptions and was able to solve previously intractable problems powerfully reinforced it. But accepting the vision and grasping the tool required a concurrent commitment to a particular understanding of representation that had been long developing in Western thought. The categories upon which the calculus operated had to be the categories of formal logic, the categories the West had explored in its epochal development of geometric proof. Such proof offered the certainty and control that the era sought, but for this system to work the things of the world and the categories by which we represented them had to be well formed. Aristotle's famous dictum that the middle must be excluded is a requirement of this sort of logic. If categories are allowed to overlap, if an entity may belong to more than one category, then anything at all can be proved: 1 can be 2 and night can be proved day.

The requirements of Geometry govern the popular and scientific notions of categories to this day. Both folk and scientific version of representation now follow the same pattern: Representations, like the objects in the world they reflect, are taken to be unified, stable, and separable. They are formally defined through the use of necessary features. A member of a category is found by determining if it has the necessary and sufficient features of the category, and elaborate hierarchies have been developed to contain super-ordinate and subordinate categories; the prototypical example is Linnaeus's taxonomy of life.

In summary, this now classical view arose during the Enlightenment in reaction to the turmoil and uncertainty of the day. A quest for certainty was made possible by the successes of Newton and Leibnitz in introducing the calculus, a tremendously successful tool that enabled its wielders to use simple laws to reliably predict trajectories of all types by dividing the smooth curve into a series of distinct and separate parts. A mechanical, reductionist vision of the world was almost inevitable, and it was aligned with a similar set of assumptions about the representations that we acquired and the knowledges that we possessed. These, too, were atomistic, complete in and of themselves, and they participated in simple, linear relations of cause which the logicists of medieval scholasticism called implication. The best knowledge was like the perfect atom or monad: complete, solid, law following and indistinguishable in type and effect from its fellows. Such knowledges could be combined to build anything, yes; but it was the clean form of logic that connected them just as causality connected the real, undifferentiated atoms of the day. Schools reflected this vision, and the most deeply embedded practices in our schools are directly tied to this pre-understanding of the world and its operation.

Of course, in our day new sciences focusing on complexity offer a different image of the world—and will call for a correspondingly different conception of representation.

Curriculum Present

> "This boy is Ignorance. This girl is Want. Beware them both, and all of their degree, but most of all beware this boy, for on his brow I see that written which is Doom, unless the writing be erased."

Dickens's ghost spoke doom as a result of children left in ignorance and want. Doomsayers in our own day accuse education in the same grave tones as Dickens's ghost. Without doubt, we so accuse ourselves. Educators have struggled against the consequences of the classical geometric vision for the lives of children—and learners of all ages. But we have not struggled consistently against the vision itself, perhaps because we have been ignorant of any alternative.

For educators the central implication of the classical vision has been category formation because category formation is less technically known as learning. Any educational mission will have to act out of some understand-ing of what categories are, how categories are acquired, and how they are used once acquired.

The classical category, like those things in the world it represents, is solid, unchanging, separable from all others and related to other categories by relations of cause or, as is said in logic classes, by implication.

Categories in the classical story are fully learned when they become fully logical. This is clearest in the work of Jean Piaget but is shot through our cultural presuppositions and is embedded even in Lev Vygotsky's classic portrayal of the word. Both radical and social constructivism are founded upon such structures. These approaches differ from traditional ones not in *what* they judge a good category or concept to be but in *how* they assert that a conventional category is most fruitfully acquired. Indeed, "discovery" methods, which focus on lists of features developed through contrast-and-compare teaching strategies, are exemplary instances of Francis Bacon's empirical method. Even more entangled with the classical vision are the current forms of schooling. Schools generally teach knowledge in a way that enacts its presumed logical nature. We often open a unit with definitions, prior to the presentation of the material to be learned. The unit is conceived as a vehicle for delivering content, gently in some cases, more didactically in others. But in any case, little that is not finally factual or does not involve good reasoning over secured knowledge is considered central to achieving the school's mission.

Presumptions about what knowledge is and what a good piece of knowledge looks like have had deep effects upon the design of instruction and the design of instructional materials. Traditional educational devices such as objective testing, the lecture format, and long, straight rows of desks in detached classrooms survive in schools in the face of vehement and sustained criticism—the most pointed of which has originated within education communities. But these tactics persist in the face of sustained critique in no small part because they are better aligned with what our culture believes knowledge to be than the alternatives offered by reformers. How we are taught and learn facts (understood as atoms), and how separable they are assumed to be from their eventual context of use is a direct product of our historically grounded assumptions concerning knowledge. Our schools are profoundly Enlightenment institutions, more deeply so than our republican form of government.

The pallor cast by these assumptions over the institutions and the practice of education is daunting, and it is the rare child who finds happiness and joy in school as a direct consequence of his or her scholastic learning. But it is not clear that it has to be this way.

Curriculum Yet-to-Come

> "Are these the shadows of the things that Will be, or are they shadows of the things that May be only?"
>
> Still the Ghost pointed downward to the grave by which it stood.
>
> "Men's courses will foreshadow certain ends, to which, if persevered in, they must lead. But if the courses be departed from, the ends will change. Say it is thus with what you show me!"

For us as for Scrooge, the ghost of the future is the one that haunts most forbiddingly. It is easy enough to share Scrooge's foreboding. As we look out over the landscape of educational reform, we can see both a path unchanged and attempts to depart from that path. Certainly the rise of constructivism, ecological education, the increasing influence of situated perspectives, the partial recovery of Dewey's legacy, and a renewed emphasis on interpretation and meaning in educational theorizing all point in the direction of a departure from the path well trod. But these steps off the path are partial and nowhere dominant or unchallenged. A steady drumbeat of attack on ideas like "relativism," "multiculturalism," "humanism," and "whole language" seems to drown out any quieter educational discourse. Encouraging thematic or cognitively oriented national standards documents from education's disciplinary areas seem to have, at best, little effect on the almost universal movement toward content-based, fact-driven standards and at worst to have spurred an unanticipated level of vitriol, which solidifies as a new "return to basics" movement. Perhaps most dramatically the national History Standards document, an interesting attempt to encourage inquiry, interpretive sophistication, interdisciplinary study, and multiple points of view in understanding our common heritage was condemned by the United States Senate with but one dissenting vote. Opponents consistently condemned theses standards by claiming that these characteristics indicated a rejection of objective, fact-based history in favor of a relativistic multiculturalism intended to introduce doubt about America's true story. Although educators may dissent from such interpretations of purposes that are widely considered central to any powerful education, it is fairly clear that American education, at least, is staying on the path.

In truth, the widespread reaction against "relativistic" ideas is easily understandable. The advocates of such ideas do dissent, however indirectly and however incompletely, from the strict classical, rationalist model outlined earlier. From the classical point of view, the advocates of a more interpretive and socially grounded approach are straying from the straight and narrow path of rational discourse. The public and the politicians are not mistaken in that regard. The discourse of formal logic is founded on a desire to find a way to *cease* to question. Those who understand otherwise mistake, in my view, the method of Cartesian questioning for its end; Descartes declares fervently for bedrock fact and deductive certainty. Doubt, for Descartes, is simply a tool to separate the wheat of Truth from the chaff of uncertainty. Those who follow in his path may reasonably affirm those same values.

What might be different? What could turn our communities from the path they are now set on? I do think we could summon up a different vision, but it is one we will have to create ourselves. In Dickens's story, no ghost appears to point the way out; that is Scrooge's task alone and one that he will have to make up as he goes along.

I do not offer a new vision of curriculum itself, only a vision of a different set of assumptions which do not drive us as inexorably down a path that leads to a focus on bare facts and straight rows of desks.

If the current ghost haunting curriculum emerges from an interlocked pattern of world, representation, and knowledge based on the strictures of geometry, then turning from that well-worn path might reasonably be expected to entail reconfiguring our understanding of world, representation, and knowledge.

Dynamics—A Changing World

It is crucial then to note that the newly emergent dynamic vision proposes a different world and different tools with which to apprehend it. On a dynamical account the world is composed of an immensely complex network of relations. The things in the world that we see are themselves composed of networks—networks which shift, driven by recursive, level crossing relations which can act over time to amplify small differences.

A different world calls for different tools with which to understand it. Where the Newtonian universe played off the activity of the calculus, the seeds of a dynamic view lay in Darwin's introduction of time in the form of recursive, level crossing relations—recursive between generations, with small genetic differences amplified and preserved, and level crossing in the sense that the larger context provided the basis for the survival or destruction of phenotypic individuals. It continued with the introduction of ecological analyses that proposed elaborate models of recursive, stability-seeking networks, which nonetheless could cycle dangerously out of control. It now moves on with the introduction of fantastically plastic computer modeling environments in which the relations can be easily specified and the computer does the almost impossible calculations that track the development of the system. It is no small irony that the development of the digital computer, in some ways the very embodiment of Newtonian-style assumptions, has enabled the explicit demonstration of a radically different framework. Ecological and evolutionary models are replacing the clockwork metaphor.

The World and the Things in It

Classical View	Dynamic View
linear	relational network
serial causality	recursive, level crossing relations
made of solid, separate objects	composed of shifting networks
instantaneous	develops over time
(small differences remain small)	(small differences may grow)
calculus	dynamic modeling
clockwork, mechanical	ecological, evolutionary

Dynamics—Representing a Changing World

That such a world will need to be apprehended differently does not, on reflection, seem surprising. The stable, unitary, context-free atoms of thought that are stored up in the mind against the day when they are retrieved have no place in a complex understanding of the world.

The logic of ecology and evolution is best represented in the realm of cognition by connectionist modeling and theories of representation. On a connectionist view, the basic operation involved in representation is pattern completion rather than retrieval from a fixed store. Such representations are radically context dependent, being constructed on the fly from elements of the individual's history and his or her immediate situation and purposes. We never experience the same individual or object twice in just the same way. Dynamics abhors stability. Crucially, such representations are associative engines in which experience, not similarity of feature, is the primary organizing principle. These representations gain their associative qualities by the very fact that they are not separate one from the other. All representations must make use of the same network of relations. Each differing representation or instance of a category is simply a particular pattern of activation constructed in response to the immediate world or imaginative recollection and uses the same elements used by other categories or instances. The associative reason and the odd, quirky, non-feature-based recall that we all experience are, in this account, not a bug but the central productive feature of the system. The dynamic vision's basic mental operations of pattern completion and associative recall encourage us to consider the evocative, associative relations that drive a poem as a much better metaphor for the structure of human reason than the geometric proof associated with the classical vision.

The Nature of Representation

Classical View	Dynamic View
retrieval	pattern completion
stable	shifting with experience
unitary, atomistic	composed of networks, dynamic
context free	context dependent
objective	unique, constructed
separate	meshed together, superimposed
rationally related and structured	association built during experience
geometric proof	poetic creation

Dynamics—Knowledge of a Changing World

But as powerful as our associative reason may be, a distressing innate instability is inextricably tied to our creative capacities. What poetry lies within us is a product of the slippery way that biological systems represent the world. There is a very real danger that subsequent experience will wash out and dilute our associations to such an extent that useful patterns of relations will be lost. Or, if subsequent experience is structured in such a way as to bias recall, experience may actually lead to incorrect attributions and even false memories. In some ways, a theory of mental activity that integrates such a wide range of *arational* findings about human cognition is an exciting advance, but it leaves us with the problem of explaining the stability of knowledge and the rationality that we do experience in our everyday lives.

Knowledge

Classical View	Dynamic View
in the mind	between world and self and other
reflects the world	practices, an activity of the world
certain	contingent upon available resources
direct perceptions, "self-evident"	socially structured expectations
showing proof	assessing the consequences
The encyclopedia	building a house

Fortunately, we don't have to figure out a way to make the productively slippery biological system internally stable. We can, instead, refer to the stability that we build into our environment through collective activity. If, following Enlightenment tradition, we regard knowledge as that stable storehouse that enables us to act consistently and accurately, we quickly realize that a dynamic understanding of this capacity must differ radically from a traditional understanding which locates this capacity in the stability of knowledge itself. Boxed in by commitments to a dynamical view of both the world and human representation, theorists who take complexity seriously, I think, have little choice but to consider adopting situated approaches to knowledge. These approaches echo the patterns already established in our discussion. Knowledge is not located in a single place in the individual mind but is distributed within an activity system that encompasses the world, the self, and the other. Crucial knowledge is structured into our environment and is something we recognize and act upon, as much as recall. I recognize how dependent I have become on my computer interface to think smoothly and accurately as I write this paper. Without the resources I have at my fingertips as I sit before the screen, I feel that I write very differently. When supporting artifacts and social situations are not available, we have a very difficult time finding and acting on the knowledge that usually comes so easily. Such a dynamical approach to knowledge also calls for a different way of discerning what makes a particular piece of knowledge valuable. The classical approach emphasizes securing the axiomatic basis for any claim about the world. A dynamic approach, founded as it is in the uncertainty of the world, finds such a claim difficult to support in most cases and prefers to ask what will be the relative consequences of adopting one position or another.

A vision of knowledge as embedded in social practice and structuring artifacts locates knowledge in activity and in interaction. Such an understanding abandons the concept of the encyclopedic storehouse of knowledge first put forward by the *philosophes* of the French Enlightenment in favor of the coordinated activity and use of embedded tools that we might find in the situated activity of a work crew building a house.

Conclusion

> "I have endeavored in this…to raise the Ghost of an Idea, which shall not put my readers out of humor with themselves, with each other, with the season, or with me. May it haunt their houses pleasantly, and no one wish to lay it."

Following Dickens's remarks in his preface just cited, I only raise the Ghost of an Idea, insubstantial no doubt but offering an alternative set of assumptions about the world, representation of the world and knowledge that may lead us to make the decision to act differently. For Scrooge to act differently, to be able to act to rescue the children of his nightmares from want and ignorance, he had to cast aside the counting house mentality that located wealth in the solidity of countable golden coins and affirm the insubstantial idea that his salvation lay in human relations. His miserly actions were a predictable consequence of his belief that he could possess wealth, just as education's actions have been a consequence of the idea that we could possess knowledge and store it up in fear against a time of need. Scrooge turned to the alternative set of assumptions and their implications that he could observe in the Cratchit family; educators must work a bit harder, drawing metaphors from multiple sources and creating patterns of meaning as we go.

Dickens's novel ends in hope and Victorian exhortation. Tim has been saved and Scrooge, having left behind the three ghosts, is able to embrace the alternative, relational spirit that animates the Cratchit family. Dickens recommends that spirit to his readers, and I can do no better than to echo his sentiment.

Notes

Of the traditions in which this text participates, Charles Dickens's Victorian moralism and the structure of his *A Christmas Carol* (1956) are used as tools to help remind us that our seemingly abstract ideas and beliefs have real consequences for the children of our communities—and for the quality of our own being in the world.

Curriculum Past: I draw my understanding of the history of ideas from the tradition grounded in John Dewey's seminal *The Quest for Certainty: A Study of the Relation of Knowledge and Action* (1929). I particularly recommend to the interested reader Chapters II & III, "Philosophy's Search for the Immutable" and "The Conflict of Authorities," for their discussion of the currents of thought that Dewey holds characterize the dawning of the modern era. More recently Stephen Toulmin's *Cosmopolis* (1990) consciously takes up and further historicizes Dewey's project. Chapter I, "What Is the Problem with Modernity," neatly places Toulmin's work in the history of commentary on modernity and points to the major conclusions of the text. Toulmin's contrast between Montaigne's reason and Descartes' ration was particularly crucial for my understanding of the intellectual underpinning and the origins of our age. For a book examining similar questions but written from a Foucaultian perspective, see: Timothy J. Reiss, *The Discourse of Modernism* (1982). From Reiss I draw the idea that modernist representation relies on an assumed isomorphism between the structures of language, thought, and the world based on the model of geometric proof. While all three of these authors critically examine the certainty that the geometric model of rationality affords, the mathematically inclined reader may prefer the account given in Phillip Davis & Reuben Hersh, *Descartes' Dream: The World According to Mathematics* (1987).

Curriculum Present: E. D. Hirsch's *The Schools We Need and Why We Don't Have Them* (1996), most explicitly his final chapter, is a site where a concerned reader may observe the current understanding—and implications for practice—of an explicitly "enlightenment" curriculum. Some may wish to delve into recent theorists' preferences for "scientific" categories based on the logical formalism of necessary and sufficient features. In education, two towering (and often contrasted) figures are Jean Piaget, upon whom large swaths of recent constructivist theory is premised, and Lev Vygotsky, who is central to current sociocultural work. For Piaget see, especially: Inhelder & Piaget, *The Growth of Logical Thinking: From Childhood to Adolescence* (1996), particularly chapter 16. For Vygotsky see chapters 5 and 6 in *Thought and Language* (1986) where he discusses his concept of the scientific category/word and its acquisition. An intriguing and readable overview of research on category formation that has deepened my considerations is George Lakoff's *Women, Fire, and Dangerous Things: What Categories Reveal about the Mind.* (1987)

Curriculum Yet To Come: A germane exploration of the stability of the American educational system and its associated practices may be found in Larry Cuban's *How Teachers Taught: Constancy and Change in American Classrooms 1890–1990* (1993). **Dynamics—A Changing World:** On the implications of adopting a dynamic worldview for understanding research and a sampling of the diverse areas in which a dynamic approach constitutes the leading edge of the discipline, see: William Bechtel and Robert C. Richardson, *Discovering Complexity: Decomposition and Localization as Strategies in Scientific Research* (1993). Ilya Prigogine and Isabelle Stengers's seminal *Order Out of Chaos: Man's New Dialogue with Nature* (1984) nicely ties the philosophical history to Prigogene's Nobel Prize-winning work. **Dynamics—Representing a Changing World:** For those interested in the debate over the nature of representation useful starting points in exploring a literature relevant to the perspective taken by this chapter may be found in Andy Clark's *Associative Engines: Connectionism, Concepts and Representational Change* (1993) (focusing on connectionist representation) and *Being There; Putting brain, body, and world together again* (1997) (which extends the framework to include issues of embodiment). **Dynamics—Knowledge of a Changing World:** Much of this section is deeply indebted to pragmatic understandings of knowledge and the allusion to Dewey's house-building activity at the Chicago Laboratory School is one sign of this. Less familiar but recommended is G. H. Mead's *The Philosophy of the Act* (1950), which makes clear the implications of pragmatism for traditional (what I have called classic) views of learning and knowledge. See, for instance, the section "The Nature of Mental Processes" for a succinct exposition of why Mead holds that the mind does not end at the skin. The elder pragmatists assumed a dynamic continuity between biology, social situatedness and individual cognition that has been seldom appreciated. More recently, researchers operating from both connectionist and situated perspectives have found their counterpart's views potentially valuable. See James V. Wertsch, *Mind as Action* (1998), pp. 51–53, for the view from the situated side of the aisle and David Rumelhart and J. L. Smolensky in "Schemata and Sequential Thought Processes in PDP Models" in volume 2 of the *Parallel Distributed Processing* (1986) tome for their view on the value of Vygtoskyian analyses.

References

Bechtel, William, and Robert C. Richardson. (1993). *Discovering complexity: Decomposition and localization as strategies in scientific research.* Princeton, NJ: Princeton University Press.

Clark, Andy. (1993). *Associative engines: Connectionism, concepts, and representational change.* Cambridge, MA: MIT Press.

Clark, Andy. (1997). *Being there: Putting brain, body, and world together again.* Cambridge, MA: MIT Press.

Cuban, Larry. (1993). *How teachers taught: Constancy and change in American classrooms, 1890-1990.* 2nd ed. *Research on teaching series.* New York: Teachers College Press.

Davis, Philip J., and Reuben Hersh. (1987). *Descartes' dream: The world according to mathematics.* Boston: Houghton Mifflin.

Dewey, John. (1929). *The quest for certainty: A study of the relation of knowledge and action.* New York: Minton Balch.

Dickens, Charles. (1956). *A Christmas carol.* New York: Columbia University Press.

Hirsch, E. D. (1996). *The schools we need and why we don't have them.* 1st ed. New York: Doubleday.

Inhelder, Bärbel, and Jean Piaget. (1964). *The early growth of logic in the child, classification and seriation.* New York: Harper & Row.

Lakoff, George. (1987). *Women, fire, and dangerous things: What categories reveal about the mind.* Chicago: University of Chicago Press.

Mead, George Herbert. (1950). *The philosophy of the act.* Chicago, IL: University of Chicago press.

Prigogine, I., and Isabelle Stengers. (1984). *Order out of chaos: Man's new dialogue with nature.* New York, NY: Bantam Books.

Reiss, Timothy J. (1982). *The discourse of modernism.* Ithaca, NY: Cornell University Press.

Rumelhart, David E., and J. L. Smolensky. (1986). Schemata and sequential thought processes in PDP models. In *Parallel distributed processing, volume 2: Psychological and biological models*, edited by D. E. Rumelhart, J. L. McClelland and the PDP Research Group. Cambridge, MA: MIT Press.

Toulmin, Stephen Edelston. (1990). *Cosmopolis: The hidden agenda of modernity.* New York: Free Press.

Vygotsky, Lev S. (1986). *Thought and language.* Translated by Alex Kozulin. Cambridge, MA: MIT Press.

Wertsch, James V. (1998). *Mind as action.* New York: Oxford University Press.

John St. Julien currently teaches courses on curriculum, technology, cognition, and social studies at the University of Delaware. His research interests focus on situated and connectionist understandings of human cognition, Creole approaches to identity, educational technology, and social studies education.

Perspective on St. Julien

Kristin Kight

> Space, the final frontier,
> These are the voyages of the Starship Enterprise,
> Its continuing mission,
>   to explore strange new worlds,
>   to seek out new life and new civilizations,
>   to boldly go where no one has gone before!

Reading St. Julien's *Haunting Curriculum*, his vision of curriculum future, and heeding his concerns about curriculum past opened an idea for me of what a preparatory school for Starfleet academy might look like. Such a school would have a clear purpose, which today's American schools do not. They suffer from conflicting goals from those of the nineteenth century progressives, to whose standards to apply, to accommodating the Americans with Disabilities Act. There is a great confusion about what the product of our school system should be. A preparatory school for the Starfleet academy, however, would have to equip students for a life of encountering the unknown, and being open to unforeseen developments. This would have to enact a curriculum, an organization of people, and learning experiences that eschewed the human attraction for comfort that tradition satisfies. Definitely not, as St. Julien puts it:

> ...an image of the world where everything has its place, where things are governed by simple and elegant laws, and where all that is necessary to know the future—and indeed the past—is a full description of the myriad solid objects that compose the world and the causal relations which connect them. (This volume)

Now we need an "ecological and evolutionary model" that allows a dynamic learning environment where positions of teacher and student, advanced student and novice can switch with each other, where knowledge is distributed within the learning group and across sources outside it. Where the Prime Directive[1] operates among learners and teachers as it will later govern unexpected encounters with new worlds. Such a school would have to promote diversity in working groups, acquisition of problem-solving skills, and an emphasis on process over specific product. Thus it would be consistent with St. Julien's vision of curriculum future.

Imagine that instead of age-segregated classes trooping through a prescribed set of courses each day, 50 minutes at a time, students from fourteen to eighteen years of age would be spending a cycle (perhaps a cycle of six days?) working on understanding and solving a question that pulls together elements of math, physics, history, literature, and language. For this example I choose high-school-aged students because this is the level where we seem to be most concerned about arranging their days predictably and their studies in accordance with tradition and are most unclear about what we want them to become. The vision of change I propose would be a problem-based approach, and would promote guided participation for younger members of the group by more experienced members, allowing the roles of teacher and learner to shift flexibly and recursively over time. Groups might find themselves solving such puzzles as this one: "Investigating the discovery of a piece of metal bearing a United States Air Force insignia, the away team finds itself trapped in the world of *The Hotel Royale*, a novel come to life." They might move from there to another puzzle incorporating botany, food distribution, architecture, math (at several levels), and cultural tastes: "Kidnapped by aliens known as Ligonians, Lieutenant Tasha Yar battles for her freedom and the welfare of a diseased Federation planet."

These two problems were taken from descriptions of episodes of the television show *Star Trek: The Next Generation*, and they are amusing as well as puzzling to solve. A curriculum need not be based on the assumption that learning is different from fun or separate from life. St. Julien suggests a basis for curriculum future in connectionist theories and context-dependent representations of knowledge. The process here is pattern completion and extension. Problems like the ones quoted here or drawn from humanity's history offer many ways for the subjects we now separate to be interwoven in more meaningful learning activities.

From the perspective of a teacher, such a curriculum would allow several aspects of professional practice that are almost impossible in curriculum present. First, this new arrangement would allow teachers to collaborate on and integrate their plans for a given cycle or unit. Second, it would allow for teachers not currently involved with a unit to take time with their assessments of a just completed one and to enhance their learning by participating in the student group while a colleague of different expertise facilitated or planned for the next cycle. Third, it would move the whole enterprise (pun intended) out of the traditional classroom and into the world, taking advantage of resources both technological and natural that seldom are used to the fullest by current school field trips. Fourth, it would allow teachers to enact lesson plans based on the dynamic view of knowledge that St. Julien recommends for curriculum future. This really cannot be done within the structure of day, class, and relationships, to say nothing of buildings that currently structure school. Finally, such a restructuring of school would help us teach our children some of the nonacademic things we lament about both families' and schools' failure to do adequately under the current system. In a context in which knowledge and responsibility are distributed across the group, such values as civility, cooperation, mutual respect, and interest in multiple viewpoints would be modeled and upheld by the very nature of the interaction necessary to solve the problem before the group.

From a student perspective it would defeat the problem of inert knowledge, or the why-are-we-learning-this syndrome. It would be much more interesting and engaging. The tendency we now have to compartmentalize the disciplines so that students are surprised to learn that spelling counts in biology, that economics (not to say math) has an impact on literature, and that the ability to communicate effectively has an important role in almost every area of life. Yes, it would involve more active participation than does the typical class in curriculum present and that means more work, but not more seat work, busywork, or worksheets.

> Held captive over an unknown planet, the away teams of the *USS Enterprise* and Ferengi starships must pass an important inquisition by a mysterious life form known as Portal, before they are allowed to continue their journeys through space.

And now to the issue of assessment. Although traditional exams would be possible under this vision of curriculum and school future, they could only play a part in assessing the gains made by students engaged in these lessons. It would be necessary to establish methods for assessing the quality of group interaction, so there might need to be a team of observers for each active group. Would such assessment be formative or summative? Both make sense here, in contrast to our current methods, which are almost exclusively summative. Assessment would need to extend to the adults involved in these lessons as well as to student performance. A portfolio of materials generated in the process of learning and problem solving would be indicated for both individuals and for the group as a whole. There is a greater opportunity in this kind of an education to teach that evaluation is an ongoing and essential part of life, and a disposition to seek it out and incorporate sensible suggestions from it benefits a person from cradle to grave. In contrast the description of the episode of *Star Trek: The Next Generation* quoted here communicates the feeling we currently have about tests.

Like St. Julien, I only offer a collection of ideas about what this vision of curriculum future might entail in practice. Sharing it with a small group of currently practicing teachers brought on a lively and good-humored discussion of the possibilities we'd like to see emerge as realities. The general consensus was that much of what is proposed here could be done now were we only to have the nerve.

Note

1 It is forbidden to all spaceships and members of Starfleet to interfere with the normal development of any culture or society. This directive is more important than the protection of spaceships or members of Starfleet. Losses are tolerated as long as they are necessary to observe this directive.

Kristin Kight is a doctoral student in the cognition and instruction program at the University of Delaware. A former high school teacher, her research interests center on problems of executive functioning in intelligent underachievers and the innovative curricular arrangements that might be helpful in their achieving academic success.

Chapter 12 Speaking of Ghosts...

Problematic: Decentering the Eye/I

> In general we feel more secure when things are *visible*, when we can "see for ourselves"....We employ visual and spatial metaphors for a great many everyday expressions. We insist on employing visual metaphors even when we refer to purely psychological states, such as tendency and duration. For instance, we say *there*after when we really mean *then*after, al*ways* when we mean at all *times*. (Marshall McLuhan and Quentin Fiore, 1967, 117; emphasis added)

> i keep recalling that Socrates wrote *nothing* and we are still recovering from the misreading by Plato. (jan jagodzinski, quoted in Pinar and Reynolds, 1992, 250)

Once upon a time, hearing was believing. But, as Donna Trueit reminds us, societies shaped by the alphabet—a medium that depends upon the eye for comprehension—reproduce a dominant discourse in which signs mediated by the ear alone are distrusted (and even, as jagodzinski suggests, "misread"). Claims to truth privilege visualization (objectivity is grounded in observation) and diminish the transitory sounds and contingent silences of acoustic space.

Ted Aoki (1991) invites us "to allow *sonare* to dwell juxtaposedly with *videre*" and to engage in a more attentive listening that "allows us to become thoughtful of how we may have become beholden to the metaphor of the I/eye—the I that sees" (185). Trueit's suggestion that *écriture féminine* offers a way of writing that, in Aoki's terms, allows *sonare* to dwell with *videre* is especially useful because it decenters the I/eye without diminishing the written wor(l)d. In this respect, we recall John Varley's (1978) science fiction story, *The Persistence of Vision*, in which he constructs a utopian community designed and built by the deaf-blind. He then explores these people's technologies, media, and modes of communication and their relations to sighted children and visitors. Donna Haraway (1989) cites Varley's story as an inspiration for *Primate Visions*, her critical feminist history of primatology and its cultural effects: "The interrogation of the limits and violence of vision is part of the politics of learning to revision" (384). In *Primate Visions*, Haraway exposes the "violence" that arises from the relationship between our vision—what, how, why, who, when and where we choose to see—and those others (human, animal) who are subjected to and objectified by our gaze. In relating the development of Haraway's politics and method to *écriture féminine*, it might be significant that her most recent book is the record of an extended conversation (Haraway, 2000).

In his introduction to this volume, Noel Gough asserts that "curriculum vision begins with an embodied eye/I." Trueit also privileges embodiment but wisely invites suspicion of the eye/I's dominance in the language of curriculum inquiry.

References

Aoki, Ted T. (1991). *Sonare* and *videre*: Questioning the primacy of the eye in curriculum talk. In George Willis and William H. Schubert (Eds.), *Reflections from the heart of educational inquiry: Understanding curriculum and teaching through the arts* (pages 182–89). Albany, NY: State University of New York Press.

Haraway, Donna J. (1989). *Primate visions: Gender, race, and nature in the world of modern science*. New York: Routledge.

______. (2000). *How like a leaf: An interview with Thyrza Nichols Goodeve*. New York and London: Routledge.

McLuhan, Marshall, and Quentin Fiore. (1967). *The medium is the message*. New York: Bantam Books.

Pinar, William F., and William M. Reynolds. (1992). Appendix: Genealogical notes—the history of phenomenology and post-structuralism in curriculum studies. In William F. Pinar and William M. Reynolds (Eds.), *Understanding curriculum as phenomenological and deconstructed text* (pages 237–61). New York: Teachers College Press.

Varley, John. (1978). *The persistence of vision*. New York: Dell.

Speaking of Ghosts...

Donna Trueit

Yes, let us consider the presence of ghosts in the curriculum, acknowledging that once upon a time something lived but was cast out and died. Something of the past dwells just beyond our consciousness. Let us indeed consider, as Bill Doll suggests, that there are ghosts, Dewey's among them, and that control is more than a ghostly reality in our classrooms. Control is present in the ways we speak, silently imposing its will through our speaking.

Let us acknowledge, when speaking of ghosts, that there are different ways of speaking and that conversation is but one.[1] Let us heed the call from William Pinar (Pinar et al., 1995), as Doll reminds us in this text, for curriculum theorists to converse, but let us avoid confusing conversation with dialogue.[2] Let us in this instance focus on conversation as its own form of expression, as a way of speaking that embodies the poetic, and later speak of the poetic as a way of summoning embodied knowledge, written as *écriture féminine*.

Walter Ong (1982) reminds us that a long time ago, there was only speech. We did not write. In this time we used language orally in certain patterns, rhythms, and forms, but with the increasing technologies of literacy, orality is unfortunately subsumed and rendered invisible. Currently, we do not recognize a difference between conversation and dialogue, but as Eric Havelock (1986) points out, in preliterate Greece, language was poetic. It did not conceive of nor have the words for dialogue in the literate Socratic style. There were no words or speech patterns to objectify a self. That occurred when speech became objectified through writing; the self became distinguished as both a subject and an object, separate from others.[3] In this context, Hamlet's famous soliloquy "To be, or not to be..." takes on special significance. Hamlet ponders not simply his existence—whether to live or die—but to do so as an acting subject (!) or as a passive object.

Ong advocates an integration of orality and literacy in order to develop both a stronger sense of self and self in the world. "Orality-literacy dynamics enter integrally into the modern evolution of consciousness toward both greater interiorization and greater openness" (1982, 179). In our classrooms, where we emphasize literacy, let us not forget orality in all its forms, recognizing the need for conversation. Let us summon the Muses: caste out of the curriculum by Plato, they dwell in conversation, inspirit conversation, breathe life into it.

Plato and the Muses

Muses are the mythical, mystical spirits of speech of ancient Greece. The muse carried messages of inspiration, virtue, and the cultural past through oral performance—elocution, song, recitation—the spoken word. Poets were trained in oral arts to perform the work of the muse and, in doing so, educated the people. Havelock (1986) surmises that as Greece moved from a primarily oral society to a more literate society, Plato realized that writing would supplant rhetorical traditions. Havelock describes the transition from orality to literacy by referencing the *Phaedo*, "the most famous of Plato's dialogues":

> In the prelude, waiting in prison for death, [Socrates] reports that in the last few days he had turned for recreation to the task of versifying some of Aesop's fables. Up to this point, he remarks, "I had thought that the supreme form of the Muses' art was really philosophy." But as he turns back to versifying, preparing for the end of life, he reverts also to those ways of orality with which he had grown up. His own previous career had exemplified as dramatically as was possible the closeness of the partnership between traditional orality and incipient literacy. His own dialectic depended upon a growing literate vocabulary. Yet he had never written a word himself. Plato's incomparable insight captures a last sense of the partnership precisely at the moment when it was to be dissolved. The orality to which Socrates briefly turned back was to fade away before the presence of its junior but now more powerful partner, just as Socrates must fade away too. By the time it was Plato's turn to leave, in the middle of the fourth century, the Greek Muse had left the whole world of oral discourse and oral "knowing" behind her. She had truly learnt to write, and to write in prose—and even to write in philosophical prose. (116)

It cannot be said that Plato didn't believe in spirits, for his mentor, teacher and hero, Socrates, had his own muse, a *daimon* called Diotima, a prophet, a visionary,[4] who served Socrates as a spiritual intermediary and interlocutor. In the *Symposium*, written by Plato, Socrates in active dialogue with Diotima, learns about eros,[5] and Plato reveals his prejudice against the ancient Greek tradition of poetry. "Diotima the prophet connects poetry, practical reasoning, art, and creativity" (Garrison, 1997, 8). Diotima tells Socrates "there is more than one kind of poetry in the true sense of the word—that is to say, calling something into existence that was not there before, so that every kind of artistic creation [poiesis] is poetry and every artist a poet" (8). Her opinion of poetry makes obsolete the epic poems, as Diotima emphasizes the spontaneity of creation[6] over recitation of historical or epic poems. Plato's Socrates, a man who did not write, is revealed in the dialogues as one who hears the voice of the Muse and is led to certain transformations as a result of conversations with her. Unfortunately, Diotima died with Socrates, and the voice of the Muse was silenced.

Plato shunned the Muses of Poetry and History because he felt that myths "needed to be good for us, beautiful to listen to, and conducive to right opinion....Only philosopher kings can censor, for only they know *the* truth" (Garrison, 1997, 7).[7] The poetic verses of the Muses carried the didactic knowledge of a primarily oral culture, the common knowledge of the rhetorical tradition, a knowledge to be absorbed rather than demanding growth, transformation and movement to the ideal *Forms*, Plato's conception of a transcendent reality. Plato criticized the poets for being imitative, managing only to copy the "natural" rhythms in their poems, and for not being truly creative, because their poems were committed to memory and later recited.

Plato's notion was that through *dialogue*, a process of active questioning and reflection, students would come to know. Dialogue is associated with the dialectic, a formalized inquiry leading to a reasoned understanding, thoughtful and engaging—not without its own sense of spirit, more aptly named by Jim Garrison (1997), a passion. Dialogue is a public, reductive process of coming to a *point* of understanding. It assumes a knowable reality, certainty, and a stable unitary self. Plato created "rational beings."

If we can agree to the influence of Plato's philosophy on education and teaching in the Western tradition as traced by scholars throughout the ages,[8] we may also agree to the significance of logical dialogue as the basis of educative language, which relegates other forms of speaking, writing, and knowing to a place outside of the academy. This creates a bifurcation of interactions, into those which are educative, the dialogical, and those which are then noneducative, which I will call *conversational*[9] and discuss later. Recognizing the distinction Plato makes between the purity and power of dialogue over other forms of interaction, the connection between the expression of the word and the value of the idea becomes even clearer. Knowing that flowed from the logical discussion of ideas transported one nearer to the Forms. Referring to Plato, Hans-Georg Gadamer (1980) explains that

> the problem of methexis, i.e., of the participation of the many in the one idea, is developed dialectically to the point where apparently insuperable difficulties result in order that the participation of the ideas in each other might then emerge as the solution. For the latter alone makes clear what knowledge, and what the logos is. (138)

Knowledge is carried in the word, the *logos*, written or spoken in the form of dialogue. For Plato, ideas that emerge from the dialectic, through dialogue, have the power to unite the many in the face of insurmountable difficulties.[10] However, as we understand today, this unity won through the power of the word universalizes and denies differences. And importantly, the idea of creating a unity demands *sharing* a vision.

In the movement from orality to increasing literacy, major changes occurred in interactions which had long-lasting effects in those fields of endeavor that are concerned with knowledge and learning. The first is that with representational thinking, the self and the mind became objects which could be investigated, known, and transformed.

Second, the rational word, written or spoken, became a metaphor for ideas and truths expressed as "visions" of which one could be certain and, incredibly, that through language one could "give" visions to others (Rorty, 1979). As evidence of this change of consciousness, recognize how literacy permeates our being, reference how incomprehensible it is to talk of ideas without using the metaphor of sight; we say "I *see*" when we understand—and the assumption is that we can and do! We discuss our *views*, our *perspectives*, and as Doll's essay indicates, our inspirations are spoken of in terms of *envisioning* possibilities or perhaps *insights*. Literacy depends upon the recognition of text, the written word (Ong, 1982). "It would seem inescapably obvious," says Ong, "that language is an oral phenomenon" (6). Orality is the use of spoken language: "Wherever human beings exist they have a language…spoken and heard, in the world of sound" (7). But he points out that scholars since the time of the Greeks have assumed, "often without reflection, that oral verbalization was essentially the same as the written verbalization they normally dealt with" (10). One small example lies in the use of the word "discourse" to represent both spoken and written uses of language. Ironically, even aphorisms, which are themselves characteristic of poetic speech, reflect the extent to which we are converts to a literate society: Don't believe what you hear. Seeing is believing. Instead of finding wisdom in voices, of the Oracles or in one's inner voices, knowledge became located outside of oneself

Finally, logic and reason embedded in dialogue was privileged over other ways of knowing and speaking, providing a framework for educated speech. Those who cannot speak to the point and use the proper language are silenced as knowers. Language is not only a way of communicating meaning: It is a means of controlling who can participate in the interaction. Since ancient times, learning has been associated with using language in a certain way. One of the ghosts of control that I perceive in the language of education exists in speech patterns that control by situating the power of ideas in the particular use of the language. One's elocution and use of language identify him or her as educated. However, this traditional understanding, originating at the time of a shift from orality to literacy, is based on an assumption that ideas, like commodities, are external to a unitary self, waiting to be discovered and transmitted. Dialogical interaction uses "the word" as an entity that sits outside of the individual and relations, capable of carrying meaning.

What has been lost in educational contexts are the voice of the muses and a sensory-intuitive and spiritual orientation to the world. Knowledge that one *feels* as a result of perceptions, intuitions, and spiritual connection was, and still is, devalued. In the following section, I will advocate for the recuperation of embodied knowledge, summoning the poetic present in conversation, a way of speaking, and *écriture féminine*, a way of writing.

Conjuring Conversation As Poetic

I suggest, playfully, that the Muse dwells in conversation. She is the inspiration of our ideas, the ones that fly off in all directions, thoughts that spring to "mind" unbidden, leaping out of our mouths. This is the work of the poetic Muse, present in the shadows of our consciousness, alive in our orality, but unacknowledged in our interactions except as aberrations[11] in our discredited discourses, gossip, chats, heart-to-hearts. Conversation is oriented to developing meaning over time, in and through relations. It is the common way of speaking, not to a "point" of understanding (although understanding certainly may occur), not "on a subject" (although this too occurs), but around and about—with no intent to determine meaning—it wanders, wonders, muses. There is a movement from topic to topic, one to the other, connected by "Oh, that reminds me…," a flow that is often recursive, picking up from previous encounters. "Conversation is a game of circles. In conversation we pluck up the termini which bound the common of silence on every side" (Emerson, 310). It is not *inquiry*[12] although it explores, queries. It is additive and divergent. Conversation does "begatting" (the oral tradition of Bible lineages) by linking together, making connections of the disparate, the ineffable. Conversation is an occasion, an event fully contextual but irretrievable, present only in the moment, because the sound of the words is instantly gone. It is both sound and silence pregnant with past, present and future—and more. Ong specifies that

> the oral word...never exists in a simply verbal context, as a written word does. Spoken words are always modifications of a total, existential situation, which always engages the body. Bodily activity beyond mere vocalization is not adventitious or contrived in oral communication, but is natural and even inevitable. In oral verbalization, particularly public verbalization, absolute motionlessness is itself a powerful gesture. (1982, 67–68)

Orally patterned thought demands that the body *express* itself. Even in its stillness—perhaps more eloquently—the body speaks. Ong notes that the rhythmic nature of orally patterned thought is linked to balance, breathing, and the bilateral symmetry of the body. Part of the rhythm of conversation comes from the back and forth as speakers respond to each other, but the other part is the rhythm within a speaker, between sound and silence. Silence is not simply the absence of speech: it signifies spaces, gaps, and discontinuities in conversation, which have significance in admitting the untidiness, complexities and resistances in real life. Silence surrounds conversation and is a part of the conversation, creating a rhythm—the rhythm of poetry—imitation of music and nature. Rhythm signifies life—the pulsing, beating, throbbing ongoingness of life in *this* world—without a care for transcendence to the next.

Socrates's musings with Diotima represent inner speech, his reflective questioning of, and meditations on, the world. To muse is to be absorbed in thought, to meditate continuously in silence, to ponder (*OED*). What is the relationship of words to worlds as inner voices play with the possibilities inherent in any moment? This is not a *prescripted* or *procedural*[13] moment; this is a moment of potential, a political space with the potential for any number of responses that will affect relationships. In our most satisfying conversations, speech is often not even coherent, sometimes only fragments are uttered, and yet participants continue to respond to each other in ways that meet their needs. Surely the Muse is at play here! We bring to each speech event all of the unspecified, diffuse feelings of the past to the present. Conversation is a process of making sense not of the words that are spoken (although it is surely this, too), so much as responding to "the other" through one's senses. Instead of responding to words, one responds to the *voice*, the call. The performative nature of embodied knowledge is in our wholly responding to the call. The relationship then of words to worlds is the bridging of the abyss, each occasion of conversation an opportunity for the past to be seen in light of the present and future relationships. It is in this place of awareness between the word and the response that the Muse inspirits conversation. In the silence is the power and spirit of the Muse, at play with possibilities, in the rhythm of the conversation.

Poetic Narrative: *Écriture Féminine*

The orality that haunts conversation abides in *écriture féminine*, writing conjured into existence by French poststructural feminists such as Julia Kristeva and Hélène Cixous. *Écriture féminine*, also known as *feminine writing* and writing *the body*, shares certain characteristics of orality with conversation, even as it has its own identifying traits. By the difference it presents to modern discourse, *écriture féminine* represents a postmodern discourse, challenging everything about the practice of writing—knowledge, knowers, what can be known, what can be written. It is not bound by the constraints of literary writing, in fact, resists all of the organizing structures of form, ideas, and expression considered necessary for *good* writing. As Lynn Worsham (1991), writing about *écriture féminine* and education, indicates, the statement "to define *écriture féminine* would kill it" typifies the resistance of *écriture féminine* to modern conceptions of knowledge, that "things" can be categorized, defined, known, meaning transmitted from my head to yours. Cixous (1976) states, "It is impossible to define a feminine practice of writing, and this is an impossibility that will remain, for this practice can never be theorized, enclosed, coded....it will always surpass the discourse that regulates the phallocentric system" (883).

Verena Andermatt Conley (1990), in discussing *écriture féminine*, describes a process through which the writer becomes free. "By virtue of its poetry that comes from the rapport of the body to the social world, *écriture féminine* disrupts social practices in the way it both discerns and literally rewrites them" (vii–viii). Because meaning is personally constructed there is no truth (in the modern sense), and yet paradoxically, it is the truth (of the moment). As a result, all writing is a creation of self,

self is created through writing, and all narrative is fiction. In its own terms, feminine writing is autobiographical in the sense that all writing is representative of a self and lends itself to exploration of a nonunitary self, subject(s) in process. *Écriture féminine* assumes that the writer is always "being born" in the process of writing.

Cixous eloquently describes the short stories of Clarice Lispector as the epitome of feminine writing. In the foreword to Lispector's (1989) book, Cixous manages, without defining, to illuminate traits which characterize *écriture féminine*. The writing cannot be followed for a plot, progressive chronological time, or sequencing of events. Instead, "the text follows movements of the body and enunciation, but it also follows thematics. Rather than a narrative order, there is an organic order" (x). The organic order she refers to is the flow of the text through its phonetics and images, the movement of pleasure, *jouissance*, the building of a climax, through a back and forth of rhythm, space, recursion, and interruptions.

Like the immediacy of conversation, *écriture féminine* writes the moment, in the moment. It speaks of the context of the present. Ong (1982) notes that "by keeping knowledge embedded in the human lifeworld, orality situates knowledge within a context of struggle" (44). In addition, the structure of orality itself is connected to "the give and take dynamics of sound; interpersonal relations are kept high—both attractions and, even more, antagonisms" (45). The violence, struggle, and hardships of everyday life which characterize early verbal art forms (as in the epic poems) are present in *écriture féminine*. Cixous's early essay "The Laugh of the Medusa" speaks of the violence, dissonance, contradiction, and agonistic tension in the lives of women in a patriarchal society. As the title suggests, the mythic female creature epitomizes the conflicting societal attitudes toward women, being the "respected" mother who gave birth to the gods but causing death to those who looked upon her face.

This classical myth could even be a metaphor for the silencing one experiences when faced with the Other, the power of the other—text, body, concept—one is left speechless. What is this silence? What are the moments of indeterminacy, undecidability and ambivalence? Julia Kristeva (1991) notes that from a psychoanalytic perspective we are "strangers to ourselves" and always will be, needing to acknowledge the "uncanny strangeness"[14] in order to be able to accept and/or develop a relationship with the Other—which is always a part of our being. Psychoanalytically, silence is dysrhythmia, not breathing, death, the anguish of the repression of the semiotic chora, insufficiencies, meaninglessness. However, for both Kristeva and Cixous, in this reduction to zero, the subject is born as inspiration.

It is in this silent space that Cixous begins to write, claiming the opportunity to explore, to speak the unspeakable, to attend to the embodied, to transgress the limits, and to confront the ghosts of control—the ghosts that reside in our ways of speaking and writing. For Cixous, our being—including sensuality and sexuality—and use of the language are inextricably linked: the syntactical, grammatical structure of discourse obstructs the expression of knowledge of the body on the inside, at the edges and as we intersect with others. Cixous situates her writing at the threshold of feeling, where voice is woven into the text. This bodily orientation to discourse is characteristic of orally patterned thought.

The connection that I make between *écriture féminine*, conversation, and the relevance to education relates to the notion that people develop intellectually as they develop in relationship to themselves and others. The question that begs asking then is, why is this not educational? Why is this process, too, not recognized as worthwhile inquiry? Conversation and *écriture féminine* provide opportunities to participate in the formation of subjectivities, to play with voices and ways of being in an atmosphere of political safety and acceptability, facilitating and easing the encounter with the stranger which is both self and other.

Let us consider using the technology of writing to write of self and other, but let us invoke the Muse, assuming that Havelock (1986) was wrong: that although she had "truly learnt to write, and to write in prose —and even to write in philosophical prose" (116)—she is still present to us in the orality of conversation and *écriture féminine*. Let us speak of our *visions*, if this be the metaphor of choice, in hopes of inspiring others, allowing that each has a unique *view*. Let us, sometimes, proliferate meanings. Let us call upon the "livelier spirits of life" (Doll, this volume) to speak of issues for which there is no single meaning, to explore our multiple understandings and ignorances of self and other. Let us claim the freedom of transgressing, playing in the silence, writing the embodied voices, talking with the subjects of our being.

Acknowledgments: Thanks to William Pinar for his encouragement and insightful comments, and to LSU curriculum and instruction graduate students for their thoughtful feedback and criticism.

Notes

[1] Nicholas Burbules (2000) identifies four forms of dialogic relations: dialogue as inquiry, dialogue as instruction, dialogue as debate, and dialogue as conversation (394).

[2] Without creating too strong a separation between conversation and dialogue, recognizing that most exchanges have elements of both and that curriculum is a very complicated discourse, I want to call attention to and explore the way "naturalized" use of language influences social and political practices to perpetuate inequities. To continue using Burbules's dialogical distinctions, and by way of distinguishing conversation as unique, I suggest that dialogue has an element of "intentionality" suggestive of a purpose and/or an agenda that I associate with control (and power).

[3] Havelock (1986) compares Homeric (preliterate) poetry (that was later transcribed) with the writings of later Greeks (Plato's Socratic dialogues) and concludes: "As language became separated visually from the person who uttered it, so also the person, the source of the language, came into sharper focus and the concept of selfhood was born" (112).

[4] The reference to a "seer" rather than the auditory "oracle" as a mode of inspiration signifies the shift from orality (associated with hearing) to literacy (associated with sight).

[5] Susan Edgerton (1996) writes: "Plato spoke of eros...erosic love for Plato was desire—love, and the search for what was lacking. Plato separated mind and body within eros by differentiating between a raving or vulgar eros (body) and a sublime eros (mind). Thus for the philosopher, love involved lacking and seeking beauty, truth, and the good" (65).

[6] According to Ong (1982) the poets had a repertoire of stock phrases related to historical events and/or characters, that they "rhapsodized"—literally, stitched together—for a particular audience and occasion, adjusting the recitation according to the audience's response.

[7] The roots of a hierarchy of knowledges lie in this statement, and one locates the buds of modernistic attitudes that are criticized from race, class, and gender perspectives.

[8] Alfred North Whitehead states that "all history is one long footnote to Plato."

[9] There are, of course, other ways of speaking, but for the purposes of this paper I will focus on conversation; the complex and fascinating history of rhetoric will not be discussed here. Rhetoric, for Plato and other Greeks of that period, represented the antithesis of the process of reasoning and logic that Plato advocated.

[10] At this point it might be suggested that the homogeneous nature of the group that attended Plato's school might have affected the validity of his observations. He did not have the advantage of testing the strength of his thesis in the presence of the diversities of race, class, and gender that are commonly a part of classrooms today.

[11] As evidence of the positive value placed on linearity and reason and the devaluing of a lack of direction or destination, "aberration" means a "straying from the path, lit. & fig.; breaking of rules; moral slip; intellectual deficiency" (*Oxford English Dictionary*).

[12] Conversation is not inquiry in the formal sense of the word, i.e., research, or in the dialectical sense of logical argumentation or disputation.

[13] Nicholas Burbules (2000) expresses concerns about "the role dialogue has played in educational and democratic theory: *proceduralism*, which elevates issues of pedagogy over an examination of the broader factors that do or do not make dialogue

possible...[and] *prescriptivism,* which despite good intents at accommodating diversity may be actually counterproductive in contexts of difference" (399).

14 "Uncanny strangeness" is Kristeva's psychoanalytic reference to the wrenching, inexpressible experience of disruption one senses, as an infant being introduced to language, that one is separate from the mother. She suggests that "otherness" is a repressed part of our being, and when confronted with any "other," one re-experiences the anguish of the breach. The encounter with the other leaves us temporarily speechless.

References

Burbules, Nicholas. (2000). Dialogue. In David Gabbard (Ed.), *Knowledge and power in the global economy: Politics and the rhetoric of school reform* (pages 393–99). New Jersey: Erlbaum.

Cixous, Hélène. (1976). The laugh of the Medusa. Keith Cohen and Paula Cohen (Trans.) *Signs, 1*(41), 875–93.

______. (1989) Foreword. Verena Conley (Trans.). In *The stream of life* by Clarice Lispector. Elizabeth Lowe and Earl Fitz (Trans.). Minneapolis: University of Minnesota Press.

______. (1994) *The Hélène Cixous reader.* Susan Sellars (Ed.). New York: Routledge.

Cixous, Hélène, and Calle-Gruber, Mireille. (1997). *Rootprints: Memory and life writing*. Eric Prenowitz (Trans.). New York: Routledge.

Conley, Verena. (1990). *Reading with Clarice Lispector.* Minneapolis: University of Minnesota Press.

Edgerton, Susan. (1996). *Translating the curriculum: Multiculturalism into cultural studies.* New York: Routledge.

Emerson, Edward W. (1968). *Complete works of Ralph Waldo Emerson* (12 vols.). In *Essays: First series,* vol. 2, 310. New York: AMS.

Gadamer, Hans G. (1976). *Philosophical hermeneutics.* Los Angeles: University of California Press.

_______. (1980). *Dialogue and dialectic: Eight hermeneutical studies on Plato.* New Haven, CT: Yale University Press.

Garrison, James. (1997). *Dewey and eros: Wisdom and desire in the art of teaching.* New York: Teachers College Press.

Havelock, Eric. (1986). *The muse learns to write.* New Haven: Yale University Press.

Kristeva, Julia. (1991). *Strangers to ourselves.* Leon S. Roudiez (Trans.). New York: Columbia University Press.

Lispector, Clarice. (1989). *Stream of life.* Foreword by Hélène Cixous. Verena Conley (Trans.). Minneapolis: University of Minnesota Press.

Moi, Toril. (Ed.). (1986). *The Kristeva reader.* New York: Columbia University Press.

Ong, Walter. (1982). *Orality and literacy: The technologizing of the word.* New York: Methuen.

Oxford English dictionary. 2nd edition, vols 1–20. (1989). Prepared by J. A. Simpson and E. S. C. Weiner. Oxford: Clarendon.

Pinar, W., Reynolds, W., Slattery, P., and Taubman, P. (1995). *Understanding curriculum.* New York: Lang.

Rorty, Richard. (1979). *Philosophy and the mirror of nature*. Princeton: Princeton University Press.

Worsham, Lynn. (1991). Writing against writing: The predicament of *écriture féminine* in composition studies. In Patricia Harkin and John Schilb (Eds.), *Contending with words: Composition and rhetoric in a postmodern age* (pages 82–104). New York: The Modern Language Association of America.

Donna Trueit is a doctoral student in curriculum and instruction at Louisiana State University in Baton Rouge. She holds an M.A. in education from the University of Victoria, British Columbia. Her current research interests are pre- and postmodern approaches to "knowing," complexity theory, and conversation.

Perspective on Trueit

Brian Casemore and Nichole Guillory

That Donna Trueit advocates for the "recuperation of embodied knowledge" charges us with returning or restoring to health a part of ourselves which has somehow been lost. In tracing the historical movement from orality to increasing literacy, Trueit reminds us that "the voice of the muses and a sensory-intuitive and spiritual orientation to the world" are lost in educational contexts. It is in these contexts that we situate our response to Trueit's chapter. Honoring as best we could Trueit's description of conversation, the two of us, former public high school English teachers, engaged in a conversation of our own—of which we provide an excerpt later in this perspective—to explore some of the ways forces of schooling impede our moving toward embodied knowledge and to think about the exciting possibilities of allowing ourselves the freedom in schools to "summon the poetic." Our own conversation tended to center around three domains of our lives in schools—time, mind-body (we intentionally connect the two), and language. Though the system of schooling is never in complete control of our being and our being-with-others, it does often get in the way of conversation as Trueit describes it. In our conversation, we talk about how forces of schooling make conversation seem too risky for us to try, how we are required to bring only our minds—not our bodies—into the classroom, how we remain isolated from others in the learning process, and how "proper language" prevents us from full participation in classroom interactions.

Despite these forces of schooling, we remember moments and spaces in educational environments in which interactions were filled with the poetic, wandered into new rhythms, and held voices in splendid relation to expressive bodies. We feel/believe Trueit's call for a recuperation of embodied knowledge can be performed through a pedagogy that encourages participation in such pockets of conversational relation. A pedagogy of this sort is not a prescription; rather, it engages curriculum with a keen awareness for the nascence of conversation and embodied expression. It is a search that admits we will not all arrive at the same understanding, that new relations will confound existing knowledge, that tensions will arise, that silence will be discovered as a profound and meaningful presence. With Trueit, we look to silences. Although schooling marks silence as lack of knowledge, as mistake, and as failure, we seek to embrace the richness of meaning in silence that pushes conversation outward, beyond centralized control.

To speak of recovering the poetic in schools is not a call to a voyeuristic excavation of student experience and subjectivity; rather, it invites, even seduces, that content into new rhythms and relations, internal and social. Such movement resists school control and the service of "ideas, like commodities...external to a unitary self" (Trueit, this volume). Curriculum becomes an invitation for students and teachers to find new relations with school subjects, psychic life, and social experience. Heightened conversation does take place in schools. And with the incursion of schooling forces, it gives way, entrusting its power to memory, history, body, and future articulations.

Nichole: Don't you think schooling gets in the way of conversation as Donna describes it?

Brian: Yes, there seem to be many forces getting in the way of conversation.

Nichole: What about the rush of time? I remember always feeling rushed in my own classroom. There was never enough time. I always felt compelled to cover what the curriculum guide required. I was driven by the clock. 8:33 A.M.—announcements; 8:47 A.M.—first period; 11:22 A.M.—lunch. I would constantly ask my students how much time we had left in a class period. I remember cutting off good lessons in the middle because I felt we had to move on to what we were "supposed to be learning." That's sad.

Brian: So there is a line of time outside of us, the hard temporal line we have to follow. Can we consider ways to give more space to the present when we are driven forward by external curriculum demands, standards—predicting and testing?

Nichole: As though there is some end.

Brian: Not only can we not stop to linger in consideration of a passage, we never can stop in silence. Something always intrudes on the silence. There is very little comfort with silence or the acknowledgment of meaningful silence. Silences are considered mistakes, a lack of knowledge.

Nichole: And wasted time and space.

Brian: We give students very little space.

Nichole: Yes, we cram so many students into a limited amount of physical space in schools, and we don't create enough opportunities for them to learn in relation, to experience what Donna calls embodied knowledge.

Brian: We ask them to bring only their minds into the classroom and leave their bodies at the door.

Nichole: Watching and listening to students before school, after school, during their lunches, in between classes, they are conversing. They know how to engage in conversation already. When the bell rings for class, students shut down the conversation and go into classes where conversation is totally removed.

Brian: So, the embodied speech is at lunch, out in front of school, on the school bus, and in the last ten seconds before you squeeze them into the classroom. In the classroom we too often pursue knowledge outside of ourselves.

Nichole: So does conversation only happen in the abstract? Is it only theoretical? Is it only here on paper? Given the system that we have now, perhaps we just aren't visionary enough to imagine something different. A recuperation of embodied knowledge obviously isn't going to fit into what we have existing already. Or, do you think there are moments or little pockets in which it takes place? I think there are.

Brian: I think that is how you identified it from the beginning, these pockets or places where it occurs. I like that image because I'm more comfortable trying to understand new relational contexts in that form —not because it's easier or more efficient but because it's small. I can see the potential because I know there is room for my participation.

Nichole: It's realizable.

Brian Casemore is a doctoral student in curriculum theory at Louisiana State University in Baton Rouge and a former classroom teacher. His current research interests are in autobiography and English education.

Nichole Guillory is a doctoral student in curriculum theory at Louisiana State University in Baton Rouge and a former classroom teacher. Her current research interests are in popular culture and education, specifically black women rappers and the pedagogies they enact around issues of representation, power and black women's sexualities.

Chapter 13 The Call from the Stranger

Problematic: Posthuman Spirituality

In the following essay, Hongyu Wang notes that in Chinese spiritual traditions, "the highest ideal is to achieve oneness between self and the universe." Maxine Hong Kingston (1977) makes a similar point in her powerful and haunting story of education as a spiritual journey, *The Woman Warrior: Memoirs of a Girlhood Among Ghosts*: "I learned to make my mind large, as the universe is large, so that there is room for paradoxes" (34). This ideal contrasts sharply with much of what passes for education in the Western tradition, in which successful achievement in learning often seems to involve the ability to shrink the cosmos to fit within the preordained boundaries of an individual's human consciousness.

To explore Dwayne Huebner's vision of curriculum as a spiritual journey, we will follow his example by introducing a stranger. Our stranger is posthuman—a cyborg—and the paradoxical universe within which the journey takes place is complex and chaotic (because this is, as it were, our "last word" in this book, we make no apology for taking the opportunity to revisit, albeit briefly, two key foci of our own curriculum theorizing; see, for example, Doll, 1986, 1993; Gough, 1995, 1998; Weaver, 1999). We argue that some of the most generative concepts for exploring our transpersonal transactions with the cosmos are provided by chaos and complexity theories, cybernetics, and cyberpunk science fiction—the latter being a literature that imagines the possible future relationships between self-organizing systems and technologies of the self. In the light of Huebner's questioning of scientism, we note that the nonlinear dynamics of the biosphere—such as the amplification of fluctuations, the emergence of bifurcations, and the immense consequences of small, low-energy effects (the "butterfly effect")—were described in literature (and not only in science fiction) long before scientists such as Ilya Prigogine provided mathematical explanations for them. But, as numerous human-initiated ecological catastrophes demonstrate, the moral imperatives that might guide our transactions with a chaotic and complex universe have received much less attention. As Bob Dylan (1965) writes: "i accept chaos. i am not sure whether it accepts me."[1]

However, a chaotic cosmos "accepts" (accommodates) the ecologically sustainable (and, in a quite literal sense, mind-expanding) operations of many insect societies. The evolution of open, nonlinear dynamic systems of communication and resource management—involving both chance and determinism—enables ant societies to resolve problems of a complexity that far outstrips the information-processing capabilities of an individual ant with very limited data. We might well ask how ants accomplish this with semiochemicals and pheromones while we have achieved so much less (relatively speaking) with our human languages and technologies. Are there practical limits to how fully we *as individuals* should aspire to "achieve oneness between self and the universe"? Or should we deliberately deploy cybernetic, genetic, and biological technologies that might enable the evolution of a posthuman "hive" mind?

Many science fiction stories rehearse the synergistic links between Prigogine's theories of self-organization and the cybernetic project to build intelligent artifacts. For example, Bruce Sterling's (1989, 1990) cosmos is explicitly "Prigoginic": Mind is a dissipative structure (itself a product of biological evolution—another dissipative structure), generating further dissipative structures such as literature and technology. More provocatively, in William Gibson and Bruce Sterling's (1991) novel, *The Difference Engine*, an intelligent artificiality elucidates a moment in its own past when a chance event (a minor fluctuation) enables its own future evolution into an intelligence that can tell its own story. Using nonlinear dynamics to explain how a machine in a far-from-equilibrium system might spring into autonomous life, Gibson and Sterling provide a plausible portrayal of being-and-becoming that transcends any attempt to essentialize such concepts in human terms.

The complex hybridization of humans and machines provides no clear boundaries between maker and made, between us and our technologies, but this is the posthuman condition that we are all part of being-and-becoming (see Hayles, 1999). The cyborg meets all of Huebner's descriptors of the stranger: Someone alien to us (but who nevertheless might lurk within us) who implies the presence of the transcendent, and embodies the unknown, the uncertain, and the unexpected. Of course, cyborgs are not the only strangers who may appear within our horizon, but in a curriculum conceived as a spiritual journey in the posthuman world, we might be wise to call upon the cyborg within us.

Note

[1] In the same place, Dylan offered the following pertinent pearl of spiritual wisdom: "i am convinced that all souls have some superior to deal with/like the school system, an invisible circle in which no one can think without consulting someone."

References

Doll, William E., Jr. (1986). Prigogine: A new sense of order, a new curriculum. *Theory into Practice*, *25*(1), 10–16.

______. (1993). *A post-modern perspective on curriculum*. New York: Teachers College Press.

Dylan, Bob. (1965). *Highway 61 revisited* (liner notes). New York: CBS Records.

Gibson, William, and Bruce Sterling. (1991). *The difference engine*. New York: Bantam.

Gough, Noel. (1995). Manifesting cyborgs in curriculum inquiry. *Melbourne Studies in Education*, *36*(1), 71–83.

______. (1998). Reflections and diffractions: Functions of fiction in curriculum inquiry. In William F. Pinar (Ed.), *Curriculum: Toward new identities* (pages 94–127). New York: Garland.

Hayles, N. Katherine. (1999). *How we became posthuman: Virtual bodies in cybernetics, literature, and informatics*. Chicago and London: University of Chicago Press.

Kingston, Maxine Hong. (1977). *The woman warrior: Memoirs of a girlhood among ghosts*. London: Lane.

Sterling, Bruce. (1989). *Islands in the net*. New York: Ace.

______. (1990). *Crystal express*. New York: Ace.

Weaver, John A. (1999). Synthetically growing a post-human curriculum: Noel Gough's curriculum as a popular cultural text. *Journal of Curriculum Theorizing*, *15*(4), 161–69.

The Call from the Stranger: Dwayne Huebner's Vision of Curriculum as a Spiritual Journey

Hongyu Wang

Alas, I cannot stay in the house, and home has become no home to me, for the eternal Stranger calls, he is going along the road.
The sound of his footfall knocks at my breast; it pains me!
The wind is up, the sea is moaning.
I leave all my cares and doubts to follow the homeless tide, for the Stranger calls me, he is going along the road.
(Rabindranath Tagore, *Fruit Gathering*, VII, 1916, 8)

Soon after I first came to the United States, I went to a potluck party at a professor's house. It was the first time I had joined in such a party, and I was at a loss. People were scattered throughout the house, in the hall, in the kitchen, and in the backyard, either standing or sitting to talk with each other. It was nothing like Chinese parties. And so many strange faces surrounded me! Quietly moving among people, listening to their talk, I could feel the flow of the party, but I was not part of it. To be among strangers—myself being a stranger to others—could be so frustrating. I honestly told the friend who took me there, "I feel like I am an outsider." After some time, music started, and some professors and students began to dance together. I was invited to join them. Gradually I began to relax and told myself: This is exactly what I want—to be in a new land and to meet strangers so that my life can be enriched.

Leaving home on a journey of exploration was a conscious choice of encountering "the otherness of the Other" (Bernstein, 1991, 66), continuously seeking a fuller self. To my surprise, four years of living with strangers in a foreign land has not only opened my heart to new ways of thinking, feeling, and being, but has also strongly urged me, as never before, to return with critical eyes to my own spiritual traditions based upon a relational view of self, reality, and cosmos. Such a spiritual journey of encountering the stranger, which is also a process of my education, has carried me to where I see both the world and the self continuously anew.

Education is inherently a spiritual quest. As Whitehead (1967/1929) says, "the essence of education is that it be religious"(14). This is to understand "religious" in the sense of listening to and responding to the call from the stranger "with reverence," to reach out for the promise and gift of new lands, and to envision education as a journey of continuously transforming the given into new forms of life.

No one has engaged in an inquiry into education as a spiritual journey as powerfully as Dwayne Huebner. Huebner has devoted much of his life to cultivating and articulating a spiritual language to talk about education, curriculum, and schooling. Drawing upon Parker Palmer's concept, Huebner uses "the stranger" (1985a, 1985b, 1985c, 1993) as a metaphor to call upon the sense of "moreness" and "beyondness" in curriculum, so that education becomes a transcendent journey (1963, 1966, 1967, 1974, 1985b, 1993, 1998) of continuously entering into the novelty, newness, and wonder (1959) of life. My personal journey of opening to "the stranger" both inside and outside of myself makes such a spiritual vision of curriculum especially appealing to me. However, at the time Huebner began writing about this idea in the context of the American curriculum field, which was dominated exclusively by technical, empirical, and scientific language, such a vision was radical. Huebner was ahead of his time when he launched a challenge to the technical foundations of education, with its emphasis on control and prediction, as early as the 1960s. This powerful, passionate, and somewhat lonely outcry against the dominant scientific and technical picture of education and curriculum is still refreshing to our ears today, when American schools continue to be dominated by the prepackaged curriculum guide, procedural teaching models, standardized testing and evaluations, and educational reform rhetoric, all of which remain chiefly concerned with raising students' academic standards.

When I first came to the United States, I anticipated experiencing an experientially based, child-centered curriculum in American schools—Dewey being the symbol of American education in Chinese educators' imagination. I was greatly attracted to the transformative power of Dewey's educational thought. It took me some time to realize, as Doll (this volume) puts it so powerfully, that Dewey's vision has been a ghost haunting the American curriculum, which has long been in the throes of the language of the technical and the procedural and of a search for the perfect methodization and standardization.

The haunting Doll sees from the ghosts of Dewey and Whitehead, in their call for the process of becoming and transformation, echoes the challenge initiated by Huebner upon dominant curricular discourses and practices. In the midst of "the moral and spiritual crisis in education"

(Purpel, 1989) and the "spiritual drabness" brought on by the "clockwork curriculum" (Gough, this volume), it becomes crucial to envision a fundamental reconceptualization of curriculum. Huebner's spiritual vision of education and curriculum as a transcendent journey is still a challenge unfulfilled. Renewing such a vision can tap into the potentiality of the present embodied in both the past and the future to allow a more vibrant life in our classrooms. Drawing upon Huebner's works and his metaphor of the stranger, this essay elaborates on curriculum as a spiritual journey.

Curricular Languages and the Neglect of the Spiritual

Huebner (1985c) claims he has spent most of his professional career searching for more appropriate or creative languages to describe educational phenomena. Acknowledging that the prevailing language of education and curriculum is behaviorism, positivism, or scientism—so taken for granted that it becomes invisible—Huebner unmasks the dominating role of such a language to reveal its nature of control. He searches for a transcendent vision of education through religious metaphors that can unfold the wonder, awe, and creativity of both the world and the child. As early as 1959, he claimed "scientific validity is not the only kind of validity. In the existential situation in which we must plan for and act with boys and girls, we must bring all of our knowledge and creative powers to bear, not just those provided by the behavioral scientist" (2). An exclusive focus on efficacy and efficiency in education leaves out the mysterious, the transcendent, and the sacred, embodied not only in art, literature, music, and religion but also in science. Huebner calls for "new concepts to deal with problems of education" (7), those concepts that can facilitate our capacity for wonder, and our active engagement with the ever-changing creative processes of the universe.

Huebner (1966) directly questions the tyranny of the Tyler Rationale imbued with the language of purpose (not experience) and learning (not understanding) and suggests alternative curricular languages. The language of objectives for controllable calculation obscures the newness embedded in lived experience. The language of learning exclusively in terms of observable behavioral change clouds children's understanding of who they are, what they can do, and what they might become. For Huebner, the language of purpose and learning locks out the uncertain, the unknown, and the mysterious, which, in turn, drains out the spirit of life and puts everything under control. In this language of control or "ghost" as Doll terms it, the future is predictable and educational processes are carried out according to predetermined procedures. Such a "ghost" of external and imposed control—"unclean spirit" Huebner would call it (1993, 410)—needs to be exorcized so that the potentiality of the present is no longer trapped by the given, and the presence of the transcendent can be illuminated. As Huebner has said (1966):

> Present curriculum language is much too limited to come to grips with the problems, or rather the mysteries, of language and meaning of the classroom. The educator must free himself from his self-confining schemas, in order that he may listen anew to the world pounding against his intellectual barriers. The present methodologies which govern curriculum thought must eventually give away. (116–17)

For Huebner, framing the languages of learning, socialization, objectives, and child development exclusively in a behaviorist sense hides from our awareness the way we exercise power over children and the way we impose our modes of life on them. When children can't match the teacher's expectation, the educator turns to three language games for help: "readiness, motivation, and discipline or control" (Huebner, 1974, 190). The teacher focuses on how to prepare or motivate children to receive ready-made materials. When these strategies do not work, learning degenerates into a discipline problem. As a result, instead of living together with children and helping them participate in the continuous reconstruction of the public world, the teacher resorts to external influence to hold children in obedience to the norm and the standard. There is little room left for anything alien, strange, or beyond the given. And the systems of grading, promotion, and credentials further reinforce these language games. Children's spontaneity and the newness the young can bring to the world are lost in the ghostly language of normative control. Schooling becomes a one-way instructional process from adult to child, which severely limits children's capacity for imagining new possibilities and their potential for transcending established forms of life.

Huebner (1985b) calls for a new dialogue between education and religious traditions. The separation of religious and educational traditions as a simplistic political convenience leaves out important and profound questions about the meaning and significance of life, and consequently deprives education of its very creative source. "To the extent that various modes of knowing are separated from religious traditions they become closed in upon themselves and lose their vitality, their 'spirit,' their creativity, and the possibility of being transcended" (348). For Huebner, our exclusive dependence upon the technical foundations of education not only leads to the undervaluing and the neglect of the spiritual in schooling and curriculum but also places moral and spiritual values under the control of scientific and developmental languages through the rhetoric of objectivity. The very idea that moral and spiritual values can be detached and taught in a scientific and technical way obscures the pervasive power of the spiritual. Therefore we need a new language about the spiritual which can bring the vitality of life and the creative power of the cosmos into education and curriculum. To unfold Huebner's spiritual vision of education and curriculum, we first need to start with how he defines "spirit" and "spiritual."

What Do "Spirit" and "Spiritual" Mean?

Though himself deeply rooted in the Christian tradition, Huebner (1985b, 1993, 1998) defines "spirit" and "spiritual" in a broad sense as vitality of life and "moreness" and "beyondness" of being, in which the given, the expected, and the known are constantly transcended. In reaching out for the otherness, the possibility of "new ways, new knowledge[s], new relationships, new awareness[es]" (1985b, 343–44) continuously opens up. Such a meaning of the spiritual, one imbued with the transformative, transcendent, and creative power of life, is no longer trapped by the exclusive and suppressive role of religious dogma—a source of tremendous fear which Americans have concerning the introduction of religious education into schooling. Beyond any particular religious tradition, "spirit" and "spiritual" identify with what is *more than* the present, more than current forms of life, and beyond the self, pointing to a transcendent dimension of human existence. In this sense then, to experience the spiritual is to venture into the strangeness of the unknown to create new ways of knowing, living, and being: "[A]n awareness that what we are and what we know can never completely contain what we might be or what we might know" (345).

In the summer of 1998, Huebner gave a lecture titled "Education: A Spiritual Journey" at the University of Victoria, Canada. Consistent with his long time devotion to cultivating a spiritual vision of curriculum, he elaborated his sense of the spiritual in a somewhat summary way. Huebner defined five capabilities of human life: (1) our capability for consciousness; (2) our capability for imagination; (3) our capability for will; (4) our capability for power; (5) our capability for love. The spiritual aspect of education is inherent in a journey of being constantly transformed by nourishing consciousness, will, imagination, power, and love in order to be open to the strangeness and the newness of both the world and the self. Such a spiritual journey has no end other than death; it is a life long process of continuous renewal and transcendence. In such a journey, we need to be willing to let go of who and what we are so that new selves can be born.

Consciousness brings self-reflectiveness, thoughtfulness, and awareness of who we are, what we might become and what we ought to be. Such an awareness of both our limitations and new possibilities is made possible by language and other symbolic forms: "They are symbols of moreness, of otherness, of the transcendent—symbols that life as lived can be different" (Huebner, 1985b, 344). There is always something more to see, to hear, and to experience. This sense of "moreness" is carried further into *imagination*, a special kind of consciousness which makes it possible to envision reality, world, and self differently. Imagination takes us beyond the known, the present, and the given to journey into new horizons of imagined alternatives. In such a journey, unexpected openings are explored; unaccustomed angles of seeing are cultivated; surprising encounters with the stranger are approached, and what is usually excluded and suppressed is uncovered in a constant search for new meanings.

Will is "the capability to want, to desire, to act with intention"(Huebner, 1998, 3). As agency, will engages us in the efforts of reconstructing the world and the self. The energy of will is called upon to make possible our capacity to let one's old self die in order to generate new layers of self, and make possible our capability of turning "despair into hope, sadness into joy, and death into life" when the engagement with the stranger shocks us into confusion and depression (Schweitzer, 1991, 142). Here, the capability of *power* to influence, construct, and change comes into play. Such power can be positive or negative. With the awareness that "with the power to influence comes the lifegiving possibility of being influenced" (Huebner, 1966, 111), it becomes essential to exercise mutual influence for creation, cocreation, and re-creation of both the self and the world. Thus, we need to be on constant alert against the abuse of power in controlling others rather than sharing the gift of life with others.

Finally, there is a capability of love, of establishing a caring and responsible relationship with others and the world. Only through loving relationships can we be attentive to and mindful of the world, affirm the presence of the other—the stranger—in our lives and understand ourselves and others more fully to promote personal transformation while participating in the reconstruction of reality. The capacity for love provides a supportive community to encourage us to risk challenges and to venture into the unknown. Imbued with the life-affirming possibility and the transcendent power of human existence, love is the source of change and creativity.

In the same lecture, Huebner points out that one of the difficulties in seeing education as a spiritual journey comes from the language of *self*, *individual*, and *identity* in the Western tradition. Such a language implies a stable self, an independent individual, and a fixed identity, which privileges constancy and completeness. It tends to block the possibility of change and transformation which makes education a journey. Huebner's critique of Western individualism brings me back to my own spiritual traditions.

The sense of an isolated individual or a unitary identity is not present in Chinese culture. In Chinese spiritual traditions, the highest ideal is to achieve oneness between self and the universe and union among the way of Heaven, the way of Earth, and the way of "man." Spirituality is embedded in an organic and dynamic interconnectedness within and between humanity and nature. The Chinese self is always in relation—to other people, to social community, and to cosmic processes. Located in the web of human and cosmic relationships and always open to the otherness of others and the world, the self is constantly renewed by participating in the creative transformation of the ever-expanding cosmos. For the great Indian poet, Tagore, the call from "the eternal Stranger" is also a call for an active engagement with eternal cosmic movement to be one with God who ceaselessly walks along the road of cosmos. With the acknowledgment of Eastern wisdom about the co-emergence of self, others, and the universe, a new sense of nondualistic spirituality based upon "sacred interconnections" (Griffin, 1990) is emerging in the West, which is embedded within the ecological interdependence of all things and the interexistence of ourselves with all other life forms. From a relational view, the self is always in a process of renewal and transformation, interactively connecting with the mysterious source of creativity and divinity.

To challenge the language of a unitary self, such as Huebner envisions, we need to introduce the stranger and the strangeness of the world into education and curriculum. Awareness of the stranger and the newness of the world can bring fluidity and movement into the self by reaching out for the uncertain, the unfamiliar, and the strange. In this way, the boundary of a fixed identity is constantly transcended and the awesome power of change is infused into curriculum. Education is about change, emergence, and transformation, which makes it a spiritual journey, a journey of nurturing consciousness, imagination, will, power, and love to reach out for the constant rebirth of the self inward and the world outward. Such a spiritual vision of education is infused with the transcendent dimension of human life, the creative energy of cosmos, and a sense of responsibility for answering the call from the other—the stranger.

The Call from the Stranger: Education as a Spiritual Journey

Parker J. Palmer (1981), in *The Company of Strangers*, suggests that in the Christian tradition, the stranger serves as a spiritual guide to shatter taken-for-granted perceptions and assumptions, to challenge conventional truth, and to bring the promise of new life. Elaborating upon Palmer's notion, Huebner introduces "the stranger" into education and curriculum to create a space for the spiritual. The stranger is someone alien to us, someone we are not familiar with, someone carrying alternative language, images, worldviews, and ways of life. In this sense, to invite the stranger into our horizon is to risk questioning our own views and ways of being. To dwell in the horizon of the stranger calls upon a new awareness of the world and opens up an alternative possibility for human life. Such an effort of "turning inside out" and "turning outside in" (Huebner, 1998) calls us to better understand who we are and what our world might be, and puts us "in a better position to dialogue, to mutually construct a new reality" (Huebner, 1985a, 336). The shared reality is marked by mutual transformation. Different from a common, sensual meaning of "stranger," "the stranger"—in Huebner's vision—implies the presence of the transcendent and embodies the unknown, the uncertain, and the unexpected. In this sense, the world can be the stranger which constantly opens up new vistas. The stranger can also lurk within us, hidden inside as what is denied, excluded, or unrealized. As Julia Kristeva points out, "to worry or to smile, such is the choice when we are assailed by the strange; our decision depends on how familiar we are with our own ghosts" (1991, 191). A journey into the inner self can be projected out into the world so that the world becomes the extension of us, and a journey out into the strangeness of the world can also extend our inner self. Such a dynamic interplay between the outer and the inner brings the stranger—it can be others, the world or ourselves—into play so that we can engage in the spiritual journey that is education. My personal journey of encountering the stranger has opened my eyes to new ways of perceiving both reality and self. It has brought awakening moments when I was shocked into new understanding and new consciousness. An engaged encounter with the stranger is a creative way of affirming the transcendent.

In this sense, education, by its essence, is a spiritual quest, a quest for transcending and transforming current forms of life, a quest for imagined possibility, a quest for dynamic connections with something larger than the self, a quest for the newness and moreness of self, others, and the world through a journey of opening to the strangeness both inside and outside of the self. Huebner (1985c) elaborates this so beautifully:

> Education is a call from the other that we may reach out beyond ourselves and enter into life with the life around us....The otherness that informs and accompanies education is the absolute Otherness, the transcendent Other, however we name that which goes beyond all appearances and all conditions. Education is the lure of the transcendent—that which we seem is not what we are for we could always be other. Education is the openness to a future that is beyond all futures. Education is the protest against present forms that they may be reformed and transformed.... Education is indeed a leading out....it is a leading out by the Otherness that is the source of our transcendence. (360–61)

Huebner (1985a) suggests that the meeting of the teacher with students is a meeting with the stranger. To acknowledge students as the stranger is to respect their own ways of knowing and being and to create room for the teacher's own transformation through encounters with the young. The language of students as "learners" deprives students of their right to participate in the construction of a shared reality and puts students under the control of adults and their established world. To challenge the taken-for-granted and bring imagination into play, the teacher is engaged in the art of education in such a way that the novelty and creativity of the young can be affirmed. For Huebner (1987), teaching is a vocation called forth by students, the content, and institutions. The call from the young invites the teacher to participate in their emerging stories, and as the teacher listens to children and makes her/his creative response, s/he is also engaged in reshaping her/his own life. Therefore, in the language of students as the stranger, teaching becomes an invitation for students to participate in a shared construction of a new reality, a joint search for meanings, and the shared activities of telling stories, recollecting memories, and imaging possibilities. Teachers and students become co-journeyers traveling on the road to the unknown.

Not only do we need to approach students as the stranger, we also need to approach the strangeness of subject matter (Huebner, 1985c) and encourage students to dwell in the space of the content as the stranger. To regard the content as the stranger to be lived with rather than as an object or a preexistent reality to be mastered and grasped initiates an effort to share a new life form and to participate in the continual creation of the world. This move from "an *I-It* relationship to an *I-Thou* relationship" (Buber in Huebner, 1959) brings the wonder, awe, and mysteries of life into an interactive mode of knowing. In this way, the task of teaching is not to teach content but to make the stranger present to children: "To bring the stranger, and the fruits of her comings and goings, into the presence of the person to be educated—to be led forth" (Huebner, 1985c, 362). The language of learning, of goals and objectives, of ends and means in a behaviorist sense intends to make everything and everyone familiar and known. It ignores the presence of otherness in our life, diminishes the need for imagining ourselves into the stranger's world, and consequently loses the power of the transcendent inherent in the coming and going of the stranger. "The religious journey, the process of being educated, is always a consequence of encountering something that is strange and different, something that is not me" (Huebner, 1993, 407–08). For Huebner, to know is to be in relation—in relation with the phenomenal world, in relation with human beings. To be in relation with other people is to come into other ways of experiencing the world for creative transformation of the self. To be in relation with the natural world is to listen to the voice of the Earth and to be in touch with the spontaneities of the universe (Berry, 1990) so that co-creation of humanity and the cosmos can be possible. And this relationship is poetically described as "a dance of love" with the stranger (Huebner, 1985c, 367). It is also a relationship constructed by and through play (Huebner, 1993). In our dancing with others and playing with the world, knowledge as a consequence of leading out to the otherness of the content is kept alive.

To leap into the unknown and to encounter the stranger can be threatening; the process of giving up some part of the self in order to create a new self can be frustrating, and the efforts of following the "homeless tide" (Tagore, 1916) can be overwhelming. To make this growing process possible and to respond to the call from the stranger in a creative way without being overpowered by the strangeness, we need a supportive community full of love, faith, and hope. For Huebner, a spiritual journey in which both the teachers and students can be open, vulnerable, and available to new ways of thinking, feeling, and living cannot be a solitary one. It needs the support of a caring and loving community in which one dares to challenge the self, to reconstruct the present, and to create new relationships. "We can face the threat of the unknown and of the stranger if we are not alone; if we are in the presence of love which affirms life" (1985c, 363). Such a community not only provides assurance that life can be renewed and enhanced rather than destroyed by reaching out to what is alien and different, it also enables one to participate in the web of sacred interconnections. It provides patience, an active and expectant waiting that accompanies love and gives hope. A community of love, trust, and patience has a healing power to bring into new unity what may be disrupted by the stranger.

In short, to imagine an educational landscape that makes room for the spiritual does not mean simply to teach spiritual and moral values; it means to infuse the spiritual into every aspect of schooling so that education can become a spiritual journey in which both the teachers and students can constantly reach beyond themselves to listen to and answer the call from the stranger.

To embark upon a spiritual quest in education, let us listen to the call from that unknown child by the sea (Yang, 1990) which speaks to me passionately:

> I don't know who that boy is
> The one playing an intriguing game by the sea
> Owner of a sand castle and daydreams
> A straw hat shading his eyes
> He's laughing robustly
> As he strolls together with the sun
> I don't know who that boy is...
>
> The handkerchief pinned to his shirt front
> Is blue as the sky emblazoned with life's mysteries
> His face is a beautiful dream
> He whispers to himself
> He has come to the world's beach
> To talk to the waves
> I don't know who that boy is...
>
> I don't know whether his basket-like heart
> Contains memories other than these
> The ocean overlaid with the rays of twilight
> Hiding laughter within an everlasting puzzle
> Even though storms hover past the horizon
> The world deserves the laughter of small children.
> I don't know who that boy is.... (135)

Let us build our school and construct our curriculum by the sea, illuminated by the sunshine the child can stroll with, lapped by waves the child can talk to; let us open a world vibrant with dreams, games, whispers, laughter, and even storms; and let us create, as Doll says, a "spirit-ful" (this volume) space for the child to journey into life's mysteries with the company of the stranger. A continuous, ever-evolving and unfinished journeying: together with the children, we are forever on the road…

Acknowledgements: I wish to thank Vikki Hillis for the loan of her personal tape of Dwayne Huebner's lecture at the University of Victoria, Canada, in 1998. I also deeply appreciate her invaluable suggestions on revising the draft of this paper. Thanks also go to Dwayne Huebner and William E. Doll, Jr., for their comments and support.

References

Bernstein, Richard J. (1991). *The new constellation: The ethical-political horizons of modernity/postmodernity.* Cambridge, MA: MIT.

Berry, Thomas. (1990). *The dream of the earth.* San Francisco: Sierra Club.

Griffin, David R. (1990). Introduction. In David R. Griffin (Ed.), *Sacred interconnections: Postmodern spirituality, political economy, and art* (pages 1–14). New York: State University of New York Press.

Huebner, Dwayne E. (1999). *The lure of the transcendent: Collected essays by Dwayne E. Huebner.* Vikki Hillis (Ed.). Collected and introduced by William F. Pinar. Mahwah, NJ: Erlbaum.

_______. (1959). The capacity for wonder and education. In *The lure of the transcendent,* (pages 1–9).

_______. (1963). New modes of man's relationship to man. In *The lure of the transcendent* (pages 74–93).

_______. (1966). Curricular language and classroom meanings. In *The lure of the transcendent* (pages 101–17).

_______. (1967). Curriculum as concern for man's temporality. In *The lure of the transcendent* (pages 131–42).

_______. (1974). Toward a remaking of curricular language. In *The lure of the transcendent* (pages 184–97).

_______. (1975). Poetry and power: The politics of curriculum development. In *The lure of the transcendent* (pages 231–40).

______. (1985a). Education in the congregation and seminary. In *The lure of the transcendent* (pages 340–52).

_______. (1985b). Spirituality and knowing. In *The lure of the transcendent* (pages 340–52).

_______. (1985c). Religious metaphors in the language of education. In *The lure of the transcendent* (pages 358–68).

_______. (1987). Teaching as a vocation. In *The lure of the transcendent* (pages 379–87).

_______. (1993). Education and spirituality. In *The lure of the transcendent* (pages 401–16).

_______. (1996). Challenges bequeathed. In *The lure of the transcendent* (pages 432–45).

______. (1998). Education: A spiritual journey. A transcript of Huebner's lecture at University of Victoria, Canada, on July 25, 1998, provided by Vikki Hillis.

Kristeva, Julia. (1991). *Strangers to ourselves.* Leon S. Roudiez (Trans.). New York: Columbia University Press.

Macy, Joanna. (1990). The ecological self: Postmodern ground for right action. In David R. Griffin (Ed.), *Sacred interconnections: Postmodern spirituality, political economy, and art* (pages 35–48). New York: State University of New York Press.

Palmer, Parker J. (1981). *The company of strangers.* New York: Crossroad.

Purpel, David E. (1989). *The moral and spiritual crisis in education: A curriculum for justice and compassion in education.* Granby, MA: Bergin and Garvey.

Schweitzer, Mary. (1991). Déjà vu. *Anthropology and Humanism Quarterly, 16*(4), 137–42.

Tagore, Rabindranath. (1916). *Fruit gathering*. New York: Macmillan.

Whitehead, Alfred N. (1967). *The aims of education and other essays* (Original publication 1929). New York: Macmillan.

Yang, Lian. (1990). Boy by the sea. In Edward Morin (Ed.), *The red azalea: Chinese poetry since the cultural revolution* (page 135). Honolulu: University of Hawaii Press.

Hongyu Wang, an assistant professor at Oklahoma State University, graduated from Louisiana State University. She has published two articles in English in the *Journal of Curriculum Theorizing*. She has coauthored two books in Chinese—*Educational Methods* (with Shuduan Lin, 1989) and *Educational Experiment and Studies on Education in the Future* (with Zhen Feng, 1998). Wang has translated into Chinese William E. Doll, Jr.'s, book *A Post-Modern Perspective on Curriculum* (Taiwan, 1999; Beijing, 2000). She has published over 20 articles in Chinese.

Perspective on Wang

Donna Porche-Frilot

> There never was nor will be a man who has certain knowledge…
> Even if he should chance to say the complete truth, yet he himself knows not that it is so. (Xenophanes, sixth century B.C., fragment 14)

> Re-examine all you have been told,
> At school, at church or in any book,
> Dismiss whatever insults your soul
> And your very flesh shall be a great poem.
> (Walt Whitman, 1855, vi)

Zenon is a name that often appears in the records of my family's genealogy; it is a word taken from the Greek *xenos* meaning "stranger." The frequency with which this name appears on my family tree (passed down through over 200 years of naming) signifies both the timelessness of my ancestors' estranged condition and a spirit of resistance they came to through seizing the unwanted mantle of "stranger." You see, I—as my mothers and fathers before me (and theirs before)—am multiracial: We are the literal embodiment of America's proverbial "melting pot." Those red, black, brown, beige, and white people who united in a multitude of complex patterns to form my corporal body came from every nation of people who ever called Louisiana "home": Native Americans, Africans, Europeans, and Caribs. What these men and women—parents, teachers, warriors, servants, craftsmen, planters, and profiteers—didn't share in ethnicity, class status, religion, or physical appearance, they shared in the lived experience of being different from those around them. The very flesh of their children, in all its variant new hues, became, and remains to this day, an icon of chaos and complexity, social rebellion, racial impurity, and a failed morality. Thus, I read the appellations of my ancestors and cousins as a way of speaking to both community and progeny about the tenuous relationship their children have with the world around them. Having obtained permanent guest status, they endured multiple positions of subjectivity: slave amongst the free, Catholics amidst the rising tide of Protestantism, black-, brown-, or olive-skinned against the pale-skinned, Jews amongst Christians, French amidst Anglo-Americans, Colored people in the white-supremacist South, and multi/interracial people living in the paradigm of "race." Variations on a theme of estrangement, giving birth to strange new selves, strange new ways of being and knowing, authored by those who bore the names that narrated their condition and experiences: Zena, Zeno, Zenothea, Zenon....

Hongyu Wang's "The Call from the Stranger: Dwayne Huebner's Vision of Curriculum as a Spiritual Journey" thus recalls for me the poetics of self-estrangement—an expression of thinking and being created by attending the phenomena of difference as a lived experience. Wang recalls a perilous moment of cultural consciousness that occurred when her Chinese self became conscious amidst a Western cultural celebration. Her status as "stranger in a foreign land" then becomes reified. With energy, sincerity, and hope, she rescues this critical personal moment from its pain and mines it for fertile new visions of the self and the student/teacher relationship. Drawing upon Huebner's spiritual vision of education and Chinese spiritual notions of a relational sense of self, she begins to construct a new, hybrid vision of the future of education and curriculum. Wang finds new language by taking up Dwayne Huebner's project to infuse curricular discourse with the language of the spiritual and the transcendental journey and adding her own cultural ideas of self as experienced through "participation in a "web of sacred interconnections." Here, she invites both teachers and students to share a transcendent journey to the self, to "participate in the shared construction of a new reality, a joint search for meanings, and shared activities of telling stories, recollecting memories, and imagining possibilities" (this volume).

I fear, though, that the notion of "teacher as stranger" must be problematized. I do believe that cultivating a sense of estrangement from self and others can create the philosophical inertia for envisioning the world and self in new ways, but practical dangers arise when we underestimate the negative potentialities of teachers taking the stance of a stranger with their students. Too much estrangement is painful and awkward; it is a feeling which Wang admits in her essay: "[T]o be among strangers—myself being a stranger to others could be so frustrating." Here she offers a tantalizing clue to the hidden complexity of her fecund proposal, but it is a point that softly slips away. In her "Call of the Stranger," Wang might have yielded some of the ways in which others inscribe estrangement on her unwillingly and how she would apply the educational philosophy of "the call of the stranger" to combat re-inscription into a state of Otherness that is not transcendent.

Few would argue with the fact that the history of education, like all other aspects of society, has long been plagued with problems that are rooted in an inability or unwillingness to deal with human differences. My earliest schooling experiences in Louisiana are indelibly marked for the multiple ways in which I was regarded, day to day, year after year, as a nameless stranger. Just a "colored girl" in a white southern school during the first year of racial desegregation, I was neither guest nor visitor but *intruder.* Besides the drudgery of being introduced and assessed each year by the same school officials, the distance between myself and my teachers was insurmountable as it was also for my rare compatriots who sat in other classrooms. Our physical and cultural differences were regularly illuminated to scaffold theories of race and myths of white supremacy. The enacted notion of the Other was—and remains—harmful to generations of children who differed from the norm by reason of religion, race, gender, sexual orientation, and/or physical ability. In fact, standardized testing, tracking, and other aspects of modernist-inspired educational systems demonstrate a perverse aesthetic for sameness—for a quelling of creativity and other divergent, spirit-filled energies—based on modernist sensibilities and the factory model of schooling. We should remember that to call upon the stranger means to conjure the hideous ghost of the Other. Perhaps we should consider the following question: Does not the act of answering the call from the Other affirm Western culture's propensity to reify otherness, to iconize human differences, and hence, create valuated categories of humanity?

And yet, I am drawn to Wang's provocation, for she genuinely seeks a new vision for curriculum theory discourse and educational practice. She opens spaces for talk about spirituality and brings alternative traditions to the table of curriculum discourse. Like a siren song, her words lure me to the beach: "Let's build our school and construct our curriculum by the sea, illuminated by the sunshine the child can stroll with, lapped by waves the child can talk to...." Let us all wonder openly and imaginatively about the need for a total transformation of schooling and curriculum, a total reinterpretation of the teacher-student relationship. But I suggest that we move beyond the simplest model of the stranger. We might reconstitute the student as our *neighbor/stranger*, whereby we can invoke the prophet's words and ask educators to look upon those who are different as their proximate other self, she whose differences you should get to know but also he whom you should love and do unto "as thy self." Perhaps we could imagine/consider the notion of stranger as guest, drawing from the best model of a culture's social possibilities, the best of social traditions, connoting hospitality, love, and care.

References

Whitman, Walt. (1855). Preface. *Leaves of grass*. In http://jefferson.village.virginia....rks/leaves/1855/text/fulltext.html. Original work published 1855. Brooklyn, NY: Thomas Rome.

Xenophanes. (1956). *Fragment 14* (ca. sixth century B.C.). In *Philosophers speak for themselves: From Thales to Plato,* 2d ed. Edited by T. V. Smith. Chicago: University of Chicago Press.

Donna Porche-Frilot is a doctoral student in curriculum and instruction at Louisiana State University in Baton Rouge. After teaching computer technology for ten years, she completed an M.A. in education at LSU. She has conducted field research on adolescent literacy in middle school settings, led teacher education workshops on technology integration, and taught in elementary school gifted programs. She is a member of the National Council of Teachers of English and has presented papers at the national convention as well as at the LSU Women and Gender Studies Conference and the American Educational Research Association National Meeting.

"Questioning is the piety of thought."

Martin Heidegger
The Question Concerning Technology

Index

COUNTERPOINTS

Studies in the Postmodern Theory of Education

General Editors
Joe L. Kincheloe & Shirley R. Steinberg

Counterpoints publishes the most compelling and imaginative books being written in education today. Grounded on the theoretical advances in criticalism, feminism, and postmodernism in the last two decades of the twentieth century, Counterpoints engages the meaning of these innovations in various forms of educational expression. Committed to the proposition that theoretical literature should be accessible to a variety of audiences, the series insists that its authors avoid esoteric and jargonistic languages that transform educational scholarship into an elite discourse for the initiated. Scholarly work matters only to the degree it affects consciousness and practice at multiple sites. Counterpoints' editorial policy is based on these principles and the ability of scholars to break new ground, to open new conversations, to go where educators have never gone before.

For additional information about this series or for the submission of manuscripts, please contact:

Joe L. Kincheloe & Shirley R. Steinberg
c/o Peter Lang Publishing, Inc.
275 Seventh Avenue, 28th floor
New York, New York 10001

To order other books in this series, please contact our Customer Service Department:

(800) 770-LANG (within the U.S.)
(212) 647-7706 (outside the U.S.)
(212) 647-7707 FAX

Or browse online by series:

www.peterlangusa.com

